D0991919

HISTORY OF WOFFORD COLLEGE

HISTORY OF
WOFFORD COLLEGE

1854 - 1949

By

DAVID DUNCAN WALLACE

of the Class of 1894

PUBLISHED FOR WOFFORD COLLEGE

By

VANDERBILT UNIVERSITY PRESS

NASHVILLE   1951

Copyright, 1951
By
WOFFORD COLLEGE

"The Christian college is the manufactory which takes the finest raw material the Church can furnish, multiplies its value a hundred fold and returns it to the Church in a life-giving stream of intelligent faith, trained power and consecrated leadership."
—Henry Louis Smith

The great possession of any university is its great names. It is not the "pride, pomp and circumstance" of an institution which bring honor, not its wealth, nor the number of its schools, nor the students who throng its halls, but the *men* who have trodden in its service the thorny road through toil, even through hate, to the serene abode of Fame, climbing "like stars to their appointed height." These bring glory, and it should thrill the heart of every alumnus of this school, of every teacher in its faculty, as it does mine this day, reverently and thankfully to recall such names amongst its founders as Morgan, Shippen, and Rush, and such men amongst their successors as Wistar, Physick, Barton, and Wood.

Gentlemen of the Faculty—Noblesse oblige.

—Dr. William Osler

in valedictory address,
University of Pennsylvania, May 1, 1889.

Wofford College Main Building

FOREWORD

By WALTER K. GREENE
(President of Wofford College)

ABOUT THREE years ago, in thinking of the many traditions and inspiring incidents that wrap themselves in benediction about Wofford College, the thought occurred to me that they should be recorded in an authoritative history of the College. I imagine this same thought had occurred to hundreds of other alumni, because one would occasionally say to me: "We ought to preserve that Wofford experience in a history of the College."

The matter was presented to the Board of Trustees, and it met with an enthusiastic reception for two reasons particularly: (1) The Board felt that Wofford had something worthy of record and that Wofford men everywhere would be grateful for the privilege of having the total life of their College in print and (2) there was a significant conjunction of the idea and the man. It was our belief that there was just the man available who could best incarnate the idea. That man is a son of Wofford, intimately related personally and officially to all those fine and noble things that lie deep in the heart of the College. That man is a rare combination of teacher, scholar, and author. He is a distinguished historian and author of the authoritative and definitive history of South Carolina. There was never a more favorable conjunction of the idea and the man in Wofford's long and proud history.

Therefore, the Board of Trustees took advantage of this fortunate situation and requested this distinguished teacher, scholar, and historian, Dr. David Duncan Wallace, to write the history of Wofford College. He accepted the responsibility, and the history, therefore, becomes another notable contribution he has made to the proud position his Alma Mater holds among the liberal arts colleges of this country.

Using the official records of the College, related manuscript material, newspapers and magazine files, etc., Dr. Wallace has written a narrative of absorbing interest to persons concerned with Wofford College or the history of Southern education. The story of Wofford's conception and development unfolds in unbroken sequence: the high purpose of its founding, the relations between the College and the Church and the wider

7

public, the heroic wartime and postwar battles for survival, and its growth under the leadership of powerful personalities. The story includes the most complete account ever written of Benjamin Wofford, the life and character of Dr. James H. Carlisle, Dr. Henry N. Snyder, and Dean A. Mason DuPre, to name a few of the men whose lives have been woven into the making of the College. Anecdotes, incidents, and humor illustrate the characters and events of a stirring story.

Every aspect of the College life lives in the hundred and fourteen thousand words of the *History*. The appendices contain tables of the enrollment and graduates of each year from 1854 through 1950; the number of each kind of degree, earned or honorary, awarded each year; the list of names, with date and degree, of every person having received an honorary degree; a complete list of Trustees from the first, with the dates of service of each; a list of all instructors since the opening of the College, with their degrees, departments, and terms of service.

Wofford College is grateful for the privilege of making the *History* available to the friends and alumni of the College under the imprint of the Vanderbilt University Press.[1]

---

1. On April 29, 1951, as this book went to press, Dr. Wallace died at his home on Wofford campus.

8

THE AUTHOR

DR. DAVID DUNCAN WALLACE was born May 23, 1874, in Columbia, S. C., the son of William Henry Wallace and Alice Amanda (Lomax) Wallace, while his parents were members of the Faculty of the Columbia Female College. From them he derived by inheritance and association high ideals of scholarship and character. His mother was one of the most highly educated women in South Carolina, not only having been carried through the whole course of the Wofford College curriculum by her grandfather, Prof. David Duncan, but having continued her studies without intermission through her life. For instance, when her son returned from his graduate studies at Vanderbilt University, she seized upon his Anglo-Saxon books and before long had written out a translation of the whole of that exceedingly difficult Anglo-Saxon poem, Beowulf. January 10, 1900, Dr. Wallace married Miss Sophie Willis Adam, of Spartanburg, who lived to July 3, 1933. Of their four children, three follow the father's profession: Mrs. Edwin B. (Sophie Willis) Clippard and Alice L. Wallace in the public schools, and his second son, Dr. Robert M. Wallace, as Assistant Professor of English in the University of Alabama. His elder son, David Adam Wallace, lost his life by the torpedoing of his ship as he was bound for service abroad in the Second World War. October 6, 1937, Dr. Wallace married Miss Maud Summers Orr, who four years previously had come from Chicago to Spartanburg with the family of her sister, connected with Converse College.

Young Wallace was virtually fated for Wofford College, with which his mother had been intimately connected through her grandfather, Prof. David Duncan, of the original Faculty, and from which his father graduated. At considerable sacrifice his parents gave him his collegiate education at his father's Alma Mater. After receiving his A.B. there in 1894, he went to Vanderbilt University, where in 1899 he became the first person to take his Ph.D. degree in History. In 1924, the University of South Carolina conferred on him the degree of LL.D. and the Presbyterian College of South Carolina the degree of Litt.D. From 1896 to 1898, he taught History and English in the Carlisle Fitting School of Wofford College in Bamberg, S. C. In 1899, he became head of the newly created department of History and Economics in Wofford College, where he continued to teach those branches, except for several years' leave of absence for historical

9

research, until retired under the age limitation in 1947. For the first half year of 1917-18, he supplied the place of the distinguished historian, Ulrich B. Phillips, in the University of Michigan, where he gave graduate courses in American History. For the four years, 1929-33, he was on leave, except for one lecture a week, for writing the History of South Carolina, and was again on leave for historical research and writing for the eighteen months ending February, 1946. Since retirement, he has taught advanced and graduate classes for three quarters during 1947, 1948 and 1950 in Emory University and, for the academic year 1948-49, taught in the College of Charleston.

It is hard to say whether Dr. Wallace has been more teacher or writer; for all his writing has contributed to his work as a teacher. Not only are his published maps designed as teaching aids, but so are the numerous maps that he made for his classroom, and the globe, 61 and a quarter inches in diameter, which he constructed, so far as known the largest classroom globe in the country. While giving full attention to classroom duties and during his leaves of absence, Dr. Wallace has written (not to mention articles in the Encyclopaedia Britannica and other cyclopedias, and magazine and other articles) a number of works, usually on Southern or South Carolina history. His doctor's thesis was on *The Constitutional History of South Carolina from 1725 to 1775*. In 1906 appeared his *Civil Government of South Carolina and the United States,* used for many years in the public schools of the State until the style of such textbooks changed to something of a different character. It is still useful as a factual summary. The appearance of his *Life of Henry Laurens* from the press of Messrs. G. P. Putnam's Sons in 1915 won wide recognition. The London *Times Literary Supplement* of April 7, 1916, considered that "every chapter adds something to knowledge," and particularly supplements Sir George Trevelyan's *History of the American Revolution* where he neglects the Southern colonies. In a review occupying more than a page in the London *Spectator* of April 22, 1916, Lord Cromer, "the maker of modern Egypt," was impressed with the account of how the errors of British politicians had helped to throw away the most valuable part of the British Empire.

The *Laurens* was followed in 1915 by another volume from the Putnam press, *The Government of England,* a concise account of the British constitution as it actually operates, without the cluttering of historical and evolutionary lumber. In 1935 appeared from the press of the American Historical Society Dr. Wallace's most important work, the *History of South Carolina,* in three large volumes, which Dr. Francis B. Simkins of the

10

University of Louisiana in *"The State"* of June 26, 1949, calls "by far the best history of any Southern State." Dr. Milledge L. Bonham, Jr., of Hamilton College, New York, wrote in the *American Historical Review* of July, 1938:

Wallace displays an amazing mastery of his sources. Often it is evident that he could have written a monograph or a treatise where he has confined himself to a paragraph or a chapter. . . . Another outstanding virtue is the fearless impartiality of the book in dealing with persons, sections, causes, and movements. No reader can fail to perceive that Professor Wallace is a Carolinian to his marrow, with a deep love for his state and its people. But it is not the blind love of the narrow partisan; he perceives and records the errors of Carolina, her leaders, her institutions. Whether it be Negro versus White, Tory versus Whig, Secessionist versus Unionist, aristocrat versus plebeian, the merits and faults of both are impartially set forth. While the reviewer does not subscribe to all the author's opinions and conclusions, he must admit that the book is as unbiased as is humanly possible.

Said Charles A. Beard in *America in Midpassage* (p. 917),

When the geography of ideas was taken into account, it was perhaps just to say that the most fertile and penetrating historical writing of the midpassage was produced by Southern investigators, such as F. L. Owsley, B. B. Kendrick, A. M. Arnett, D. D. Wallace, Rupert Vance, and C. Vann Woodward, to make a selection.

There is now in process of publication by the University of North Carolina Press an abridged edition in one volume of the large three volume *History of South Carolina.* Dr. Wallace in 1935 prepared a set of large maps illustrative of South Carolina History, which were published by the Denoyer-Geppert Company for use in colleges and schools, presenting graphically the development of political, economic, and historical forces. He has also written two histories for which no publication arrangements have been made, *The Life of General Martin W. Gary,* and *A Hundred Years of Gregg and Graniteville.* His dramatization of the latter was presented several times to crowded audiences on the occasion of the centenary of the Graniteville Company. This side line was natural; for whatever he writes he sees, and makes his reader see, dramatically.

A good part of the two years, 1949-50, was used in writing the *History of Wofford College.* It contains the fullest account ever written of Benjamin Wofford, besides an account of all phases of college life, including the overcoming of hardships, the manifestation of human interests, and the realization of academic and religious aspirations.—W. K. G.

PREFACE

IT HAS been a great pleasure, personally and professionally, to trace the life of Wofford College through almost the first century of its existence. Perhaps I should not have been asked to write this history. I am too much of the professional historian, trained in the severe school of critical analysis and objective judgment, to practice indiscriminate worship or to describe characters in the style of tombstone obituaries, as writers of books of this kind seem sometimes to think is proper. I have finished my task, and what have I done? Given, I believe, a truer and better balanced picture of the leading characters connected with the history of Wofford College than has ever been done before, disagreeable to sentimentalists, but unavoidable if we are to seek historic truth. Also, I fear, I have offended some old friends, which is part of the price the sincere historian must pay; shocked traditionalists, which is badly needed, and, let me venture to hope, impressed thinking men with the fact that there is no permanent safety for Wofford College or justification for the sacrifices of a loyal constituency except for Trustees and Faculty to join to high moral ideals vigorous intellectual life. Real interest in our past is one way of showing that we are really alive.

The most useful source of information has been the Minutes of the Board of Trustees, because they are the most complete and best kept of our records. But even they at certain periods leave much to be desired. Long resolutions "spread upon the Minutes," informing us that such and such a deceased member was various kinds of a good and valuable man, are of little value to the historian; while tantalizing are such entries as that the reports of the President and Treasurer of the college were read and received as information, without the slightest clue as to what the nature of the information was. Often, however, the reports of the Trustees or President or the Conference Educational Committee to the Conference as recorded in that body's printed *Minutes* come to our rescue. I congratulate the future historian, and through him all who may be interested in our history, that President Greene insists that the good plan generally followed in the past, of the information itself being spread upon the minutes, shall be followed in future.

My own connection with the college as student and teacher covers more than half its life span, and through the papers and recollections of my

13

ancestors reaches back through my great-grandfather, a member of the first Faculty, to the beginning. I have also enjoyed intimate association with numbers of men for long periods connected officially or otherwise with the college. Others to whom my thanks are due for supplying documentary or other material are President Walter K. Greene, Dr. H. B. Carlisle, Treasurer J. K. Davis, Librarian Miss Mary DuPre, Prof. Herbert Hucks, and the late President H. N. Snyder and Dr. A. M. DuPre. My wife Mrs. Maud Orr Wallace has been of invaluable assistance in reading the proofs. I thank Mr. Robert H. Willis for his skill in producing or reproducing a number of photographs, and the editors of *The Bohemian* for permission to use several pictures from that publication.

D. D. Wallace

Wofford College, November 1950.

CONTENTS

15

CONTENTS

CHAPTER I

WOFFORD ANCESTRY AND BACKGROUND

SAID Dr. James H. Carlisle, "Benjamin Wofford united three words not often found together: a rich Methodist preacher." Who was this man and how did this come to be?

The Woffords were of that great tide of migration from the British Isles such a large portion of which flowed mainly into Philadelphia and drifted along the Piedmont plateau into the colonies to the southward. Two Wofford brothers from Northern England settled in Pennsylvania, near the Maryland line, says the Spartanburg Wofford family tradition. More definite is the statement of a Wofford descendant Mr. J. W. Gladney of Phoenix, Arizona, whose family tree says that Absalom Wofford (1690-1750) of Cumberland County, England, settled with his wife Sara in Prince George's County, Maryland, and had at least one son of the same name as one of the five who are known to have come to Spartanburg, and, like him, was a Revolutionary soldier. [1] This is in harmony with the statement of the very reliable Landrum's *History of Spartanburg County* that Col. William Wofford, the eldest of the five brothers who came here, was born near Rock Creek, Maryland, about twelve miles above the present city of Washington, October 25, 1728. One of the Spartanburg Woffords settled in the Friendship neighborhood, one near the present Woodruff, one on Enoree River, one near the present Glendale, and one, Joseph, in whom we are most interested, near the site of the later Hill's Factory on Tyger River. William, Joseph, James, John, and Benjamin are names scattered abundantly among their descendants. William and James were Deputy Surveyors, whose names are signed to plats in the State archives from the early 1760's. [2]

These Woffords were substantial citizens, some of whom occupied official positions and several of whom prospered materially. Ensign Campbell of the British army during the Revolution says that Col. William Wofford was a rich Tory at whose house the Ensign's troops obtained abundant refreshments. Clearly Campbell fell into confusion as to Col.

---

1. The genealogist Mr. Leonardo Andrea, who prepared recently an extensive Wofford genealogy, to whom I am indebted for the data concerning Absalom Wofford, is uncertain whether to believe the five Woffords who came to Spartanburg County the sons of this Absalom, or of a William Wofford; inclines toward the latter.

2. A. S. Salley to D. D. Wallace.

Wofford's politics. Draper in his *King's Mountain and Its Heroes* gives an account of Col. William Wofford's services in the American forces. He built Wofford's Iron Works on Pacolet River, which the British burned— further evidence of the fact that William Wofford was on the American side.[3] Numerous grants of land were made to Woffords from the 1760's on, some of them quite large, especially those to William and James. Joseph, in whom we are more interested, was by no means so prosperous as some of his brothers. We find a grant to him in 1793 of 61 acres on Tyger River, though surely he must have owned land long before that, and in 1795 one for 417 acres on Two Mile Creek in Spartanburg County, and in 1797 one for 370 acres in the same county. These data, taken from the Grant Book in Columbia, are not conclusive as to all property owned by the Woffords, for they take no note of inheritances or purchases, but merely serve our purpose of showing the general material welfare of the Wofford clan.

The Census of 1790 gives the following data:

	Free white males 16 yrs. and over	Free ditto under 16	Free white females	Slaves
John Wofford	4	—	3	2
Capt. James Wofford	3	2	8	—
Benjamin Wofford	3	2	5	9
Jeremiah Wofford	2	—	1	—
Joseph Wofford	2	2	5	5
Absolem Wofford	3	3	3	—

Joseph Wofford, the father of the founder of Wofford College, was a Captain in the American forces in the Revolution. An indent in the records acknowledges a debt to him by the State of £42 and interest for services in Col. Roebuck's regiment since the fall of Charleston on May 12, 1780. Another indent, which he sold to Ferdinand Phinezy, is assigned and signed in Wofford's own hand.

Another brother, Benjamin, illustrated the division of families which made the Revolution largely a civil war. The papers of the Council of Safety of December 9, 1775, tell us that Capt. Benjamin Wofford had been brought down to Charleston by a party of rangers and confined in one of the officers' rooms by order of Col. Huger.[4] It runs true to form that one of the richest, if not the richest, of the family stood with the Tories,

---

3. The Revolutionary records in Columbia show indents issued to one William Wofford, a private, and one to Captain William Wofford, the latter for service in Col. Roebuck's regiment; also indents for services by several other Woffords. *Landrum's History of Spartanburg County,* and the *History of the Wofford Family,* published by the Wofford Memorial Association in 1928, give data on names and locations of settlements.

4. *S. C. Historical and Genealogical Mag.,* III, 198, Oct., 1902. Also *Wof. Fam. Hist.,* 13, 50.

i.e., the conservatives. Benjamin suffered the loss of his estate of 1,065 acres by the Confiscation Act of 1782, though it does not appear from the records whether his lands were actually sold before the general pardon of the Tories some years later.[5] Benjamin's petitions for pardon were several times refused. The family tradition that he was last seen standing on the deck of a ship in Charleston harbor (presumably fleeing with the British army on its withdrawal in 1782) is not sustained by his own statement in his petitions of 1789 and 1792 in the Historical Commission office in Columbia, numerously signed by his neighbors, that he never left the State, but returned to his family and put himself on the mercy of his country. We find him in 1786 and 1790 shrewdly buying up indents (the certificates of the State's indebtedness for services or supplies during the Revolution), which were finally paid by the United States government when it assumed the State debts incurred in the struggle for independence. He must not have been such a hateful character, despite the fact that his conviction as to the best way to preserve freedom for Americans differed from that of the other Woffords; for his brother Joseph "stood for him and asked for mercy for him during the Revolution when Benjamin was arrested," [6] and gave his son born during the war his Tory uncle's name.

Joseph Wofford, the father of the founder of Wofford College, was born in 1741 and lived at least until 1826.[7] According to Dr. Benjamin Wofford, nephew of the founder, Joseph Wofford was a small man, round shouldered, quick of movement, irritable in disposition, quick to resent, quick to forgive.[8] He married in 1768 Martha Llewellyn, daughter of Hugh Llewellyn, whose father was born in Wales.[9] She was born in Pennsylvania of Quaker parents and was brought while young by her father to South Carolina. Joseph lived in Spartanburg County, not far from the south side of Tyger River. Though "by no means a wealthy man," [10] in the Revolution he was Captain of a company in Col. John Thomas, Sr.'s, Spartan regiment, for which the district was named in 1776. On one occasion while he was hiding out for safety the Tories, led by Capt. Nat Young, watched his house closely; for they knew that he had an urgent reason for wishing to be at home. Having observed him enter, they captured him and threatened to

---

5. *Statutes at Large*, IV, 519; VI, 632; Confiscation records. Mr. Andrea, cited above, for Confiscation records.

6. Andrea.

7. Benjamin Wofford, the founder, says in an obituary of his mother dated May 18, 1826, in the *Methodist Magazine*, IX, 358-9, that at his mother's death, March 24, 1826, his father was eighty-five. (Erroneously printed 83 in *Wofford Family*, 55.)

8. *Wof. Fam.*, 39.

9. Andrea, quoting J. W. Gladney of note 1 above, as to Hugh's father being born in Wales.

10. B. L. Allen, son of Emanuel Allen, who was an intimate friend of the founder and married his niece, in *Hist. Wof. Fam.*, 125.

hang him. Mrs. Wofford, lying in childbed, called to Young to come to her. As he sat on the edge of the bed, she pled with him for the life of her husband: "Nat, if Joe is killed tonight, it will kill me. I cannot survive the shock. So you will have to give account at the Great Day, not for killing Joe alone, but for two others. It is murder, Nat, and you know it. I plead tonight for the life of Joe, my life, and for the life of my babe." "Captain Nat had once sued for her hand and her love, and he was touched by her helpless entreaty. He pledged her that not a hair of her husband's head should be hurt; and, true to his word, he allowed Joe to escape. That night Benjamin Wofford, the founder of Wofford College, was born." [11]

Capt. Joseph Wofford bore to his death scars about his head and neck received during the Revolution; but he lived for at least 85 years and reared six children.

The house in which the child was born that night of October 19, 1780, has long since disappeared. It stood on the southern side of Hill's Bridge Road, as it is now called, two or three hundred yards southeast of Tyger River, and about a third of a mile southward of Tabernacle Methodist Church.[12] Benjamin Wofford's mother was a deeply religious woman, who had deliberately chosen the Methodist instead of any of the other faiths that had been urged upon her. For many years her husband was so determinedly irreligious that he would not allow her the means of riding to church, several miles away; but, says Mr. B. L. Allen, he would habitually relent (or, we might better say, repent) and call one of his sons to go with the team after his mother. Once when the children were all away he went himself and heard enough of the sermon to make him a changed man. "Until 1802," says Benjamin Wofford in the only article known to have been written by him, "she traveled alone in Zion." In that year, he says, she had the happiness to see her husband and most of her children brought, under the preaching of Revs. George Dougherty and Lewis Meyers, into the fold. Her prayer that at least one of her sons should be called to preach was answered in her son Benjamin. She died a rejoicing Christian March 24, 1826, as she and her husband were reading together Clark's Commentary.[13]

Benjamin Wofford, as he himself tells us, was converted under the preaching of Rev. George Dougherty, one of the leading Methodist ministers of the South Carolina of that day, and Rev. Lewis Meyers. He joined the church under the pastorate of Meyers. "In August following,"

---

11. *Wof. Fam. Hist.,* 47.
12. Mr. Samuel T. Lanham to D. D. Wallace.
13. Wofford in *Methodist Mag.,* IX, 358-9 (Sept., 1826).

under the preaching of Dougherty and Mark Moore at "perhaps the first camp meeting held in South Carolina," he felt the call to preach. Several months later he was licensed by Dougherty, his Presiding Elder, to exhort. Something drew the young man of twenty-five to the West, and we find him during the first half of the year 1806 applying to Presiding Elder William McKendree of the Cumberland District in the Western Conference for work. McKendree assigned him as an assistant to Rev. Jesse Walker, who was serving the Hartford Circuit in Western Kentucky.[14] Wofford ranked as an exhorter, intending at the next session of the Conference to apply for admission on trial. On the second day of the Western Conference (therefore September 16), 1806, he is listed as tenth among twelve applicants for admission on trial on the recommendation of their respective District Quarterly Meeting Conferences. The entry in the Conference *Minutes* reads:

"Benjamin Wofford came from South Carolina, as a licensed local preacher, into the bounds of the Western Annual Conference, and was imployed [sic] by the presiding elder of the Destrict [sic], to ride Hartford Circuit, and from the Quarterly Meeting Conference of said circuit obtained a proper recommendation. The Annual Conference think proper to admit him on trial, upon condition that he provide, as soon as may be, for the emancipation of his two slaves, now in South Carolina."[15] Two days later we have this entry: "William McKendree proceeded to read one letter addressed to Benjamin Wofford, on the business of his two Negroes in South Carolina, and advises him to measuer's: [sic] thay [sic] may secure there [sic] emancipation." A year later, i.e. September 17, 1807, we have the final reference to our friend: "The papers respecting Benjamin Wofford read and the Conference agreed to admit the settlement."

We can only infer what "the settlement" was. Wofford apparently continued to work in the Western Conference as an exhorter under McKendree's direction for some months into 1807; for his most intimate friends say he worked there "during the year 1806 and part of 1807."[16] July 30, 1807, he married Miss Anna Todd, the daughter of Thomas Todd, the

---

14. The idea of many persons generally well informed on church history that Benjamin Wofford "traveled a wilderness circuit that stretched from Nashville on the Cumberland to Cincinnati on the Ohio" (Dr. Snyder's *Educational Odyssey*, 111) is entirely erroneous, and arises from confusing Wofford's circuit with Presiding Elder McKendree's district, which the Western Conference *Minutes* of 1806 show contained eight circuits, of which Wofford's Hartford Circuit was one. Dr. Carlisle's vague statement in the *Southern Christian Advocate* of Deecmber 1, 1883, that Wofford "did missionary work under Wm. McKendree (afterwards Bishop), whose district included large portions of Kentucky and Ohio," might be taken to mean that he worked all over the district. The Doctor presumably had access to the Western Conference *Minutes* only in the condensed form, which do not show the details of Wofford's assignment to one circuit as an exhorter assisting the regular preacher. *The Carolina Spartan*, Oct. 28, 1885, quotes Dr. Carlisle as saying in an address on Benjamin Wofford, "he traveled a circuit reaching from Nashville to Cincinnati."

15. *The Rise of Methodism in the West, being the Journal of the Western Conference* 1800-1811, edited by W. W. Sweet, p. 114.

16. Judge J. Wofford Tucker, in *Hist. of Wof. Family*.

richest man in his section. We may assume that his own possession of only two slaves argues that he brought small possessions into the union. His parents were not rich, and he was not yet 27. His bride was just 23, having been born July 23, 1784.[17]

It is impossible to doubt that Wofford's leaving his active religious work was chiefly due to his desire to marry. If the only impediment had been the ownership of slaves he could have met that by electing to preach in South Carolina instead of the West. "Locating," i.e., retiring from the active ministry, as a result of marriage was in that day of small salaries and vast circuits so common that Bishop Asbury, like David on one occasion falling into exaggerated language on the untruthfulness of all men, lamented, The devil and the women will get all my preachers!

The relation of slaveholding to the ministry, which here entered into the career of Benjamin Wofford, early rose to vex the Methodists and ultimately led to the division of the church. Wesley, Asbury, and Coke, like Washington, Jefferson, and Patrick Henry, were all strongly unfavorable to the institution; but the Methodist leaders, particularly Coke, were more willing to do something about it. Asbury, though feeling strongly, was more prudent, while Coke's agitation was so ardent that he was threatened in Virginia with mob violence and legal prosecution. The early persecution of the Methodists in Charleston was largely due to their being considered abolitionists. As early as 1780 the informal conference of Methodist preachers in Baltimore declared that all traveling preachers in the denomination owning slaves ought to be required to free them. The Conference which in 1784 gave the church its national organization established the rule that all Methodists must take this self-denying step where the law permitted emancipation; but the impractical nature of such an extreme caused its suspension in six months regarding lay members; and in 1808 the General Conference felt obliged to rule that each Conference should be allowed to deal with the question as it saw fit.[18]

Wofford's marriage was of vast importance, not only in his own life, but in that of many others besides. Thomas Todd built a home, known as "the red house," for the young couple, where they lived until Mr. Todd's death July 2, 1809, after which they moved into the home of his widow and lived with her until her death in January, 1818. Says Mr. B. L. Allen:

17. B. L. Allen in *Hist. of Wof. Family*, 126, on the Todds. Allen was the son of Emanuel Allen, intimate friend of Wofford, who married the niece who lived with Mr. and Mrs. Wofford and bought Wofford's old home place when Wofford moved to a new home to the southward. Judge J. Wofford Tucker, great nephew of Wofford, is authority for the other statements from 1802 through Wofford's retirement, except for the exact statement regarding Wofford's conversion, which is from his obituary of his mother.

18. McTyeire, *Hist. of Methodism*, 375, 380, 536.

"After the death of Mrs. Todd, Benjamin Wofford and his wife continued to live at the old homestead, inheriting all the property of Thomas Todd. This inheritance was the nucleus on which Benjamin Wofford built —the nucleus which gave Wofford College to the South Carolina Conference."[19] At that time ownership of the wife's personal property, and the management, but not the ownership, of her real estate, and the control of its income, belonged to the husband, an arrangement which in this case by no means endangered the estate.

By all accounts Anna Todd was an exceptional woman. She was so widely beloved for her numerous works of kindness that, at her death, October 2, 1835, the little church was incapable of containing the mourners, so that the funeral service was held beneath the roof of a large barn then under construction. A persistent tradition credits her with a large part in planting in Wofford's mind his interest in education. Dr. James H. Carlisle, writing in the *Southern Christian Advocate* of December 1, 1883, in referring to Mrs. Anna Todd Wofford, speaks of "the plans of benevolence which Mr. Wofford and his wife had begun very early to devise."[20] In another article he says that Mrs. Anna Todd Wofford "is believed to have suggested or strengthened the definite purpose to promote education."[21]

The Woffords had no children; but, feeling the need of young life in the home, he persuaded his widowed sister Mrs. Nancy Tucker, says Mr. Allen, to allow one of her daughters to live in his home. The daughter Nancy accordingly lived with the Woffords until her marriage to Emanuel Allen, the father of the Mr. B. L. Allen quoted above. Emanuel Allen bought the place where Wofford then lived, Wofford reserving only the burial plot, when Wofford moved a few miles to the southward, where he made his home until he moved to the town of Spartanbnrg in 1840. From about 1833 to '36 he spent the winters in Columbia.[22]

May 7, 1817, Wofford and his wife gave an acre and a half for the erection of a Methodist house of worship, which he always called "the chapel," though Rev. William Martin later named it Grace Chapel. Membership having drifted away, it has long been abandoned. "In it he worshipped and preached for years," says Mr. Allen, but with what regularity and on what terms we do not know. Dr. James H. Carlisle, repeating family tradition, says that he labored there as "local deacon." As a matter of fact, Bishop Asbury ordained Wofford deacon at Bethel Academy

---

19. *Wof. Fam. Hist.*, 126.
20. Reproduced in *Hist. of Wof. Fam.*, 65-9.
21. *Ib.*, 69-70.
22. Dr. J. H. Carlisle in *Ib.*, 67-8, on Columbia residence.

November 18, 1814, proving that, regardless of his having been denied ordination in the West because of holding slaves, his religious interest and his determination to preach continued.[23] The late Major A. H. Kirby, who was all but 22 years old when Wofford died, writes that "he was after the old type of Methodist preachers (then a local preacher), and was very earnest though somewhat methodical in style of preaching." Dr. Carlisle says, "As a preacher he was earnest and practical."

The Conference which met in Columbia, December 25, 1816, admitted Benjamin Wofford on trial. He was appointed junior preacher on Enoree Circuit, in which his home lay, for the year 1817, and as junior preacher on the Reedy River Circuit for 1818. At the Conference meeting at Camden, December 24, 1818, he was ordained elder and was sent for the year 1819 again as junior preacher on Reedy River Circuit. At the end of this third year of service as a traveling preacher of the South Carolina Conference, in the region near his home, he was located by the Conference meeting in Charleston, January 13, 1820.[24]

Wofford's first wife, Anna Todd, died October 2, 1835. September 6, 1836, he married Miss Maria Sevier Barron, daughter of Dr. Barron of Virginia, whom he met while traveling in that State. She was 33 to his all but 56.[25] Her portrait, painted by W. K. Barclay, of Columbia, S. C., in 1844, shows her as still a woman of considerable beauty and distinct refinement. In both his marriages Wofford illustrated that common occurrence of a man of ability out-marrying himself socially. This portrait and the one of her husband painted by the same artist at the same time were given to Wofford College in 1883 after Mrs. Wofford's death by Mrs. Mary R. (Wells) Agnew, the niece of Mrs. Wofford.[26] The young and beautiful Mrs. Wofford, though a woman of sterling character and devoted to her husband both in sickness and in health, did not like the quiet life in the remote and sparsely settled region below Tyger River. Wofford himself seems to have found it irksome; for he had, for three or four years before

23. This ordination was not at Annual Conference. The fact and the date are from an article by "A Friend," in *Southern Christian Advocate* of March 28, 1851—evidently a very intimate friend, all of whose statements subject to verification are correct.

24. *S. C. Conf. Minutes.*

25. I thank Miss Willie Wells, of Morristown, Tenn., a relative of Mrs. Wofford, for the day and month of Mrs. Wofford's birth June 5, 1803, and for her middle name, Sevier, both taken directly from the family Bible. The minutes of the Spartanburg lodge of Masons July 7, 1851, speak of the letter received from Mrs. Maria Scott Wofford; but the transcription of the letter has Mrs. Maria S. Wofford, the same as she signed herself in deeds recorded in the Spartanburg County records. I thank Rev. M. B. Gass, of Bull's Gap, Tenn., pastor in 1949 of the Antioch Methodist Church about ten miles northwestward of Greeneville, Tenn., and his successor, Rev. E. C. Trentham, for inspecting the tombstone, which, however, does not give the data supplied by Miss Wells; and Dr. Anna Wells Agnew of the State Hospital in Brooklyn, N. Y., a grand niece, for much assistance. The surmise that Mrs. Wofford met her husband at a camp meeting in Virginia which she often attended is from another great niece, Mrs. Myra W. Steele.

26. *So. Ch. Ad.,* Jan. 17, 1883, and J. H. Carlisle in *ib.* Dec. 1, 1883.

his second marriage, been spending the winters in Columbia. His home in Spartanburg village, a large square, plain two-story house, torn down within my memory, stood about in the roadway of the present St. John Street Extension, and faced Magnolia Street. Dr. Robert E. Cleveland's house was on his north, the Russell house to his south, and the Simpson Bobo house (later moved to his, i.e., the eastern, side of Magnolia Street to make way for the courthouse) was diagonally across the street—distinctly an upper class neighborhood. Few today know why Wofford and Short Wofford Streets bear those names.

A sort of innate talent and love for making money early turned Wofford to business and finance. We find him connected with the first cotton mill erected in Spartanburg County, the little 489 spindle factory erected in 1816 by Philip Weaver, one of the textile pioneers, two groups of whom came to Spartanburg from Rhode Island at this time. The fact that Wofford, December 17, 1818, sold to Nathaniel Gist the sixty acres along Tyger River containing the South Carolina Cotton Manufactory would indicate it was his land, and perhaps his money, which supplemented Weaver's technical skill.[27] Wofford's experience with the textile industry was not encouraging, for Weaver's enterprise did not prove so successful as did that of the Hills just a little later a few miles up the river. Wofford's conservative nature turned to banks and money lending. We infer that it was only as landowner or money lender that he was connected with Weaver's enterprise. He seems to have steered clear of the speculations in land and railroads at which so many in his day made and lost fortunes, though at times he owned considerable land. Compounding his interest and dividends was his safer and surer plan. His executors, for instance, sold his stock in three banks in Columbia and Charleston for more than $60,000.

But Wofford was not interested solely in money lending. While very much of a combination of a Benjamin Franklin economist and a Methodist Puritan, he was, like Franklin, very much of a patriot. On one occasion, when the Indians on the Southern border, apparently in the Seminole War, were on the rampage, Wofford was on hand at the muster ground where militiamen from lower Spartanburg and part of Union assembled. To meet the immediate expenses for the equipment of the quota of men called for a collection was taken up. "The soldier spirit was upon him," says his nephew Judge J. Wofford Tucker. "When the lines were established and the bugle sounded, he threw a $100 bill into the collector's hat, mounted his fine bay

---

27. D. D. Wallace, *Hist. of S. C.*, II, 411, with citation to Spartanburg County records. No land seems to have been acquired by the Weavers until eight months after the above sale. Weaver's mill was on a creek running into Tyger River from the south.

horse, and gallantly rode along the lines calling for volunteers." Ten times as many men as were called for responded.[28] Wofford was a great admirer of Calhoun and said to him the last time he saw him that if he was elected President he would go to see him inaugurated, but that otherwise he would have no interest in going to Washington.[29] We are not surprised, therefore, to know that Wofford was a member of the defeated Nullification ticket for Spartanburg for the Convention of 1832.[30]

---

28. Judge Tucker, in *Wof. Fam. Hist.*, 58. Tucker says that he remembered the incident as a boy and was thrilled.
29. *Ib.*
30. Major William Hoy, *Historical Reminiscences*, MS., lent me by Mr. Robert J. Gantt.

CHAPTER II

BENJAMIN WOFFORD FOUNDS A COLLEGE

TO HIS contemporaries, the outstanding fact in Wofford's life was his propensity and gift for making and saving money. But deep in his mind, and known to only a few friends, was the purpose of accumulating and using money for some religious or educational purpose, with finally a preference for the latter. Dr. Carlisle thinks that his character may have been influenced in this direction by the two primitive Methodist preachers under whose preaching he was converted, George Dougherty and Lewis Meyers. Dougherty was an unflagging apostle of education. The plain, humble Meyers, with his tiny income, managed to save a few hundred dollars, which at his death he gave for widows and orphans. From one of these men, says Dr. Carlisle, Wofford may have learned to save and spend money wisely; from the other to value education for enlarging the life of the individual and the church. To this I think we must add the belief, supported by a widely held tradition, that his wife Anna Todd stimulated his interest in education, as well as, through her inheritance from her father, having supplied such a large part of the foundation fortune which constantly grew under her husband's management and rendered possible transforming an ideal into a reality.

Wofford was solicited by Stephen Olin, President of Randolph-Macon College, chartered in 1830 and opened in 1832, or by its financial agent, Rev. William M. Wightman, to contribute to the support of that institution, and did, like several other South Carolinians, give $1,000;[1] but he was not inclined to make an institution so far away the medium for realizing the plans maturing in his mind. By 1844, stimulated perhaps by the crisis in the life of the church connected with the separation in that year of its Northern and Southern branches, he seems to have come to a definite conclusion. It has always been assumed that in trying in 1844 to buy the Limestone Springs Company property at the later Gaffney he was seeking to obtain, at a most attractive bargain, as it would have been, a site for the college which he had determined to found. Dr. Carlisle's expression is that his intention was to give it to the Conference for educational purposes. The company had in

---

1. Statement by Dr. J. H. Carlisle.

27

1835 erected on the ample grounds around the limestone spring a large brick summer hotel and a number of cottages. When after a brief period of success the company failed the Bank of the State of South Carolina held a mortgage for $21,200 it had lent on the property, and in 1844 was offering it for sale to satisfy the remaining part of the debt. Mr. Wofford offered to pay the amount, $10,000; but when the time came for final settlement a difference arose over a small amount of interest. Both sides stuck to what they considered their rights and the trade was called off. The property went to Dr. Thomas Curtis, an able and learned English Baptist clergyman, and his clergyman son William in 1845 for $10,000, who at once opened the Lime Stone Springs Female High School, which eventually grew into the present Limestone College.[2]

Benjamin Wofford was apparently thus definitely planning as early as 1844 to found a college. He told his friend Rev. H. A. C. Walker in 1849 that he had long considered doing this, but had been deflected by the adverse opinion of a friend to devoting his fortune to serving the church in other ways. It was the exact shape of his beneficence, and not the intention to act for the good of his fellow men and his church, which at times appeared uncertain. He considered himself as an agent and trustee. He once said to me, writes his great nephew Judge J. Wofford Tucker, "It is growing on my hands. Here is nearly $150,000. Every year it is augmented. I must leave it behind me, so [as] to do some good. What shall I do with it?"[3]

It was Wofford's friend and fellow minister who finally focused his mind on the plan for a college. Dr. James H. Carlisle, in an article entitled "An Interesting Question Partly Answered," quotes a paper dictated to him by Rev. H. A. C. Walker May 3, 1884, and never before published.[4] Rev. Walker said:

"In 1849 I was Agent in favor of one of our Christian enterprises,[5] and turned aside to share my friend's love and hospitality for a day and night. He was then very feeble in age and in suffering, though he could rise from his bed and move about in his house—even exerting himself to a seat in the

---

2. Dr. J. H. Carlisle in *Hist. of Wof. Family,* 71; W. C. Taylor, *Hist. of Limestone College,* 9-12; Spartanburg County mesne conveyance records, Mortgages, Books X, 299; Z, 547 and DD, 636, 638.

3. Tucker as above, p. 61.

4. The original MS. of Walker's statement is in the college archives, in Dr. Carlisle's handwriting and signed tremblingly by H. A. C. Walker. I use the MS., as the printed article differs, quite materially, in one or two places from the original. Dr. Carlisle's article in the *Southern Christian Advocate* is reprinted in *History of the Wofford Family,* 69-75.

5. The American Bible Society, the Doctor's article interjects in parenthesis.

yard, taking me with him. Entering into conversation, he leading, we spoke to this effect:

" 'Brother Walker, my time is short; I want to give the greater part of my property to our church, and I desire to advise with you how to dispose of it.'

" 'This takes me by surprise, my dear Brother Wofford; but if I can aid you, I shall be at your service.'

" 'I want to divide it out to church societies—to all, or select, and in proportion, or proportionally.'

" 'I do not know about that, Brother Wofford. What amount do you give in all?'

" 'One hundred thousand dollars.'

" 'If you divide this amount as you propose among the church societies, you give where it will do good in several places, limitedly and comparatively little. Why not found a college—spreading widely—working, increasing in power and goodness through the ages as they come?'

" 'I had thought of that once, long since, but when I proposed it to Brother W——, he bluffed me so that I thought that there was no wish of having a college.'

" 'Be assured, Brother Wofford, you misapprehended Brother W——, for he earnestly desired a college within our Conference bounds, and still greatly wishes it.'

" 'Assured of what you say, I am quite pleased that a college should be founded.'

"Brother Wofford continued conversing with me on the subject. He expressed himself gratified, and said, 'Now, Brother Walker, as you must go today, will you write me in full what you have said and send me the paper?'

" 'I will, with great pleasure.'

" 'Brother Walker, be prompt—time is short—mine is near its end.'

"After a cordial separation, I went away, to meet him no more till I stand at the pearly gates."

The interview was out of doors, probably in the mild weather of summer or autumn, 1849, and hence only a few months before the date of Wofford's will, February 1, 1850. The college owes only less to Rev. H. A. C. Walker than to Benjamin Wofford himself; for without Walker's firm and sensible advice Wofford's beneficence might have become a shower so thinly spread as to evaporate with only a fraction of the benefits that would flow from a reservoir of refreshment and strength.

It was indeed as Wofford said: "Time is short—mine is near its end." "A Friend," evidently a very intimate friend, writes in the *Southern Christian Advocate* of March 28, 1851, of Wofford's last days and illness. He was taken sick October 18, 1850, and for the next six weeks was in "extreme physical suffering." Violent paroxysms of vomiting continued from the first until three hours of the end. "It would be paying but a merited tribute to his pious and accomplished wife to say that she attended him constantly and untiringly, as no one else could have done, never leaving his room unless compelled to do so by imperious necessity. She was to him a messenger of mercy and comfort; indeed he would have no one else to minister to him." He would frequently urge that she must take care of herself. He asked for friends to come and sing and pray with him. When a third physician, in addition to the two who had been serving him, was called in the hope that something might be done, his answer was, "You cannot live, you must die—I hope, Mr. Wofford, you are prepared for meeting your God." "Yes," replied the dying man, and passed away in perfect confidence and peace. It was Monday morning, December 2, 1850, at half past six o'clock.[6]

Wofford's was an active mind, said the local newspaper, with pure republican principles and imbued with prudent firmness and ardor for the rights and interests of his native State. His hospitality is remembered by thousands. By his express wish he was buried in the little plot at the old home which was built for himself and his first wife by her father, in which already lay Thomas Todd, his wife, and their daughter. On a visit to Emanuel Allen, who had bought the place, with whom he usually spent a week every year, pointing to the three graves, he had directed Allen to build a wall enclosing them and space for a fourth grave. "When I am dead, bury me there," he said, pointing to the vacant space. Allen called his attention to the inferior quality of the brick he had bought for the wall and said that more money should be spent, so as to make it durable for all time, and suggested that a monument might sometime be placed over his grave. Wofford replied, "No, that will do; I do not want a monument nor anything expensive about my burial place." [7] On the plain stone, which he had directed should be placed at his grave, were inscribed the words, believed to have been composed by his great nephew Judge J. Wofford Tucker:

6. See also *Spartan*, Dec. 5, 1850, reprinted in Wofford Catalogue of 1870-71, 19; also see *So. Ch. Ad.*, Dec. 13, 1850. An article in *Spg. Herald* Nov. 5, 1922, apparently by J. H. Carlisle, Jr., errs in saying that Wofford died in the Trinity house (a printer's mistake probably for Twitty house, which stood where the post office now is).

7. B. L. Allen, in *Hist. of Wof. Fam.*, 129-30.

BENJAMIN WOFFORD FOUNDS A COLLEGE

ENTOMBED BENEATH
ARE THE MORTAL REMAINS
OF
THE REV. BENJAMIN WOFFORD
SON OF
JOSEPH AND MARTHA WOFFORD
WHO WAS BORN
THE 19th DAY OF OCTOBER, A.D. 1780
AND DEPARTED THIS LIFE IN THE FULL
TRIUMPHS OF THE CHRISTIAN FAITH
THE SECOND DAY OF DECEMBER,
AGED 70 YEARS, ONE MONTH AND 13 DAYS.

*For 48 years he was a member of the Methodist Episcopal Church,
for 16 years a minister of the gospel; he gave to the country and the
church an institution for the benefit of which countless thousands, yet
unborn, may have reason to be thankful and reverence the donor's name.*
PEACE TO HIS ASHES

On Founder's Day, October 19, 1920, the remains of himself and his wife Anna Todd were moved to Wofford College Campus.[8]

The closing words of the epitaph point out the one fact without which Benjamin Wofford would not be remembered. So exclusively has this act been noticed that the man behind the gift has become a sort of abstraction. His last will and testament has been spoken of as though it contained little besides his bequest for the college, whereas it contains many points illustrating his character as a man, who, though deeply devoted to one aim, yet was marked by the common aims and purposes of humanity.[9]

Item 3. I give to "my dearly beloved wife Maria S. Wofford" the house and lot where we live in the village of Spartanburg, with all its furnishings, valued at $4,000; also my carriage and all live stock, valued at $1,000; also two slaves valued at $1300 and $1400; also $10,000; also fifty acres of land above the village which I bought of E. C. Leitner.
Item 4. To my friend and "connexion" Emanuel Allen $1000 and two slaves.
Item 5. To my nephew Major Harvey Wofford $1,000 and four slaves.
Item 6. To my brother Joseph Wofford $1,000.
Item 7. To my kinsman Dr. Benjamin Wofford $1,000 and the note and interest of about $1,000 that he owes me.
Item 8. To my kinsman John Wesley Wofford $1,000.
Item 9. To my kinsman Jeremiah Wofford $1,000.
Item 10. To my kinsman Joseph Wofford $1,000.

8. Faculty Minutes.
9. Will; also papers of Benjamin Wofford's executors in Probate office, Spartanburg.

31

Item 11. To my niece Mrs. Bennett $500.

Item 12. To my niece Mrs. John Lankford $500.

Item 13. To my niece Mrs. Willis Leyton $500.

Item 14. To my niece Mrs. Coleman C. Leyton $500.

Item 15. To my niece Jane Wofford $500.

Item 16. To my sisters Ann Tucker and Rebecca Mullinax each an annuity of $100 during life, funds to produce same to be invested by my executors.

Item 17. To my sister Martha White and all her children living at my death $3,000 to be equally divided among them, except that none of this to go to Mrs. Harvey Wofford, as she is otherwise provided for.

Item 18. To Samuel W. Tucker and his two sons, $1,000, to be equally divided among them.

Item 19. To Mrs. J. M. Lanham, $300.

Item 20. To Anna W. Tucker $500.

Item 21. To Joseph W. Tucker (i. e. J. Wofford Tucker) $1,000.

Item 22. To Mrs. Rebecca Gillam $300.

Item 23. To Mrs. Patsy Powell and her two daughters, to be divided equally, $300.

Item 24. To the American Bible Society $1,000.

Item 25. To the South Carolina Missionary Society $4,000.

"*Item 26.* For the purpose of establishing and endowing a college for literary, classical and scientific education, to be located in my native District Spartanburg, and to be under the control and management of the Methodist Episcopal Church of my native State, South Carolina, I order" $100,000 to be delivered to trustees, half, if so much shall be required, for lands and buildings, and the balance solely for the purpose of an income-producing endowment. If the estate falls short of the amount of bequests, the shortage shall be made up from the bequest to the college. (There was no shortage.)

Item 27. My executors are to dispose of the balance of my estate not specifically devised at public sale on one and two years' credit, with interest from date of sale.

Item 28. If my estate exceeds these legacies, my executors shall apportion the surplus among all the legatees, except that none of the surplus shall go to my wife, the Bible Society, the Missionary Society, or the college.

Item 29. I appoint my nephew Major Harvey Wofford and Dr. Benjamin Wofford my executors.

The will was approved in common form December 11, 1850, and in solemn form March 14, 1851. The bequests totaled in value approximately $149,000.

Wofford's gift was so large for the time that it attracted wide notice outside the State. The statement has been made for years in the Wofford College Catalogue that no Methodist in America, perhaps in the world, had previously made such a large gift for education. Few indeed anywhere in the United States had made such a large single gift. I recall only that of Stephen Girard in 1831.

The next large gift for education in South Carolina was that of Mr. Ephraim Baynard in 1865 of $166,000 to the College of Charleston, which virtually saved the institution. Among the more notable gifts for education in later years in South Carolina have been those of Thomas G. Clemson, D. E. Converse, Major J. L. Coker, and A. B. Murray, the donations of the last of whom for various public purposes exceeded a million dollars.

Wofford's will reveals other strong characteristics of the man besides his love for education. The wide distribution of bequests to relatives and friends expresses a strong family feeling and the strength of his friendships. Remembering the Bible and Missionary Societies is indicative of his comprehensive view of religious interests. The most remarkable feature of his will is the comparatively small bequest to his wife, which raises in my mind a question to which I have no answer: did Mrs. Wofford already own property inherited from her father in Virginia or otherwise obtained? I surmise that she must have had something of her own, based on the slight information we have as to her father's having been a man of means. Dr. Anna Wells Agnew of Brooklyn, great niece of Mrs. Wofford, writes that at marriage her grandmother and Mrs. Wofford shared some slaves, indicating that the Barron family possessed some wealth.[11] Mrs. Myra W. Steele, another great niece of Mrs. Wofford, writes that Dr. Barron endowed a hospital for Mexican war veterans, and that his daughters spent the winters in Washington.

When the will became known Mrs. Wofford was naturally very angry. Out of an estate of approximately $150,000 Mrs. Wofford was given about $17,500 (estimating the fifty acres of land at twenty dollars an acre). It has been blandly, I may say almost apologetically, assumed by many that the "twenty-five to fifty thousand" not bequeathed to the college went to the widow; but such was not the case. It was a bitter pill to see practically $28,000 distributed to friends and relatives in sums too small to be of much significance to anyone in particular, and moreover with the provision that if the estate turned out to be worth more than anticipated the surplus should go to those persons, but none of the surplus to her. Mrs. Wofford would doubtless have agreed that the principle laid down by her husband's friend Rev. Walker, namely, that it was wasteful to distribute his public benefaction among a large number of church societies, might have been equally well applied to the distribution of that part of the estate going to individuals.

It has been said that every man has the right to make his own will, and,

---

11. Dr. Agnew to D. D. Wallace, July 17, 1949. The statement by Mrs. Myra W. Steele also comes through Dr. Agnew.

as suggested above, Wofford may have had reason of which we do not know for the comparatively small provision for his widow. And, we must remember, $17,500 had then a value of at least three times that sum today. Wofford had been accustomed to a simple manner of living, and to his economical mind $17,500 may have appeared sufficiently generous for a woman's needs.

Mrs. Wofford's feelings of disappointment extended to the college; but, Dr. James H. Carlisle told me, we flattered her, gave her a prominent place at commencement, etc., and she soon came to take pride in the institution. Dr. Anna Agnew, of Brooklyn, N. Y., writes me of the pride which her great aunt, Mrs. Wofford, took in the college. Mrs. Wofford moved to Clifton, New Jersey, near Passaic, where she lived with her niece Mrs. Martha R. (Wells) Agnew, with whom she later moved to North Hudson, Wisconsin. There she died January 13, 1883, in the eightieth year of her age. By her request she was buried in Antioch Church cemetery, about fourteen miles northwestward of Greeneville, Tennessee, due doubtless to the fact that that had been the residence of her sister Mrs. Felix Wells, the mother of her beloved niece who paid her long visits in Spartanburg.[12]

After Mrs. Wofford's death Mrs. Agnew gave the college the portraits of Mrs. Wofford and Benjamin Wofford by Barclay. Some correspondence preceded Mrs. Wofford's consent that the pictures should go to the college, she insisting that her picture must hang in the college beside that of her husband, as she considered herself the co-founder because of her not having contested what she considered the unfair will of her husband.[13]

The portraits are said by Dr. Carlisle to have been considered good likenesses. The pity is that the only two pictures we have of Benjamin Wofford (the other being a pen and ink drawing of William H. Scarborough, which I discovered in possession of his granddaughter, Mrs. W. H. Stuckey, of Ridge Spring, S. C., and by permission had photographed) represent him as almost a physical wreck, in advanced life, though, even at his best he must have been plain. He was sixty-four when the Barclay, the worse of the two, was painted. He was six feet, two inches, in height, very spare, and was inclined to stoop. A cinder from a blacksmith's forge having in his early life destroyed the sight of his left eye,[14] he usually wore large green glasses. Though of limited schooling, he was fond of serious reading.

12. Mrs. Myra W. Steele, great niece of Mrs. W., on burial place. *Sou. Ch. Ad.* Jan. 27, 1883.
13. Dr. J. H. Carlisle in *So. Christian Ad.* Jan. 27 and Dec. 1, 1883, on age and date of death of Mrs. Wofford and the presentation of portraits; Dr. Anna W. Agnew, Mrs. Wofford's great niece, on Mrs. Wofford's attitude, relations, and place of burial.
14. The Scarborough likeness, which is with clear glasses, shows it to have been his left eye.

Benjamin Wofford

From an India ink draw-
ing by William H. Scar-
borough; belonged to the
artist's recently deceased
granddaughter, the late
Mrs. W. H. Stuckey of
Ridge Springs, S. C.

Benjamin Wofford

Portrait by W. K. Barklay
in 1844. In Wofford Col-
lege Chapel.

Sample of Benjamin Wofford's writing

He was agreeable in social intercourse, and young men found him a wise counselor and helpful friend.[15]

Several instances of his helpfulness to young men come down to us directly from the persons concerned. Major A. H. Kirby, who lacked a few weeks of 22 when Wofford died, writes, "he was of a very friendly disposition, frequently indulging in pleasant jokes with his intimate friends and companions, and, as I remember him, was inclined to notice children and young people with whom he came in contact. I well remember, when I was a clerk in a store, his coming around and giving me advice in the matter of economy—telling us never to waste anything, not even a nail." [16]

Another incident was related to me by Mr. Ed. L. Archer about his father and Benjamin Wofford. It was a case of diamond cut diamond, in which John B. Archer was one diamond and Benjamin Wofford the other. Mr. Wofford came into Archer's saddlery shop one day and said:

"John, why don't you enlarge your business?"

"Haven't the capital, Mr. Wofford."

"Well, I'll lend you whatever you need. How much do you want?"

"Three hundred dollars, Mr. Wofford."

So the small loan, all that the craftsman with his small shop cared to risk using successfully, was forthcoming, at the usual rate of interest. When the time for settlement arrived, Archer counted out to his rich friend the amount, principal and interest. The amound laid down was a "bit" (twelve and half cents)[17] too much. Mr. Wofford fumbled in his pocket for the change, and, not finding a "bit," remarked, "Oh, well, it's a small amount," and put out his hand to rake in the money. Quick as a flash the saddler's hand fell upon his. "No, Sir!" said Archer; "That bit's mine!" And so it remained, and we may believe that ultimately the transaction was settled with proper exactness.

We have another chapter of the story of the harness shop. Wofford said to Archer one day, "John, that is going to be a valuable lot some day. You had better buy it." Archer replied that he did not have the money. Mr. Wofford replied, "I will sell it to you and wait for the money." The records show that on November 1, 1849, Wofford conveyed the lot on the southeast corner of Jail Street (now called Wall Street) and Morgan Square to Archer for $1,000, to be paid in installments, the debt being secured by mortgage. So much for the record; now for the tradition, which says

---

15. Dr. J. H. Carlisle, in *So. Ch. Ad.*, Dec. 1, 1883, *Hist. Wof. Fam.*, 65 ff.
16. *Hist. of Wof. Fam.*, 76.
17. Half cents were coined through 1857, though never a twelve and a half cent piece, answering to the eighth of the Spanish dollar, officially eight reals (royals), on which our dollar was based.

that when Archer made his final payment he lacked three cents. Mr. Wofford replied, "That's all right about your owing me three cents, John, but don't forget to pay me the interest on the three cents." Which shows that Mr. Wofford was capable of a sort of grim joke, and did not mind having the reputation for skinning a flea.[18] Some of the stories handed down of Wofford's stinginess are so extreme as to bear the marks of gross exaggeration, or even inventions to illustrate this trait.

Major William Hoy relates an incident illustrating Wofford's fair dealing. Hoy held a note of a gentleman who was perfectly "good," but was slow pay. Needing the money, he offered the note to Mr. Wofford. Mr. Wofford calculated the amount of the principal and interest at $207, and paid Hoy $200 for the note. He held it quite a while.[19]

The only continuous handwriting by Benjamin Wofford which I have seen (for his will is in his lawyer's hand), is a paper addressed to the two magistrates and three freeholders constituting the court which had tried, convicted, and sentenced to death Wofford's Negro John for raping a white woman. Wofford tells them in a paper dated October 6, 1827, written in a fair hand, with several simple words misspelled, that he had appealed the case to Circuit Judge Richard Gantt, who refused to disturb their verdict, and that he is now taking the case to the Court of Appeals in "Collumbia," and warns them against proceeding to execution until final decision by that court. Examination of the records fails to find anything further. Various interpretations of Wofford's position are possible, some to his credit, some to his discredit, according to the circumstances, of which we are ignorant, and therefore express no judgment, further than to note the confirmation of the lower court by Judge Gantt. It is interesting to note that Gov. Bennett incurred heavy censure for trying to save a favorite slave convicted of participation in the Vesey plot of 1822.[20]

Benjamin Wofford, says his relative and intimate friend Judge J. Wofford Tucker, "was a man of uncommon energy of character, . . . possessed of a fund of strong, practical *common sense.* . . . He rarely failed in adopting the proper means to the attainment of his ends, and his efforts were generally attended with success." He was an economist: "he acquired money and he saved money." He hated waste even in little things, considering it almost a sin. Stewards calling on him to make up the deficit on the

---

18. The facts of the sale and mortgage are taken from the records by Dr. H. B. Carlisle, and were given me Feb. 11, 1949; the story about the three cents is from Mr. J. H. Carlisle, Jr., in *Spartanburg Herald* Nov. 5, 1922.

19. Maj. Wm. Hoy, Historical Reminiscences, MS., 113.

20. I thank Mr. Robert J. Gantt, grandson of Judge Richard Gantt, for a photostatic copy of Wofford's paper.

preacher's salary noted that he would not light another candle until the old one had completely burned out; but he could be relied on to make up the deficit. He would carefully husband the last fine particles of his smoking tobacco. He would pick up a stray pin, though he could write a check for buying a pin factory. When rallied on his economies he would quote Franklin's maxims on thrift. He was criticized as being a rich preacher with no children who lent out large sums and charged interest on them. He realized that the responsibility of being rich imposed the obligation to use his wealth for worthy and unselfish purposes.[21]

Wofford's human side has been neglected amid the mingled sneers at his narrow economies and the paeans on his consecrated benefactions. As a matter of fact he was a man of strong family feeling and strong friendships. His marriage to his pretty young Virginia second wife, all but twenty-three years his junior, eleven months after the death of his first wife, was quite human. His numerous personal bequests and his calling so many friends to be with him in his last illness testify to the wide reach of his human affections. Though the ties of the old rural home remained strong, he felt a strong desire to benefit the town into which he had moved. He often declared to his intimate friends that he desired the college to be a benefit to the town where he made his home as well as to the church at large.[22]

No summary of Benjamin Wofford's life and character is better than that by Mr. John B. Cleveland in his address on Founder's Day, October 19, 1888, at the laying of the cornerstone of Alumni Hall, largely the gift of Mr. Edgar Lycurgus Archer of the class of 1871, the son of the saddler of the story above. Mr. Cleveland, himself a successful businessman and a liberal donor to Wofford College, too modest to allow the amount of his gifts to be known or his name to be placed upon the Science Hall which he built, could understand better than some others the character of the man of whom he spoke. Said Mr. Cleveland of Wofford:

The older he became, like Stephen Girard and Johns Hopkins, the more misunderstood and misinterpreted by some he became. His thrift was called avarice; his economy, selfishness; his business exactness, meanness. He went about, it was said, with his Bible in one pocket and his shaving machine in the other. They called buying notes "shaving them" in those days. And yet, let us suppose that he was not all these. Would we be here today? Would Dr. Carlisle, and Dr. Whitefoord Smith, and all those whom we honor and love, would they be with us here today? How has this selfishness become, when shown in its true light, the greatest of unselfishness! How has this avarice become the greatest

21. Judge J. W. Tucker in *So. Christian Ad.,* Jan. 17, 1851.
22. *Ib.*

and most conscientious example of liberality ever shown in this State! Contrast this life with what it might have been, or with the life of other men who are proud to call themselves just and liberal. He could have had the fat of the land, fine equipages, fine clothes, fine furniture, the reputation of a "good liver." He might have been at the same time the pride and envy of his neighbors. But his true nobility, his unselfishness, his great liberality, despised all this. That pleasure was only for one, the denial was for many.

Is there one here today who doubts that he rightly judged? We understand him: we interpret his aim, his work. We now see and appreciate what those of his own day did not—his personal sacrifice and unselfishness. In December, 1850, his death is announced in the village paper in a paragraph hardly as long as the pencil which wrote it, while several issues before are as black as a pall in memory of two local politicians whose names are not familiar to ten per cent of this audience. So it will always be. . . . Keen, shrewd, hardfisted old Ben Wofford lives today and will live while the broad acres of his spendthrift neighbors have gone years ago under the hammer of the sheriff, or, worse still, have melted under the appetites of unworthy sons. They had also their fun; but can anyone deny now which was the better judge of the article—the plain, unostentatious parson, or the neighbor who despised him, and who believed and acted on the principle "after me the deluge"? . . .

While Benjamin Wofford had the thrift to make money, he had moral courage to practice the economy to preserve it. It may be said that Mr. Wofford exhibited the highest type of selfishness when he endowed what he knew would perpetuate his name. There is no evidence to sustain such an idea. On the conrary, so far as can be gathered from his will and our knowledge of the man, nothing was purer than his intention. There is no suggestion in his will that the college should bear his name. There is no wish expressed in any way that it should be identified with his memory. The trustees are not hampered with any provision or condition which is inconsistent with the highest and most disinterested motives. . . .

. . . In reviewing the character of Mr. Wofford we are apt to regard him merely as an abstraction. . . . To get on the inside, you touch as lively a bit of humanity as ever responded to an impulse. Quick, alert, sharp-eyed and keen, full of energy and push, restless to be doing something, and that something— well, just as he built fences and walled springs; and just, too, as he would shave your note had he the chance. You may possibly think of yourself as a man of industry, of energy, of determinatiion to get along. Now intensify this a great deal, and you have Mr. Wofford. . . .

Today how has his influence grown! . . . But what a harvest! See the influence of a man who acted.[23]

That Wofford should so long have entertained the purpose of doing something for his church with his money indicates his purposeful and consistent character. His act was no afterthought of a man who had accumulated a

---

23. John B. Cleveland, in *Hist. of Wof. Family,* 85-92.

fortune; a steady purpose impelled him in the accumulation. My theory is that Wofford withdrew from the active ministry for two reasons: first, his marriage, which in addition to other difficulties soon imposed upon him the management of his wife's property; second, he must soon have realized that he was not gifted for the pulpit; but he felt nevertheless a called man, and finding that he had the talent for money-making and liking it, he dedicated himself to serve the church in that way. He did not put his hand to the plow and turn back; rather he turned his plow into another furrow.

CHAPTER III

LAYING THE CORNERSTONE, 1851

THE FOUNDING of Wofford College, though a notable event, was not something new and strange in Methodist history. In England the foundation of the first Methodist school was laid a month before the laying of the foundation of the first Methodist chapel. In 1785 was begun in Maryland Cokesbury College, the first Methodist college in America. Burned in 1795, probably by incendiaries, and rebuilt and accidentally burned, its career was brief, but its successors were numerous. In 1795 Bishop Asbury founded his Mt. Bethel Academy in Newberry County, S. C., the first Methodist school in the State, which for twenty-five years or more served a wide constituency.[1] Tabernacle in Abbeville County (called from 1800 to 1868 District) followed in 1821, succeeded in 1824 by Mt. Ariel, which grew into the George Dougherty Manual Labor School, and finally into the Cokesbury Conference School.[2] The movement was nation-wide, and was participated in by all the Protestant denominations, striving to educate the people long before the State took up the duty. The driving power back of the movement was largely the determination to combat the aggressive deism which throughout the eighteenth century and well into the nineteenth conducted a distinctly anti-Christian campaign, as illustrated in South Carolina by Thomas Cooper as President of the South Carolina College from 1821 to 1833. Says Dr. W. W. Sweet, "the great college building era in the Methodist Episcopal Church was the twenty years between 1820 and 1840." "By 1840 there were at least twenty-eight academies, seminaries, and manual labor schools in operation under Methodist auspices, each of them sponsored by an Annual Conference." "The oldest Methodist institution of college grade in the South is Randolph-Macon, . . . intended to serve Methodists both in Virginia and the Carolinas," opened in 1832. The years from 1840 to 1860 were also important, seeing in the North the establish-

---

1. Rev. John O. Willson, D.D., address before the S. C. Conference Historical Society in 1914 on *Methodism and Education;* Rev. C. E. Peele before the same body in 1934 on *The Dougherty Manual Labor School and the Cokesbury Conference Institute.* George Dougherty (1772-1807) is sometimes spoken of as the founder of the Mt. Bethel Academy; but Bishop Asbury's *Journal* shows that he had labored for the establishment of the school for several years and that he formally opened it March 19 (not 20), 1795, more than three and a half years before Dougherty became a Methodist Minister. Clearly the idea of Dougherty's having founded the school arises from his well-known enthusiasm for education and his earnest work for its support after he became a minister.

2. H. N. Snyder in Methodist Sesquicentennial volume, and preceding note.

ment, among others, of Ohio Wesleyan University in 1844, Illinois Women's
College, now McMurray, in 1846, Northwestern University in 1851, Iowa
Wesleyan in 1854, Baker University in 1858, and also two theological
seminaries; and in the South Trinity (now Duke University) in 1851, Wofford in 1854, and Central in Missouri in 1855. Emory in Georgia had been
in operation since 1836.[3] In 1836 Wesleyan College for women was
chartered in Georgia, the first chartered college in the world granting college degrees to women. In 1843 it was taken over by the Methodist Church
under the name Wesleyan Female College.[4] In 1854 the South Carolina
Conference had under its patronage three colleges operating or authorized,
for women, one being in its North Carolina territory, one in Columbia,
and one in Spartanburg.

The terms of Benjamin Wofford's will were simple and direct. In it he
appointed Revs. William M. Wightman, H. Bass, W. A. Gamewell, J. H.
Wheeler, W. Barringer, H. A. C. Walker, John Porter, and Messrs. Major
Harvey Wofford, H. H. Thomson, J. Wofford Tucker, Clough Beard, and
Dr. Benjamin Wofford, as temporary trustees to receive from his executors
the sum of $50,000 for securing land and erecting buildings for the college,
who, after performing that duty, should turn over the property to the
regular Board of Trustees. The regular Board, consisting of thirteen persons, were to be elected by the South Carolina Annual Conference for a term
of two years and were required to submit to the Conference annually an
itemized financial report. This not only assured the church control, but enabled it at the end of any two year period to make a clean sweep of the entire
Board. It is a tribute both to the conduct of the Trustees and the self-re-
straint of the Conference that this power has not been abused. After the
regular Trustees had received the physical property, the executors were to
deliver to them the sum of $50,000, to be used solely as an income producing
endowment, to which was to be added as endowment any unexpended part of
the $50,000 for buildings and ground.[5]

December 16, 1851, the charter of the college was granted by the legislature without opposition, in contrast with the experience of Erskine College
some years before, to which the legislature, jealous of rivals of the State
college, refused a charter for many years. The Conference meeting at Georgetown December 10, 1851, having elected the first regular Board of Trustees,
their names (eight ministers and five laymen) were inserted in the charter:
Reverends William M. Wightman, D.D., H. A. C. Walker, W. A. Game-

---

3. W. W. Sweet, *Methodism in American History,* 211, 215, 218, 222.
4. Wesleyan College catalogue.
5. The part of the will relating to the college is printed at page 21 of the catalogue of 1870-71.

well, Charles Betts, James Stacy, A. M. Shipp, T. R. Walsh, H. H. Durant; and Messrs. J. Wofford Tucker, Simpson Bobo, Harvey Wofford, E. C. Leitner, and Clough [S.] Beard. The charter grants the right to confer the usual college degrees and repeats the words of the will fixing the term of office for Trustees at two years and their obligation to render annually a financial statement to the Conference. It does not forbid a term of more than four years for any Professor or officer, though Wofford's will does. The charter was to run twenty-one years and until the adjournment of the next General Assembly thereafter. At the end of that time, we may add, it was renewed until repealed.

Though the will only required that the college should be located within the bounds of Spartanburg District (as the counties were called between 1800 and 1868), Wofford took it for granted that it would be located in the town of Spartanburg. The Trustees, however, acting under the freedom allowed them, considered whether location in the town or the country would be better. Dr. Wightman consulted Dr. Stephen Olin, President of Randolph-Macon from 1834 to 1837 and then the President of Wesleyan University in Connecticut. He strongly advised location in the town as more stimulating to intellectual life and better for morals and conduct.[6] A wealthy citizen of the Glenn Springs community offered a gift of $5,000 if the Trustees would purchase a tract of 200 acres for locating the college there.[7] The citizens of Woodruff also made a try; but the advantages of location at the courthouse and the liberality of the citizens of the town in offering to present the needed land as a gift turned the decision in favor of Spartanburg. Three tracts were considered, belonging respectively to Messrs. Thompson, Kirby, and Jesse Cleveland. Mr. Thompson went so far as to cut away some of the timber on his elevated plateau west of the present Charleston and Western Carolina Railroad so as to exhibit the grand view toward the village;[8] but the Trustees selected the Cleveland tract, on condition that the owner would open a street around the college land and give a right of way to certain streets to and from the location. Mr. Cleveland agreed to accept $50 an acre, and himself contributed $200, and the contract was closed April 17, 1851.[9] July 3, 1851, they bought from J. W. Tucker 200 acres of woodland lying about a mile and a half north of the college as a source of firewood for the Faculty, Dr. J. H. Carlisle told me—a site many would think as to topography and under the changed conditions of today

---

6. *Life and Letters of Olin,* II, 443.
7. *So. Christian Ad.,* March 28, 1851.
8. Dr. J. H. Carlisle to D. D. Wallace.
9. Temporary Trustee Minutes.

would be a much better location for the college itself than the spot on which it was built.

The Trustees showed lamentable lack of foresight by requesting a tract so small that within a few years it was necessary for the college to purchase adjacent tracts to prevent the establishment of undesirable neighbors virtually at the doors of its buildings, not to speak of the needs for expansion. The original campus of about thrity-six acres was of most unfortunate shape.[10] The narrow strip ran eastward from Church Street in such a way that the line was about three hundred feet in front of the main building, and so close did it come to the back of the premises, Dr. J. H. Carlisle told me, that a gentleman could almost have stepped from his carriage to the Doctor's well, which was within forty-nine feet of the house. There was no provision for playgrounds, no provision for future growth, no prudent extension of bounds as protection against undesirable neighbors.

Although the contract for erecting the buildings was not signed until July 29, 1852, the cornerstone was laid July 4, 1851, with imposing ceremonies. The Spartanburg lodge of Masons, organized in 1849, were proud of such an opportunity early in their career to exercise their impressive rites, conducted by their Worshipful Master William B. Seay. Mrs. Wofford was given an honored place, for which she expressed her thanks to the lodge. Never had the village of Spartanburg witnessed such a scene of community activity and joy. Early in the day at the corner of Church and Main Streets an immense concourse assembled from Spartanburg and neighboring Districts and from North Carolina (a large part of which was then in the South Carolina Conference). Several bands contributed to the noise and happiness. The procession was headed by the Sons of Temperance, like the others, in full uniform or decorations, followed by the Odd Fellows, then by the Masons, next the Board of Trustees and clergymen, and finally the ordinary citizens, all making a procession a half mile long, flanked by a line of carriages equally long moving beside them. At least 4,000 persons were estimated to be present.

The cornerstone of polished granite was presented from his quarry about two miles distant by Major H. K. Dean. "A leaden box was enclosed in its center in which were deposited 1st a copy of the Holy scriptures, 2d

---

10. The original deed describes the bounds and states the area to be forty acres and a fraction, and the cost $1835. A plat by Dr. James H. Carlisle in the front cover of his MS. early history of the College states the area as thirty-six acres. His seven angles and seven lines differ (in some instances quite appreciably) from those of the deed in almost every case. Apparently Prof. Carlisle made his own survey by the actual corner markers. Dr. J. Frederick Messick, Professor Emeritus of Mathematics in Emory University, using Prof. Carlisle's figures, logimarythmacally calculating from west to east finds the area 35.8 acres, and from east to west 36.8, the difference being due to a difference of 6.3 feet in the length of a line, due, he considers, to the angles being stated no more exactly than quarters of a degree.

a copy of the last will and testament of Rev. Benjamin Wofford, 3d a silver medal containing an inscription of the name of the founder of the college, the amount bequeathed, the date of the ceremonies and names of the Building Committee, 4th a copy of the *Southern Christian Advocate,* 5th a copy of *The Spartan,* 6th a police report of the statistics of the Town of Spartanburg, 7th Constitution and By-Laws of the Spartan Division of the Sons of Temperance, 8th a manuscript record of the Morgan Lodge of Odd Fellows, 9th a silver medal, with suitable inscriptions of the Masonic Order, 10th a box containing two locks of hair, one of the founder and the other of his widow." There were deposited a coin and various other articles by individuals.[11]

An article in the *Spartanburg Daily Herald* of June 10, 1906, giving no author or authority for the statement, says that the cornerstone was placed in the southeastern corner of the building. Modern search has failed to discover the cornerstone, nor have the oldest persons now living whose associations with the college go back many years before the coat of plaster which now covers the outside of the walls, ever seen it. Masonic usage would have placed it in the northeastern corner of the building unless some such consideration as the facing of the building dictated some other corner. The Minutes of the Lodge give us no hint on the point.[12] Two surmises occur to me. First, since the cornerstone was laid before the contract for the building had been signed, with the purpose, perhaps, of having the great occasion on the 4th of July, it may have been laid either in the ground, or so near the ground as to be permanently obscured. Second, the stone may have been so located as to be enclosed within the walls when the exact spot for them had been fixed.

The laying of the cornerstone was preceded by the address of the day by the Chairman of the Board of Trustees Dr. William M. Wightman, as always with his utterances direct and able. He said, verbatim as indicated by quotation marks below, and when not so indicated said in substance:[13]

"The college structure which is to rise in majestic proportions and elegant finish, on this foundation, will combine Temple and Academy: will be sacred at once to religion and letters. . . . It is impossible to conceive of greater benefits, to the individual or to society, than those embraced in the gift of a liberal Education, combining the moral principle which grows out of a knowledge of Christian truth, with the enlightened and cultivated understanding which is the product of thorough scholarship. . . . Wofford College, I need hardly remind you,

11. *Spartan,* July 10, 1851.
12. Conversation with Mr. S. T. Lanham, of the Lodge.
13. Printed in full in *Spartan,* July 17, 1851.

will be a *denominational* College. . . . Its chief patrons will be found among the members and friends of the Methodist Episcopal Church. . . . It will be known throughout the United States as a Methodist institution of learning. It will thus sail under no doubtful flag, and will doubtless be ready to show that flag in the smoke of battle as well as in the summer of prosperity.

"I make this frank and distinct avowal on the present occasion, for two purposes. First, that I may avail myself of the opportunity of saying, in behalf of that religious organization, that its leading principles are abhorrent to sectarian bigotry, and breathe the true spirit of catholic liberty, of universal good will. While its simplicity, directness and rigour, render it the religion emphatically adapted to the masses; while its history shows that its power of expansion is unlimited, and its grasp upon the popular mind, peculiarly powerful; while it has poured into the bosom of society, a tide of enlightening and saving influences, and sent its streams of living water far and wide, into the deserts of popular ignorance and vice; at the same time it challenges comparison with all other forms of modern Christianity [on freedom] from the despicable artifices of party recrimination, the reprisals of sectarian selfishness, and the haughty tone of ecclesiastical exclusiveism. . . . In the spirit of these broad and liberal views, we shall open the doors of this Institution to any of the youth of this country who may apply for admission, not only without demanding any tests of dogmatic opinion, but also without any attempt to alienate them from the religious views in which they may have been brought up. . . .

". . . I beg leave to remark with equal emphasis, that no Faculty who may be placed in immediate charge of the Institution, may be considered to have performed their duty ably and well, who do not exert their best and most strenuous efforts to make it a place of *Christian* education. We shall expect them to be men whose heart is in this work; and whose examples will carry it on as well as their teachings.

"This sort of education is the emphatic want of the age and time. We have no faith in the capabilities of mere intellectual training, apart from the vital and genuine elements of religious truth, to bless the individual or society—education which makes men *polished and powerful,* but Christian education alone makes them good. . . .

"And let me ask, what higher boon could patriotism desire for the country, than the erection and multiplication of similar seats and centres of popular education? Need I point your attention to the fact that republican forms of government are adapted only to a wise and virtuous people?" The republics of antiquity were distinguished for intelligence and culture; they fell because their civilization was not permeated with a pure religious principle. Our age is in no danger of going back to the crude forms of idolatry of ancient times, but we are in as great danger from the idolatry of materialism, the utilitarian. On the other hand, socialistic nostrums are advanced which aim that "foreign pauperism might revel in the spoils snatched from the earnings of honest industry."

Experience has taught us that the best political constitution in the world is not sufficient, unless supported by the primitive law of justice and morality, founded on a firm belief in immortal life, to protect us from injustice and corruption. Alarming is the influx of aliens, many of them from the dregs of European pauperism, and without training or the understanding of the principles and proc-

45

esses of self-government, in the coming conflict between labor and capital. "Totally unfit for self-government, with instincts favorable to the wildest agrarianism, they are a floating mass of inflammable materials, thrown into American Society, which may be taken up into the most dangerous combinations when the open collision comes between fanatical free-soilism and the reign of constitutional law."

"Our dependence, in fine, should be less in the material—more in the moral; less in arsenals and navies, more in *men* of the right spirit—most of all in the God of nations." We spend enough on the maintenance of one war ship to support twenty colleges, and pay her captain twice the salary of a college president.

I hope that our meeting today will be the precursor of another, at no distant day, to mark the breaking of ground for the railroad to connect this great district with the rest of the State, unite our sections, and promote the development of the industrial pursuits and the mighty agricultural and manufacturing possibilities of this part of our State—"the steam engine, mighty agent of physical and industrial development—the College, still mightier agent of a higher—more desirable moral and intellectual development—necessary both, let me say it with emphasis, to enable us to meet our proper responsibilities, keep abreast of the advance of the times, and fulfill a great and happy destiny. . . .

"We may lay our hands upon all the elements of prosperity and press them into the service of human improvement and consecrate them to the glory of God, by the true advancement of society. With ampler resources we may multiply schools, adopt better systems of agriculture; invest home with richer charms; cultivate literature and philosophy; and unite intelligence in firm wedlock with religion, thus purifying the world's spirit, and leaving behind us the enduring monuments of usefulness.

". . . And now having drawn upon your patience thus far, we address ourselves to the task of laying this corner-stone. We lay it for the honor, and in the name of the Holy Ghost, for the good of posterity we plant the foundation of this Institution. After the lapse of ages, and amid whatever chances or changes may in the eventful future befall our social and our political institutions, may this corner-stone support a fabric still flourishing in its early freshness. And sooner crumble this solid granite into dust, than perish from the minds and hearts of our countrymen and successors, the great principles which have this day been enunciated, and which lie at the foundation of all our virtues as individuals—all our greatness and glory as a nation!"

Those "chances and changes" which the speaker feared might "in the eventful future befall our social and political institutions" were tragically near. The same issue of *The Spartan* from which we have Dr. Wightman's address teemed with bitter attacks on each other of the two factions in South Carolina which were struggling, the one to bring about immediate secession of the State alone, the other to delay action until other Southern States were ready to join in the great adventure for the preservation of "Southern rights." Dr. Wightman spoke, as of something inevitable, of "when the open collision comes between fanatical free-soilism and the reign

of constitutional law." Already in February, 1851, in the election of delegates for a State Convention the immediate secessionists had won an overwhelming victory; and when the Convention met, only the refusal of Georgia
and Mississippi, on whom they had relied, to join forced them to wait until
the whole South came to their view. Dr. Wightman, while not an extremist,
was throughout his address thoroughly Southern in viewpoint and sympathies.

CHAPTER IV

THE SIX YEARS BEFORE THE STORM
1854-60

THE SPARTAN of July 10, 1851, says of the Wofford College main
building, "A beautiful drawing of this magnificent structure, exe-
cuted by Edward C. Jones, Esq., of Charleston is before us." The edifice,
continues *The Spartan,* is 226 feet long; the chapel 48 by 80 feet; the
museum 30 by 37; library and chemistry lecture room and two society
rooms each of the same dimensions; eleven recitation rooms 22 by 24;
twelve Professor's rooms 12 by 22; two study rooms 20 by 60, etc. The
towers are called 100 feet high. There will be five handsome residences for
Professors.

Edward C. Jones was one of the leading architects of Charleston. He
designed the original building of Furman University, now called Furman
Hall, on somewhat the same plan, though more slight, as Wofford. The
most beautiful monument of his skill is the magnificent Trinity Methodist
Church in Charleston (built as the Westminster Presbyterian Church, and
later sold to the Methodists), a perfect example of the Greek Corinthian
temple, dedicated February 3, 1850.[1]

The builders, say *The Spartan,* were Messrs. Clayton & Burgess of Asheville, N. C. I have (as referred to in the note) the contract, which bears
only the name of Clayton. Tradition has it that the workmen were Negro
slaves; but whether that applies to only the common laborers or to the
skilled workmen also I cannot say.[2] The walls are of great thickness, and
fortunately so; for the material is so inferior that, as the Trustee Minutes
reveal, repairs were soon necessary. The rear wall of the west wing soon
had to have a new foundation, Prof. D. A. DuPre told me; and in his manuscript notes left of these early years for his children he states that during
construction the western tower collapsed and killed one man. The bulging
south wall of the west wing, saved from collapse by inserting heavy iron
binding rods, still bears testimony to the soft brick which, contrary to the

---

1. Miss Beatrice St. Julien Ravenel, *Architects of Charleston* (1945), 204, passim. Jones'
original specifications, signed by him, have come down to me from my great-grandfather,
David Duncan, the first Treasurer of the college. I am giving those and other early papers
to the college.
2. Conf. Mins. 1854, 22; Catalogue 1872, 18; Trustee Mins.

architect's orders, were used for the interior of the walls. Only the outer and inner facing of brick in the thick walls of the residence long occupied by Dr. Carlisle, and now by the writer, wherever occasion has called for piercing them are found to be hard burned brick, the inner brick being sun dried brick joined by mud. Not unnaturally the west wall of this house had to be underpinned, Dr. Carlisle, his son told me, finding it expedient to abandon for a time that side of the house.[3] Fortunately oak and long leaf pine were then abundant. They were not made by man, and still are sound.

The building committee, doubtless motivated by economy, must share the blame with the contractor. They permitted modifications of the architect's specifications, such as reducing the depth of the foundation, and permitting tenpenny nails, instead of twentypennies, for certain purposes. Though they did not direct the use of soft brick, they did not prevent it. After all, it is a marvel that, with the limit of $50,000, they were able to erect the buildings which they did. Tradition says that the contractor lost money. $1,250 or more was left over from the building fund, to be added, the will required, to the endowment. It was used, as the first misdirection of endowment funds, $250 for Professors' salaries, and $1,000 to purchase scientific apparatus, the will specifically forbidding the use of endowment for any purpose but the production of income.[4]

In 1876 Captain Boutelle, of the United States Coast Survey, while making observations from a tower erected on the roof of the college chapel, from which lights were flashed to the stations on Hog Back and King's Mountain, ascertained the exact position of the building as:

Latitude North . . . . 34 degrees, 57 minutes, 32 seconds.
Longitude West from Greenwich . . 81 degrees, 56 minutes, 7 seconds.
Time West of Greenwich . . . . 5 hours, 27 minutes, 36.5 seconds.
Time West of Washington . . . . 19 minutes, 24.4 seconds.
Ridge of roof of chapel above sea . . . . 878.8 feet.
Ridge of roof of chapel above ground . . . . 62.25 feet [5]

The buildings were not complete when the college opened its first session, August 1, 1854. Not until January 1, 1855, did the temporary Trustees turn over the property to the permanent Trustees. The executors delivered to the permanent Trustees $50,000 in notes, bonds, and cash.[6] This en-

---

3. Mr. Albert Simons, the Charleston architect, tells me that sometimes such construction was due to the difficulty of transporting hard brick from a distance, and that both here and in Europe it sometimes led to grave defects.

4. Trustee Mins.

5. Wofford Catalogue 1895-6, 23.

6. Tr. Mins.

dowment was, at the request of the Trustees, supplemented by the South Carolina Conference in 1853 by the gift of $11,000, being half the Centenary Fund, plus $85.50 interest, on the condition that this should be considered as providing free tuition for all sons of Methodist ministers attending the college. (The college itself later extended this privilege to the sons of all ministers.) A gift of $5,000 about the same time from Mr. George W. Williams of Charleston, the income of which was to be used for the support and education of one or more candidates for the ministry, brought the endowment to $66,085.50. The request that the President travel, so far as his duties permitted, in order to raise the endowment to $120,000 by the sale of scholarships—a plan then and earlier tried elsewhere—accomplished something.[7] At the request of the Trustees the Conference in December, 1859, appointed Rev. H. H. Durant as Agent to raise the endowment to $200,000, a movement which for a year made encouraging progress in securing pledges; but alas, for reasons we know too well, most of these were never made good.[8]

From the first the Trustees lent endowment money in a few cases to members of their own body and to at least two members of the Faculty, of course with security. Occasionally done in later years, it was opposed as bad practice by Dr. Snyder on his becoming President and, with the hearty concurrence of the Board, was discontinued. The loans to the two professors and the members of the Board were, after the War of Secession, written off, which at least had the excuse that the college owed much more than the amounts involved to the professors as back salaries, and that the trustee had donated to the college far more than the amount of his loan.[9]

Our narrative is hurrying in advance of events. Let us return to November 24, 1853, when the permanent Trustees held their first meeting at the Conference in Newberry. All were present except Shipp and Leitner. They elected as President and Professor of Mental and Moral Science Rev. William M. Wightman, D.D., the outstanding member of the South Carolina Conference, editor of the *Southern Christian Advocate,* and later a Bishop; as Professor of Ancient Languages David Duncan, A.M., then holding the same chair in Randolph-Macon College; James H. Carlisle, A.M., as Professor of Mathematics, who had taught four years in the Odd Fellows' School in Columbia, and five years in the Columbia Male Academy in

---

7. Conf. Mins. 1854, 22.

8. Trustee Mins., Dec. 3, 1859; Dec. 14, 1860. These additions to endowment are itemized in an address before the S. C. Conference Historical Society, November 4, 1914, by Dr. John O. Willson, reprinted in *Hist. of Wof. Fam.*, 78-84. Trustee Mins. Nov. 24, 1853; July 10, 1859; Conf. Mins. 1854, 22, etc.

9. Trustee Mins. Jan. 2, 1855; July 1, 1859; Dr. Snyder to D. D. Wallace.

Hugh Ratchford Black Infirmary. One of the original Faculty houses built at same time as Main Building, all of same type. This house occupied successively by Profs. David Duncan, F. C. Woodward, J. A. Gamewell, A. M. DuPre and J. L. Salmon.

Columbia; Warren DuPre, A.M., as Professor of Chemistry, Mineralogy, etc., then head of the female academy in Newberry; Rev. A. M. Shipp, A.M., as Professor of English Literature, then holding the chair of History in the University of North Carolina. Commented *The Advocate*, "If they all consent to serve, Wofford College will have a noble Faculty." Rev. Shipp declined the position, and Prof. DuPre was granted absence on leave.

Thus, when the college opened its first session, August 1, 1854, it was with only three instructors, clean cut, clean-shaven, upstanding men (for the bearded era was still in the future): President Wightman, aged 46; Duncan, aged 63; and Carlisle only 29.[10] The first day seven students were enrolled, all in the Freshman and Sophomore classes. A few days later two more entered. Thus the population stood until the opening of the spring term in January, when additions brought the total for the year up to 24.[11] The second Wednesday in January, 1855, a preparatory department was opened under Mr. Robert W. Boyd assisted by Mr. Herman Baer, and enrolled 34 pupils. With the determination not to derogate from the standing of the college, the professors took no part in preparatory teaching until the hard years following the War of Secession. In July, 1859, the Trustees even moved the preparatory department from the college building into the village, we may infer in order totally to protect the college from being lowered in public estimation by too close association with preparatory work.[12] The homes of the total of 69 for both college and preparatory classes were as follows: Abbeville District 6; Barnwell District 1; Charleston District 2; Chester District 3; Colleton District 3; Fairfield District 1; Georgetown District 1; Greenville District 2; Laurens District 4; Marion District 1; Orangeburg District 3; Richland District 1; Spartanburg District 24 (all but 5 in the preparatory department); Sumter District 2; Union District 7; North Carolina 4; Georgia 2; Tennessee 1; Mexico 1. The wide distribution of the students in the college classes is significant; and significant also is the fact that the huge Spartanburg, including then a large part of the present Cherokee, had only 5 in the college classes as against, for instance, 6 from Abbeville. Taking into consideration the distances, the relative numbers are doubtless significant of the then state of relative culture.

It is interesting to note how the small but able faculty impressed at least one youngster, one of the four who drove from Shelby, N. C., to enroll in

10. Rare old photograph for their appearance.
11. Dr. J. H. Carlisle's MS. history of the college to 1869; Faculty report to Trustees November 1855; register of students, which, incidentally, is not complete.
12. S. C. Conference Minutes, 1859.

January, 1856. He wrote forty-one years later, including in his description two professors who were not present until several months later:

My eyes stared wide-open as I looked half-scared into the faces of my new teachers, by far the greatest men I had ever yet seen. I can see them to-day. I love now to see them in imagination as I then saw them face to face: Dr. Wightman, self-poised, scholarly, *suave,* finical, always equal to any occasion, uniformly ponderous and always overwhelmingly great in thunderous public speech; Prof. David Duncan, at this time the most learned of the *pentarche* (PATENT APPLIED FOR) and the faultlessly fine gentleman, neat almost to nattiness in his well-fitting garments and spotless linen, witty but not wordy, a stalwart hater and hitter of shallow sham and show; Dr. Whitefoord Smith, neither a student nor a scholar, but an aesthete "to the manner born," the inspired declaimer of South Carolina Methodism, the high-toned gentleman of unchallenged integrity, the sweet-spirited Christian of unaffected humility and meekness, powerful in public discourse but most of all powerful in prayer,[13] the Christian Knight, without fear and without reproach, the "Rupert of debate"; Prof. Warren DuPre, a sweet-spirited Christian of the old school of the low country, South Carolina gentry, a fluent and thoughtful speaker of graceful English, ever an object-lesson as he walked the campus as to the significance and purpose of a Christian education; Prof. James H. Carlisle,—well, I'll spare his characteristic modesty. I have no delicacy about saying what I feel in his case; but he has, so I curb my pen.[14]

We may add something from other sources on the original Faculty. As indicated, Dr. Wightman was a man of power. In a camp meeting sermon at Cokesbury, August 4, 1838, though Negroes were present, as usual, in their appointed places, he denounced the opposition, which was voiced by some persons in the up country, to the Methodist missions to the slaves on the great low country plantations, a work very dear to his heart and recognized by religious leaders of other denominations and the wealthy planters as of the most beneficial character. The missions, he said, would make the Negroes better servants in the up country as they had below. He respected all men, irrespective of their color, he continued. These words, uttered in the presence of slaves, roused strong protest, which brought from him a strong reply.[15] Bishop Wightman was born January 29, 1808, in Charleston, S. C. He died in Charleston February 15, 1882.[16] He graduated at the College of Charleston in 1827. He was for three years from 1834 Financial Agent of Randolph-Macon College and for the next two years

---

13. He is said to have sometimes prayed fifteen minutes in an ice-cold chapel.
14. An Old Boy, in *So. Christian Ad.,* August 12, 1897. Might have been one of the other four coming then from North Carolina; but the style is decidedly that of Dr. S. A. Weber.
15. D. D. Wallace, *Hist. of S. C.,* III, 510, citing *Greenville Mountaineer* of Aug. 24, Oct. 26, Nov. 2, 1838; *S. C. Conf. Memorials,* 1839.
16. Memorial tablet in Trinity Methodist Church, Charleston, S. C.

Professor of English there. He was eminently successful as a college President, both at Wofford and at Southern University, to which he went from here as its head from 1859 to 1866. In 1854, he was, says Dr. Thomas O. Summers' in fact elected Bishop; but one of the ballots clearly intended for him was written "William M. Bishop," and so was not counted. He was elected in 1866.

Bishop Wightman was a man of vigorous, even powerful, physique, and, we may add, of vigorous, even powerful, emotions, which, however, he kept well under control. Says Dr. Summers, "There was a volcano in his breast."

An intimate friend and next door neighbor, Prof. Carlisle, and a younger friend, Charles Forster Smith, have left interesting recollections of David Duncan, which we may weave together along with some facts which I derived from members of his family.[17] David Duncan was born in northern Ireland, in 1791.[18] His father was at the same time a Presbyterian elder and a Methodist class leader, before the Methodists had developed from a reforming religious movement into a distinct denomination. The young man was educated at the University of Glasgow. He entered the British navy as a midshipman March 25, 1810, and served three years. On the death of the purser he reluctantly accepted, on the imperative command of the Captain, the position of purser, in which he won the praise of the commander of the warship *Helder* in a certificate of June 3, 1812. Thus began a long course of trust officer in charge of finances, for which his exquisite handwriting and his business ability fitted him. In 1817 a classical teacher in Norfolk, Va., wrote to his old pastor in North Ireland for an assistant. The pastor sent out David Duncan, who intended to remain for a year. He soon became principal of a prominent classical school in Norfolk, from which he was elected, in 1836, to the chair of classical languages in Randolph-Macon College, then situated in Boydston, Va., with Stephen Olin as President and Langdon C. Garland (the later Chancellor of Vanderbilt University) and William M. Wightman among the Faculty. Probably the association with Wightman led to his being invited to become a member of the first Faculty of Wofford. Duncan was the first member of the Faculty

---

17. Dr. Carlisle's article, written on the night of the day of David Duncan's death, is in *So. Christian Ad.*, of Nov. 12, 1881; Dr. Charles Forster Smith's article is in *Wof. Col. Jour.*, June, 1889.

18. The difference in tradition as to birthplace of David Duncan seems to be definitely settled by his registration as a student at Glasgow University: "David Duncan Filius natu secundus Davidis Mercatoris, in parochia de Donnough in Comitatu Donegal." (Assistant Registrar of Glasgow University to D. D. Wallace, 28 Oct., 1949.) His gravestone says County Donegal. Dr. J. H. Carlisle and some of Prof. Duncan's descendants seem therefore to be mistaken in giving County Armagh as his birthplace. But Dr. Carlisle was a man of great accuracy, and was for many years the next door neighbor and intimate friend of David Duncan.

to reach the campus, says Dr. Carlisle, and took up his residence in the house now used as the Hugh Ratchford Black Infirmary. Though teaching until eighty-six years of age, he refused to the last to give up his third story recitation room in the eastern wing of the college. He was diffident and self-distrustful to a marked degree, so much so that to lead chapel prayers was always a trial, says Dr. Carlisle, which is supplemented by the statement of Charles Forster Smith that he never knew him to appear before the public but twice; first, in his inaugural address on "The Claims of Classical Learning," and second, in acting as a member of the examining board at the South Carolina College in 1859. Smith emphasizes his absolute punctuality and his immaculate neatness in dress. He was not an original thinker, continues Smith, but a very broad reader of the classics and was a great lover of fine bindings. There are stories of how he sometimes slipped in such treasures hidden from the eyes of his thrifty wife. Dr. Carlisle thought that his classical library was perhaps unequaled by any other private collection in the South. In conclusion, says Dr. Carlisle, "He had fewer of the failings of extreme age, whether physical, mental, or social, than anyone I have met. . . . He kept up his fresh interest in life to the last. . . . He was a lover of good books to an almost romantic degree." He was very generous, but completely unostentatious with it.

The third teacher with whom the college began was the clean-shaven young man of 29, James Henry Carlisle. On graduation he had been offered the principalship of the Odd Fellows School in Columbia, his Assistant being his close friend John H. Logan, later the author of the *History of Upper South Carolina.* Four years later, he was elected to the Columbia Male Academy, where he taught until coming to Wofford.[19] Young Professor Carlisle had already established a reputation as an eloquent and inspiring speaker on religious and moral subjects. While teaching in Columbia, he made an address before the Society of Missionary Enquiry of the Presbyterian Theological Seminary which was so highly thought of as to be published in the *Southern Presbyterian Review,* and published in the *Southern Methodist Quarterly Review* an article on The Essays of John Foster "which was universally praised and admired." [20] He was one of forty-one teachers, all men, who in July, 1850, at the call of Gov. Whitemarsh B. Seabrook met in Columbia "to consider the subject of Free Schools, the preparation at home of elementary and other books for the use of our schools, the best mode of insuring the progress of education, and other kindred matters." Dr. W. A. Leland was elected President and James H. Carlisle

19. J. H. Carlisle, Jr., *op. cit.,* 113-4.
20. C. F. Smith in *Carlisle Memorial Volume,* 24.

Secretary. Evidently few if any teachers from the miserable "free schools," sometimes even called by Governors in official statements "pauper schools," were present; but the roll contains the names of numbers of outstanding teachers of the time. The Teachers' Association died in a year and a half from lack of interest; but it, as did its later successful successor, found James H. Carlisle among its leaders.[21]

In a brief manuscript history of the college down to 1869 by Dr. James H. Carlisle we are told that the college building was not finished until several months after the opening. The east wing was finished first. For the first two years chapel was held in the easternmost room on the third story. On Sunday, June 24, 1855, and Wednesday, June 27, occurred the first commencement, which was of high order. Examinations occupied Monday and Tuesday. On dedication Sunday, June 24th, President Wightman preached an eloquent sermon, rich in historical illustration and spiritual power, from the first verse of the 80th Psalm: "Give ear, O Shepherd of Israel, thou that leadest Joseph like a flock; thou that dwellest between the cherubim, shine forth." Then the Chairman of the Board, Rev. H. A. C. Walker, "called the assembly to their feet, and in a brief form of presentation and invocation offered the Chapel to God." Wednesday morning a procession formed at the corner of Church and Main Streets and marched to the college. There being no graduate, the three Faculty members delivered addresses of about fifty minutes each. President Wightman spoke of the mission of the institution and defended the church college idea with some warmth, alluding to the complete lack of Methodists on the Faculty of the State college and pointing out the peculiar advantages offered by Wofford.

Prof. Duncan, a ripe scholar of sixty-four years, spoke on the nobility and value of the classics in a finished address, at places spiced with his keen native wit. Prof. Carlisle, tall, imposing, modest, followed, as a hearer expressed it, "in one of his own happy efforts, at once profound, simple, and delightful." The subject matter was moral and philosophical, "at times thrilling." A distinct contrast, which, he said to me, he felt without throwing it into prominence, was presented in his close with a portion of the address of President Wightman. "He extended a fraternal hand to all similar institutions" and paid "a tribute to the South Carolina College—in some sort the mother of us all said the orator, and hoped that when Wofford College should be celebrating its fiftieth anniversary, as the State College is doing this year, that institution, still flourishing and vigorous might be celebrating its hundredth." He lived to see his hope fulfilled when Wofford at her semi-

---

21. D. D. Wallace, *Hist. of the S. C. Teachers' Association* (1924), 5, 6, *passim*.

centennial conferred the degree of LL.D. on President Benjamin Sloan of the University.

The young Professor of thirty had chosen his line. There was nothing but maturity to be added in the next fifty years.[22]

The Faculty of three with which the college began August 1, 1854, was supplemented in August, 1855, by Prof. Warren DuPre, who had been allowed, at half pay for the first half of 1855, to travel in the North and purchase scientific apparatus, during which time he also studied under the famous chemist and geologist Benjamin Silliman at Yale. Prof. DuPre was already well known as one of the leading teachers of the State. He was one of the forty-one referred to above who met in Columbia in 1850 to form a State Teachers' Association. He was born at Mt. Pleasant, S. C., January 24, 1816.[23] When he was elected to Wofford he was head of the Newberry Female Academy, after having taught in Charleston and in Randolph-Macon College. He was the first occupant of the house immediately east of the main building, occupied for so long by Dr. H. N. Snyder, from which he moved to the house immediately to the west of the main building, later occupied by his son, Prof. D. A. DuPre and of recent years by his distant kinsman Dr. A. Mason DuPre. The first death among the campus community came with the loss soon after his arrival of Prof. Warren DuPre's eleven year old son.[24] "An Alumnus" writes in the *Wofford College Journal* of November, 1889:

I do not suppose anyone lived a more temperate life than Prof. DuPre, yet he had every appearance of a high liver, not unbecoming. . . . The kindness, the gentleness in his look cannot be described; his person, his presence all spoke it. There lay his heart upon his sleeve, and such a heart! So big, so pure, so true! . . . Prof. DuPre was irresistible—a spontaneous flow of esteem or rather affection which felt itself more than half way met.

Prof. DuPre having taken up his duties in August, 1855, and Dr. Whitefoord Smith his in the middle of the spring term in 1856, the second year's commencement exercises, July, 1856, included the inaugural addresses of these two belated additions to the Faculty. Says the correspondent of the *Greenville Patriot:*[25]

---

22. The account of the commencement is from my article in the history of the College in *The Aurora*, the first Wofford annual (1904), based on account in *So. Christian Ad.*, of July 5 and 12, 1855, and Dr. J. H. Carlisle's MS. hist. of the college to 1869.

23. Died Ap. 25, 1879.

24. Dr. J. H. Carlisle's manuscript history of the college to 1869; Prof. D. A. DuPre's written recollections. Prof. DuPre also records the death of someone (Finley by name) who fell from a tower window. I knew of this, but not the name, from my mother. The bars across the tower windows were placed there by Prof. D. A. DuPre at my suggestion to prevent such accidents, which the position of the windows rendered not unlikely.

25. Reproduced in *Charleston Courier,* August 20, 1856.

The President of the college introduced to the audience Mr. Warren DuPre, Professor of Geology, Mineralogy, &c., who entertained the audience for more than an hour with an elaborate and well written address in defence and advocacy of the branch of science over which it is his province to preside. . . . The speaker succeeded in uniting and holding the attention of his audience, notwithstanding the frequent employment of terms, familiar only to geologists and scientific men. The address was interspersed throughout with brilliant passages, by way of practical application of geological truths. Here the speaker treated the coincidence between geological truth and Divine revelation, showing that science, instead of being an antagonist against revealed religion, as some would have us believe, is really one of its strongest allies, that while a prurient philosophy has entered unbaptised upon the work of research in the earth, contributing the results of its investigation to strengthen the usurpations of atheism and infidelity, it has only been necessary for Christianity—inspired with the spirit of its author—to enter those holy walks, and it has traced out the footsteps of a God, and compelled science to pour out her libations upon sacred altars, and do homage at the shrine of revelation. . . .

The President introduced Dr. Whitefoord Smith, Professor of Belle Lettres. We have always been an admirer of this gentleman and consequently were prepared to be pleased before he had uttered a sentence; but our expectations exalted as they were, fell below the point he reached before the address was concluded. In our humble judgment, it was the most finished production we ever heard from him.

The aim of the address seems to be mainly to rescue the study of Polite Literature from the subordinate position to which the sordid utilitarianism of the present day seemed inclined to consign it. The argument was logical and conclusive, the illustrations apposite and beautiful, and the language such as would be employed by an accomplished Belle Lettres scholar. The speaker's plea in behalf of the grand old Anglo Saxon, which groans beneath the burden of *foreignisms* foisted upon it by the progressives of the present day, was earnest and powerful. His satire upon the pleonasm and fustian of latter day speakers and writers, was marked by the severity that the subject merited, while at the same time it was characterized by a spirit of playfulness that elicited a smile from every hearer.

The defectiveness of primary education was another branch of the subject which the speaker handled with admirable skill. The address throughout evinced eminent ability and was delivered in Dr. Smith's happiest style—and left the impression upon the mind of everyone present, that he was eminently qualified to fill the chair of Polite Literature.

Another feature of the second commencement was the speech of the first graduate of the college, Samuel Dibble of Charleston. Dibble had been a leader in the rebellion of the Junior class in the College of Charleston shortly before the commencement of 1855 because of the Faculty's having, quite justifiably, required the withdrawal of a disorderly member of the class. After negotiations involving the Trustees and the City Council (for the institution was owned by the city), and the Faculty, in which the students acted on the South Carolina assumption that as gentlemen they were fully on a par with the Faculty and must be so treated, the class were permitted to return; but several, including Dibble, declined to do so. Dibble, being a Methodist, came to Wofford. He took the Junior studies with that class and at the same time completed privately the studies for the Senior class.[26]

The praise heaped on Dr. Whitefoord Smith by the correspondent of the *Greenville Patriot* expresses the opinion generally held of him in his prime. It is hard for those who knew him only in the years of decrepitude of his later life to realize the man that he was in his prime. He did not, like Duncan and Carlisle, ripen into a well rounded and vigorous old age. Born November 7, 1812, he lived to April 27, 1893. He was of distinguished Scotch ancestry. His oratory either in the pulpit or on civic occasions, was a remarkable example of fluent, polished elocution, expressed in the purest English with the most perfect enunciation, and illuminated by great emotional power. Says Rev. A. J. Stokes, "That prince of orators, William C. Preston, said on one occasion, that he would like to exhibit Whitefoord Smith at the international oratorical contest in Paris as a specimen of American oratory. At another time, after lecturing fervidly on elocution and eloquence before his class, he said, 'Go and hear Whitefoord Smith as an illustration of all I have said.' " Admirers in Charleston, where he repeatedly served as pastor, in order to keep him permanently, offered to build him his own independent church, but his loyalty to Methodism would not permit him to accept such an offer. Failing health limited his activities, rendering it inadvisable, for instance, for him to continue accepting membership in the General Conference, so that he had been retired to the position of a supernumerary for several years when elected as a professor in Wofford College. After serving for a few months as the first President of the Columbia Female College in 1859-60, on account of insufficient strength for executive duties, he resigned in February, 1860, and was in April, 1860, re-elected to Wofford, where he continued to teach, barring a period during the Civil War, until 1885, when he became Professor Emeritus until his death in 1893.[27]

Dr. Smith was supreme in reading hymns or masterpieces of literature. A prominent clergyman once remarked that he never realized the meaning of a certain hymn until he heard Dr. Smith read it. He would at times re-

---

26. Prof. F. A. Porcher's Memoirs, in *S. C. Hist. and General Mag.*, XLVIII, 21-23 (Jan., 1947); Wof. Trustee Mins. July 15, 1856; J. H. Easterby, *Hist. of College of Charleston*, 134-5.
27. A. J. Stokes, In Memoriam to Whitefoord Smith, S. C. Conf. Mins. 1893, 33-35; Mrs. M. A. Graeser in *So. Christian Ad.* Aug. 12, 1897. The Columbia Female College had a much larger opening than Wofford had had.

peat passages from the great poets at length to an admiring group of students, either in classroom or on the campus. The style of his preaching did not appeal to his Scotch-Irish colleague, David Duncan. After one of Dr. Smith's sermons in the chapel (a regular Sunday afternoon function in the early days), a student said to Professor Duncan, "That was a wonderful sermon!" The old Scotch-Irishman stopped long enough to say, "Vox! Vox et præterea NIHIL!" It is said that Professor Duncan's ideal of a preacher was illustrated by a humble country minister of the time.

Dr. Smith was very nervous and completely lacking in humor. His fear of thunder and lightning was excessive. A mischievous student would sometimes say, Professor, it looks like it is going to storm. Dr. Smith, seeing some clouds in the sky, would dismiss his class and hurry home, where he would in a thunder storm collect his family in a room with solid blinds closed and lamp lit to obscure the lightning flashes, and as the Almighty beneficently watered the earth, would desperately pray for safety, while he was in less danger than he incurred every time he drank water from his well. An old pupil, after describing Dr. Smith's wonderful charm as a teacher of English literature, tells of his conduct on discovering in a student's book the following lines:

> Who was Holm?
> A critic bold and rare,
> A judge with a wig
> Who could dance a jig,
> Drain a marsh, carve a pig,
> And frame a law with care.

The skit was aimed at Henry Holm, Lord Kames, whose *Elements of Criticism* Dr. Smith used as a textbook. "The Doctor resented this as a personal reflection, and the hour was spent in the vindication of his favorites, Lord Kames and Mr. Blair." [28]

The curriculum, heavily loaded with classics and mathematics, was the diet at that time ordinarily furnished by first-class colleges. Admission was by examination, and not by certificate from preparatory schools. Among the requirements for admission were Algebra through quadratics, four books of Caesar, six books of the Aeneid, Sallust, Cicero's Orations, six books of Xenophon's Anabasis. Such pabulum is almost the complete bill of fare through the Junior year; but Chemistry was prescribed for Juniors. The only references to English are Rhetoric in the second half of the Sophomore year and the requirement of composition and declamation throughout

---

28. An Alumnus, in *Wofford College Jour.*, June, 1893, 295.

the course, "and the Senior class deliver original speeches." The Senior year broadens out into something more modern, including Natural and Moral Philosophy, Evidences of Christianity, Political Economy, Mineralogy, Geology, and a second year of Chemistry. From January through December, 1855, the presence of a bright young converted Jew, Herman Baer, made it possible to offer as electives French, German, and Hebrew, extras which the Trustees soon discarded. Without entering upon the controversy regarding the value of the classics, we may remark that the students of that day at least had the opportunity to acquire a sufficient skill in them to make the reading of them a pleasure on account of their content, instead of being, as under reduced requirements, too often a mere persecution while meeting the supposedly decent minimum of acquaintance with cultural studies.

The catalogue of 1858 contains the rule that it is considered an impropriety for students to attend any quasi theatrical or other amusements which take their money on the plea of furnishing amusement, or any lectures, whatever their professed object, without the sanction of the Faculty. It was declared an impropriety for any student during term time to attend any dancing school without written permission of parent or guardian previously communicated to the Faculty. Prayers must be attended both morning and evening, and church on Sunday. Professors found it prudent to carry a pocket Testament, as miscreants, not approving of the injunction to pray without ceasing, sometimes hid the chapel Bible.[29] Keeping a book out overtime, or taking out too many books at a time, incurred a fine of one dollar—quite a penalty, considering the then value of the dollar. In sum, concluded the rules, students are expected at all times "to display that delicate regard for the rights and feelings of others, which is the sure test and unfailing characteristics of *the* GENTLEMAN."

Expenses were low: tuition and contingent fees respectively $25 and $2 for the half year. The Trustees rejected the dormitory and mess hall plan, this, like the locating of the college in the town instead of the country, being on the advice of Stephen Olin, on the theory that the influence of life in families would be better, in addition to saving the college large expense for buildings.[30] Board was from $10 to $12 a month. The Trustees resolved, July 10, 1860, that if the students cannot get board at $12 a month, they will consider opening a college mess hall. The Faculty reported to the Trustees, December 14, 1860, that a number of students have been diverted to other institutions, and others have been compelled to remain at

29. Dr. J. H. Carlisle to D. D. Wallace.
30. *Life and Letters of Stephen Olin*, II, 443; reproduced in *Spartanburg Herald* Sept. 5, 1926.

home, by a rumor that board would be advanced to $15 a month. The Faculty succeeded, at the cost of considerable hostile feeling on the part of leading boarding-house keepers, in having board remain at the old figure. Soon students were allowed to occupy some of the unused "recitation rooms" at a merely nominal rental. Four boys occupying one of these long apartments would sometimes divide it by a chalk line, across which no trespassing was allowed.[31]

The first catalogue, i.e., for the year 1855-56, defines the first term as extending from the fourth Wednesday in August through the second Wednesday in December, and the second term from the second Wednesday in January through the fourth Wednesday in June—dates, however, which were soon changed. Beginning with 1856 the college opened October 1, and commencement was carried far up into July; but climate soon forced it back into mid-June. The Trustees soon abolished the month of holiday between the two terms and sought to have only three days' intermission at Christmas; but student protest ended this proposal before it went into effect. The catalogue of 1870-71 announces a holiday of two weeks at Christmas, a practice which may have originated earlier, as we have no catalogue between 1861 and 1871, though for some of those years we have a single sheet circular by way of announcement.

The Conference at this period had a committee of three for each of the four institutions under its charge. The report on the final examinations which they witnessed at Wofford at the commencement of 1856 convinced them of the thoroughness of the teaching. The Freshmen were rigorously examined on the first eight books of Homer, Horace as far as the Epodes, Geometry throughout, and Smith's *History of Greece*. There were eighteen applicants for the Freshman class from the preparatory department, of whom, after a rigid examination by the college Faculty, only twelve were admitted.[32]

Beginning college work in the heat of August was held responsible for the extraordinary amount of bad health during the first and second college years. One student died in the spring of the first year and four others out of the little group of twenty-four were obliged to withdraw on account of impaired health. Two students died in September, 1855, and another soon left on account of feeble health.[33]

In the springs of 1857 and 1858, and particularly in the fall of 1859, the college experienced remarkable religious revivals. Said the Faculty to the

---

31. W. H. W. to D. D. W.
32. *So. Christian Ad.*, July 31, 1856.
33. Trustee Mins. Nov. 30, 1855; Nov. 21, 1856.

Trustees: "The end we all aim at, is the connection of thorough intellectual training with a pervading religious influence; and we should feel that we have failed in the main, essential point, if with progress in study, we could perceive no growth of Christian principle among the young men entrusted to our oversight. The Faculty are happy to say, that during the term now closing there has been a gracious revival of religion among the students." [34]

Of the revival of November, 1859, Dr. Carlisle writes, November 14, 1859:

During this week the college was favored with the most remarkable season of religious interest we have known since its opening. It began without any special effort on the part of the ministers. Service has been held every night in the Methodist church and a noon prayer meeting daily. The students have held prayer meetings frequently among themselves. . . . A great many already members have been quickened and converted and twenty-one admitted to the church. . . . The Female College shared largely in the benefits.[35]

The Spartanburg Female College, some of whose buildings still stand in the village of the Spartan Mills, the present owner of the property, was opened by the South Carolina Methodist Conference in August, 1855.[36] Some apprehended danger from having a college for young women so near one for men; but during the entire time that the Female College remained in operation these fears proved groundless. In about 1873 the Female College, having been for several years under private management, was closed on its owner's being made President of the revived Columbia Female College, which the church had opened in 1859, but which had been closed as the result of the war until 1873.

Though the students of Wofford have been of unusually good behavior, still boys are boys, and hence problems were not far in the offing. One of the first concerned the "commencement party" which they requested permission to hold at a local hotel on the evening of commencement day in July, 1856. The Faculty consented on condition that both the committee on arrangements and the hotel proprietor pledge themselves that there should be no intoxicants or dancing. This arrangement continued for many years.[37] Less lovely sides of human nature were also in evidence. In the second year a prep student was dismissed for immorality, and in the third year one prep and one college student for some misconduct. In the spring of 1859 a college student was suspended for intoxication and fighting with

---

34. Trustee Mins. July 7, 1857; July 13, 1858.
35. Dr. Carlisle's MS. history of college to 1869.
36. Conf. Mins., 1855, 37.
37. Faculty report to Trustees July 7, 1857; Dr. Carlisle as above.

a knife. May 14, 1860, a committee informed the Faculty that the student body unanimously refused to associate with two students, who thereupon withdrew. The circumstances indicate that it was not the fact that they had been drunk, but the fact that they had shamelessly lied to the Faculty when questioned, that disgusted the students; for the South Carolinians of that day one was pardonable, but not the other.[38] Dr. Carlisle, years later, when President of the college, would sometimes say that he always had hopes for a young man until he would deliberately look him in the face and lie. That was something which many an errant one acknowledged it was impossible to do.

The college in early years pursued the custom of awarding first and second honors to the best and second best members of the graduating class. Perhaps the following incident in 1858 helped to account for the later President Carlisle's aversion to the custom, and his dislike for medals and all other invidious marks of distinction. In 1858 two Seniors were so dissatisfied with the distribution of honors that they withdrew from college. The Faculty, in view of their both being first grade men, recommended that the Trustees should grant them their diplomas if they should apply; but the tougher governing powers rejected the suggestion.[39]

From the first, salaries were fixed at $1,800 for the President and $1,500 for the Professors, but not for many years was income sufficient to make good the promise.[40] The Faculty suggested that an Agent be appointed to raise funds for increasing the endowment, as has been narrated elsewhere. The income of the college for the entire first two years was $10,231.76, being about $2,000 short of enough to pay salaries in full. By July, 1859, back salaries amounted to $6,602, for which notes were given the Professors. The nearest approach to payment of a Professor's salary before 1859-60 seems to have been $1,341.61, in 1858-59; but in 1859-60 the Professors were paid 110.5 per cent.

The eighteen existing alumni proved their loyalty by requesting in July, 1859, permission of the Trustees to organize an Alumni Association. Accordingly, on July 12, 1859, they met in the college chapel, organized, and elected Charles Petty President, M. B. Tarrant Secretary, and the eloquent William M. Martin Orator for the next commencement, and adopted the motto, majestic in sound and beautiful in meaning, Τρόφιμοι τόν τροφὸν

---

38. Trustee Mins. July 15, 1856; July 7, 1857; July 13, 1858; July 11, 1859; July 9, 1860; Dr. Carlisle as above.

39. *Ib.*, July 13, 1858.

40. *Ib.*, Nov. 24, 1853.

τιμῶμεν, that is to say, freely, We the adopted honor [the mother] who nourished us.[41]

We may note here as an evidence of the intellectual interests of these early Wofford students how early they organized themselves into literary societies for practice in debate, essay writing, oratory, and parliamentary practice. The Calhoun Society, all but as old as the college, was organized in September, 1854, at the suggestion of Prof. Carlisle, with eight men present at the first meeting. Prof. Duncan suggested several names, among them Calhoun and Legare. The members unanimously chose Calhoun. After rejecting the suggestion for a badge by a committee, the Society adopted the palmetto tree, it is said, but without authority stated, as suggested by Samuel Dibble. Eloquent of the social habits of the time is the purchase of thirty spittoons in 1855-56. It is to be hoped that the members were good marksmen; for the fine for spitting on the floor was fifty cents, quite a sum of money at its then value.

In October, 1858, fifteen men organized another society, named, it is said, at the suggestion of Prof. Carlisle, Preston. Prof. Duncan is said to have suggested a badge, a gold crown. The bust of Patrick Henry was a gift from Preston, a great nephew of Henry, with the words, "Give this bust of Patrick Henry to the Preston Literary Society of Wofford College and say to those dear boys, 'God bless them.'" A good deal of rivalry and some bad feeling arose between the societies because the Calhouns, through their greater numbers, elected all marshals, managers, and speakers for public occasions from their ranks. It was finally arranged that each society should elect half and alternate in electing the chief marshal.[42]

At the commencement of 1859, the college lost its first President, the able and aggressive Dr. William M. Wightman, and its eloquent and cultured Professor of English Dr. Whitefoord Smith. Dr. Wightman resigned to accept the presidency of the newly organized Southern University at Greensboro, Alabama, where he remained until elected Bishop in 1866.[43] Dr. Smith, after having in 1857 declined a chair in the South Carolina College, now resigned to become the first President of the Columbia Female College, both acts expressive of his devotion to his church. Dr. David S.

---

41. Trustee Mins.; Alumni Asso. Mins., Vol. 1 (1859-1915).

42. Dr. Carlisle's MS. history for dates of societies; catalogue 1871-2; Dibble and the badge in *Wof. Col. Jour.* May, 1890, with no authority stated. Most of the other data are from article by J. Wright Nash in *Wof. Jour.* June, 1889, evidently based on information from older persons, and article in same issue by W. F. Fooshe, presumably from similar sources. Dibble did not come to Wofford until about a year after the Calhoun Society was organized.

43. January 19, 1864, Dr. Wightman donated to the college the note which he had held since his resignation here for $1459.59 back salary, which with interest amounted to $1917, with the proviso that $50 of it go toward a monument for Wofford men who died in the war.— Treasurer's papers, Wofford College.

Doggett of Virginia declined the offer of the chair of English, and for the next year Profs. Duncan and Carlisle being engaged every hour, the English classes were taught by the new President, Dr. Shipp, and Prof. DuPre. Dr. Smith's strength proving unequal to the burden of the presidency, he resigned it in February, 1860. He was asked to return to Wofford, which he did November 20, 1860.[44]

As the young college faced the future—unknown, and yet known to be of great glory or great calamity—it had behind it six years of, on the whole, encouraging history. Speeches by students on public occasions gave little signs of consciousness of the seething fires of sectional strife soon to burst into eruption. Typical oration subjects from 1854 to 1860 were Consequences of Marathon, Conscience, My Mind to Me a Kingdom Is, Dangers and Duties of Educated Men, Marius Sitting Among the Ruins of Carthage —reflections of the curriculum rather than of contemporary life. Calculated to shock men into keener realization of immediate problems was the opening of railroad connection with Columbia—November 25, 1859—a day of speeches and general holiday.[45] Endowment was approximately $69,000, and pledges for more were coming in. The student body had increased every year, rising from 24 to 76. High standards of scholarship had been maintained by a Faculty of unusual ability and culture, who rigorously held themselves to purely college work, though they governed the preparatory department without teaching in it. The Library contained about one thousand volumes, and a good beginning had been made toward a scientific museum through the donation of the Indian and mineral collections of Dr. J. H. Dogan and the purchase for $500 worth of scholarships, of the minerals of Dr. Andrews of Charlotte.[46] Co-operation between the church, Trustees, and Faculty had been perfect and the attitude of the public was cordial. Methodists had cause to be well pleased with their colleges.

---

44. Trustee Mins., Dr. Smith's letter of acceptance in *So. Christian Ad.,* also Mrs. M. A. Graeser in *ib.,* Aug. 12, 1897.
45. Dr. Carlisle, as cited above.
46. Trustee Mins. Dec. 2, 1859, on Library; Nov. 19, 1854, on Dogan; Jan. 2, 1855, on Andrews. Catalogue of 1871-2 seems to err in dating the purchase from Andrews 1869.

CHAPTER V

CIVIL WAR AND RECONSTRUCTION, 1861-75

ON THE resignation of President William May Wightman the Trustees chose as his successor Rev. Albert Micajah Shipp, D.D. Dr. Shipp was an accomplished scholar, deeply imbued with the classical tradition. He was born of excellent North Carolina stock June 15, 1819. He attained considerable fame as a preacher; but in 1848 his voice became so weakened from a throat affection that he could no longer preach continuously, and naturally, with his scholarly equipment, turned to teaching. He was President of the Greensboro Female College in 1848 and '49, and from 1849 to '50 Professor of English Literature and History in the University of North Carolina, and from 1850 to '52 Professor of French and History and during 1853 to '59 Professor of History in the University. It will be recalled that he had been invited to become Professor of English in the original Faculty of Wofford College in 1853, but declined. Chosen to the Presidency in 1859, he accepted. Dr. Shipp represented South Carolina in every General Conference from 1850 through 1888, the year before his death.

As a commentary on the frame of mind cultivated by the curriculum of that day, young men continued, as war hovered on the horizon, even in May, 1860, to deliver orations on "The Deserted Halls of Alhambra," "Washington Irving," and "Omnia Mutantur et Nos Mutamur cum Illis." But another speaker in this Senior exhibition discoursed on "There Is a Spirit in the World Like to Subterranean Fire," a prophetic title whether he intended it so or not. As early as March, 1860, the Faculty granted a petition from the military company recently organized in the village, which a number of the students had joined, to use the extreme western room on the third story as an armory.[1] President Shipp wrote to Governor Pickens suggesting that they be released and formed into a company of students to be at the Governor's command. To this the Governor, January 28, 1861, readily agreed, and urged that young men in college should remain at their work, as their education was essential to the public welfare. President Davis also protested against students leaving college for

---

1. Dr. J. H. Carlisle's Ms. hist. of college to 1869; Dr. Shipp to Gov. Pickens, Apr. 12, 1861.

war: "The farmer who 'grinds his seed corn' will reap no crop next year, and will deserve no compassion."

By January, 1861, 79 students had matriculated and college exercises proceeded satisfactorily until the battle of Fort Sumter, April 12 and 13, after which excitement prevailed during the rest of the session; but conduct was so good that no student had to be summoned before the Faculty. Commencement exercises were dispensed with, but a class of 15 of more than usual promise were given their diplomas.

On the attack on Fort Sumter the students sent to Governor Pickens a delegation, again asking that he would accept their services; but his advice was, as before, to remain in college. When the college year closed 29 students, including the Seniors just graduated, had joined the Confederate army in Virginia. When college opened October 1, 1861, over 40 had enlisted, leaving only 33 in classes. Of these more than half left after the Federal capture of Port Royal, November 7, 1861. "Most of them went in a body to attach themselves to Capt. J. A. Leland's Company in Manigault's Battalion for the defense of the coast between Charleston and Georgetown." Only eleven Freshmen and Sophomores were present when the term closed December 13, 1861, and only eight at the end of the session in July.[2] The first martyr in the Southern cause was William Maxwell Martin, a Wofford graduate of 1857, who had developed into a gifted poet as well as orator. His graduation speech, The Calico Flag, says Dr. Wauchope, "produced a sensation in its way beyond anything in the annals of the college." He died February 21, 1861, of illness contracted from exposure on duty at Fort Moultrie, standing by his cannon through the cold, damp night.[3]

In 1861 the Trustees authorized the Faculty to open a school for the local community; but the small prospects of drawing patronage from the schools already existing led the Faculty to use their permitted discretion to refrain, stating that they would, if the Trustees saw fit, relinquish a proportionate part of their salaries.[4] The length of the war was foreseen by few; still less its outcome. The bulk of the college endowment was invested in Confederate bonds. The securities owned by the college at the close of the War of Secession included $85,897 of Confederate bonds and certificates, $1,297 in Confederate money, and bank stocks of $17,525 par value, all of which were ruined by the war. A number of municipal or railroad

2. Dr. Carlisle as above; Report on Com. on Ed., *S. C. Conf. Mins.* 1861, 41-4; Faculty report in Trustee Mins.

3. G. A. Wauchope, *Writers of S. C.,* 296.

4. Dr. Carlisle as above.

bonds were in the hands of the Treasurer in 1877 or 1878, which probably were obtained before or during the war, although they may have been donated later. It is correct, therefore, to say that the endowment was swept away by the war, although it was not all invested in Confederate bonds.

In 1859-60, as noted above, the Faculty, never before paid in full, received an amount equalling 110.5% of that year's salary. In the early years of the war hopes were high. The campaign ordered by the Conference in 1859 at the request of the Trustees for increasing the endowment to $200,000 succeeded so well that during the conflict, says Dr. Carlisle, gifts and pledges and bequests to mature largely exceeded $200,000,[5] in securing which President Shipp rendered great service. We have the following list of subscriptions and gifts in Greenville and Spartanburg Districts: Simpson Bobo, $12,500; G. Cannon and G. Finger, $2,500; John Bomar, D. E. Converse and J. C. Zimmerman, $3,000; J. and J. D. Bivings, $2,000; J. and J. W. McMaken, W. A. Finger and W. H. White, donation in domestic manufactures, $2,000; James L. and A. Hill, cash, $1,000; James McMaken (additional), $2,000; William Lester, A. H. Lester and George Pegues, $1,000; Rev. W. L. Pegues, $1,000; Rev. Charles Betts, $1,000; Rev. J. R. Pickett, $1,000; Robert Bryce, $1,000; J. H. Dingle, $5,000.[6] By July 5, 1864, the Trustees found themselves able to pay all expenses and salaries in full, in depreciated Confederate money, of course.

The diminution of enrollment required some adjustment of the Faculty. Dr. Whitefoord Smith was assigned to a church. Prof. DuPre volunteered and was assigned to salt making on the coast. October 1, 1863, finding only 18 students in attendance, the Trustees resolved, as it was impossible on the income available to pay salaries, 1. That any students attending college should be taught in connection with the high school to be organized and governed by Prof. Carlisle, assisted by Prof. Duncan, as their college duties may allow; 2. That the President shall, with the sanction of the Conference and Bishop, solicit for the imperative increase of the endowment; 3. That the Bishop be requested to reappoint Dr. Smith to a pastorate;[7] 4. That Prof. DuPre be requested to continue his salt making; 5. That salaries of Professors shall be paid, as before, but that any other earnings a Professor might make should be counted as salary. Finally,

---

5. Dr. Carlisle as above; Wof. Col. Catalogue 1871-2, 21.

6. I cannot tell whether the amount after two or three names means that each gave that sum or that they did so jointly.

7. He was assigned to the church in Spartanburg.

inflation having played havoc with purchasing power, the salary of the President was raised from $1,800 to $2,500 and the salary of a Professor from $1,500 to $2,000, and tuition was increased to $100. July 5, 1864, a special appropriation was made of $1,250 for the President and $1,000 for each Professor, at a time when the Confederate dollar was worth twenty cents in gold. Tuition was raised to $150. Eleven students were reported in college during the past year, and 47 in the high school. The high school saved the college from closing entirely; for during the year 1864-5 there were no students in the college classes. November 18, 1864, salaries were further increased to $3,200 and $2,500.

Since I have taken the trouble to dig out the facts from the Treasurer's books, I may as well give them in detail to the reader. The salaries of the Professor in the college for the early years were as follows:

For the collegiate year 1854-55 $1169.39, being   % of the $1500 salary;
For the collegiate year 1855-56   1119.90, being 74.6 % of the $1500 salary;
For the collegiate year 1856-57   986.00, being 65.6 % of the $1500 salary;
For the collegiate year 1857-58   1306.90, being   % of the $1500 salary;
For the collegiate year 1858-59   1300.60, being 89.44% of the $1500 salary;
For the collegiate year 1859-60   1658.01, being 110.5 % of the $1500 salary;
For the collegiate year 1860-61   1453.85, being 96.9 % of the $1500 salary;
For the collegiate year 1861-62   956.30, being 63.75% of the $1500 salary;
For the collegiate year 1862-63   1216.40, being 81.   % of the $1500 salary;
For the collegiate year 1863-64   2378.00, being   % of the $2000 salary;
                        and $1196.45 on back salary.
For the collegiate year 1864-65 $3113.00, being   % of the $2500 salary;
                        on salary and $749 on back salary; only Carlisle and Duncan teaching prep school, were paid salaries for 1864-5.
For the collegiate year 1865-66   482.42, being 32. % of the $1500 salary;
For the collegiate year 1866-67   637.52, being 42.5 % of the $1500 salary;
For the collegiate year 1867-68   653.49, being 43.56% of the $1500 salary;
For the collegiate year 1868-69   776.86, being 51.78% of the $1500 salary;
For the collegiate year 1869-70   853.59, being 56.9 % of the $1500 salary;
For the collegiate year 1870-71   1002.10, being 66.8 % of the $1500 salary;
For the collegiate year 1871-72   1208.67, being 80.57% of the $1500 salary;
For the collegiate year 1872[8]   1102.62, being 77.17% of the $1500 salary;
For the collegiate year 1873   1224.75, being 81.65% of the $1500 salary;
For the collegiate year 1874   1262.94, being 84.2 % of the $1500 salary;
For the collegiate year 1876-77[9] 1062.03, being 70.8 % of the $1500 salary;

8. President Shipp, who took over the books on the resignation of Prof. David Duncan as Treasurer, in 1872, was no such bookkeeper as was Prof. Duncan, who was a perfect model, both in method and in beautiful execution. Dr. Shipp states salary for the calendar, not college, year.

9. Again the academic, instead of the calendar, year. From 1865 the table assumes the stated salary to be $1500, although the inflated war figures were not officially changed back to $1500 until 1870.

For the collegiate year 1888-89   1050.00, being 70. % of the $1500 salary;
For the collegiate year 1889-90   1326.07, being 88.4 % of the $1500 salary;
For the collegiate year 1890-91   1500.00, being 100. % of the $1500 salary;

Lee's surrender and the flight of Jefferson Davis across northwestern South Carolina into Georgia brought soldiers on both sides to Spartanburg. The Citadel and Arsenal cadets were encamped on the Wofford Campus, where Governor Magrath made them a fiery speech, telling them that we would fight the Yankees beyond the Mississippi; but the approach of Federal cavalry from North Carolina sent the Governor scurrying to Greenville, a little south of which the cadets fired, so far as I know, the last shots of the war in this State, as the cadets of 1861 had fired the first shot of the war at the *Star of the West* in Charleston harbor; but not one poor Citadel boy, who, ill with fever, had been taken to the home of Prof. J. H. Carlisle to die. Prof. Carlisle and others of the Home Guard were sent up the road to meet bushwackers said to be approaching from North Carolina. Serious was the situation, and serious looked the tall Prof. Carlisle, utterly unsuited for war-like pursuits, as his friends laughed afterwards, with the knees of his long legs sticking up over the shoulders of his horse, Old Bald. The alarm proved groundless and the Home Guard marched back without either victory or defeat. Old Bald died before the Yankees really did arrive, and so saved himself the humiliation of capture; but the invaders forced Dr. Shipp to receive a raw-boned animal in exchange for his excellent horse, which naturally bore the name of Old Yank. [10] That experience was common when Brevet Brigadier General William J. Palmer's brigade of cavalry in pursuit of Jefferson Davis at about 2 o'clock on the afternoon of April 30th occupied the town unopposed. By strict orders no private property was to be molested, an order only slightly violated except as to horses and mules. President Shipp obtained from the General for the college and residences guards, who occupied the hallways and behaved with perfect gentility, except for the appropriation of some books from the society libraries, perhaps to while away the time. The troops left the next day.[11]

The invaders included some printers and a humorist; for they issued from the office of *The Spartan:*

10. Dr. Jesse Cleveland is authority for the Home Guard expedition.—J. H. Carlisle, Memories of Wofford College, MS., 134-5.

11. *Spartan*, May 4, 1865; Prof. D. A. DuPre's notes on his life for his children, for which I thank Mrs. Helen DuPre Moseley.

EXTRA EDITION!
Sunday, April 30, 1865

KIND READERS:

While writing this we smell the battle afar off, and on every breeze is borne to our ears, the thunder of the Captains and the shouting. Already in our mind's eye, we behold the hungry villains devouring our substance: already do the doleful brays of our mules made captive reach our distracted ears, and admonish us that the time to take these valuable animals to the mountains has arrived.

There no longer remains any doubt of the approach of the Yankees; and as the Assyrians came down like the wolf on the fold, so will the vandal hordes of Lincolndom descend upon Spartanburg, unless something is done to prevent it. There is no time left for indecision or delay. Rise men of Spartanburg in your might, and gird up your loins for the conflict, go forth and smite the invaders. . . .

In the mean time your editor will retire to a safe place in the vicinity and await the result with anxiety. If our brave, but alas, small force is successful, in resisting the Yankee advance, we will return—if not . . .

As we write news has arrived by a reliable gentleman, that France has formed an alliance offensive and defensive, with Col. Thomas commanding the Cherokee Indians, and one hundred thousand gallant copper colored patriots, armed with tomahawks and scalping knives, are now marching on New York City. Great consternation prevails in the North. This glorious item of intelligence should nerve the arms of our brave defenders to strike to the last.

As the Spartans of old choked up the pass of Thermopalae with the Persian dead, so let us imitate their glorious example and cover our hills and valleys with the carcasses of these miscreants. How truly the poet says:

> " 'Tis great for one's country to die."

We trust that our readers will appreciate the grandeur of the sentiment, and that they will not be backward to offer up such an insignificant thing as life upon the altar of Southern Independence. On Spartans, on!

N.B.—Since writing the above, we learn that the report of the alliance between Louis Napoleon and Col. Thomas is untrue. This is greatly to be regretted. Our devil, who is possessed of a fine literary taste, has been reading an ancient poem entitled Hudibras, and has just read aloud the following passage from the same,

> "He that fights and runs away,
> Will live to fight another day;
> But, he that is in battle slain,
> Will never, never, fight again."

After thinking the matter over, we have come to the conclusion that there is much truth in the above lines, and accordingly advise our friends to refrain from hostilities.

It was feared that the Federals might imprison Prof. Carlisle as he had been a member of the Secession Convention. He refused to hide when urged to do so as the enemy approached, saying that if they took

71

him it would be at his own fireside, and not from some gully or cave in the woods. When news of their being near reached the schoolroom he dismissed the boys, with directions to go straight home. Little Waddy Thompson sidled up to him and said, "Professor, if the Yankees take you I hope they will be kind to you." [12] They did not molest him in any way.

By December, 1863, several hundred dollars had been raised for a monument to the Wofford men who had died in the war; but nothing came either of this or of later proposals for such a purpose. At the Alumni meeting at the commencement of 1894, for instance, it was proposed to raise funds for such a purpose. A visionary member urged that it should be a building, on which my father remarked that this was simply killing the whole plan by attempting too much. I have been able to add a few names to those previously published of Wofford men who died in the Confederate military service, a roll of honor of at least thirty-five names, which we record with deep emotion:

L. Manning Austin, Freshman in 1857-8; died July 13, 1863, of disease contracted in camp. (Secretary of Faculty J. H. Carlisle's record.[13])

James Austin Bailey, Junior in 1859-60; died at home May 25, 1863, of illness contracted in the army. (Secretary J. H. Carlisle's record.)

John George Barber, Sophomore 1860-61; Killed instantly at Battle of Dranesville, Va., December 30, 1861. (Secretary J. H. Carlisle's record.)

Howard Simpson Bobo, killed instantly in Battle of Deep Bottom (or Fussell's Mill), Va., August 16, 1864. (Secretary J. H. Carlisle's record; Calhoun Society Memorial page in Minutes of 1867.)

Andrew Thompson Bowie, Sophomore 1860-61; died January 22, 1863. (Calhoun Society Memorial page in Minutes of 1867.)

Theodotus LeGrand Capers, class of 1860; killed at Second Manassas, August 30, 1862. (Minutes of Wofford Alumni Association July 10, 1867, have penciled note saying that T. L. Capers, Whitefoord A. Smith, and J. J. Palmer were killed by the same shell.)

John Moore Carson, Sophomore in 1860-61; died June 23, 1864. (Calhoun Society Memorial page in Minutes of 1867.)[14]

Epaminondas Washington Davis, class of 1860; Lieutenant Davis was killed by a cannon ball June 30, 1862, near Richmond, Va. (Secretary J. H. Carlisle's record.)

Thomas Elijah Dawkins, class of 1860; killed at Second Manassas, August 30, 1862. (Secretary J. H. Carlisle's record.)

---

12. J. H. Carlisle, Jr., Memories of Wofford College, MS., 137, 139.

13. Secretary Carlisle's record states that P. B. Austin died in October, 1862, but makes no reference to war.

14. D. D. Chandler and G. W. Clarke are marked dead on Preston Society rolls shortly after the war, but nothing is said regarding when or how they died.

Thomas Carey Duncan, class of 1860; killed June 30, 1860, near Richmond. (Secretary J. H. Carlisle's record.)

Andrew Soule Durant, Freshman class of 1860-61; died in hospital in Richmond July 2, 1864. (Secretary J. H. Carlisle's record.)

William Turpin Hardy, class of 1861; killed near Chancellorsville, Va., May 3, 1863. (Secretary J. H. Carlisle's record.)

Felder David Houser, Junior class of 1860; left to join army; died at home April 19, 1862, having gone home to recruit his health. (Secretary J. H. Carlisle's record; Com. on Ed., S. C. Conf. of Dec. 1862, list him as having died for his country. Calhoun Society Memorial page erroneously gives date of his death as that of G. M. Houser, who left College on account of poor health and died of consumption, according to Secretary J. H. Carlisle's record. Neither his nor any other record mentions war service for G. M. Houser.)

Richard Ragan King, class of 1859; died of diphtheria in hospital Oct. 2, 1862. (Secretary J. H. Carlisle's record.)

Maynard Cooper Layton, Freshman 1860-61; died in camp hospital near Lookout Mountain, Georgia, October 18, 1863. (Secretary J. H. Carlisle's record; Carlisle Society Memorial page in Minutes of 1867 says he died October 9, 1863.)

William Maxwell Martin, class of 1857; died February 21, 1861, of illness contracted from exposure on duty at Fort Moultrie, S. C. (Secretary J. H. Carlisle's record.) "The first martyr of the Confederacy."

Eli Hoyle Miller, class of 1859. Education Com. of S. C. Conf. in Minutes of December, 1862, lists him as having died in the war that year.

Sergeant Horace Asbury McSwain, Junior 1860-61; captured the flag of a Michigan regiment, for which he was commended by Gov. Pickens and eulogized by the S. C. House of Representatives, who ordered that his name be stamped on the flag and engraved on its staff. After a distinguished career he was killed in his eighth battle, Second Manassas, Aug. 30, 1862. (Secretary J. H. Carlisle's record, quoting House of Reps. Journal of 1862, page 315. McSwain was a member of Company K (Spartan Rifles), Palmetto Sharpshooters.)

James Alexander Moore, class of 1858; (Ed. Com. S. C. Conf. Minutes Dec., 1862, lists him as having died in the war.)

Francis Lewis Moore, Freshman 1860-61. (Education Committee as above.)

Zachariah Linden Nabers, Junior class of 1860-61. (Secretary J. H. Carlisle wrote in college register, "Died of wound May 21, 1863." Naber's niece, Mrs. Carrie Nabers Skelton, of Hartwell, Ga., writes me that he was killed at Manassas.)

Nicholas David Oglesby, Sophomore in 1858-59; killed at Battle of First Manassas, July, 1861. (Secretary J. H. Carlisle's record.)

Albert Maximilliam Padgett, Sophomore 1860-61; died January 3, 1863. (Minutes of Education Committee as above in December, 1863, list him as having died that year in the war. Date from Calhoun Society memorial page.)

James Jerman Palmer, class of 1860 (erroneously printed German in *Southern Christian Advocate* article of July 27, 1911, and so copied ever since. His signature and all early college catalogues have the name Jerman. Killed at Second Manassas Aug. 30, 1862.—Secretary J. H. Carlisle's record.)

William Smith Patterson, Freshman 1859-60. Served well from early in war; was killed on north bank of James River October, 1864. (Secretary J. H. Carlisle's record.)

Robert Lemuel Pearson, Freshman 1860-61. "Died of camp fever in Virginia, Sep. 26, 1862." (Secretary J. H. Carlisle's notation in college register. Catalogue erroneously gives Samuel as middle name. No other Pearson in catalogue or register before 1865.)

Taliaferro Simpson, class of 1861. (Education Committee for 1863 as above have him as having died in war that year.)

James Marshall Smith, Freshman 1859-60; died of wound June 2, 1862. (Secretary J. H. Carlisle's record.)

Whitefoord Andrew Smith (Son of Dr. Whitefoord Smith), Freshman 1860-61. (Calhoun Society memorial page in minutes of 1867. "Fell at Second Manassas."—Secretary J. H. Carlisle's notation on college register.)

Joseph Smyley, Freshman 1860-61; died May 28, 1864. (Calhoun memorial page as above.)

Abram Samuel Summers, class of 1861; killed in Confederate service by accidental discharge of a pistol by a friend. (Secretary J. H. Carlisle's record. His name is sometimes misspelled Abraham; he signed it Abram.)

Sumter Wickham Tarrant, Sophomore 1860-61; died November 12, 1861, in army hospital from effect of measles. (Secretary J. H. Carlisle's record. Calhoun Society memorial page says he died November 17, 1861.)[15]

J. E. Walker, preparatory classes 1857-58; killed instantly near Petersburg, Va., July 21, 1864. (Secretary J. H. Carlisle's record.)

Benjamin Wofford Wells, Junior 1860-61; died at Richmond, Va., Oct. 29, 1862. (Secretary J. H. Carlisle's record.)

James Emory Williams, class of 1861; in cavalry; died of fever May, 1862. (Secretary Carlisle's record.)

John Melvin Zimmerman, Junior 1860-61; died at Richmond, Va., June 30, 1862. (Secretary J. H. Carlisle's record.)

Russell Daniel Zimmerman, Sophomore 1860-61; killed May 7, 1864, near Petersburg, Va. (Secretary J. H. Carlisle's record.)

The college had lived gaspingly during the four years of war, and only the high school conducted during 1864-65 by Professors Carlisle and Duncan enables us to say that it is the only men's college in the State that did not close its doors. It was a sad meeting of the Board of Trustees, at the usual commencement time, if meeting it could be called with only the three members living in Spartanburg attending out of the thirteen. At the meeting during Conference in November, 1865, only four could be gathered, all of whom were ministers and so due to be present anyhow. The Faculty seemed more hopeful than their employers, who for years attended Board meetings in small numbers; for in those days expenses of Trustees were not paid, and even Trustees had to

---

15. A. J. Tolleson, Junior 1859-60, is marked dead on Preston Society roll shortly after war; no mention of war.

Faculty of 1867—Left to right: Whiteford Smith, English; James H. Carlisle, Mathematics; David Duncan, Ancient Language; A. H. Lester, History and Biblical Literature; Warren DuPre, Natural Science; A. M. Shipp, Mental and Moral Philosophy.

pinch. The Faculty reported that they had begun the new session September 4th, a month early, with flattering prospects, as there were the usual number in the high school and some members of the Freshman, Sophomore and Junior classes. But for fifteen years the history of the college was the short and simple annals of the poor. Education in the South was in ruins. The University of Alabama, for instance, had been burned, and at re-opening two professors and one student appeared. In 1873-4 it had only 53 students and in 1875-6 only 111, and these mainly in the preparatory department. The University of North Carolina had 80 students in 1870, and was closed from 1870 to 1875, as was the University of South Carolina for some years before 1883. [16] It was a period in which the schools of the churches rendered a very valuable part of their service.

One wonders how, on the fractions of salaries that were paid in these years the families of the professors lived. The axe had to be wielded by hands more accustomed to the book or the pen. Professor Carlisle, for instance, was to cut the wood for the family; but after a short experience the tall, unathletic scholar announced that someone else would have to do that. [17] Prof. Warren DuPre the chemist was more fortunate and could turn his wood splitting to making matches, thinking perhaps, like a British statesman proposing a tax on matches, *e luce lucellum* (from light a little profit), thus proving from the classics the superiority of the sciences. Differences arose among the Faculty as to whether the limited funds should be assigned to each professor in proportion to the size of his family, as with Conference aid to needy preachers, or to each man equally as their work was equal. Generally, strange to say, those with large families favored the former plan, those with small families the latter.[18] The Conference came to the rescue. The South Carolina delegates to the General Conference pledged their Conference to give $3,000 for the Faculty and to enact an annual appropriation of $5,000 for the college. [19] The December, 1866 South Carolina Conference, in response to an appeal from their Educational Committee, voted to raise at least $5,000 for the support of the Faculty, to be divided into seventeen parts; 5 parts for President Shipp; 4 for Prof. DuPre; 3 for Prof. Whitefoord Smith; 3 for Prof. Carlisle, and 2 for Prof. Duncan—clearly as to these funds acting on the plan of relief for needy preachers; but it was years before an impoverished

16. Mims, *History of Vanderbilt University*, 79-81; Greene, *Hist. Univ. of S. C.*
17. J. H. Carlisle, Jr., to D. D. Wallace.
18. D. A. DuPre to D. D. Wallace.
19. Trustee Mins., July 4, 1866.

people made good more than a small part of such promises. [20] How badly Conference help was needed is indicated by the fact that tuition fees yielded not over four hundred dollars per Professor. [21] No catalogue was published between 1861 and 1871 though for at least two years, one apparently being 1868-69, there was issued a little two sheet folder.

It was impossible under conditions existing immediately after the War of Secession to keep up the ante-bellum practice of the college of Professors abstaining entirely from teaching preparatory classes. In January, 1867, Prof. Warren DuPre took charge of the classical school (i.e., the preparatory classes), with Prof. Duncan assisting in languages, and Prof. Carlisle in mathematics. For several years, and through the 1866-67 year there was no occasion for a college Faculty meeting. [22] In October, 1868, the college opened with increased attendance. Arrangements had been made for John W. Shipp to take charge of the preparatory classes, thus leaving the college Professors free for their own departments, except that President Shipp and Profs. Warren DuPre and Carlisle continued to teach some prep classes in "language," Latin, and Mathematics. More or less teaching by college Professors of preparatory classes (sometimes called "introductory" and "sub-introductory"), with one or more teachers also for the preparatory classes, continued even after the creation of the Wofford Fitting School in 1887, which will be described in due course.

In the early years of the college the Faculty took a much more active part in conducting the institution than later. The annual and semi-annual reports to the Trustees were the Faculty's reports, signed by the President on behalf of the Faculty. The Faculty were ocasionally invited by the Trustees to meet with them. Suggestions of college policy frequently originated with the Faculty. For instance, on their recommendation, July 4, 1866, the five Trustees present adopted their recommendation to create a chair of History and Biblical Literature, and to elect to it Rev. A. H. Lester, and to establish a divinity school to be conducted by Professors Shipp, Smith, and Lester. Apparently it continued only a few years and amounted to little except specializing in religious subjects.

In 1868 a few students began a prayer meeting in the room of one of them. Attendance rapidly increased and interest was so lasting as to

---

20. *Ib.*, Dec., 1867. Prof. Lester was omitted, doubtless for the reason that at the time he was possessed of ample means. For a while at least Prof. Lester taught at part salary on this account. Prof. Duncan had some real estate and accumulated bank stocks in Virginia.

21. Report Com. on Education, S. C. Conf. Mins. 1868, 32.

22. Dr. J. H. Carlisle's MS. on early history of the college.

lead to the founding in 1879 of the college Y.M.C.A. The Association was active in Sunday schools and the neglected parts of the town. For some years it secured a preacher to address them at commencement, Rev. A. Coke Smith being the first. In 1889, it sent, by request, representatives to organize a Y.M.C.A. at Furman University. Seven-eighths of the students were at that time members. [23] Religious life during the period ran strongly. The Faculty reported to the Trustees December 17, 1874, that a recent revival in the town church had resulted in the conversion of almost all the students who were not already church members.

All whose recollections went back to the days shortly following the War of Secession recalled that the maturity of character of the ex-soldier students gave to college life a notable earnestness, industry, and elevation. The Faculty reported in 1866-67 that the work of the students, particularly those who had returned from the war, is better than in former years, and their conduct exemplary. "The students govern themselves." But, though they maintained former standards of scholarship, they found it necessary, they told the Trustees, December, 1867, to admit irregular students who wish to take only certain studies; in other words, as we see from other passages, more and more were finding it impossible to master the Greek and Latin, and so had to be satisfied with the inferior degree (first conferred in 1870), as it was then considered, of Bachelor of Science instead of the traditional Bachelor of Arts. The classics were omitted from the B.S. course and bookkeeping, history, or such studies substituted. A student who had successfully pursued the A.B. course through his Sophomore year was allowed to shift to the B.S. Between 1884 and 1931 the college did not offer the B.S. Degree. German was allowed to be substituted for Greek in the A.B. course. For long the classics held their primacy. The commencement program for 1868, for instance, reads as follows:

REVERENDO ALBERTO M. SHIPP, D.D.
FACULTATIS PRAESIDI
OMNIBUSQUE SENATUS ACADEMICI SOCIIS
UNIVERSIS DENIQUE HUMANITATIS CULTORIBUS
EXERCITATIONES HASCE

---

23. W. H. H. in *Wof. Col. Jour.*, March, 1889. Minutes of the early Y.M.C.A. were found in 1902. Prof. W. C. Herbert, in Wof. Jour., Dec. 1902, says that first entry in these minutes is Dec. 13, 1879, which records adoption of a Constitution and election of officers, H. C. Folk being elected President.

JUVENES HODIE PRIMI GRADUS IN ARTIBUS HONOREM PETENTES
ELLISUS BUTLER CANNON
BARHAMUS WILLIS FOSTER
GULIEMUS CLARK KIRKLAND
RICARDUS DAVIS SMART
REVERENTER DEDICANT

Two of the graduation speeches had subjects stated in Latin; a third was on The Glory of Athens, and the fourth was on Laudable Ambition. Almost the only familiar feature is Watts's hymn, still sung at commencements, beginning

> From all that dwell below the skies
> Let the Creator's praise arise.

All this was

HABITA IN COMITIIS
WOFFORDENSIS COLLEGII
DIE JULII OCTO, ANNO SALUTIS, MDCCCLXVIII
RERUMQUE PUBLICARUM FOEDERATARUM
AMERICAE
SUMMAE POTESTIS
XCIII

—"Americae Summae Potestis!" How terribly these words had burned into their consciousness from 1861 to '65; but accepting this Mighty Power of America (which we translate sovereignty of the United States despite John C. Calhoun's argument, which guns had conquered, that no such thing existed), these men continued their devotion to the sovereignty of the mind, or, as they called it, Humanitatis Cultoribus. It was a sad time, but a glorious sight.

President Shipp, but none of his successors, delivered the farewell address to the graduating class in Latin. I have no commencement programs before 1858, and none for the 1860's except '60, '68, and '69. Watts's lines were used in 1860. Occasionally after that the programs do not include these lines in the specified hymns, but from 1875 onward their words of solemn praise have risen at every commencement. I can neither confirm nor deny the statement of J. H. Carlisle, Jr., further than indicated above, that they were used at every commencement from the first.[24]

But life at Wofford in those grim days was not all drab. There was no glee club; but in the late '60's the rich voices of John B. Cleveland, Dan

24. J. H. Carlisle, Jr., *Memories of Wofford College*, M.S., 42, *passim*.

DuPre, Dolph Foster, Trapier, Lewis Jones, Ed Chambers, and Dick Smart serenading the belles of that day were sweetly remembered by them as grandmothers. Said one of the chorus to me years later, I don't remember much about our programs except that we didn't sing any religious songs. Young men sometimes rose into poetry in inviting young ladies to parties.

During the difficult war years the two societies united, and were referred to as the Consolidated Society. The Preston minutes of October 4, 1867, begin with the statement, "The Society for the first time since November 9th, 1861, met, and all the members, eleven, were present." The Calhoun minutes continue through December 15, 1863. Their next entry is in March, 1866; and October 5, 1866, they voted to notify the Consolidated Society of their withdrawal. For a long time the societies, with hardly any rivalry from other forms of intellectual or social diversion, were taken for granted and enthusiastically supported as voluntary organizations. June 25, 1872, the Trustees voted that they had proved themselves of such value that the Faculty ought not to permit any student to remain in college who declined to unite with one of them. They continued very active and effective parts of college life until a decline began in the 1890's. Their later history will be sketched in due course.

It was during these hard years that the college became possessed of its first telescope. As the institution could not afford even such an important aid to teaching, Professor Carlisle gave lectures on astronomy for a small entrance fee in Spartanburg and nearby towns, and with the proceeds bought, April 16, 1869, for $150.00, the three inch glass telescope which served until replaced a few years ago by a larger instrument. The college gave the old one to Dr. Carlisle's grandson, James H. Carlisle III, who had already made quite a good one for himself out of a pasteboard map shipping tube that I gave him and some glasses that he had.

Greek letter fraternities were in 1869 introduced, when W. A. Rogers, a student coming here from William and Mary College, Virginia, led in organizing Delta chapter of the Kappa Alpha fraternity. Chi Psi also came in 1869, Chi Phi in 1871, Sigma Alpha Epsilon in 1885, Pi Kappa Alpha in 1891, and Kappa Sigma in 1894. To these, which existed here at the time of the exclusion of fraternities in 1906, will in due course be listed fleeting chapters before 1906 and those instituted after the re-admission of fraternities in 1915.

The Education Committee of the Conference reported in December, 1870, that the college had opened with 123 students, a few of them in the preparatory department. "The past year, all things considered, has been one of the most successful in the history of the college"; nothing seems lacking except better finances. Salaries were changed at this time from the meaningless inflated figures of the war period back to the original $1,800 for the President and $1,500 for the Professors; but for many years these figures were almost equally meaningless. Though the Conference showed its good will by voting generous educational assessments, the collections amounted to only a fraction of the figures named. In 1870 the college received from this source about $1,500. Tuition fees brought in about $3,500, whereas $9,300 was needed for operating expenses, not to mention the need of a building repairs fund, without which dilapidation was threatened.[25]

Rev. John R. Pickett, one of the Trustees, dying March 15, 1870, left his estate to his wife with the requirement that it go after her death to the college. By 1893 $7,808.65 had come to the college. The Alumni Association pledged itself in 1872 to raise $50,000 in two years, and by January 1, 1875, had secured pledges to the extent of $57,563; but collections must have been poor; for Prof. W. W. Duncan, the Financial Agent of the college, reported in June, 1877, that all of the college's available assets, including ante-bellum notes and bank and railroad securities, did not in his judgment exceed $33,000, aside from real estate, library, apparatus, notes received for tuition, etc.[26] On this foundation three Financial Agents, all of them future Bishops—Duncan, Smith, and Kilgo—were to begin the building of the modern endowment.

The year 1875 saw the resignation of the college's second President, Rev. Albert Micajah Shipp, D.D., to become a Professor in the theological department of the new Vanderbilt University. He had succeeded during the war in securing large pledges to the endowment.

A disagreeable incident in connection with the change of administration was the anger of the retiring President at his successor, Dr. James H. Carlisle, whom he quite unjustly considered responsible for the dropping at the same time of his son John W. Shipp, a good scholar, but a notoriously poor disciplinarian, from the principalship of the preparatory department. Dr. Carlisle felt the injustice deeply. Seeing Dr. Shipp's carriage coming up the road, taking him to the train for Nashville, Dr. Carlisle went to his front gate and waved an adieu. Dr. Shipp gave no response. The breach was never healed. Later when the two men met on the Vanderbilt University campus, Dr. Carlisle extended his hand with the words, in substance, Dr. Shipp, it will not do for two men occupying the positions that we do in the church to allow any misunderstanding to keep us apart. Shipp

25. Trustee Mins., Dec. 8, 1870.
26. Trustee Mins., and Alumni Asso. Mins., of indicated dates.

refused the proffered hand and walked away, eventually to his classroom to teach young preachers theology or Christian charity, which? The opinion of an old student seems to show some insight: "No one suspected Dr. Shipp of being cold or haughty, yet his dignity was of the chilling kind which gets you at once on stilts." [27]

Dr. Shipp's ten years in the Vanderbilt University theological department (as Dean for the last three years) ended with his resignation at the demand of Bishop McTyeire, who was by direction of Commodore Vanderbilt virtually dictator, the Bishop frankly saying that he must have a Dean of greater ability. In December, 1876, the South Carolina Conference requested Dr. Shipp to write the history of Methodism in South Carolina. This he did, despite the pressure of his work at Vanderbilt, and stipulated that any profits from the book should go to the benefit of aged preachers. It was published in 1883 and constitutes the fullest work on the subject, though the pressure under which it was composed caused it to be badly organized. After his retirement from Vanderbilt University Dr. Shipp lived as a superannuated minister in Marlboro County, S. C. He died at Cleveland Springs, N. C., June 27, 1887, from an illness incurred from overexertion in helping a neighbor extinguish a forest fire.[28]

27. First incident, Dr. Carlisle to Dr. Snyder, and Snyder to D. D. Wallace; Dr. H. B. Carlisle on the Vanderbilt campus incident; "An Alumnus" in *Wof. Col. Jour.*, Nov. 1889, 9.
28. A. M. Shipp, by D. D. Wallace, in *Dictionarary of American Biography*; Dr. J. W. Kilgo to D. D. Wallace on Bishop McTyeire's attitude.

CHAPTER VI

DR. CARLISLE BEGINS HIS ADMINISTRATION
1875-1890

THE ELECTION in 1875 of Dr. James H. Carlisle, of the chair of Mathematics since the opening of the College, as President in some ways occasioned not a ripple upon the stream of college life. The old pleasant personal relations, the old quiet endurance of the hardships of the times, the old absorption in an ancient classical curriculum and the cherishing of standards of religious earnestness and personal honor continued. But in an important respect the advent of the new President marked an era, for it opened to him the unrestricted opportunity to put into operation his own ideas of discipline and character building, and especially through his wonderful chapel talks to create an atmosphere for the entire campus life to a degree that would not otherwise have been possible. This was, we may believe, what mainly determined him to accept the position. In the years ahead calls were to come from other institutions, in particular from his alma mater, the University of South Carolina; but he had chosen his work and stuck to it—the work of educating men in a small college by close personal contact, with a minimum of executive management.

Dr. Carlisle was not, in fact, a college president of the modern kind, the rather autocratic executive of the distinctly business type who exercises, with the willing consent of the Trustees, leadership in finance, in the choice of the Faculty, and in the shaping of general college policy, so long as he proves an executive success. Dr. Carlisle's greatness as a leader is of the type of Socrates surrounded by his friends or Jesus enlightening and elevating his hearers and educating the chosen twelve to carry on after he was gone. He was no more an executive than they were; but that is no reflection on either them or him. Like them, he was without ambition. He correctly described himself as not an administrator, but an educator. In what counted most, the stimulation of the best that was in young men, he was supreme.

While emphasizing the moral aspects of the man it is necessary to remind those who did not personally know him of the depth, vigor, power, and quickness of his mind. His memory was marvelous. There was no confusion. He either knew that he knew a thing or that he did not know it. But it was not a bold, inquisitive, or laborious mind. It was acquisitive rather than productive, conservative and cautious to the point of intellectual timidity except where moral issues were involved, when it was clear and uncompromising. A favorite motto (not a motto of men who enlarge the circle of human knowledge) was that it is as satisfactory to a healthy mind to know that there is an explanation as to know what the explanation is. He belonged to the ages of faith and diffused faith around him. He was no organizer or driver or accumulator of endowments; but it is his peculiar glory that he was, and is, "the spiritual endowment of Wofford College."

"The Doctor": the men of the present and the just departed generation always called him that. He was given the degree of Doctor of Laws by Southwestern University of Georgetown, Texas, in 1870. Year after year he pointed out to the Trustees the needs of the institution, emphasizing the necessity of enlarging the endowment; but so disagreeable was it to him to ask for money that he rarely did other than general exhortation to obtain it. He told me that when he was a young teacher in Columbia he would almost rather have gone to work again to earn it than to ask his patrons for what was due him. Another illustration directly from him: He told me that on one occasion as he and a wealthy banker, long prominent on the Board of Trustees, were walking up to the college, the Trustee said earnestly, "Doctor, I know a plan by which we can endow the college!" The Doctor smiled as he related it. "I thought to myself," he said, "Brother —————, I know a plan by which we could very easily endow the college." That he did not say to the Trustee what was the nature of the plan in his mind was perhaps a fault for a college President, but could a man who would have said it be his kind of college President?

So much of Dr. Carlisle for the present, so that we may the better understand him and judge of events during his administration.

The first commencement, 1876, under Dr. Carlisle's presidency was somewhat different from those that had gone before. He delivered his address to the graduating class in English, and not in Latin, as had been President Shipp's custom. In two other particulars this commencement was notable. First, the graduating class of twenty-one was the largest up to that time and contained a number of men who were destined to take a conspicuous part in the history of the coming generation. Second, the commencement orator was the Republican Governor of South Carolina, Daniel H. Chamberlain. To understand this we must recall that in 1876 the white people of South Carolina were sharply divided between the Straightouts, who favored an uncompromising fight to expel the "Radicals" and Negroes from control of the government of the State, "from Governor to Coroner"; and the

83

Fusionists, who, pointing to the failure of every such effort in the past, considered that the only immediate hope for better conditions was for the whites to unite with the small reforming element among the Republicans to re-elect Chamberlain, a man of great ability who had enraged the corruptionists of his own party by his efforts for reform. He spoke at Wofford, Erskine, and Furman, and declined an invitation to Charleston only because his presence in Columbia was necessary to oppose the corruptionists, from whom he said, "the civilization of the Puritan and the Cavalier, of the Roundhead and the Huguenot, is in peril."

Governor Chamberlain's address at Wofford, on the Influence and Effects of High Literary Culture upon Civilization, the gallant ex-Confederate soldier Hugh L. Farley, then editing *The Spartan,* described as "above and beyond anything like criticism from us. We cannot do justice to it by any words of praise," and so he would shortly publish it in full. I have been told that on the warm summer day Chamberlain, the most hated man in the house, was also the coolest; and that he was invited to dinner at the home of Prof. W. W. Duncan, long famous for its hospitality.

The new President soon had a largely new Faculty. Besides the resignation of the former President, Professor Lester had resigned December 1, 1873, to resume the active ministry.

About April 1, 1876, Prof. Warren DuPre departed to be President of Martha Washington College for young women at Abingdon, Va. His son, Daniel Allston DuPre, studying in Edinburgh on leave of absence from his work in the preparatory department, was asked to continue his preparation for teaching all the natural science courses when he should return to Wofford, as he did April 1, 1877, after an absence of approximately two years of study at Edinburgh and travel in Europe.[1] At the same time as the new President came the brilliant Charles Forster Smith as Junior Professor of German and Latin, soon shifted to his specialty, Greek. June 26, 1876, while still lacking four days of twenty-four years of age, he was made full Professor, though at slightly lower salary than the older men, but raised to the same amount June 11, 1878. Prof. William Wallace Duncan (December 20, 1839-March 2, 1908),[2] son of Prof. David Duncan, arrived from his pastoral work in Virginia and took up his duties as Professor of Mental and Moral Philosophy January 1, 1876. Joseph Augustus Game-

---

1. Trustee Mins. June 27, Dec. 17, 1875; June 25, 1877. Statement by Prof. D. A. DuPre's daughter.

2. The date of Bishop Duncan's birth is taken from the family Bible, in his father's handwriting. The error on his gravestone of stating it as Dec. 15 is due to the member of the family whom Mrs. Duncan asked to prepare the inscription. I have seen errors of five days, three years, and ten years on the monuments of distinguished men, in having which corrected on the stone in the latter two cases I participated.

William May Wightman
President, 1853-59

James Henry Carlisle
President, 1875-1902
President Emeritus, 1902-9

Albert Micajah Shipp
President, 1859-75

well entered the service of the college as teacher in the preparatory department in October, 1875. In November, 1876, William M. Baskervill joined the Faculty as teacher of the younger classes in Greek, all the Latin classes, and classes in the critical study of English, and French for Seniors.[3]

There was need in 1875 of this young blood. Though maturity, and even venerableness, contribute something not to be had otherwise, it was time for Wofford to take in some younger men in touch with newer methods. As late as 1880 the catalogue recorded as former Professors only Warren DuPre and A. H. Lester. President Carlisle, always the youngest of the "old Faculty," was vigorous at 55; Dr. Whitefoord Smith, often feeble, was 63, and was to give up half his work in 1882 and to retire completely in 1885. Prof. David Duncan, always the oldest of the "old Faculty," was extraordinarily vigorous at 84 and was to teach part time for two years more until in 1877 he asked to retire on account of failing eyesight. In 1872, at the age of 81, he had given up the treasurership and had asked to be given half time work.

How these Professors managed to live on their partially paid salaries in the hard years before the late '80's is a puzzle; but how they managed to accumulate considerable libraries is a mystery. Professor Duncan in 1879-80 gave over 1,200 volumes, the bulk of his classical library, to the college. The portrait of him by Albert Guerry in June, 1881, shortly before his death the 31st of the following October, was paid for by the college in recognition of his long service and this gift. "My boys," as he called them, liked as always to "get it back" on the teacher who sometimes shot his keen humor at them. Said one on the morning of a big snow, "Professor, I thought I would never get here this morning. Every time I'd take a step forward I'd slide two steps backward." "Well, how did you ever get here?" asked the Professor, thinking to puncture that little witticism. "Professor, I just turned around and started back home," and the student had scored one. The agile Professor Duncan and the less vigorous Dr. Smith differed in temperament as in physique. As. Dr. Smith was driving his leisurely old grey horse down the street one day, he called to Professor Duncan, who was pegging along on foot, asking if he would ride. "No, thank you," replied Duncan; "I'm in a hurry."

Charles Forster Smith, W. W. Duncan, and W. M. Baskervill were able men, and moreover Duncan was invaluable for his work as Financial Agent in putting the college on a firmer financial basis. Smith and Baskervill were scholars of a new type at Wofford, representing the enthusiasm then

---

3. Trustee Mins. June 25, 1877.

stirring among young American educators for thorough university training. Smith,[4] after graduating at Wofford in 1872, had studied at Harvard and in Germany during 1874 and '75. Coming to Wofford in October, 1875, to relieve Professor Duncan of some of his Greek classes (as well as to teach German), and on the veteran's retirement in 1877 of all his Greek, he taught at Wofford for four years, 1875-79, and returned on leave to Leipsic for 1879-81, in which latter year he took there his degree of Doctor of Philosophy. The Wofford catalogue carried him for a few years as a former Professor of 1875 to 1881; but as a matter of fact he did not teach here after the beginning of his leave in 1879, but went for a year to Williams College, from which he went to Vanderbilt University and from there to the University of Wisconsin, where he taught as one of the leading Greek scholars of the country until his retirement in 1917.[5]

Another vitalizing addition to the Faculty came with the election in June, 1878, of young James H. Kirkland as tutor, with work and salary to be fixed by the Faculty. He and James C. Klugh in 1878 were the first alumni to receive from Wofford the degree of Master of Arts on postgraduate studies, instead of merely on application three years after graduation. June 12, 1882, by vote of the Trustees "the salary of Professor James H. Kirkland was fixed at fifteen hundred dollars" (a full professor's stipend), and from that time he appears in the catalogue as Professor instead of as formerly Assistant Professor. He was then twenty-three years, nine months and three days of age, being thus the youngest full professor in the history of the college, distancing in the race for juniorship Charles Forster Smith, a full Professor at twenty-three years, eleven months and twenty-six days, and Henry Nelson Snyder, a full Professor at twenty-five years, seven months, and twenty-three days.

For five years Kirkland taught at times Latin, Greek, and German (principally the latter two), and June 18, 1883, took leave of absence to carry out his long cherished purpose of study at Leipsic, where in 1885 he received the degree of Doctor of Philosophy. He was asked in 1886 to accept the chair of Latin at Vanderbilt University, where his election as Chancellor in 1893 began a career notable in American educational history. Chancellor Kirkland never lost his interest in Wofford College, nor could Wofford lose her affection and her pride in him as once of her Faculty and as her most distinguished alumnus.

---

4. Charles Forster Smith (June 30, 1852-August 3, 1931) was the son of a Methodist preacher, and descended from a Smith family prominent as wealthy planters and business investors in ante-bellum South Carolina. He was not connected with Prof. Whitefoord Smith. His younger brother Perrin Smith (Wofford, 1884) was one of the greatest paleontologists of his generation.

5. *Who's Who in America, Vol. 16, Dictionary of Amer. Biog.*

In one of his addresses at Wofford (for he favored us on several important occasions) Dr. Kirkland beautifully expressed his affection for the old college. He described the dream that came to Xenophon in the darkest days of his leading the betrayed and imperiled Greeks back to their home. He dreamed that he was in his native land and saw his father's house, "the home of his childhood, bathed in supernal light." He rose from the ground where he had been sleeping, "strong for new duties and courageous for new dangers." "This incident," said Kirkland, "has found its counterpart in my own life; for often after days of peculiar trial and exhausting toil, the sweetest gift that sleep has brought my wearied spirit has been the vision of childhood's home and a renewal of associations long broken. Today my dreams are realized; once again I walk this sacred campus; and with every step, Antaeus-like, I feel new strength enter my frame, new courage my heart, and the tones of the old college bell seem to ring out a kindly greeting to the long absent son." [6]

William M. Baskervill, who, as noted above, joined the Faculty in November, 1876, though by no means the superior, if indeed the equal, intellectually of Smith and Kirkland, the other two young scholars bringing to Wofford the breath of the new learning, was able, on account of the state of English studies at the time to make a more important contribution to the curriculum and methods of teaching than either of the others. As a student at Randolph-Macon, with the instinct of the genuine scholar who seeks the knowledge that he desires rather than academic degrees, he took advantage of the elective system to confine himself to languages and the lectures on Moral Philosophy of the brilliant President, James A. Duncan, the most gifted of the five sons of David Duncan of Randolph-Macon and Wofford. Therefore he did not apply for the A.B. degree, a lack in his insignia which Wofford in 1878 honored herself as well as him in amending by conferring upon him the degree of Master of Arts. He studied at Leipsic for the two years 1874-76, and was induced, at the instance of Charles Forster Smith, to come to Wofford in November, 1876, to relieve Smith of some of his Greek and to carry an assorted cargo of languages in addition. After the two years 1876-78 at Wofford he returned to Germany, where the death of his young wife in childbirth so grieved him that he returned to the United States in February, 1879. For the two years 1879-81 he was again at Wofford. In the summer of 1880 he returned to Leipsic for his examination, and so became the first teacher at Wofford bearing the degree of Doctor of Philosophy. From 1881 to his death in 1899 he was at Vanderbilt, where he became one of the major

6. Mims, *Life of Chancellor Kirkland*, 68.

forces in the training of scholarly teachers and the inspiration of Southern authors.

There was no such revolution possible in the other languages as was then taking place in English. Baskervill came to Wofford with the determination to spread the new learning of Anglo-Saxon, historical grammar, and the direct study of the literature itself instead of the study of critics' or historians' description of the literature. In this he was the disciple of T. R. Price, then of Randolph-Macon, whose methods of English teaching were an important event in American education. In every age there is a peculiar vitality to whatever newly stimulates the mind. It may be Greek in the Renaissance or Greek and Hebrew in the Reformation, as dead as either might become in the universities after they had lost their power to give new ideas; and now the vitalizer was English language and literature. The Wofford Faculty sympathized, and placed in their catalogue for 1876-77 (the first to which Baskervill had the opportunity to contribute) a page and a half signed by him, which is so progressively revolutionary as to require quotation complete. "English Philology," it is entitled, and runs as follows:

I cannot better explain the purpose of this new study than in the words of my teacher Prof. T. R. Price, now Professor of Greek, University of Virginia, formerly Professor of Greek and English, Randolph-Macon College, Virginia:

"The Faculty, in adding this new study to the established studies of the College, have endeavored to remedy a defect that has been long felt and bitterly regretted by cultivated men, as the chief fault in collegiate instruction; for the study of English in the College may, as our experience has shown, be regarded as useful, both as means and as end. As the means of insuring an easier and sounder progress in other studies, and especially in the study of other languages, the scientific study of the English, by preparing the mind for the reception of other sciences, by sharpening the intelligence and by stimulating the powers of thought and expression, has shown itself to be of the highest utility. But, beyond all that, the Trustees and the Faculty are profoundly convinced that the opportunity of careful and exact study of our own language as an end in itself, is the greatest benefit that our College can bestow upon her sons. Thus, in doing this, they are helping to solve the much-mooted question of practical education and are removing from the collegiate system the reproach that, both in England and America, has of late brought upon the Colleges well-merited censure. Young men, born into the possession of a language that comes down to them fraught with the wealth of a splendid history, and into the enjoyment of a literature that throws open to them the highest models of moral and intellectual greatness, ought not, for lack of teaching, to be suffered to leave College, knowing many other things, indeed, but unskilled in the use of their mother tongue, and with far less knowledge of their own rich heritage than of the treasures of foreign lands. It ought no longer to be seen that young men, at the end of their studies, should often be unable to write a letter decently, or to express with ease, or even with correctness, the knowledge they have won. The study of the

English should, on the contrary, wherever English is spoken, enter as the leading element into every system of liberal education, and keep pace in its advances with the age and progress of the student. For, in practical value, it of course surpasses, and in scientific value, as part and means of mental discipline, it at least equals the study of a foreign tongue. The college appeals, therefore, with hope and confidence to its friends and to the public to sustain it in this effort to place side by side with the Latin and the Greek, with the French and the German, the philosophical and literary study of the English."

Though the new subject matter and methods marked a great advance, we must not suppose that Wofford students had previously had no advantages in the study of English literature. Prof. Whitefoord Smith, the teacher of English for many years, and still giving his courses, was possessed of fine literary taste and the power of inspiring his pupils with the love of good reading. The condition of the books, both in the college and in the society libraries, bears testimony of extensive use. Charles Forster Smith was surprised in the 1870's to find a Junior class in Latin complain that he gave too short lessons,[7] surprising indeed for one who in later life proclaimed from the Wofford platform: "I teach the first third of the class, for that keeps the second third on their toes, and the Lord have mercy on the last third, for I never could." (Better, in my opinion, is the rule of Kant: Teach the middle part of the class, for the geniuses can take care of themselves, and there is no hope for the dunces.)

What the custom of Prof. Baskervill while at Wofford was in the matter of assigned reading I do not know; but it is surprising to find Mr. James H. Carlisle, Jr., who graduated in 1885, writing that during his whole course not a Professor ever referred him to a book in the library, nor did he ever see a student reading in the college library. Dr. H. B. Carlisle of the same class confirms this in substance, but points out that at that time there was much more reading in the literary society libraries. I can say that the condition of the literary society books in the early '90's showed considerable use in the past, and also that there was at that time considerable use of them. The college had not in earlier decades made proper provision for use of its library. Though at times some member of the Faculty was called librarian, not until 1896 was a regular librarian employed. In the early '90's (how much earlier I cannot say) there was a good collection of magazines, and the library was open for a good part of each day.

Baskervill stimulated both Faculty and students; and, we may say, it was creditable to the Faculty that they so heartily welcomed his contribution. He did not win all hearts, however, for he allowed too free a rein in the class

---

7. Mims, *Life of Kirkland*, 33.

room to his impatience and sarcasm. One student who did not take to his innovations was Henry H. Kinard, whose dissent written on the blackboard was a good deal better than most of the screeds with which the "March colts," as he calls them, kicked back at the Professor. His poem reads as follows:

ANGLO-SAXON AND DUTCH

This is taught by Baskervill
Who goes for it with vim and will
And tries so hard his class to inspire
With his Anglo-Saxon fire.

Alas, alas, his fire is spent
On those who have but little bent
For Anglo-Saxon and all such
Connected with the hated Dutch.

Professor's been to Germany—
And thus the reason you can see
Why Anglo-Saxon and its kind
Have been instilled into his mind.

The class heeds not his high behest,
But utters up a strong protest
Against each foolish innovation
Brought hither from the German nation.

As the young Professor's sarcasm grew bitter, Kinard confessed his authorship, and was sternly informed that he must appear before the Faculty. The President's expression was severe, as his long index finger extended to an unusual height along his temple—a sure sign of the gravity of the occasion. "What are you before the Faculty for, Mr. Kinard?" he asked. "Writing poetry, I answered solemnly," records Kinard. "They say that Dr. Carlisle never laughed in the presence of students, but I made his face volley and thunder. With a sweep of his arm he groaned 'You may go, Sir;'" and that was the last of it.[8]

A disagreeable incident in Baskervill's career at Wofford arose in connection with his awarding of the David Duncan Greek medal for the best Greek student in the Junior class. Baskervill had taken over Greek for Charles Forster Smith on Smith's return to Germany to finish his doctorate. He awarded the medal to Thomas C. Duncan, the grandson of the founder of the medal and son of the then Professor of Mental and Moral Philosophy, and Financial Agent of the college, W. W. Duncan. Of the class of eleven

8. H. H. Kinard to D. D. Wallace Jan. 26, 1918, writing what he had long ago related to me orally.

Juniors only one besides Duncan returned to graduate, and he only by the compulsion of his father (though one other returned, but did not complete the year [9]), so indignant were they at the medal's not having been awarded to D. E. Hydrick, who went the next year to Vanderbilt and won the Greek medal there. Dr. Carlisle was always averse to formal distinctions between students, and opposed prizes, etc., as leading to ill feeling, and did not hesitate to ridicule distinctions in scholarship measured in decimal points. "Is that tragedy or comedy?" he would say. So strong did his feeling become in later life, when he had ceased to attempt specific instruction and occupied his time discussing moral issues or college problems, that he declined to mark his students in any way except to give all second grade, and that only because the Secretary insisted that he must have some grade for the record. We may be sure that the withdrawal of two Seniors early in the college history because of dissatisfaction with the awarding of first honor, and the Tom Duncan incident, colored his address before the National Educational Association in 1882 against prizes in college.

Discipline in the '70's and '80's was often sterner than that accorded Kinard for his poem, particularly if a moral issue was involved. Dr. Carlisle related in my hearing, with the air of being somewhat ashamed of the incident, that the Faculty had once sent a boy home for going to the circus. Prof. Whitefoord Smith, he explained, had told his class that any student who went to the circus would be dismissed, "and the Faculty thought that they had to stand by him."

Arthur Gaillard Rembert, the later distinguished teacher, like some other fine students, once ran afoul of Faculty displeasure. He and a fellow student, Tom Hill, having gone through the act of one grossly insulting the other on the floor of the literary society, engaged in a mock duel with blank cartridges behind the college. The shirt of one of them was stained red, for impressing their fellow students, who rushed up and were terribly scared at the supposedly desperate condition of the man being borne away, and hastened to spread the terrible news. Dr. Carlisle, with his affection for every student and his horror of the duel, an old South Carolina custom on the wickedness and folly of which he often spoke with great impressiveness, was deeply shocked. But for the fine record of Rembert as a student, probably both miscreants would have been sent home.[10]

On another occasion Rembert fell afoul of the wrath of the Doctor, who had been incorrectly informed that Rembert had on a picnic freely imbibed

9. J. H. Carlisle, Jr., Memories of Wofford College, MS., 55.
10. Dr. H. B. Carlisle especially; but the story is widely known. More detailed account by J. P. Wightman of the class of 1883 in *Wofford College Journal*, summarized by J. H. Carlisle, Memories of Wof. College, MS.

of "mountain dew." So earnestly did the Doctor denounce to him his conduct, without waiting to give the accused the opportunity to defend himself, that young Rembert finally said, "Doctor, if you will not hear my statement, I will not hear yours," and walked out of the room.[11] Very disrespectful, doubtless, but very much in the style of the low country gentleman, whose self-respect is maintained irrespective of relative rank. Not unlike Samuel Dibble's declining to return to the College of Charleston on account of a difference with the Faculty. The quiet, impassive boy seldom gives the college any trouble, but seldom does he give it much else. A famous Dean once sighed, "I have just been sending home some of the future leadership of the country." (Undergraduates omit this passage.)

A different sort of problem arose regarding student conduct in 1884. November 29th of that year an election was held as to whether the town of Spartanburg should by local option be made dry. Disgraceful scenes were enacted—Negroes herded to the polls, floaters swilled with liquor. Twelve students, presumably ardent drys, voted. The result was reported as 336 for the drys and 332 for the wets. The wet Mayor, Col. Joseph Walker, backed by a majority of the Council probed the contested voters, who, lawfully and properly, refused to answer the question of how they voted. The Council resolved that such conduct should be punished by imprisonment as contempt. Excitement was intense as the Council, day after day, examined witnesses and challenged voters. Dr. Carlisle, Prof. Wallace Duncan, and Prof. Woodward were among those examined. The Mayor at last gave one of the students two minutes in which to answer as to how he voted. As the audience waited tensely for the result Mr. John B. Cleveland, though not then a member of the Council, whispered something to the Mayor. Whatever it was, the Mayor decided not to jail the student. In speaking in chapel on the incident Dr. Carlisle said, "I had determined that, if that young man had been jailed, I would ask the privilege of sharing his cell." The chapel custom of that day of no applause was burst wide open that morning. Dr. Howard B. Carlisle asked Mr. Cleveland many years later what he had whispered to Mayor Walker. Mr. Cleveland replied, "I told him he had better go slow." The Council reversed the result of the election by declaring it a wet victory by a majority of six. This was annulled by Judge W. H. Wallace; but the victory of the drys was brief. November 27, 1886, the wets won by 395 to 332.[12]

Library facilities were limited in the 1870's. The catalogue of 1876-77

11. Narrated to D. D. Wallace by Dr. H. N. Snyder.
12. Spartanburg City Council Minutes, Dec. 3, 1884, *passim;* Nov. 29, 1886; Dr. Howard B. Carlisle to D. D. Wallace.

states that the library of the college and of the two literary societies totaled about 5,000 volumes. Requirements for the A.B. degree were as follows: In the Freshman year, Mathematics, Greek, and Latin each 4 hours a week, and English 2; Sophomore year, Mathematics 4 hours a week and Greek and Latin each 3; Rhetoric 2 and English 2; Junior year, Greek and Latin each 3 hours a week; Chemistry 4; Natural Philosophy (or, as we would call it, Physics) 2 hours for half the year and Logic the other half for 2 hours a week; Senior year, Mathematics 2 hours a week; Moral Philosophy and Metaphysics 4; Evidences of Christianity and Criticism (i.e., literary criticism) 3, all being required, and two of the following electives: Geology 3 hours; Political Economy 2; German 2.

From the information at our command, the entrance examinations of the early days were oral. Apparently before 1860 they were stricter than later; for it is recorded in one year that of the 18 candidates coming up from the college's own prep department only 12 were admitted after being examined by the Faculty. After the War of Secession the woeful lack of preparation on the part of students, which the Faculty said could hardly be imagined by one not a teacher, compelled a relaxing of standards. The entrance "examinations" in effect became hardly more than a form and great reliance was placed on the ability of earnest young men to make up their deficiencies. In many cases this faith was not misplaced.

A tightening up came with the new Professors Charles Forster Smith and Baskervill. Mr. James H. Carlisle, Jr., tells us that they introduced the system of written examinations. They were sometimes quite severe. In one case a student began his examination at seven in the morning and finished by lamplight. The Faculty soon limited them to three hours.[13] The Faculty reported to the Trustees June 25, 1877, that in most departments written examinations had been introduced, with good results. The catalogue of 1876-77 states that examinations, chiefly written, are given in February and June, and that students failing are required either to take the class over or are conditioned on the subjects in which they fail.

Also smacking of this newly imported influence is the "school system," which went into effect October 1, 1880. After Dr. Carlisle and other members of the Faculty appeared by invitation before the Trustees to explain the proposal at the June, 1880, meeting, it received unanimous endorsement.[14] The plan went into effect October 1, 1880. The old organization

13. J. H. Carlisle, Jr., *op. cit.*, 92, 94.
14. The custom for many years of publishing the catalogue after commencement and calling it (for instance) the catalogue "for the collegiate year 1879-80," but including in it professors elected at the recent commencement or, as in the present instance, a new system that had not been in effect during 1879-80, is quite confusing. The present custom of saying catalogue for 1944-45, announcements for 1945-46, had not arisen.

of students in rigidly divided "classes" of Freshman, Sophomore, Junior, and Senior, was abandoned, and their names were printed alphabetically in the catalogue regardless of age or standing, with the names of the "schools" in which they were studying after each name. The catalogue explained that the system had been adopted to meet the needs of patrons. In their life-work French and German may prove to be more important than Latin and Greek, while English is now regarded by all thinking men as an absolute requirement. It is the intention to put these new studies on an equality with the older ones. Under the old four years course each student had to take certain prescribed courses, keeping always with his class. Professors were often forced to sign diplomas for men whom they knew to be deficient in their departments. Owing to deficient preparation in Greek many students become "irregular," become discouraged and stop college. The change in system will not affect the quality or quantity of work required for the A.B. degree. It simply means that the student will not be required to be studying a certain Latin book at the same time that he is studying a certain book in Mathematics. When he has completed the prescribed course in any school he will be given a diploma signed by the Professor involved and the President, and will receive his A.B. or A.M. degree when having completed the required number of courses for the one or the other.

The nine departments are to be called schools. The school of English (No. 6) alone receives special explanation. The Faculty, it says, in requiring this course have sought to supply a long-felt want, for neglecting which until the recent past both English and American colleges have been justly blamed. Having now for three years given this course, and having found it to work well here as elsewhere, the Faculty are prepared to recommend it to institutions throughout the country. It includes Shakespeare's and Chaucer's works, Anglo-Saxon, Bain's Composition, etc. The other English courses (School No. 8) were under Dr. Whitefoord Smith. The degrees granted would be Graduate in a School, Distinguished Graduate, Bachelor of Science, Bachelor of Arts, and Master of Arts.

I may safely use the snack of higher criticism of literary productions which I learned under Dr. Baskervill at Vanderbilt to convict him of undoubtedly being the author or a contributor to this description, though others of the young newcomers are strongly under suspicion. Baskervill was simply telling of the exact plan by which he had acquired his training in languages at Randolph-Macon, voluntarily neglecting to take any courses which he did not feel that for his purposes he needed, and so not applying for an A.B. degree.

The Faculty loyally tried to make a success of a system clearly much better adapted to advanced university work than to an A.B. college course. The system continued through the college year 1883-84; but the catalogue for that year (published after commencement) announced that "the elementary character of its matriculates, and the limited number of its instructors, have constrained Wofford College to abandon the School System. It now offers to its students two parallel courses of study, both leading to the degree of Bachelor of Arts." One consisted of the old standard courses, with not quite so much science as the other; the second differed only in having a little more science and substituting German for Greek. A few years later the alternative was changed to consist only of the substitution of two years of German and two of French for the three years of Greek (which, of course, had been preceded by a preparatory course in Greek, which was not the case with the modern languages).

During the experiment with the "schools," and in all from 1881 to 1888, the college was served by another able Virginian, also a student of the great English teacher Price, Frank C. Woodward, who enthusiastically carried on the new teaching of English inaugurated by Baskervill. The college was still in hard lines and attendance was not encouraging. On Woodward's leaving to accept a professorship in the University of South Carolina the Trustees felt that they had secured a drawing card in the North Carolinian Prof. A. W. Long. Long was a competent scholar, but he did not fit in here, as he later freely confessed.

As part of the effort to improve educational conditions in South Carolina the first of a series of State Normal Institutes, or summer schools, was held under the direction of the State Department of Education at Wofford College in 1880, with State Superintendent of Education Hugh S. Thompson, Edward S. Joynes, Henry P. Archer, R. Means Davis, Louis Soldan, and W. H. Witherow as the instructors. There were eight of these early Institutes, all but two being held in Spartanburg or Greenville because of their good summer climate, the other two being held in Columbia and Charleston.[15] Some years later the State Department of Education conducted a State Summer School at Winthrop College. This lapsing, Wofford College took advantage of the opportunity and conducted a summer school in 1909 and 1910, but unwisely ceased when Winthrop College in 1911 began her own summer school, which has continued ever since. The later history of the Wofford Summer School will be noted in due course.

The period of the middle and later 1880's was not a happy one. There was

15. D. D. Wallace, *Hist. of S. C. State Teachers Asso.*, 24-25; college catalogues.

not perfect harmony among the Faculty. President Carlisle, doubtless for reasons satisfactory to himself, sometimes failed to carry out orders which the Faculty had voted. Professors Frank Woodward and W. W. Duncan became so impatient of this as to protest to the President. Finally, about 1885, the Doctor wrote out his resignation, stating that he was withdrawing because of lack of harmony in the Faculty; but before presenting it he showed it to his most intimate associate among his colleagues, Prof. D. A. DuPre. Prof. DuPre protested against such action. "Why, Doctor," he said, "don't you know what would be the result? You would not be allowed to resign, but the other two men would necessarily do so." The Doctor dropped the idea of resigning.[16]

From various sources we know that there was great student dissatisfaction with several recent additions to the Faculty, and in general much bad feeling and lack of college spirit. But the alumni were loyal. At the 1888 commencement they determined to reorganize their Association and to organize local Associations in every county of the State, and subscribed $10,000 for a dormitory (Alumni Hall), collections for which, however, did not prove sufficient for the four story structure. Later Edgar Lycurgus Archer of the class of 1871 made up the deficit. After the fire which injured it the night of January 17-18, 1901, it was renamed, against his protest, Archer Hall.[17]

Plainly the better times that were definitely marked by certain changes in 1890 were on their way. But first we must turn back to note certain problems that have been passed over so as not to break the narrative of the academic development.

---

16. Conversation with Dr. H. N. Snyder.
17. In 1949-50 the name Archer Hall was transferred to what had always been called the DuPre house, which had been equipped after Dr. A. M. DuPre's death as the administration building. It had previously been occupied by Prof. Warren DuPre and his son Prof. D. A. DuPre.

CHAPTER VII

FROM BAD TIMES TO BETTER TIMES
1875-89

THE FORWARD moves narrated in the last chapter were not accomplished in a vacuum. The trying and at times desperate financial conditions of the 1860's and '70's continued with little abatement well into the '80's. Under their stress the college long went uninsured, until in 1876 an alarm of fire in the town caused the Faculty on their own responsibility to have it insured. April 1, 1881, the first fire occurred on the campus when the residence occupied by Prof. D. A. DuPre, just west of the main building, burned. It was rebuilt, using the same walls.[1]

Of the few thousand dollars left of the original endowment several thousand dollars of personal notes were after some years canceled.[2] As related above, the Alumni Association, in 1872, under the leadership of Prof. Robert W. Boyd of the preparatory department, pledged itself to raise $50,000, and soon had subscriptions for more than the amount; but panic of 1873 played havoc with collections. Tuition fees fell from $6,104 in 1874 to $2,235 in 1875. In the year 1876-77 only 44.4% of the stipulated salaries were paid.[3] Financial Secretary W. W. Duncan reported to the Trustees June 25, 1877, that the entire assets of the college, aside from real estate, library, apparatus, notes receivable for tuition, etc., would not exceed $33,000.

June 11, 1878, after mature consideration, the Trustees canceled the pre-war notes of James H. Carlisle for $800, of Warren DuPre for $3,000, and notes of Simpson Bobo and A. Walker for $3,000. The college owed the professors many times the amounts of their notes, and Bobo had, during the war, given the college in Confederate bonds, valuable then, many times the amount of his note. Dr. James H. Carlisle once said to me that Bobo's gift in bonds equaled $30,000. He was at that time the largest donor since Benjamin Wofford. Nevertheless lending to Professors or Trustees was a bad practice. Dr. Snyder told me that on becoming President, Bishop Duncan, then chairman of the Board, and several members of his family

1. Trustee Mins., Dec. 15, 1876; June 13, 1881.
2. Catalogue 1871-72, 21.
3. Trustee Mins. June 25, 1877; Alumni Asso. Mins. June 26, 1872.

were borrowers from the endowment. Dr. Snyder was warned of the danger of offending the Bishop. He nevertheless told the Board that he disapproved the practice. The Bishop replied that he was perfectly right, and promptly had the debts in question, which were well secured, paid off.

The income of the college for the year 1876-77 amounted to $2,171 from tuition, $2,492.33 from interest on bonds (i.e., mainly personal notes, then often called bonds), and $1,029.48 from the Conference assessment, totaling $5,692.81. From this there was paid to the Faculty $5,532.33. Figures for the year 1880-81 were:

From invested funds	$1,596.48
Tuition fees	3,629.95
Educational collection	2,420.97
Miscellaneous	2,659.74
	$10,307.14

Salaries of Faculty, $8,333.65, etc., leaving balance of $466.41 on hand.

The several Financial Agents appointed before W. W. Duncan had labored under great difficulties, as indeed did he; but his enormous energy and slowly improving times gave him better success. A young professor of the period cynically wrote to Dr. Kirkland at Vanderbilt:

Dr. Duncan fumes and fusses and labors unceasingly about the endowment, but I fear it will not do much after all. Anyhow his exertions for the church and education will hardly go unrewarded. The next General Conference will doubtless give him a bigger place for which he will be well fitted from his long endowment-drumming experience.[4]

The prophecy was soon fulfilled; for Dr. Duncan was made Bishop in 1886, and Wofford had to look for another Professor of Mental and Moral Philosophy and Financial Agent. It found him in another brilliant preacher and future Bishop, A. Coke Smith, who, more eloquent but less stalwart than the vigorous Duncan, almost broke his health down at the task. Smith worked at the task from 1886 to 1890, and then served for a few months as one of the Missionary Secretaries for the church, after which he taught in the theological department of Vanderbilt University from 1890 to '92. Never fitting well into the limitations of academic life, he returned to the pulpit and was made Bishop in 1902. Born September 16, 1849, he died at the age of only fifty-seven, December 27, 1906. Then came the volcanic John C. Kilgo, another future Bishop, whose tempestuous eloquence and restless energy, offending some but winning many, made him more success-

---

4. Mims, *Life of Kirkland*, 27.

ful than either of his predecessors. Income for the year 1881-82 had risen to $11,763, which included $1,221.73 borrowed from the investing fund, which was really not income at all, tuition fees $3,853.79, interest $2,284.40, and the Conference educational collection $2,472.08 and smaller items. Salaries totaling $8,405.24 were paid to a faculty of seven.

The evolution of what became Wightman Hall, an economical eating place for poor students, seems to have begun with the Whiteside Brothers, Zach and "Zeb," of the class of 1877. They were the first students to cook meals in their room in the main building. About 1878-79 six others followed suit. It worked so well that others joined, and it grew to such proportions that the college recognized and helped.[5] The Faculty report of June 12, 1882, says that during the year 1881-82 twenty or more of the students united to secure a good man cook and provide their own meals at about seven dollars a month.[6] The college furnished them the large ground floor room opening through a door into the eastern tower, and a wooden shack for a kitchen. I well remember in the early '90's the plain dressing and the look of determined character of the men who ate at Wightman Hall, as it was called. In 1900-1 it was furnishing meals at $6.50 a month, including a dollar a month from each boarder for the cook.[7] In the catalogue from 1901-2 through 1907-8 it was called College Hall, at which time it was discontinued.[8]

In those hard years several men carried the economy of eating in their own rooms to such a point as to impair their health. The story of the Whiteside boys (though I never heard that they injured their health by any kind of economizing) has been made widely known through Dr. John G. Clinkscale's delightful historical novel, *"How Zach Came to College."* These two North Carolina boys from Green River Cove, Zach T. and his brother A. S. Whiteside, having brought their produce to town, as they camped near the college heard the bell. Being told that it meant that there would be speaking in the chapel that night, they went, and came away determined that they would one day stand on that platform; and they did, and graduated in 1877, Zach maintaining in his speech The Intellectual Equality of the Sexes, and his brother speaking in favor of Intellectual Inequality of the Sexes. Zach became a Baptist preacher, and his brother a good citizen farmer in their native valleys.

---

5. J. H. Carlisle, Jr., Memories of Wof. Col. MS., 69-70.
6. Daniel C. Roper, *Fifty Years of Public Life*, page 24, errs in saying he "helped organize an eating club among classmates," in the autumn of 1884. It was not composed of "classmates," but of members of any and all classes. Mr. Roper apparently merely joined it and had no part in organizing it.—Trustee Minutes, June 12, 1882.
7. *Wof. Jour.*, June, 1889; Oct., 1899, etc.
8. *Wof. Col. Jour.*, Oct. 1908, 29.

The story of Dr. B. B. Lancaster, a physician from North Carolina, though falling later in time, may be related here. Dr. Lancaster, though a practicing physician, lacked a college education. He had his patients who owed him carry lumber, window frames, etc., down to Spartanburg, where he erected in the pines along the northern side of what is now Dewey Avenue a three room cottage, lined with tar paper. There he and his wife and their son lived while the son studied in the Fitting School and the father earned his degree at the college, graduating in 1901. His determination to complete his schooling at a German university was frustrated by his death a few years later. He was a man of sterling character, great determination, and considerable intellectual ability, and, despite this seriousness, an agreeable companion. It was embarrassing to me as a young Professor during my first two years to teach a man of such maturity of character and so much wider experience of life than myself. Nothing could have been more admirable than the propriety and tact with which the older man adapted himself to the situation.

In December, 1882, the South Carolina Conference:

Resolved, 1. That the Conference raise an endowment fund of one hundred thousand dollars for Wofford College during the next two years, and that this fund shall be known as the Centennial Endowment of Wofford College.

Resolved, 2. That in order to carry out the foregoing resolution, the Conference instruct each preacher to appoint a small committee in each church of his charge, to aid him in taking up a collection of at least one dollar for each member annually, for two years.

The Centennial Endowment was planned in celebration of the one hundredth anniversary of the organization of the South Carolina Methodist Conference in 1785. In a long article in the *Southern Christian Advocate* of January 27, 1883, Dr. Wallace Duncan detailed a plan by which each of the 50,000 Methodists in the State might be induced to do his or her part. Sad to say, plans depending on the co-operation of large numbers of people proportionately never succeed. Doubtless those who devise them merely use the per capita basis as a standard of reasonableness in presenting the total of their aim, and of inducing many small givers to contribute something. The success of the movement, urged the Faculty, might involve the very existence of the college. Year after year Financial Agent Duncan brought in increasing amounts; but still the goal was far away. Total investments amounted in June, 1885, to only $45,420. As so often in Wofford endowment campaigns, hard times palsied the hand of generosity. During the year 1885-86 the total income for current expenses was $8,417, of which the

Conference Educational collection brought in $2,421.35, tuition $2,360.30, and interest on investments $3,422.66—a small improvement over the income of $7,823 for the year ending June, 1879. For the year 1886-87 the Faculty received 76½% of their stipulated salaries, an improvement indeed over the 42.5% of twenty years before, but in 1888-89 only 70%. Beginning with 1890-91, 100% was paid. In one at least of these hard years President Carlisle declined to accept more than the share of a Professor, says family tradition; though in other years our records, which are not complete, show that he received, as was proper, the same proportion of his stated salary as did others.

A grievance deeply felt by the denominational colleges of that day was free tuition so frequently granted by the State University. June 16, 1885, the Trustees appointed a committee to meet with similar committees from other denominational colleges to urge upon the legislature the injustice of the practice. A similar fight was being carried on in some other States, and was to grow more bitter in the 1890's in both Carolinas under the brilliant and aggressive John C. Kilgo. In 1886 the Trustees resolved upon a loan for poor students at 4%, loans to be granted a student for the expenses of only four years, and to be repayable in four years.

Conditions were so serious in 1886 that President Carlisle, speaking in the annual report of the Faculty, urged action on the Trustees with unprecedented earnestness for one living as nearly as any man not a hermit could above the thought of money. He wrote:

No words from us can be necessary to impress upon your body the responsibility, which the present condition of the college imposes upon all its friends. Without using words lightly, we may say that we have reached a crisis in its history. When the church at large begins to look among our earliest graduates for the men to place in the very highest positions of responsibility and labor, we may see that the past is beginning to yield its mature fruit. The present and the future are making new demands upon all engaged in the great work of Christian education. The position of affairs around us in our own State, as well as the circumstances of our whole country, are just now suggestive and significant. This is not the time for indifference or for slack and feeble measures or work. Our church and country will reap a few years hence as they [sow] today. Benjamin Wofford was in advance of his generation in his enlarged views of education, and in his confidence in the church which had nourished him. Will not the Carolina Methodists of to-day build on his foundation? Let not his native State be among the last portions of our country to be blessed by the widening stream of liberality which he may almost be said to have opened. With an increasing feeling of interest in the College and an enlarged view of the grand possibilities before it, we promise your body all the help we can give you in building up the great interest committed to our care.

101

There were enrolled in 1885-86 only 72 students and the next year only 64. The average enrollment for the eight years 1868-69 through 1875-76 was 95.6; for the twelve years from 1876-77 through 1887-88 only 73.2. In a sort of desperation the Trustees passed a series of resolutions, several of which deserve mention:

As the decreased patronage is partly due to the inability of patrons to pay the cost of board and tuition, we plan a dormitory for sixteen students, room in it to be rented at the same rate as charged for rooms in the college building, i.e., one dollar a month per student.[9]

The Faculty should visit churches in Spartanburg and neighboring counties, and especially District Conferences.

Elect a Faculty who will inspire the fullest public confidence (clearly hitting at a young Professor of very poor teaching ability, whose resignation was at once received).

Fees to be collected in advance, but if necessary parent to give a note at ten per cent, with penalty of exclusion of the student if not paid by the end of the year, but not to apply to worthy young men giving their own notes.

Faculty to meet at least once a week, and all discipline requiring suspension or withdrawal to be only by vote of a majority.

To further popularize the institution encouragement should be given the Faculty to develop the gymnasium, and arrangement should be made on the campus for "manly exercise."

The next year a device tried elsewhere was suggested, but happily not adopted, namely, to increase the number of the Trustees. Instead the Conference was requested to appoint an advisory board, consisting of one person from each county of the State. For a short while such a plan operated. For instance, in June, 1888, fifteen men, spoken of as members of the advisory board and visitors, met with the Trustees. Apparently not until 1888 did the college pay the expenses of out-of-town members of the Board of Trustees, which perhaps accounts for the fact that it was necessary in June, 1884, to make the sole entry that, due to lack of a quorum, the annual meeting was not held.[10]

Whether the passing of the depression of 1886, or whether the earnest pleas were bringing results or whether the contagious personality of Dr. A. Coke Smith, as he circulated around the State, was in part responsible, or

---

9. Reducing tuition in 1888 from $60 to $40 a year failed to bring a compensating increase in enrollment. S. C. Conf. Mins. 1888, 17.

10. Trustee Mins. June 11, 1885, on payment of Trustees—but June 17, 1891, I find the Board ordering that hereafter traveling expenses of the Trustees in attending meetings be paid, thus clearly covering the case of non-"out-of-town" Trustees attending meetings at Conference, etc. In earlier years it had been customary for a Conference committee of visitors to inspect the college.

the better feeling of South Carolinians, as a politician might contend, at there being in the White House the first Democratic President since 1861, the commencement of 1888 seemed to mark a new era. The presence of many ministers especially, as well as other visitors, was encouraging. Said an account in the Charleston *News and Courier,* never had such enthusiasm been shown by the alumni, who resolved to organize local associations all over the State. E. L. Archer started an alumni fund by subscribing $500, and Dr. Herman Baer, the Charleston wholesale druggist, and Dr. A. Coke Smith followed with like subscriptions, and soon $5,100 was pledged.[11] When it was learned that the Trustees had resolved to build three cottages for dormitories, a call meeting of the alumni was held which requested the Trustees to allow the almuni to construct a dormitory instead, which was agreed to, and so the Alumni Hall was born. The cornerstone was laid on Founder's Day, October 19, 1888, with ceremonies and addresses expressive of pride in the past and of confidence for the future.

The resignation of Prof. W. W. Duncan on his election as Bishop in 1886 removed from the Faculty a wholesome and vigorous personality who, like his successor Dr. A. Coke Smith, was too individualistic to fit perfectly smoothly into academic grooves. Dr. Duncan occupied the enormous three story brick house intended for the President, in which Presidents Wightman and Shipp had lived; but Dr. Carlisle, not equipped for extensive entertaining, preferred not to move into the grand mansion. The dining room on the first floor and the reception rooms on the second extended the entire length of the southern side. The abounding hospitality of Dr. Wallace Duncan and his charming, stately wife fortunately was not limited by the compensation received from the college. Dr. J. J. Lafferty of the *Richmond Christian Advocate,* the literary society orator at the June, 1883, commencement, was greatly embarrassed when he found he had brought the wrong speech; but he nevertheless had a good time, for he was entertained at the home of his former fellow Virginian. He wrote: "At Dr. Wallace Duncan's there were twenty or thirty at meals. Three tables—kin people, old friends, and visitors. The happiest gathering I ever saw. And yet he, in every letter, urged, 'Bring your wife and daughter.' The house of Duncan has always been that way." [12] And so, we may add, it continued to the end of Dr. Duncan's life. There was hardly a day when the arrival of several unexpected guests would have caused embarrassment. His hospitality included the high and the humble, the popular and the unpopular.

We must not be misled by Dr. Lafferty's account into supposing that

---

11. *News and Courier,* reprinted in *Wof. Jour.* of Jan., 1889.
12. Reprint in *So. Christian Ad.* June 30, 1883, from *Richmond Christian Ad.*

hospitality was limited to "the house of Duncan." At commencement until comparatively recent times Faculty members and their wives filled their tables with commencement guests. The times were simpler, but for that very reason commencement entertainment was more elaborate. A popular visitor needed an engagement card to keep his bids to dinners and suppers straight. Needless to explain that the Trustees were favorites, and long-enduring friendships were formed by their stopping with the Professors. The necessary change, demanded by the mounting mass of business, of housing them at a hotel has made for more effective administration, but has somewhat transformed the Trustee from an intimate personal friend to a far-removed abstraction of fearsome potentiality.

Prof. W. W. Duncan's successor, both as Professor and as Financial Agent and Secretary, Rev. A. Coke Smith, D.D., was a brilliant preacher, aged then 37. He had just "almost killed himself saving souls" in one of the greatest revivals in the history of Charleston, and proceeded almost to conclude the suicide process by his labors for raising the college endowment in addition to his duties as teacher. In August, 1888, the Trustees resolved that he should suspend all work except such as his physician should allow. In December, 1888, Rev. John C. Kilgo was elected special agent to assist Dr. Smith in canvassing for the endowment. We can judge of the heartbreaking character of the work from Kilgo's statement in February, 1893, that he had raised $24,295.85 for the endowment, only one person having given as much as $500 and fewer than twenty-five having exceeded $100.[13]

Support of the college was still quite inadequate. In 1889 the effective endowment was $52,647; for imperious necessity had, as on various occasions, led to "borrowing" from the endowment to meet upkeep or repairs, acquiring the Fitting School property, etc.[14] Still, with 1888 and '89 the skies were brightening. A commodious dormitory had been erected. An important move of the period was the creation in 1887 of the Wofford Fitting School. The initiation of this important step came from the Faculty, under the leadership of two of its newer members, A. Coke Smith, seconded by Frank C. Woodward. The Faculty suggested that these two gentlemen explain the idea to the Trustees, which they did at the meeting of June 13, 1887.[15] After hearing the two professors the Board resolved to establish the Wofford College Fitting School, and to buy for the purpose from Rev.

13. Garber's *Kilgo,* 10-11.
14. Tr. Mins. June 9, Aug. 7, 1890; June 15, 1891, etc.
15. D. M. McLeod as Alumni Editor of the *Wofford Journal,* June, 1900, p. 158, says that Dr. A. Coke Smith was responsible for the founding of the Fitting School.

R. C. Oliver the three large brick buildings and ample grounds of the old Spartanburg Female College, now a part of the Spartan Mill village. An appeal to the Methodists of the State easily secured the necessary funds, and so the old female college plant became an adjunct to Wofford College instead of continuing as it had been for a while under Reverend Oliver, as an orphanage.

The school was under a Board of Control, subject, of course, to the college Trustees. The services were obtained as Headmaster of Prof. Arthur G. Rembert, a fine type of low country gentleman, a Wofford graduate of 1884, who combined with a high degree of scholarship the qualities of a superb schoolmaster. The school opened October 1, 1887, and was an immediate success, proving how correct had been the idea that few adequate high schools then existed in the State; and the very high percentage of the graduates who entered Wofford proved also the correctness of the view that the college's own fitting school or schools would help to build up the declined patronage. The move distinctly raised the college in public estimation. In 1891-92 the Fitting School had 90 students taught by its own five instructors. Due to the growth of the modern public high schools the number had gradually sunk by 1894-95 to 50. In 1894-95 that *bete noire* of the modern standardizers had reappeared in professors in the college giving instruction to preparatory classes. Dr. Carlisle was giving lessons in Bible study and Professor Gamewell in Latin. In the summer of 1895 the school was moved to the college campus and lodged in Alumni Hall. Prof. A. Mason DuPre was in 1895 added to the Faculty as Second Master, and took up his lodgings in the building. On Headmaster Rembert's resignation in June, 1897, Professor DuPre became Headmaster and remained such until 1912. The Headmaster and one full time teacher in 1898-99 were being assisted by five of the college professors. The school shared the growing prosperity of the college, and in 1910-11 was using the services of only one college professor, Prof. Rembert in Greek. That year it registered 175 students. Headmaster Rembert had been also Professor of Greek in the college since the resignation of Prof. E. B. Craighead in the summer of 1893 to become President of Clemson College.[16]

Following the fire which on the night of January 17-18, 1901, burned the third and fourth stories of the Alumni Hall, the new Fitting School quarters, now called Snyder Hall, were built. In this building, and the now two story Alumni Hall, rechristened Archer Hall, and a recitation hall to its north, the school continued until discontinued in June, 1924. The growth of a good

16. *Wof. Jour.*, June, 1893, 333; Oct. 1893, 34.

public school system rendered the Fitting School less needed, and the enlarged enrollment in the college demanded its quarters for dormitories. Headmaster W. C. Herbert, who had since 1918 been conducting the Fitting School with excellent success, was transferred to the college as Professor of Mathematics and Greek, with his work later shifted to the Department of Education.[17] As a hard-worked servant he was also for years Registrar, and for the year 1925-26 served as Dean. He was followed as Dean by Dr. A. M. DuPre (1926-40); then came LeRoy H. Cox, and in 1942 Dr. C. C. Norton.

Dr. Carlisle's reaction to the Fitting School fire supplied a striking illustration of his lack of the business executive's prompt and resourceful way of meeting a crisis. He looked completely prostrated as the Faculty met to discuss the situation; and when a fine new building soon rose to afford the School bigger and better quarters he said happily, "I did not know where the money was to come from, and I do not know now where it came from."— What are Trustees for if not to save a choice spirit like his from being cumbered with such matters?

The Carlisle Fitting School of Wofford College, named in honor of the great teacher, was established in Bamberg in 1892 as part of the effort on the part of the college to draw a well prepared class of students. Another school for the Peedee section was discussed, Bennettsville and Florence being generally mentioned, but nothing was done in that direction. The citizens of Bamberg donated four acres of land, worth, with the building on it, $5,000, and $10,000 in cash, General F. M. Bamberg being the largest contributor.[18] Hugo G. Sheridan, a famous schoolmaster from Orangeburg, was the first Headmaster. He was followed in 1896 by Mr. W. E. Willis. My first teaching, as Instructor in English and History, was there, so that I know something of the difficulties under which the school labored, including the competition of a very active rival in the same town under the friendly co-operation of the Baptists. Wofford received some excellent material from the Carlisle School, but, quite naturally, never in the same amount as from the school in Spartanburg. Unlike the Wofford Fitting School, Carlisle was co-educational and served a very useful purpose for the adjacent counties in those days of inadequate or no high school facilities in small places and rural districts. The growth of a good high school system—one of the outstanding educational advances in the last generation—rendered it less and

---

17. The following complete the list of Headmasters of the Wofford Fitting School besides A. G. Rembert and A. M. DuPre already noted: J. M. Steadman, Jr., and A. W. Horton, Associate Masters 1912-13; A. W. Horton 1913-15; F. P. Wyche 1915 to his death Feb. 10, 1918; A. M. DuPre in charge the balance of the school year; W. C. Herbert, 1918-1924.

18. Trustee Mins. June 11, 1892.

less needed. In the five years from 1920 to '24 enrollment dropped from 254 to 102; fewer graduates were going to Wofford, and the school was accumulating a deficit. It was in 1932 leased to Prof. James F. Risher, the last Headmaster under Wofford College management, and in 1938 was sold to him, and has since been conducted by him as a military preparatory school drawing patronage from a large number of States and some foreign countries.

The old Cokesbury Conference School was for a while about the 1890's under the control of the Wofford College Trustees; but the same forces that eliminated the two fitting schools have caused that to merge into the local public school system of the community.

An addition to the intellectual life of the college in this period was the *Wofford College Journal*. Prof. A. Coke Smith urged the idea to his younger brother, the later United States Senator Ellison D. Smith, who accordingly took a leading part in the movement which led the two literary societies to vote in October, 1888, to establish *The Journal*. The first monthly issue is dated January, 1889, with Ellison D. Smith as Editor-in-Chief and the later President of Duke University, William P. Few, as an associate editor. The first issue was made up chiefly of articles by Professors, though two editorials ran true to form for the future careers of their authors: The Blair Bill, by Ellie Smith and the Wofford College Reading Room by Will Few. The future Bishop E. D. Mouzon also appeared as an associate editor. The future Bishop in his first number shot out a vigorous attack on college fraternities, to which a representative of the fraternities as vigorously replied in the March issue. In the March number John H. Marshall, Professor of English, wrote approvingly of the growth of intercollegiate athletics in American colleges and wished for such a development at Wofford. Headmaster Rembert of the Fitting School replied with warmth—we may almost say heat—with the forcefulness of his acute mind, saying very positively about all the bad things that can be said about the abuses connected with intercollegiate sports and arguing for physical exercise in moderation and the supreme interest in the intellectual and moral aspects of college life. Rembert was at the height of his ardor for scholarship. Many years later he said to me, "I suppose it is well for a man to feel at one time in his life that the most important thing in the world is Greek, even though he may later see that it was not quite that." Marshall, much more the man of the world, replied more moderately, and therefore more effectively, holding that the undoubted advantages of athletics were unattainable without intercollegiate contests. Rembert came back with a lengthy reply in October. Marshall might have enjoyed a quiet smile if he had witnessed in the early years of the 1900's Rembert as Chairman of the Faculty Athletic Committee fighting with all his ingenuity and earnestness for everything connected with Wofford's intercollegiate teams. I have always thought that the extremes to which he went as Chairman of the Athletic Committee in this regard were more the expression of the thoroughness with which he did anything which he undertook rather than an inherent love for athletics.

The participation by Professors in the *Journal* soon became only occasional; but it continued to be a chief arena for student opinion on athletics. Unquestionably physical exercise had been neglected in the early years of the college. The sickness frequently commented upon by the Faculty can hardly have been entirely unconnected with that. The much more frequent deaths then than later among the students were, however, doubtless due in large measure to the general ignorance of sanitation and preventive medicine. And, we may remark, conditions at Wofford were in no way peculiar in those regards.

The beginning of extra-campus athletics, says Dr. Howard B. Carlisle, was games of baseball between the students and the Federal soldiers stationed in Spartanburg for a while during Reconstruction. The students sometimes employed the soldiers' military band for their entertainments. Mr. S. D. Schofield says in his M.A. thesis, The History of Wofford College, that the first baseball team at Wofford, "the Pioneers," was organized in 1869, but that intercollegiate games did not begin until about 1886 and did not become an important part of college life until about 1896. Quite naturally Prof. Marshall was chosen as manager of the baseball team organized in 1889, and also of the football team, and won great commendation from the students for his activities for athletics. December 14, 1889, Wofford beat Furman in football 5 goals to 1, at the encampment grounds (at the present Hayne). *The Baptist Courier* commented that it was greatly to the credit of the Furman boys that they gave more attention to the cultivation of their heads than their feet—a glory which they have since lost if we are to judge by their successes on the gridiron in more recent years. In a second game in Greenville, January 14, 1890, Wofford again took the honors by 2 goals to 1. The *Wofford Journal* attributed Wofford's success to their being a heavier team and to their having been coached by a Yale man.

The Faculty expressed disapproval of intercollegiate sports and athletics languished. "Breathing—the only exercise at Wofford—football and baseball are no more," lamented *The Journal* in November, 1892. Mr. Evins, who has consented to train us, says he can't make a football team out of a half dozen men. But soon the tide rose again. At Thanksgiving, 1893, Furman beat Wofford at Greenville 18 to 4; but in the autumn of 1895 Wofford

108

trounced Furman 44 to 0, and beat South Carolina in the contest of November 14, 1895. Defeat by the University of Georgia moved the students to raise money to employ William Wurtenbaker as coach.

Football in that day was extremely rough, broken bones and even deaths occurring with disturbing frequency. The Board of Education of the South Carolina Methodist Conference in December, 1896, denounced the game as brutal, wasteful of time and money, a hindrance to intellectual pursuits, and destructive of morals; and therefore recommended that the college authorities forbid it at Wofford. The demand was complied with; but the Conference of December, 1899, resolved that so much of the report of 1896 as recommended that the authorities "entirely prohibit" football at Wofford be rescinded, and that the regulation of football and other games be left entirely to the Trustees and Faculty. The *Wofford College Journal* of October, 1900, announces that football has been re-introduced and has already produced some good results. Interclass games flourished, but no games with other institutions were allowed until after considerable agitation, in response to a unanimous petition by the student body, the Trustees rescinded the prohibition, November 26, 1913, playing to begin with the fall of 1914.[19]

There occurred about 1900 a series of victories in baseball, based largely on the possession of several remarkable pitchers. Gus Chreitzberg of the class of 1895 is considered by some fans the best of them all; certainly he was the most powerful, throwing a ball of great swiftness. A little later came the best balanced team, perhaps, Wofford ever had. Outstanding was Fayssoux DuPre of the class of 1902, backed by a remarkable catcher, F. H. Hudgens (1902), and supported by a team captained by C. B. Burnett as an almost faultless first baseman and a group of players offering not a weak spot. They lost only two games in three years—one to Trinity and one to Cornell.[20] DuPre, though without Chreitzberg's physical strength, was unrivaled among college pitchers of the State in the wizardry of his curves. It was facetiously said that he had made his father more famous than had all the Professor's years of teaching. The possession of such a team of simon pure college players was sometimes used by friends of other teams as justifying their hiring players, as otherwise this unfair distribution of talent left the outcome of the game a foregone conclusion.

The Wofford College Lyceum was organized by Prof. J. A. Gamewell in the college year 1898-99, and became an important part, both as entertainment and as intellectual stimulation, in the college life.[21] There had

19. Trustee Minutes; *Wof. Col. Jour.*, Dec. 15, 1913.
20. Walter K. Greene, the second baseman, to D. D. Wallace.
21. Wof. Catalogue, 1898-99, 31; 1908-9, 42.

earlier been a sort of informal lyceum consisting of lectures of various of the college Professors, sometimes participated in also by prominent citizens of the town. For instance, in the winter and spring of 1890 Dr. Carlisle lectured in the opera house on Orion, many of his statements being incredible, said the reporter, were it not for the known character of the speaker. Major D. R. Duncan, long a Trustee of the college, followed with a disquisition on the tariff and tariff history. Prof. D. A. DuPre lectured next on ancient and modern methods of illumination. The series was in the interest of the city Y.M.C.A.[22] More directly a forerunner of the lyceum was a series of lectures in the college chapel by various Professors, for instance, during 1893-94, which must have had some virtue, for today, fifty-five years afterwards, I distinctly remember some of the points in them. I can never forget Dr. Carlisle's saying that some of the patriarchs would today be sent to the penitentiary for some of their conduct (Father Abraham himself, for instance, was not entirely innocent); and that it is as satisfactory to a healthy mind to know that there is an explanation as to know what the explanation is. Both of these were quotations by the Doctor; for he was much given to quotations, but to quotations well worth quoting. The latter quotation is more expressive of the type of his mind and faith than any other one statement I ever heard him make.

The Lyceum became Prof. Gamewell's chief interest. To bring to the college notable speakers was to him a delight; and with notable success did he pursue his aim. Although there was a Lyceum committee, he really did the work and let the younger members who desired changes understand that he knew better than they what the collegiate and general public wanted. The earlier years of the Lyceum were the best; for at that time it was possible to secure intellectual leaders of national fame. Such were Woodrow Wilson, Lyman Abbott, George Kennan, Wilfred T. Grenfell, of Siberian and Labrador fame respectively, Hamilton Wright Mabie, Vachel Lindsay, Carl Sandburg, Henry van Dyke, and William J. Bryan. Eventually the radio and other means of public address militated against the lyceum platform. Men of national leadership declined to undergo the inconvenience of following a lyceum circuit when they could sit in a radio studio or even in their own offices and receive more for broadcasting to the millions than they would get in a long tour of the lyceum platforms. It became more and more difficult to secure the great popularizers of literary, moral and scientific leadership; but the institution still forms a useful part of the college program. The Lyceum constituted Prof. Gamewell's greatest contribution to the intellectual life of the college.

---

22. *Wof. Jour.*, Feb. and March, 1890; *ib.*, 1893-94.

Financial conditions were improving in the late '80's, but in some respects the Faculty was not. Prof. A. W. Long, who taught English here from 1888 to 1890, in his *Son of Carolina,* published in 1939, says: "I had not in these two years impressed Wofford College very strongly, and assuredly it had not impressed me." "It was intellectually in slack water. Every brain was sealed up tight in its own little can. I hear it has been vastly improved since my day." [23] Although the most unfavorable expression about the college that I have ever read, by one who failed to enter into the traditions and spirit of the place, it contains enough truth to make Wofford men sit up and take notice. Though there were several men of first class ability then connected with the college, it was a period of transition and uncertainty, with at least four short time birds of passage who, thinks Dr. Snyder, "rattled around" in the places of abler predecessors.[24] Perhaps they rattled around not so much on account of their size as because they were unattached. J. Wright Nash of the class of 1890 was the leader of a student movement to get rid of these gentlemen.[25] Dissatisfaction must have been strong indeed for even the plain-speaking Nash, Editor-in-Chief of the *Wofford College Journal,* to write in December, 1889, under the heading, "Will the Trustees Read": "How much like 'dumb driven cattle' are we students who have no appeal to higher authority when an imposition has been committed? . . . Whatever the Faculty may learn of a Professor they feel a delicacy in reporting it to the trustees simply because it is none of their business." Appeal to the Trustees is impracticable, for they rush away as soon as attending to necessary business and know nothing of what is going on in the college. "In order to have competent men in the several departments and the best work done by such men, the Trustees should visit the institution at any and all times during the year, drop into the recitation rooms unexpectedly and learn what kind of work is being done there. . . . We beg the Trustees to be more vigilant and make some needful changes. They must do this if they wish to keep the standard of Wofford College where its reputation demands that it should be."

We shall see how well the Trustees, whether they read Student Editor Nash's editorial or not, soon acted in harmony with it.

---

23. Long, *Son of Carolina,* 189-90. Long was later instructor for three years and precentor for eleven in Princeton University. (Dean J. D. Brown of Princeton to D. D. Wallace, March 10, 1948.) He was the friend of Presidents Theodore Roosevelt and Woodrow Wilson, and had a varied literary career, including the publication of three anthologies.
24. *Educational Odyssey,* 63.
25. So Dr. Snyder told me.

CHAPTER VIII

DR. CARLISLE CLOSES HIS ADMINISTRATION
1890-1902

THE SESSION of 1890-91 began with a largely new Faculty. Dr. A. Coke Smith had resigned to become one of the Missionary Secretaries of the Southern Methodist Church. Resigned also were Professors Granville Goodloe in Greek, A. W. Long in English, and John H. Marshall in French and German. President Carlisle was still described as Professor of Mathematics and Astronomy; but (to recall a favorite quotation of his from Kant, "the starry heavens and the moral law" as the two sublimest facts in the universe) he was more and more devoting his teaching to the moral law and less and less to the stars and geometrical figures. He had never neglected the moral law; but in his earlier years he had been an exact and exacting teacher of mathematics as well. Profs. Daniel Allston DuPre and Joseph Augustus Gamewell, gentlemen of the old stamp, were in charge respectively of sciences and Latin. It was this year, 1890, that Prof. DuPre was given the additional duty of Treasurer (following A. Coke Smith), with supervision of grounds and buildings thrown in.

Prof. DuPre stood in closer personal relations with Dr. Carlisle than did any other member of the Faculty, as was natural from their long associations and personal qualities. But the Doctor played no favorites in any improper sense, but treated all members of his Faculty with sincere friendliness. If he entertained a prejudice against a man when he became a member of the Faculty, as he sometimes did (for he took no part in selecting his Faculty as Presidents generally do), he generously recognized the man for what he was when he came to know him as a colleague.

After the resignation of the three young Professors referred to above, the Trustees waited until August 6th to choose their successors. That day they elected E. B. Craighead Professor of Greek and French, and Henry N. Snyder Professor of English and German. The next day they chose Samuel R. Pritchard Assistant Professor of Mathematics. Professor Snyder, twenty-five years and seven months of age, was the youngest full Professor in the history of the college except Charles Forster Smith and James H. Kirkland, who were given that rank a little before reaching twenty-four. The coming of these men opened a new era in the history of the

112

college. Craighead and Snyder as the more striking personalities were advertised over the State as wonderful finds; but it must not be forgotten that the less spectacular Pritchard was as well fitted for his work as they were for theirs. Both Craighead and Snyder were gifted as public speakers. Craighead was of the florid style. An able, strong-willed man, he was so combative that he quarreled himself out of one presidency after another and finally founded a newspaper to flay his enemies. He left Wofford to become the second President of Clemson College (H. A. Strode having served before its opening), to which he was elected June 21, 1893, and served until the acceptance of his resignation July 7, 1897, to go into effect September 1 following. He rendered useful service there by insisting on high standards of scholarship for the young institution.[1]

Dr. Snyder on the other hand displayed more wisdom. He was tact, judgment, moderation personified. He was a most accomplished artist in the spoken word. He had the gift for catching the gist of any subject and the spirit of any occasion, unlike some more weighty orators who are disappointing except when roused on something in their own peculiar realm. He understood as perfectly as a movie producer how to play down to the level of an average popular audience. It was what in his situation he needed to do, but it was a poor way to cultivate his really considerable mental abilities. He would take an idea, dissect it, turn it over and over, until the simplest mind comprehended and hence felt both gratitude and admiration toward the speaker who had so entertained and enlightened him. This gift does not imply that Dr. Snyder lacked resources for higher tasks. When in contact with minds of his own caliber, as in a General Conference of the church, he was capable of weighty thoughts forcefully expressed.

Dr. Snyder was supreme in exposition, persuasion, and charm, but not in rough and tumble give and take. He needed to be listened to respectfully and sympathetically. I never saw him show up poorly but once, and that was when he was put forward by the prohibition forces in a heated political convention, under heckling and interruption, to lend his prestige to closing the debate. Though capable of meeting aptly many occasions on which his predecessor would have shown up less happily, he was incapable of the flashes, illuminating and awing like lightning, which often burst from Dr. Carlisle like inspired utterances from a Hebrew prophet.

Of course the young Professor Snyder had not then fully developed these talents; but from the first he was supreme as a teacher of English literature. His capacity for entering into the spirit of an author, and his own gift of

---

1. Clemson College Trustee Minutes; *Dictionary of American Biography*. Dr. Craighead died Oct. 22, 1920. *So. Ch. Ad.*, Nov. 4, 1920. Born Mch. 3, 1861.

lucid, engaging exposition made his class to a student capable of the appreciation of literature a labor so delightful that the hitherto unprecedented loads of reading that he prescribed seemed hardly a burden. The era before the coming of Charles Forster Smith, Kirkland, and Baskervill into the Wofford Faculty may be called (in the terminology of European history) the ages of faith; those young scholars with a new sort of equipment inaugurated the Early Renaissance, and with these new younger men of 1890 began the High Renaissance. We are now in Modern Times; and what Modern Times are to be the future must tell. But let us remember, as we said in commenting on Smith, Kirkland and Baskervill, that there were good things here before they came. Spartanburg was already proud of Wofford. It was in the 1880's that John S. Reynolds, later Reporter of the South Carolina Supreme Court, lived for a short time in Spartanburg. Says Dr. W. W. Ball: "After two months, one of his friends, meeting him in Columbia, said, 'Why, John, I thought you had gone to Spartanburg to grow up with the town—now I hear you are back to stay—what's the matter?'

" 'Yes, I've come to stay.'

" 'Well, what's the matter with Spartanburg?'

" 'Spartanburg is all right, George, but I found I couldn't live there without accepting three dogmas.'

" 'Yes; what were they?'

" 'The first was that Wofford College is a greater institution than Oxford, the second that Dr. Carlisle is a greater mathematician than Copernicus was, and the third is that Coke Smith is a greater pulpit orator than the Apostle Paul—and I'll be damned if I could subscribe to them.' " [2]

The Trustees were proud too. They pasted into their Minutes at about this time the picture of the college, the list of Trustees and Faculty, and the really fine commencement program of 1891 with Bishop Galloway as preacher and John Temple Graves (the elder) as deliverer of the literary address. In 1890-91 they had been able to pay the Faculty in full for the first time since the War of Secession. [3]

Another all but new member of the Faculty was Rev. John C. Kilgo, who had been made assistant to the Financial Agent in 1888. Born July 22, 1861, [4] he was now in the full tide of his restless energy. He left college in 1881 after finishing the Sophomore class and soon became one of the outstanding leaders, both in Conference affairs and in strong preaching. His

2. W. W. Ball, *The State That Forgot*, 20.
3. Trustee Mins. June 10, 1890; June 15, 1891.
4. He lived to August 11, 1922.

voracious mind demanded more, and as one means of attainment he asked his friend Snyder to take him through a course in English literature. Dr. Snyder relates that it was a battle royal, in which he fought to save from overthrow the great makers of English literature from a fighting critic who would take nothing for granted. Sometimes until two in the morning he would fight to make the fighting Kilgo see that Tennyson was not "just sweetened water," that Browning was not just "hiding kindergarten religious stuff in words jumbled so that nobody could understand what they meant," that Shakespeare was not "too much sound and fury." But toward Thomas Carlyle, another stormy petrel, his attitude was different: "What a preacher he might have made, had he not fooled himself into being a writer, a wordmonger." [5] How he ever missed the point that of all things Carlyle was a preacher is hard to understand.

So far as Professor Kilgo's duties as Financial Agent permitted, he was a stimulating teacher in the classroom. I have seen him almost fall asleep in his chair, rouse himself, and go on in a way that was not, that day, particularly inspiring. His preparation for his department, and in fact his general education, were slender; but his vigor and common sense were a saving element both in Economics and in Philosophy. Though he had finished only the Sophomore class at Wofford, the college recognized his later acquired scholarship by giving him A.M., in 1892.

During his stay at Wofford and later as President of Trinity College (the present Duke University) Kilgo was the aggressive leader of the war of the church colleges against the State institutions. Both the selfish and the religious motives were frankly avowed. It was unfair for the State to subsidize colleges out of the taxes paid in part by patrons of church institutions, which were gasping for breath, and yet were supplying the State with the larger portion of its college trained citizenship; and the State institutions were denounced as "Godless." Instances were emphasized of profane or intemperate teachers, and above all the influence of the deist (described as an infidel) Thomas Cooper, who in the first third of the nineteenth century had brought the South Carolina College almost to ruin by his attacks on organized Christianity and its "hireling clergy." Dr. Carlisle took no part in the controversy, although his faith in the efficacy of education under definite religious influence was profound.[6]

The personalities of Dr. Carlisle and John Kilgo were so different as to make co-operation difficult. The Doctor's ideal was to *be;* Kilgo's was to

---

5. Snyder, *Educational Odyssey,* 64-66.
6. Kilgo's fight on the State colleges in the two Carolinas is treated in Dr. Snyder's *Educational Odyssey,* 142, 184 *passim,* and extensively in P. M. Garber's *John Carlisle Kilgo* as Trinity President.

do, and his sharp tongue did not hesitate to express his opinions. Kilgo's aggressive nature, his appreciation of the power of money and his admiration of strong, aggressive moneymakers, made him impatient of Dr. Carlisle's inactivity toward such aims. Kilgo's love of a fight and the bitterness which he exhibited toward his enemies contrasted strongly with Dr. Carlisle's passivity and his charity toward those with whom he differed most widely.

The Faculty at Wofford in 1891 was largely new, but not so the Trustees. One of the existing members had been elected in 1854, one in 1870, two in 1874, one in 1875, two in 1877, two in 1884, three in 1886, and one in 1887. It was not to be supposed that this could please a man like Kilgo. At the December, 1892, Conference every Trustee but four dating from 1887 or earlier was left off. Dr. Carlisle was highly displeased. One of the demoted was his brother and another bore the name of Benjamin Wofford. Kilgo got the credit for the manoeuvre, though it was rumored that another important alumnus inspired the move. Kilgo was suspected of scheming for the presidency. "If that young man wants my place he can have it!" said Dr. Carlisle hotly to his most intimate friends. In addition the Doctor was shocked by such disrespect for tradition. Kilgo was so indiscreet as to sneer in the presence of students as he chatted with them on the college portico (myself being one of the little group), "Why should I want the presidency? I see more people than he does as I travel over the State."

Dr. Snyder intervened: Kilgo must go to see the Doctor and assure him that he had no such intentions. Kilgo went, and after two or three tempestuous, exhausting hours the two men understood each other better, but never cordially. The Wofford system worked more smoothly when its forces of attraction and repulsion were no longer under the necessity of adjusting the movements of two inharmonious bodies of that size. Dr. Carlisle spoke highly of Kilgo's character and ability when consulted by the Trinity Trustees.[7]

After Professor Kilgo went in 1894 to Trinity College as its President, though freer to move in his own orbit, it was not with smoothness. Like Craighead after his leaving Wofford, he was a fighter, and a bitter and powerful one; but, whereas Craighead was beaten, Kilgo won. Kilgo's acceptance of the call to Trinity was a bold move, in which doubtless his ambition to accept a dare and his unpleasant relations with Dr. Carlisle at Wofford both played a part. Bishop Duncan, when consulted, pointed out the difficulties. Trinity then had an endowment of $22,500 and a debt of

7. Garber, *Kilgo*, 26-27.

Faculty of 1891. Standing (left to right) : S. R. Pritchard, Assistant Professor of Mathematics; H. N. Snyder, Professor of English and German; the Rev. J. C. Kilgo, Financial Secretary and Agent, and Acting Professor of Metaphysics and Political Science; E. B. Craighead, Professor of Greek and French; J. A. Gamewell, Professor of Latin and Secretary of Faculty.

Seated (left to right) : The Rev. Whitefoord Smith, Emeritus Professor of English Literature and Elocution; Dr. J. H. Carlisle, President, and Professor of Mathematics and Moral Science; D. A. DuPre, Professor of Chemistry, Physics, and Geology, and Treasurer.

$40,000. Kilgo's winning the confidence and support of the Dukes, then disaffected to the college, spelled victory.[8] It was with deep satisfaction that after he was made Bishop in 1910 he could look back upon an achievement which ultimately made Trinity in the transformed Duke University the most heavily endowed institution in the South with the exception of the University of Texas.

The westernmost brick residence (next to the southernmost Fitting School building now called Snyder Hall) was built in 1892 for Professor Kilgo.

Two circumstances prevented Dr. Carlisle's performing as often as he would have liked, and as others would have liked, the service of bringing the college to the attention of the public by his personal presence, always impressive from his stately figure and his eloquence; first, he shrank from publicity; and, second, he was a sad victim of train sickness. Yet until well on in life he went through with it anyhow. As late as October, 1891, the *Wofford Journal* tells us that "Dr. Carlisle has sacrificed his feelings, and gone out over the State to speak for Wofford." He attended several District Conferences and made several educational addresses in various parts of the State. In October he and Professor Kilgo attended the Second Ecumenical Conference in Washington, where Dr. Carlisle made a "magnificent" address of welcome to the British delegates. "Where have you been keeping him," asked a Northern delegate, "that we have never heard of him?"

Emphasis upon religious life has always been strong at Wofford. In the spring of 1891 there was a season of unusual religious interest in both the college and the Fitting School, and again much the same the next year. Notable was the Leftwich meeting, touching powerfully both the college and the community in the spring of 1894.[9]

Wofford's first intercollegiate debate took place in Greenville in the crowded opera house between Wofford and Furman April 21, 1893, on the query, "Resolved, That the tendency of modern thought is toward socialism." [10] A powerful debater upholding for Furman the thesis that it was so tending was the later prominent Baptist preacher Dr. C. E. Burts. Wofford contended the contrary through the voices of W. A. Pitts, H. Zach Nabers, Preston B. Wells, and D. D. Wallace; and, to the belying of all subsequent history, the committee under the chairmanship of President Winston of the University of North Carolina gave the decision to Wofford. That afternoon the Wofford baseball team overthrew the Furman. Inter-

---

8. Garber, *Kilgo*, 84, 100.
9. Fac. report, Trustee Minutes June 15, 1891; June 12, 1893; *Wof. Col. Jour.*, May, 1894.
10. Preston Society Mins.

collegiate debates were revived much later, and in them Wofford has shown up well. Sad to say they now attract so little attention as to draw the merest handful of students as listeners.

The present writer caused a slight ripple in the unusually smooth course of college life by an indiscretion in January, 1894, as editor of the *Wofford College Journal*. One of his hates has always been special privilege or the abuse of privilege, and in the expression of his dissatisfaction he has sometimes tended to be extreme. In those days the different members of the Faculty subscribed to various magazines and placed them in the reading room for general use, each Professor if he chose at the end of the year keeping his contribution for his own.

The editor vigorously criticized the taking out of magazines for indefinite periods by both students and Faculty, but centered upon the Faculty as perhaps the worse offenders and certainly as setting a very bad example and interfering with a useful student habit of reading. He concluded, "Let us have no more vexatious, unjustifiable and injurious abstraction of magazines."

I have never understood that the ordinary members of the Faculty took much offense, perhaps because they recognized the justice of the complaint; but Dr. Carlisle was deeply moved. The word "abstract" he considered an insult to the Faculty members. I do not suppose the Doctor himself had ever practiced the habit I denounced, for he enforced upon himself the highest standard of propriety and regard for others. It was really worth a good deal to witness in person the Doctor's magnificent indignation, even though directed against one's self: the intense earnestness, the flashing eye, the distended nostrils as he breathed aloud like an excited horse. I was under suspension for a few days and suffered greatly under the sense of unjust treatment for a well-intended attack on an unjustifiable practice. A simple statement to the Doctor that I had no intention of reflecting upon the character of any Faculty member healed the breach. I saw joy in the old man's face as beautiful as his indignation had been magnificent—I will not say awe-inspiring, for it did not inspire awe, but only curiosity and self-defense. It was a satisfaction to find that, however improper my language may have been in pursuing a proper purpose, I was hardly out of the way at Vanderbilt University when a better system of administering the reading room was instituted. Some of the students condemned the strong language I had used, but most seemed to take less interest than in a question of the eligibility of a baseball player. Wofford students have always been characterized by great respect for authority. A student rebellion against a legitimate Faculty action, such as led by Samuel Dibble at the College of Charleston, is almost inconceivable here. Our sudents come from a religious and social stratum notable for its orderly conduct and its respect for authority. Moral for future editors: be careful as to the propriety of your language; and be careful how you sacrifice yourself for people who don't care.

There was one feature of the *Journal* that year to which no one could take exception; that was the very valuable June, 1894, issue, for which I take no credit to myself further than the fact that I took advantage of Professor Snyder's having that spring set his Senior class in English to making studies in South Carolina literature and history, and used the best of them to make up my final number.

It was at this time that a forward step was taken in uniting the libraries of the two societies and of the college. The agreement, after long discussion, was reached in October or November, 1894. The college's collection was stated as about 4,000 volumes. That of the Calhoun and Preston Societies respectively equaled about 2,300 and 1,700.[11] The growth of the library has been continuous, and at an increasing rate in recent years. The total number of volumes July 31, 1949, was 45,804; or omitting public documents 40,174. The small number of public documents is accounted for by the fact that several decades ago the United States government dropped the library from its depositories to which it sent practically all government publications free, as we were not willing to supply the enormous amount of shelf room needed. The valuable collections of the Conference Historical Society have been kept in the fireproof vault of the library building, the vault being the gift of the children of Rev. James W. Kilgo, D.D., long a Trustee of the college, for the primary purpose of the preservation of those books and records. Since the doubling of the size of the library building and the extensive interior changes in the old portion in 1949 the entire building is fireproof.

The library has received a number of valuable additions by gift or bequest. The earliest consisted of more than 1,200 volumes given by Prof. David Duncan in 1879. In 1894-95 Col. R. L. Coleman gave a sum of money for enlarging the quarters of the library, which was then housed in the main building. During the year 1902-3 two valuable collections were received: more than 800 volumes bequeathed by Rev. J. Thomas Pate, consisting of a well selected body of literature, theology, history, and popular science. The same year was received the Herman Baer Collection of 435 volumes, mainly bound magazines and books in French and German. On his

---

11. *Wofford Jour.*, Dec., 1891; Nov., 1894; Trustee Mins., June 7, 1895. It is impossible to ascertain the exact number of volumes at the time of consolidation. The college catalogue states that the combined libraries totaled about 8,000 volumes. The most accurate statement regarding any of the three collections is for the Preston, placing it at a little less than 1,700. The Calhoun therefore apparently included about 2,300 volumes.

death March 2, 1908, Bishop W. W. Duncan bequeathed a large part of his valuable library to the college. After the death of Dr. James H. Carlisle October 21, 1909, his children, Miss Sallie and J. H., Jr., gave the college the bulk of his library, 2,276 volumes. In a mistaken idea of honoring the Doctor the college fitted up a room in the library which was rarely opened, to resemble the Doctor's study, with the result that the books have been of little use, as is likely to be the case whenever a donation is kept "intact" (which means significantly untouched) in the main body of a public library. The largest collection ever donated to the library consists of about 3,000 volumes given by Dr. A. G. Rembert, one of the greatest readers and lovers of books in the history of the college. Consisting of the selections of a broad-minded scholar in general literature, English and American fiction, psychology, philosophy, Latin, and Greek, it is unexcelled in usefulness by any other collection ever received. Mr. Warren DuPre bequeathed $500, to which his widow (the daughter of Bishop Duncan) added $500 for purchases and also $1,000 as an endowment, the proceeds of all of which have been used principally for modern American literature. The daughter of Mr. Samuel Dibble, the first graduate of the college, established a similar arrangement, $500 for immediate purchases and $1,000 for endowment for books in the department of English Language and Literature. Bishop E. D. Mouzon bequeathed more than a thousand volumes, and the children of Rev. E. Toland Hodges, long a Trustee of the college, presented to the college his library of 1,800 volumes, to which they made annual additions. The Robert T. Fletcher Collection was established by his Sunday school class in commemoration of this Wofford student who gave his life for his country in France in 1918. Rev. Mark L. Carlisle and others have also made valuable additions.

The use of Alumni Hall by the Fitting School necessitated providing other dormitories for the college students. June 11, 1895, the Trustees ordered the erection on the campus of an adequate number of cottages of six to eight rooms. In addition one or two adjacent houses were bought. Thus largely were the students housed until the opening of Carlisle Hall in 1912.

The Treasurer's report of June 15, 1891, showed total income for the past collegiate year of $12,518. Tuition and Conference collections both showed improvement, being respectively $3,604 and $3,214. Salaries paid amounted to $8,800; balance on hand $1,182. Endowment totaled $50,916, not including railroad stocks of $5,400 nominal, but doubtful real, value, and notes of $400. The college owed banks $3,199. Continuing improvement is shown by the balance sheet of June, 1894:

Received interest	$3,870.72
Conference Collections	2,128.74
Tuition	4,037.91
Past Tuition	313.52
For Expenses	1,618.52
For Supplies	1,335.23
Col. R. L. Coleman Donation	200.00
From Alumni Hall	304.27
	$13,808.91

Paid Salaries	$9,529.20
Paid Expense	1,681.33
Paid Sundries	1,556.90
Balance on hand	1,041.48
	$13,808.91

We have noted the lack of provision for physical exercise in the early years of the college, and of demands by the students that the want be supplied. It must have been as early as 1880 (but I have no exact information) that the western one of the two long rooms under the chapel which had earlier been used for the preparatory department was fitted up with simple gymnastic apparatus. With its skimpy equipment, dirt (covered with sawdust) floor, and poor ventilation it was quite unsatisfactory and after a few years was virtually abandoned. Largely through the urging of Capt. W. E. Burnett of the class of 1876 the Alumni presented to the college, January 21, 1897, their gift of a real gymnasium, the building now used as a recreational hall. The Trustees in June, 1900, named it the Wilbur E. Burnett Gymnasium for the principal contributor, and paid the remaining $1,625 of the total cost of $3,202.[12]

As intercollegiate athletic contests multiplied and rules as to the eligibility of players, etc., became more complex, discussions on contested cases became a large and irritating part of Faculty meeting debates. Relief from this vexation came only with the turning over of all such questions to the Athletic Committee.

Just to keep the record straight, we must remark that even in this enlightened modern period student pranks showed little tendency to disappear.

---

12. *Wof. Col. Jour.*, Oct., 1896; Trustee Mins., June, 1897; *So. Christian Ad.*, June 21, 1900. Prof. H. T. Shockley calls my attention to the college catalogue's stating the date of the building of the gymnasium wrongly, as he remembers using it five years earlier than the stated date. Examination shows how the error arose: The 1896-97 catalogue says that a gymnasium, "complete in all its appointments," has been built. The 1900-1 catalogue states that a gymnasium "has been built on the campus and named for Captain W. E. Burnett." The catalogue of 1920-21 says "this building was completed in 1902 and named for Captain W. E. Burnett." This error, illustrating well one way in which historical errors arise, was repeated for many years, until finally allusion to the date was dropped.

How normally decent young men can bring themselves to harass a saint like Dr. Carlisle, or even less sensitive souls, is a question the answer to which we must leave to the psychologist, normal or abnormal as the case may be. But in 1898 about six weeks before he would have graduated, a fine young man painted Dr. Snyder's perfectly innocent, well behaved cow; of licking off which paint said cow languished and languishing did die. Not to encourage such amusements, but to reassure parents whose sons may become transgressors, we note that in 1934 the same Dr. Snyder, then President, recommended, and the Trustees confirmed, that the painter had shown himself such a living example of the fine qualities of Wofford men that he be given his diploma; and so from thenceforth, as not before, Marvin W. Adams' name appears in the catalogue at the head of the class of 1898; and moreover that fall the Conference elected him a member of the Board of Trustees! (Said the famous Professor Jowett of some such pranks at Oxford, "I see the mind of the University has been expressing itself.")

My cows in the early 1900's fared better, one led up the steps to the second story porch of the main building, and another even placed in the college chapel, largely, no doubt, for the fun of seeing the Professor get the animal down. I quietly went to church at the 11 o'clock hour, and left during the first hymn to assist, without any students observing, two colored men get the cow down; for, as easy as it is to lead a cow up, it is impossible to persuade her to descend. Each foot must be lifted and put carefully in place, step by step. To my surprise, half the student body beat me to the college and shouted advice on how to do it.

More serious was the shooting scrape into which a gentleman, now an honored retired Colonel with a distinguished career in the judicial department of the United States Army, got with an uninstructed youth of the town—the age-old town and gown conflict. It was terrible on the old Doctor, and we relate it only to prevent undue pessimism as to how much worse are these than were the old times, and to lend support to the hopes and faith of parents of today.

An extracurricular activity of a more civilized kind was the trip in which the whole student body was invited to journey to the South Carolina Interstate and West Indian Exposition in April, 1902. I was appointed to arrange the trip, secure transportation, accommodations in Charleston, etc. A large proportion of the student body went, and behavior was perfect except for one young South Carolinian's throwing a biscuit at a colored waiter whom he thought disrespectful. I still prize the beautiful set of Shakespeare which the students presented me on our return. A special feature of the trip was Prof. D. A. DuPre's escorting his class of Senior scientists to the museum

122

and the phosphate beds and manufactories.[13] I was proud on summing up my accounts for ticket sales that I had not made an error of a cent; but on getting back home was somewhat taken down as a businessman to find that I had given the railroad agent a check on the wrong bank.

The relations of Wofford to the Columbia Female College on several occasions called for adjustment. June 17, 1891, the Wofford Trustees received from the sister Methodist institution a protest against Wofford's injuring the Methodist women's college in two ways: first, the names of two Wofford Professors appeared in the catalogue of Converse College, an institution "essentially anti-Methodistical"; and second, Wofford College laboratories were allowed to be used for the instruction of Converse students. Thus Columbia Female College was probably deprived of Methodist students who might otherwise go there.

The Trustees replied that Prof. D. A. DuPre's name appears in the Converse College catalogue without his authority, and, as to the laboratories, he allows Converse students, on paying the regular fees, to witness experiments which he has prepared for his Wofford classes. It is hoped, said the Trustees, that this will explain the situation satisfactorily. Nevertheless a few years later Prof. DuPre ceased his service to Converse.

A more serious question, that of admitting women to Wofford, was discussed in the Wofford Trustee meetings at least as early as 1894; for in that year Trustee C. G. Dantzler moved that women be admitted. It was not acted upon, and in 1895 he withdrew his motion. By vote of June 14, 1896, women were admitted to the Junior and Senior classes; but none appear in the next year's catalogue. Three enrolled as Freshmen in 1897, two of whom duly graduated in 1901—Misses Puella M. Littlejohn and May Duncan Wannamaker. In June, 1897, the Trustees appointed a committee to confer with a committee from the Columbia Female College on the educational interests of the Conference. June 13, 1898, the Trustees resolved that, in view of the resolution of the Conference in 1897 favoring the admission of women to all classes at Wofford, this should be done. On motion of Rev. W. R. Richardson, such an enthusiast for coeducation that he seemed to expect to see the halls of Wofford crowded with women, the Trustees authorized the raising of $10,000 for building them a dormitory; but no provision for their housing was ever made. Coeducation made little progress at Wofford, although almost all the girls who came made excellent students, and not the slightest untoward incident ever occurred. The first woman graduate was in 1901; the last in that period in 1904. The Faculty did not

13. *Wofford Journal*, April, 1902, 45, 47.

like it; the boys did not like it; the little handful of girls felt isolated. It was ordered that no more should be admitted unless 18 years of age and in the Junior or Senior class, which effectually stopped it. Since then the only woman student in regular fall-winter-spring terms has been Miss Caroline E. DuPre (Mrs. E. E. Wells), daughter of Dean A. M. DuPre, who graduated in 1934.

A feature of Wofford life that was already assuming creditable proportions and was soon to develop still more was Wofford graduates pursuing their studies further in universities. It was stated in the *Wofford College Journal* of March, 1889, that not until 1872 had a Wofford graduate continued his studies at a university. Twenty were listed who had since that date studied either in professional schools or in advanced literary or scientific courses. Of these figures I have made no test; but we know that from that date there has been an increasing number of our graduates who have taken advanced university work.

In June, 1897, the Trustees instructed a committee to report on whether it was practicable to establish a chair of History and Political Economy. Since the beginning of the college these subjects had been tossed from one professor to another, according to their fitness or the time at their disposal. Quite naturally the teaching of History particularly amounted to little more than the assignment of some brief standard work on Greece, Rome, England, or the United States. Professor Snyder argued for the History and Political Economy, partly doubtless because it was practical to use the instructor in these to assist him in his heavy duties in English. Prof. D. A. DuPre desired a man who could add Biology to the curriculum. Both chairs were soon established, that of History and Economics in 1899, to which D. D. Wallace, just taking his doctorate at Vanderbilt University, was elected. Wallace thus became the first Ph.D. to teach in the college since Baskervill, who took his degree at Leipsic in the summer of 1880 while teaching at Wofford, and was the first instructor to hold the degree while teaching here. I was warned that Dr. Carlisle was somewhat apprehensive about me on account of the offense I had occasioned him while editor of the college *Journal,* but soon had the satisfaction of knowing that he was pleased with my work and influence. His cordiality toward me left nothing to be desired. A. B. Cooke, Professor of German and French in Wofford from 1895 to 1908, was our next Professor to take the degree, as he did in 1901, and was followed by C. B. Waller in 1904 (Ph.D. from Vanderbilt in 1903) as the third in the modern crop of doctors. "The Ph.D. rash," as Dr. Snyder called it, had broken out and was later to become a veritable epidemic. There were great personalities at Wofford both before and after the "Ph.D. rash" broke out, and it is personalities and not degrees that make the college. Nevertheless the demand that young scholars shall pursue their studies until they have won the degree assures at least a certain professional training for their work; and moreover there is nothing that can stir their scholarly instincts and abilities like association with alert young men keyed to the highest pitch of intellectual activity, both by their own work and the friction of mind on mind in an atmosphere the tang of which will extend its influence to the end of their lives.

An important addition to the Faculty in 1899 was Prof. John G. Clinkscales as Professor of Mathematics. He was put in the place of Prof. W. G. Blake, not on account of any deficiency in Blake as a mathematician, but because the college needed Clinkscales' remarkable talent in addressing popular audiences, in making friends and attracting students. He did not denounce the State institutions, as had his predecessor in the field John C. Kilgo, as he could not well have done even if he had been so inclined, as he came to Wofford from a chair in Clemson College. Dr. Carlisle, of course, had nothing to do with displacing Blake, or in seeking to strengthen the field agency; for many of the ordinary duties of President he simply would not perform. His sense of propriety and human justice was deeply shocked by the treatment of Professor Blake, though toward Professor Clinkscales personally he was perfectly friendly. Dr. Clinkscales, both as Professor of Mathematics at Clemson and as a speaker, was already widely known, and he proved, not only a most amiable member of the Wofford community, but a valuable representative in the field, winning and holding friends for the college.

Dr. Herman Baer, long a member of the Trustees and in his youth instructor in German and Hebrew in the college (for he was a converted German Jew), was thanked in June, 1900, for the handsome bronze tablet which he had had erected in the lobby of the main building. The very exact and somewhat blunt old gentleman walked up to inspect his gift, commemorating the "benificence" (as he had not written it) of Benjamin Wofford. He placed his finger on the guilty i in the middle of that word, and uttered with disgust and most appropriate emphasis the one word "BenIficence!" and stamped away with his heavy stick striking the floor with more than its usual force. And there to this day is the guilty i, polished by many an accusing finger.

At Dr. Carlisle's first commencement as President in 1876 he handed a diploma to George E. Prince. At his last in 1902 he handed a diploma, with appropriate remarks, to Prince's son, Norman L. Prince. In the audience sat Dr. Samuel Lander, the founder of the institution now called

125

Lander College, young Prince's grandfather, who, fifty years before to the day, had received his diploma from Randolph-Macon College. Dr. Carlisle asked the ladies in the audience to rise in honor of the man who had given such service in the Christian education of women.[14]

June 9, 1900, Dr. Carlisle handed the Trustees his resignation as President, but at their request allowed it to remain on the table for twelve months. In June, 1901, at their urgency, he allowed it to remain unacted on for another year; but in June, 1902, he insisted that his resignation be accepted, though he was willing, he said, to render such other service as he might be able.[15] He insisted on resigning, he said, while he still knew that he ought to resign. The Board accordingly accepted his resignation and elected him Professor of Astronomy and Ethics, with the right to reside so long as he desired in the house which he had occupied on the campus since the founding of the college. Thus closed the laborer's task in the twilight of a beautiful life, awaiting for a few years yet the evening bell.

---

14. J. H. Carlisle, Jr., *op. cit.*, 87-8.
15. Dr. Carlisle's resignation lay before the Trustees for two years (and not for three years, as Dr. Snyder states in his *Educational Odyssey*, page 95).

Chapter IX

DR. CARLISLE AS A TEACHER *

NO ONE can be satisfied with any account of Dr. Carlisle as a teacher; for the writer if successful must present perfectly that very real but very elusive thing personality. Dr. Carlisle after a long life of constant devotion to a great task left nothing in written form as an adequate monument to himself. His literary output was trivial in comparison with his ability. His public addresses were not connected with such events as to lead to their perpetuation in popular fame. His few little books, which we will notice in the next chapter, misrepresent rather than indicate his intellectual resources. His contributions to the religious press, particularly his "Practical Application" of the lesson in the *Sunday School Magazine,* though of value to thousands of readers at the time, form no permanent or systematic body of writing. His life was a part of the immense contribution of labor and character to keep the church militant and the individual upright and active. He thus made his large contribution to the vast unselfish sacrifice which good men and women of each generation make in order that there may be, if possible, future generations better than theirs.

At the height of his maturity and activity Professor Carlisle put his ideal of the work of the teacher into an address before the Educational Institute of South Carolina (a sort of forerunner of the State Teachers' Association), December 21, 1870, in Columbia, on the subject, "Some Mistakes the Young Teacher May Make":

The term machinery is often applied to the apparatus and helps which are resorted to for the purpose of extending the efficiency of educational plans. Thus used, the term is convenient and useful, but dangerous. A school furnished with all needful appliances . . . is not a loaded cannon, which a child, or a coward, can discharge with as much efficiency as a giant. It is rather an arrow, which, however keen and well feathered, can have no force which did not, in some shape, slumber in the arm that sent it. All educational schemes must be worked by living force. And perhaps this cannot be done without an earnest and real, even painful, expenditure of effort. . . .

Robertson, of Brighton, was mortified when his friends condescended to praise

---

* This chapter is taken largely from the chapter on Dr. Carlisle as a Teacher which I contributed to Dr. Watson B. Duncan's *Carlisle Memorial Volume.*

him. He said, "Here I am, spending my heart's blood to be the religious teacher of this people, and they praise me as a pleasant speaker!"

And Ruskin seems to approach the same great truth from a different direction, when he says, "We continually talk of taking up our cross, as if the mischief of a cross was its weight—as if it was only a thing to be carried, instead of to be crucified on!"

Do these utterances offend or startle any teacher? Why should they? Unless we are trying to rise into this region of effort and achievement, our daily business is a commonplace trade, a sleight of hand, as unmeaning as if we were drilling monkeys or training parrots. . . .

Up to a certain point . . . you need not enquire what trade or calling your pupil intends to follow. He ought to be educated not simply or chiefly because he intends to be a farmer, lawyer, or statesman, but because he is a human being, with capacities and powers, with inlets of joy, with possibilities of effort and action which no trade or calling can satisfy or exhaust. . . . It is very easy to declaim against utilitarianism, but who will advocate a system which has no utility in it? . . . Is an education to have no reference whatever to the probability that the subject will live in America, Africa, or Jupiter? or whether he will probably live on air, manna, or bread earned in some honest calling?

We must recall the perilous conditions in the South Carolina of that day, and to a degree in the world at large, to appreciate his closing paragraphs:

Those who, thirty years hence, will correct, perpetuate, or intensify the evils supposed to exist in these representations, are now on the benches of your schools. Any evil passion which will then fearfully shake the frame-work of society, is now slumbering in a schoolboy. . . . Every pupil now untaught, or badly taught, adds one to the fearful possibilities against us. Remember that while education (if you will sufficiently enlarge and dignify the term) may save us from untold evils, eulogies on education never can. You cannot, of course, by anticipation or rehearsal, take your pupils through the crises awaiting them, but you may do much to impart or strengthen the spirit, which will fit them for the future. They will live hereafter in a land of outward plenty. So teach them that they will not mistake plenty for prosperity, a voluminous census report for an inventory of happiness, the means of good living for good living itself. Your pupil may live in an hour of sadness in his country's history. Let him know and exhibit, that there is nothing in common with the deep, sincere sorrow of the disappointed lover of his nation and race, and an outbreak of vulgar passion or mortification. Let him know that to the patriot,

"Grief should be like joy, majestic, equable, sedate,
Confirming, strengthening, cleansing, making free,
Strong to consume small troubles."

His life may be spent in a majority. Let him be so taught that he may avoid the dangers of uncontrolled power. If the desired prize of victory, either by the ballot-box or the battlefield, is allotted to him, let him seek earnestly the rarer

128

gift, the wisdom to know how far to press it. Let him rise to the elevation where he may say to his weaker antagonist, "I have disarmed you by force, I will conquer you by just and fair treatment."

Or he may, in his opinions, be in a minority. Let him know the privileges and responsibilities of his position there. Let him be able to say, "I cannot fawn, or cringe, or flatter. I will not mock, or curse, or revile. My maturest views of man and government, of history and society, must be entirely reversed, before I can expect a just and stable government, with the measure you propose. But I will trample under foot the base suggestion to madly hasten the ills which, I fear, are imminent. I may be a disappointed, even a wronged and outraged man. But I am not, therefore, a reckless, frenzied man, willing to bury society in ruins, if I may but crush others with myself."

He can learn to oppose, not in a personal, passionate spirit, but his opposition must be calm, strong, sincere, well-defined. And even if he lives in an historical crisis, where his country finds neither "strength in her arm, nor mercy in her woe," there remains to him, then, the last, and perhaps the noblest triumph of patriotism. Let him stand, calm in his own integrity, and "gaze on successful tyranny with an undazzled eye."

Let us teach the pupil by precept and example, if it may be, to be exacting on himself, yet lenient to others, pure yet tolerant. For, one thing is certain. All shades and phases of opinion will be represented among our forty millions of citizens . . . those who think it may be proper, after a while, to take on some ballast, when we have spread all our sails, and those who think "all sail and no ballast" is the very perfection of government, or that, by a happy compensation in political mechanics, the sails *are* the ballast; . . . the young man who cannot be made to feel a fear, and the old man who can scarcely be induced to indulge a hope: all these must live together. And they must do so without poisoning the well-springs of society, or bringing on a state of anarchy and lawlessness, where every man gazes defiantly or suspiciously in the face of his fellow. CAN THIS BE DONE? Are there moral forces active or slumbering, in our modern society, sufficient to carry it through the strain now upon it? That question, in some form, meets the thoughtful observer of life every hour of the day! "He may be unwise who is sanguine, but he is unmanly, unpatriotic, and unchristian, who despairs!"

Let it be our constant aim, that every day spent in the recitation room may tend to furnish those results which the Prussian king demanded from his university—"FRUITS, GENTLEMEN, FRUITS IN THE SOUNDNESS OF MEN."[1]

The whole of the quotation is expressive of the thoughts of good men in the crisis of Reconstruction then gripping the country. The last paragraphs express his theory of the proper attitude and conduct for Southerners suffering under that galling yoke, an attitude expressive of his piety and passivity and the personal self-respect of the good man whose mind is its own place.

Another address of a teacher to teachers was that which he made July 13, 1901, before the State Teachers' Summer School held at Con-

---

1. *Addresses of J. H. Carlisle,* 93-107.

verse College with the then unprecedented enrollment of 614 ("the largest number of South Carolina teachers ever gathered in one room," he said), which he called Regrets of an Old Teacher. It is not up to his usual standard; for how could one who had the right to express so few regrets have much to say on that subject? Towards the end he became more confidential:

Now, I want to get a little closer to you still, and leave the third and second persons and use the first. I should say in all sincerity and with regret, looking back through all the crises and collisions of a teacher's life, I have been wrong about as often as my pupils have been. I have spoken improperly to them, I believe, as often as they have spoken improperly to me. I have not the slightest regret for having taken too much interest in any human being. That is never to be regretted. The regret is deep on the other side.

And he concluded with his great confession: "Now, my dear young friends, teachers, it will be my regret through the few years that may be granted me that the influence, conscious and unconscious, the tuition, conscious and unconscious, that have gone out from me as a teacher have not been higher, nobler, purer."

This is beautiful in a way, but how excessive the humility of a good old man heaping undeserved blame upon his own head! We must judge a man by the circumstances and his age. He would hardly have expressed such paralyzing passivity while the fires of his vigorous years still burned. How unlike the stupendous energy and healthy self-confidence of Paul, who had so much more to confess: "I have fought the good fight; . . . henceforth there is laid up for me a crown of righteousness."

Dr. Carlisle sometimes read to his class a little poem entitled "The Bird with the Broken Pinion," which related how the writer had found a little bird with a broken wing, had cared for it, and, when it had been healed, released it; "But the bird with the broken pinion never soared so high again." [2] The force that the Doctor could put into that last line was impressive. His meaning was to impress upon the boys what a crippling scar even once falling into vice left upon the soul. I asked him one day (though not, of course, right after his reading the poem) whether it was not possible that a man falling into sin, like Peter denying his Lord, might not through soul-searching repentance and strengthened determination, be a better and stronger man than he was before. He thought for a moment, and replied, "Yes, that is possible." I felt that I had scored one on the bird with the broken pinion theory, but I did not dare to say so, and besides, would not willingly have said anything that would

2. The poem is in Dr. Watson B. Duncan's *Carlisle Memorial Volume*, p. 169.

be unpleasant to him. The same thought the Doctor emphasized by frequently quoting the phrase from St. Augustine, "It is one thing to rise again; it is another never to have fallen." I recall how pleased he was when I mentioned that I had read that classic of the soul's experience.

Dr. Snyder has fortunately jotted down almost at the moment of their utterance some of the gems that fell from Dr. Carlisle's lips in his chapel talks: [3]

Onerous duties frequently done soon sweeten into the joys of high privilege.

To be the roommate at college of a low, vile blackguard is a dear price to pay even for an education.

Three men commit a crime. Each is guilty of the whole of it. There are no vulgar fractions in sin.

In almost every case a young man fixes in college the two points of the straight line that determines the direction of his after life.

Scholarship and character are too close together for a young man to build up the one and at the same time tear down the other.

There is danger that the colleges are turning out every year accomplished tramps, with Latin diplomas in their hands, to swell the vast and increasing army which must either beg or steal.[4]

One may conceal some crime from the policeman, the Governor, the President. Between him and them it is somewhat of an equal contest; at least it is man to man. But woe to him who enters into a contest with his maker!

If this country is ever going to ruin, it will not be from lack of Greek, Latin, and mathematics but from lack of a basis of honest character.

When character once begins to disintegrate, there is no telling just where the breaking will show itself.

An insult is never an excuse for taking human life. Time will cure the wound of the insult, but will only deepen the stain of the blood.

There are two classes of college students that cannot afford to spend much money—those who have worked hard and made their own money and those for whom somebody else has worked hard and made money.

The management of that perplexing and delicate matter of money is rightfully the invariable test of character, for it is at this point that scholar and sage, poet and schoolboy must touch common life and bear its strain.

A man may be able to tell in six languages why he cannot pay his debt; but the debt, if ever paid, is paid in solid, everyday American gold and silver and greenbacks.

While you are planning to spend a dollar foolishly, your parents are planning how to save a dollar to keep you in college.

There are very few fears for the young man when the simple faith of his

---

3. W. B. Duncan, *Carlisle Memorial Volume*, 93-6.
4. That is an unusual piece of pessimism for Dr. Carlisle, not in accord with the hopefulness based on his vigorous Christian faith. One of the most uneasy comments that I ever heard him make on the worst features of contemporary life he ended with the words: "Our Lord knew all things, and yet he was no pessimist."

childhood seems to be shaken by the trade winds of a critical attitude or by the gusts of earnest enquiry or even by a cyclone of ardent doubt, provided he keeps the foundations of his moral character firm and strong.

When a young man begins to drink, the trouble is not that he will become a drunkard. But I have fears of something far worse. Society and home training have so frowned on drinking that every step a young man takes in that direction is an act of deception. And so character is weakened at its most vital point, and he becomes a liar instead of a drunkard, or more probably both.

The State Legislature has about ten insignificant places to offer, paying from forty to sixty dollars. There are about four hundred young men and young women applying for those positions, which last for only about six weeks. Is it possible that a considerable number of young men are finding in life no fixed positions for which they are thoroughly prepared, but are floating about in that vast mass which pauperizes society and enriches jails! At any rate, I have a faith, as strong as my faith in the providence of God, that society always has a proper place for the young man who can pay his way in force and integrity of character.

So many young men, after a college course in which integrity has been shattered and character tarnished, write to me for recommendations for responsible positions, implying that a word from me can supply what they have not and what they did their best to destroy, or else implying that the higher qualities of character and conduct had grown up in them, as Jonah's gourd, in a night. Not so! Not so! Will you never learn that the high matters of conduct and character are not the fungus growth of a night, of two nights, of three nights, but are the result of the slow, silent processes of the years, renovating, purifying, strengthening, and toughening the whole nature through strenuous endeavor?

Thomas Carlyle said that it was not a sign of strength when a man had convulsions so that it required seven men to hold him, but that true strength is the daily, earnest bearing of burdens so that we become strong under them. So the real student is not the one who has "convulsions" of study on stated occasions—examinations and such like—but he who does his daily duty earnestly, manfully, and thus by a gradual process feels himself growing and expanding under them.

I am not talking to the educated young white man who can tell an outright untruth. There is nothing in him to talk to. You cannot raise him with a lever because there is nothing to rest your lever on. Sometimes your leg or your arm "goes to sleep," as the saying is. It needs vigorous rubbing or a sudden strong blow to wake it up. Conscience, alas! sometimes also "goes to sleep" and needs a sudden strong shock to wake it up; but the hardest sleeping conscience to wake is that which has been lulled by habitual lying.

That is a wonderful phrase of Nehemiah's about consulting with himself. To hold a mass meeting of the powers of one's nature, to go into a solemn committee of the whole upon the state of one's self, not a committee in which the anarchy of one's impulses, appetites, and desires holds sway, but a committee presided over by the sovereign will, illuminated by the imperial intellect, and guided by the keenly dividing dictates of the divine conscience—this is a high consultation with one's self.

Mr. N. D. Lesesne of the class of 1892 recalls the striking phrase of the Doctor's: "You have been through college; but has college been through you?"

I may add several striking passages from my own memory:

The temple of your soul is become a menagerie for the obscene reveling of every unclean beast!—*Sunday School lesson talk, denouncing vulgarity.*

A selfish man can get anything he is determined to have in this world except happiness.

By all the possibilities of failure, by all the splendid possibilities of success, by all in the present life and all in the eternal, I charge you every one to be a man! Farewell.—*Baccalaureate address to class of 1896.*

Dr. Carlisle was above all else a teacher; by deliberate choice he refused to be anything else even when made President. He said to Dr. Snyder, when the latter was considering an offer of the presidency of another institution, "I have had to face similar crises in my career. Each time I have raised the same question: Was I by choice an educator or a college administrator? If I chose to be the latter, a college administrator, it didn't matter much whether my stay at a particular institution should be long or short. It would be determined largely by prestige or salary. But if I was to be an *educator,* that was something very different. Education is a process, and requires time, much time, for one to see the results of his labors—five years, ten years, and even twenty years after his students leave college. He has to wait patiently on the slow years to get the measure of what he has been trying to do. For better or for worse I've been an educator, not an administrator, and I do not regret the choice." [5]

The Doctor spoke little of the future life, on the ground doubtless that if this life were lived properly the future would be properly taken care of. One day in class, as his eyes looked into the distance, as his mind was looking, he said very quietly and very earnestly, "I cannot see how the future life can be other than progressive development of the mind toward, but never attaining, the perfection of the Infinite." No harps; no white robes; no shouting of hosannas, but continuous development of mind and soul.

Another illustration from Dr. Snyder shows how Dr. Carlisle left some of the most important functions of a college executive to others. In conversing with the President young Professor Snyder was led by

5. Snyder, *Educational Odyssey,* 103.

some remark to ask, "Were you not consulted about my election?" "No," said President Carlisle, as hardly another college president in the United States could have said in similar circumstances. I have gathered that it was generally much the same with him.

Dr. Carlisle met public occasions splendidly, impressively. Few men could pack so much in a few winged phrases and leave an audience so thrilled with the sense of great thoughts worthily uttered. But this was not except on rare occasions his best; for his highest inspiration was not the crowded auditorium, but the group of students to whom, as a perpetual generation of youth, he had devoted himself with a devotion second only to parental affection. Some who knew the great teacher only at a distance, or perhaps in the mellow years of old age, thought of him as a benign old man of antique, seer-like wisdom, loving the good and full of gentleness. They overlook his strength, which was as large an element of his character as his goodness. He was a man of power, capable of passion, anger, and fire.

Students sometimes felt the scourge of his indignation, and sometimes, as with any man of strong temper and sensitive honor, felt it unjustly; but no man was more magnanimous to make amends. An illustration, related to me by Mr. H. H. Kinard, who was present, which occurred when the Doctor was about fifty-five will suffice. The Doctor had said, "Close your books," and had begun the recitation. Soon he noticed a student on the back bench with head bent down, looking into his book. Of all things the Doctor hated sulking meanness or any form or deception. With grief, indignation, or whatever more respectable word you may choose to designate it (the boys said simply "he was mad"), he raked the offender with a terrible fire. When he was fully roused, though with perfectly maintained dignity, Dr. Carlisle's harnessed emotions champed like a war horse's, well simulated by his flashing eye and audible breathing. At length he paused. The student said calmly, "Doctor, I did not hear you say close your books." The effect was like that of a stunning blow. Rising from his chair, with extended hand he walked to where the student sat and grasped his hand, saying with feeling that made every man present suffer with him, "I beg your pardon! I beg your pardon!" The middle-aged man who related this to me seemed to think it the greatest thing he ever knew the Doctor to do.

One other instance may be cited, arising not from acting too sharply on a misunderstanding, but from impatience with inattention. A very dignified, well-behaved student was asked by the Doctor in the Bible study class to go to the board and locate on an outline map the position

134

of Damascus. The student ridiculously placed it in about as wrong a position as was possible. The Doctor perhaps felt, What does all that I have been trying to do for this student amount to? He lit into the youth in an overwhelming way and at length paused and looked far away out of the window. The student said humbly, "Doctor, I told you I was not prepared today." The Doctor flashed back, "There are some things a Sophomore ought to know without being prepared!" I liked the condemnation of negligence, even though its severity was excessive, especially from a teacher who was systematically neglecting in his Astronomy class to see that his students got the best he could give in imparting a knowledge of one of the noblest of sciences. It was well that the hot temper, like steam in a boiler, was there; and only rarely, as in these instances, did it blow the safety valve. With his great powers in his late 60's completely unimpaired, the disinclination to systematic exertion was very strong.

A man changes from decade to decade, and hence, in part, the differences in the accounts we have from old students of Dr. Carlisle as a teacher. For instance, those of long ago say that he talked very little. That was in his younger years, when he rigorously held students to the assigned tasks and required them, without assistance from him, to go satisfactorily through their demonstrations. My father, a graduate of 1871, thought that he might well have unbent to give the bungling student a helpful word; but his rule then, rarely departed from, was, Let the man learn to stand on his own feet. As late as the middle '80's, says his son, that was still his practice. He explained everything thoroughly and then sent the men to the board. If the boy could not come through the only words were, "You may take your seat." Once he broke his rule and asked the floundering youth in the Algebra class, "What is your trouble, Mr.——?" The distressed boy replied, "Well, Doctor, I've tried my best, and I can't get shed of X." [6]

Students of the 1850's spoke of the Doctor as a man of few words in the classroom. Others of a much later date remember his discoursing freely, with the textbook counting for little, on anything bearing on character or conduct in college life, public events, religion, or practical morality. It of necessity sometimes became somewhat tedious. On one such day in 1894, I remember, an indiscreet youth suggested that the Doctor let the class go. There was profound silence, as the Doctor, with a stern countenance, looked through the window into the distance. The

6. J. H. Carlisle, Jr., *op. cit.*, 181.

tenseness was broken by some tactless fellow's suggesting that we might find some better use of the time. There was no word, but such a look! The hurt old man curtly dismissed the class, who slipped out of the room feeling very, very small.

Even in those days the Doctor at his best was a power. There was the direct influence of soul on soul, through the potency of the larger, richer, nobler soul inspiring the best in the other. He saw, and made his pupils see, the glory in our common life, the awfulness of sin, the sacredness of human relations. Many a day as I sat in my alphabetical place in the back of his classroom, as he made more intense the consciousness of the divine in and near one's self, the physical view of classmates and classroom swam into oblivion as a luminous pathway united him and me.

The Doctor frequently expressed his faith that a young man in passing from the simple faith of childhood to maturer religious life would safely work out his doubts provided he kept himself morally straight. Of the nature and substance of doubts he said little or nothing. He sought to quiet the restless, doubting spirit, not by information or explanation, but by exhortation to believe, as in one of his favorite quotations, "It is as satisfactory to a healthy mind to know that there is an explanation as to know what the explanation is"—a very prudent prescription, partaking more of a sedative than a stimulant and not likely very much to enlarge the scope of human knowledge.

The Doctor's method was the personal touch, and sometimes it was a very keen, direct touch, as when he said to a young man, "You drink; you gamble; you are a profane swearer." The man reddened with indignation and said, "Dr. Carlisle, who has been informing on me?" The Doctor replied, "I know the community from which you come, and I know that the men of your community never let a young man reach the age of eighteen without educating him in those vices." Years afterwards in relating the interview the man said, "I have not from that day to this gambled, touched liquor, or sworn an oath." [7]

The Doctor's great aversion was to lying. In a sort of Methodist "class meeting" with the Sophomores in the early '80's he asked young Smith, "Do you smoke?" "Yes." "Do you dance?" "Yes." "Do you play cards?" "Yes." "Do you curse?" "Yes." The Doctor looked long and intently at him, and said, "Well, Mr. Smith, I must say you are a very truthful young man, or you would not have answered me as you have. Always keep this foundation stone in your character and you will be safe; but let it dis-

---

7. H. N. Snyder to D. D. Wallace.

appear, and your character will fall into ruin." The man's later life showed that he did keep the foundation stone true and was a useful man.[8]

The personal touch, as we said, was the key to the Doctor's method in education. Daniel C. Roper spent the Freshman and Sophomore years at Wofford in 1884-85, but transferred to Trinity College because of typhoid fever's killing his closest friend and roommate. He was awed when the six foot, four inch Dr. Carlisle stopped him on the campus and began a conversation with the observation that it was a fine morning. Young Roper agreed. Then the Doctor said, "I wonder if you have a special thought for this fine day." Naturally he did not. Dr. Carlisle continued: "Let me suggest to you that you never leave your room in the morning without having one. It will keep you encouraged and balanced. Since you don't have one today, let me give you one." "Yes, Sir," said Roper with some confusion, while the Doctor regarded him, he thought, with close scrutiny; but that was merely the Doctor's habit of observing anything closely, but not severely. The Doctor continued, "The way you approach people in early life will decide your destiny. Since there are only two ways of approaching people, it is very important that you consider them and make no mistake. One way is negative, the other positive. Under the negative, you approach people suspiciously, impressing upon them that you lack faith and confidence in them. You will not get their co-operation and you will fail. Under the positive, you will approach people with confidence and faith that will prompt them to believe in you and follow you. You will thereby establish confidence, co-operation, and leadership, and you will succeed." That was much more like a classroom lecture than the Doctor's usual manner with a Freshman personally; but at all events, Mr. Roper tells us, he never forgot the words, and that often in after life they served him well.[9]

The Doctor knew each student personally like a father—much better than most fathers. Mr. Roper gives the much quoted saying of the Doctor that "When two hundred and fifty students enter the front door of Wofford College, I go out of the back door." His wonderful memory allowed few of his old pupils to escape him in after years. I tried to get him to tell me of any method he had; but he would go only so far as to quote an old school-teacher whom he had had: "Your memory is like a dog: trust it and it won't bite you." The swiftness and precision of his mind in the realm of

---

8. J. H. Carlisle, Jr. *op. cit.*, 179. The Doctor's efforts at improving men did not always succeed so well. On one occasion Squire S_____ noticed some fence posts piled in the Doctor's back yard and told young Jim to ask his father what he would take for them. Jim returned with the word that "Father says tell Squire S_____ that if he will come to church with his wife next Sunday, he will give him the fence posts." The Squire replied, "Tell your father he asks too much for his posts."—*Ib.*, 201.

9. Daniel C. Roper, *Fifty Years of Public Life*, 22-23.

his peculiar talents was remarkable, and yet in others he was notably lacking. He could not tell one tune from another, and in mechanics, though a mathematician, he was as helpless as a little child. His son said to me, "You might not believe it, but Pa had so little mechanical ability that he could hardly tie a knot in a string." In politics, social problems, government, and business, he practiced a modesty and self-distrust which prevented the output from such great faculties as the world expects from one so gifted. The explanation, I believe, was partly his indisposition to systematic intellectual labor, and partly in his absorption in moral and religious interests. Yet such questions must be met and solved, and if not by the wise and good then by whom? I remember Dr. Carlisle's saying in the Faculty group, at a time of public perplexity, "I believe there is no situation into which an individual or a nation can be thrown but that there is a possible solution in intelligence and righteousness." [10] He chose to make his contribution to good government by sending into public life men imbued with proper principles rather than by seeking to act directly himself. We must respect his opinion as to the best method in which to expend his influence.

The Doctor's chief heroes were Paul, Wesley, Washington, Lee, and all mothers. He idealized womanhood so far that he shunned the thought of women's being capable of any wickedness or weakness. With unrivaled power he presented the appeal of mother to what is most generous in young men's characters. His power and aptitude for giving a moral turn to any subject was illustrated as one winter night in 1894 his Senior class in Astronomy watched him point out the various constellations with a sweep of imagination that gave some realization of the grandeur of creation. "And yet, young men," he said, turning his eyes from the stars to us, "not all of them together are worth one human soul." Without another word the lecture was over. What in another's mouth would have been a flat, stale, canting commonplace was in his a burning truth. The dignity and worth of the human soul could never be cheap after that.

Dr. Carlisle, by the force of his personality, educated his Faculty as well as his students, mainly by example, but sometimes also by keen observations or pungent sayings. For instance, the young and ardent Professor Snyder was lamenting one day in Faculty meeting the deficiencies of some of the students. "Oh," he said, "just to have a perfect student!" "Ah," said the

---

10. A modern form of Dr. Carlisle's principle is expressed in the words of Konrad Andenaurer, Chancellor of the new German republic, in *Time*, September 5, 1949: "Christianity is a dynamic spiritual force that outlives all politics. Christianity is the answer to all ideologies. The only possible hope for peace and order in Europe lies in a federated Europe based on Christian ideals."

old President, "but the perfect student might demand a perfect Professor." There might be a sharper reproof, edged with a touch of sarcasm, as on the following occasion: The Doctor was evidently inclined to stretch mercy as far as the law allowed for a student deficient in his studies whose services were needed on the baseball team. Falling into an expression which was often on his lips, he said: "Taking account of all the equities of the case, what can we do with this young man?" "But, Doctor," said a young Professor, "this does not seem to be a case where equity applies. Equity is designed to relieve the manifest injustice which arises from the universality of law, and there are no such circumstances in this case. The law simply cuts this man off." The President was startled. He looked fixedly at the Professor, and then repeated his question in about these words: "In the light of this learned and enlightening definition of equity, what do you think best to do in this case?" Yes, he educated his Faculty, and, I do not doubt, with the model consciously in mind of the education of the Twelve by the Master.

The Doctor's method of discipline, like his teaching, was the personal touch. First came the personal appeal in his private study. He sought not to put chains on the man, but to work change in the man. If this appeal failed, it was a hard case. Report to the Faculty might follow; and if all failed the father would be asked to withdraw the student. The Doctor's method was to bring the offender to see his wrong, to repent of it, and to make a sincere and solemn promise of amendment. Whatever might be the limitations of this method in a larger institution, in the Wofford of that day it produced a degree of good order hard to find equaled elsewhere. The Doctor would say, "He will find his level"; and "The world is very ready to accept you at the valuation which you put upon yourself."

Despite his abhorrence of seeking money for himself and his aversion to seeking it directly for the college itself, Dr. Carlisle realized its importance and often insisted to young men that honestly to make money and save money might be an imperative duty. He never wearied of urging upon young men the importance of having a *magnum opus*—a great and worthy task to draw out all a man's powers. It was remarked once in the presence of an eminent Judge that it was strange that the Doctor himself never had a *magnum opus;* for he never put his hand to any intellectual task worthy of his powers. Perhaps, said the Judge, he considered that his work for young men was his *magnum opus.*

No account of Dr. Carlisle would be complete without reference to his almost life-long service as a Sunday school teacher. Not only that, but when addressing general audiences on Sunday he would often, if not generally, take the Sunday school lesson of the day as his subject, with the purpose, I surmise, of dignifying the Sunday school as a part of the church's work. His Sunday school class generally consisted of a large part of the student body of the college. His style here was intimate, almost, we may say, conversational in form, though more of continuous lecture than in classroom, where he invited discussion. That Sunday school hour was one of the most precious sources of inspiration available to the Wofford student.

Dr. Snyder relates that when he was coming to Wofford College as a young Professor Charles Forster Smith said to him of Dr. Carlisle, "You will find him the most of a New Testament man of any you have ever known." And so in truth he was. Dr. Carlisle was great chiefly by the depth and thoroughness of his consecration. Few men are willing to pay what he willingly paid to be what he was in character.

CHAPTER X

DR. CARLISLE'S LIFE AND CHARACTER
1825-1909

DURING the seven years that remained after his retirement from the presidency Dr. Carlisle lived up perfectly to his remark to his successor, "I want you to understand that President Emeritus means ex-President." The Doctor's protest when he heard that someone proposed to write his life, that there was nothing to write, that he was only a teacher, went too far, for it amounted to asking that no one should ever write the history of Wofford College. A good part of that life is found in the preceding chapters; but there are aspects of the man that did not readily fall in with the course of our narrative, but should be related.

James Henry Carlisle was born in Winnsboro, South Carolina, in a plain cottage near the center of the town, May 4, 1825. His grandfather James Carlisle came to Winnsboro, S. C., in 1818 from County Antrim, Ireland, that fruitful source of so much of the Scotch-Irish stock that has played such a part in American history. When he died, September 22, 1833, in his 68th year, he left a widow, six sons, and one daughter. His son William, who was born in Ireland July 26, 1797, and died March 28, 1867, was the father of the future President of Wofford College. William Carlisle's wife, Mary Anne Buchanan, of the same Scotch-Irish stock, was born February 16, 1801, and died June 19, 1858.

The Carlisles were plain folk, the head of the clan of emigrants being a shoemaker, and his son William a carpenter until, under the freedom of that day, he became in 1832 a physician, and after carpentering on people for sixteen years obtained a diploma in 1848 from the Southern Botanical Medical College of Macon, Ga.[1] The facts of his ambition and energy are attested by his own rise in the social scale and his sending his brilliant sons to the South Carolina College. The greater influence seems to have come from James's mother, who was a very strong character. From her he inherited the stoical restraint with which he accepted either joy or sorrow.[2]

It has been said, but mistakenly, in speaking of the goodness and loving-

---

1. Prof. W. S. Morrison and others, especially Prof. Charles Forster Smith, in Watson's *Carlisle Memorial Volume*, 14-18, 22.
2. J. H. Carlisle, Jr., Memories of Wofford College, MS. A large part of this MS. was published serially in the *Spartanburg Herald* during the latter part of 1922.

kindness of the great James H. Carlisle that he was "slow to anger." From a child he had a hot Scotch-Irish temper which at times, even after the long discipline of a Christian life, would flash out. On one occasion a teacher, Mr. Hudson, ordered little James as a punishment to write on his slate, "I am a goose," and show it to the girls. James said, "I will not." "Why?" asked the teacher. Snapped back James, "Because it's a lie." [3]

Quite different was the conduct of another teacher when James had come to be a large boy, who realized that his pupil was anything but a goose— Professor Leland.[4] James had stopped school to clerk in a store. One autumn day Professor Leland called him outside and said, "James, you are too bright a boy to stop school, and if it is for financial reasons, we can arrange that." "Yes, that is the reason," replied James. So he went back to school and ultimately on to the South Carolina College, the later University.[5] He rode his horse to Columbia and registered late in February as a Sophomore. He has been heard to say that he could not have passed an entrance examination. In private he was more self-revealing. They tested me, he said, and found me unprepared, but said, "We will give you a trial." Says his son, "Father would smile when telling this and say, 'They never mentioned the subject afterwards.'" [6] Well they might overlook the subject for the future; for in due course he graduated in December, 1844, with second honor. The result of his being given a trial, thinks his son, influenced his own conduct later toward ill-prepared boys; but I may say that he exercised his charity judiciously and never believed a student could jump over the college building, as I have heard him say, just because he believed he could.

Dr. Carlisle's son relates that one of his father's college mates said to him, "Carlisle, there are two kinds of aristocracies in South Carolina, one aristocracy of money, to which I belong, and one of brains, to which you belong." [7] The same story is related of an earlier brilliant poor boy at the college, James L. Petigru. I wonder did rich young aristocrats keep this formula for complimenting brilliant poor boys, or did Mr. Carlisle, Jr., hearing his father repeat the story about Petigru, confuse it in memory with its having been said to his father, as it quite justly could have been said?

---

3. J. H. Carlisle, Jr., *op. cit.*, 107.
4. Not unlikely the Dr. A. W. Leland who served as President of the first teachers' meeting in South Carolina in 1850.—D. D. Wallace, *Hist. S. C. Teachers' Asso.*, 6.
5. J. H. Carlisle, Jr., *op. cit.*, 105-6. The oft repeated remark that he entered the Sophomore class "half advanced" presumably means that he entered when the college year was half over, which is the fact; or it may mean he was half prepared.
6. J. H. Carlisle, Jr., *op. cit.*, 105-6.
7. J. H. Carlisle, Jr., *op. cit.*, 112.

A story illustrating Professor Carlisle's attitude toward promising young boys comes to mind here. He found that the son of a poor woman in Columbia whose son went to Professor Carlisle's school had mechanical talent, and so got him employment of a humble sort in the shops of the Greenville and Columbia Railroad at Newberry (or more correctly its suburb called Helena). The boy rose, through engineer, etc., and became ultimately the General Manager of the Southern Railway system. He never failed to send his old teacher every year a pass over the whole system.[8]

Young Carlisle's graduating speech, December 2, 1844, was on "The Character of Shelley's Writings." [9] This utterance of the nineteen-year-old boy gives the trend of his entire later life. It is marked by his striking power of phrase; but most significantly it voices his supreme spiritual optimism and his abhorrence of a life philosophy of discontent, pessimism, and rebellion. "If we find in Shelley no attempt to heal the woes of which he made such loud complaint, then indeed all his rhapsodies and tears over the miseries of man will make little impression upon us. They will only remind us of someone who, if he had the power, would strike out from the Heaven the Sun and then weep that the world was left in darkness. . . . To which of his writings would you go for support in those days of darkness and weariness which come upon all, when hope seems prostrate, your energies lifeless, your strength failing and for a moment the whole world tottering in its course? His writings tend only to kindle in the reader a morbid sensibility, a restless disposition, which leads him to mope about like Hamlet and complain that all things are flat, stale and unprofitable. And if he should become so deeply imbued with those sentiments as their unhappy author he would spend his whole life in the paroxysm of a long, unquiet, fitful fever; he would bear with stoic pride the ills of life which were inevitable, but every blow of chastisement which he received would only exasperate him and lead him with daring presumption to look up and demand the reason why the blow was given. . . . He taught that infamous doctrine which abolishes the family, teaching men utterly to disregard, or at best but lightly esteem, that sacred institution which to us is the source of all that dignifies, adorns or embellishes life. Now, if he hurled this shaft against the purity and peace of society it will console us but little to learn that he threw it *skillfully* or even that the shaft was wreathed with flowers. . . . They cannot say of him, what may

---

8. J. H. Carlisle, *op. cit.*, 115.
9. Before 1866 the S. C. College session began Oct. 1 and ended July 1, with commencement the first Monday of the following December. The Legislature being in session helped make it a great occasion.—*By-laws S. C. College;* Green, *Hist. Univ. of S. C.*

be said of the true reformer, At his death he left the world some better than he found it." [10]

Dr. Carlisle's favorite poet, says Charles Forster Smith, was Cowper, the one whom he most frequently quoted; which is simply an illustration of the fact that his esteem for literature was more governed by moral than aesthetic consideration. A passage often on his lips at home is significant of his character:

> The daily round, the common task,
> Furnish all we ought to ask:
> Room to deny ourselves,
> A path to lead us nearer God. [11]

In 1848 he married Miss Margaret Jane Bryce of Columbia. Their four children were born after they came to Wofford. Two died in infancy. A daughter, Sarah Herbert, and a son, James Henry, lived with him until his death. His wife died during the Christmas holidays, 1891. The parts of his life related in the previous chapters as part of the history of the college can easily be fitted into the continuous story of his career. We are interested here in the man himself rather than in the Professor or the President as part of an institution. "Dr. Carlisle was a man of commanding appearance and would at once attract attention in any crowd. When he entered the General Conference in Atlanta, Dr. Cunnyngham, who had never seen him before, remarked: 'There's a man!' He was six feet, four inches in height and weighed about one hundred and ninety pounds. His head was unusually large, or rather long, so that it was often difficult to get a hat (it must have been at least an eight) to fit him. His hair and beard were dark; the former worn moderately long, the latter full, but never long. His eyes were gray-blue and his most striking feature, bright and ordinarily calm and gentle, but brilliant when he was thoroughly aroused. His movements, as natural and dignified as his form was stately, on great occasions seemed majestic, though all unconsciously so." [12]

The last remark is very apt. Among great men the Doctor's nature seemed, in spite of his extraordinary modesty, instinctively to rise to its natural level. Such an occasion was when, along with Bishop Atticus G. Haygood as clerical messenger, he was sent by the Southern Methodist Church as lay fraternal representative to the General Conference of the Methodist Episcopal, or Northern Methodist Church, as we call it, in

10. J. H. Carlisle, editor: *Addresses of J. H. Carlisle*, 11-15.
11. J. H. Carlisle, Jr., *op. cit.*, 213.
12. Charles Forster Smith in *Carlisle Memorial Volume*, 27-28.

Cincinnati in May, 1880. His address on that occasion represents, to my mind, the high-water mark of his eloquence and mental outlook. Unfortunately, we must confine ourselves to short passages from what he said: [13]

Mr. President, Fathers, and Brethren: A few weeks ago a sick man rode into the depot of a Southern city. Calling for one of his own faith, he introduced himself as a dying Methodist preacher from the North. He was kindly received and had such attentions as he needed. This incident was scarcely worthy of all the notice taken of it by the newspapers North and South. It would mortify us to learn that anyone was surprised at the reception given to a strange brother. It is very certain that a minister from the South, crossing the line into your border, under similar circumstances, would receive precisely similar treatment. To the dying Christian all the kindness shown was of little value. If he had been met with coldness, with positive rudeness and insult even, supposing that possible in a Christian land, he would still have died in peace. It is the living who need kindness, recognition, and confidence.

It is an era in the history of both parties when one million human beings speak through any medium to two millions, and say, *We are brethren.* . . . One of the saddest results of recent events is that some in every part of our country have lost confidence in their fellow men, their fellow-citizens, their fellow-Christians. There is a loss greater than that. Some have lost their power to confide in others. This, if general, would be national bankruptcy in its most dreadful shape. There is, however, even a loss beyond that. Some have lost the wish to confide in others. They are not only reconciled to their disability, but they glory in it. They represent a class described by Arthur Helps as men, who, imprisoned in their prejudices, like madmen mistake their jailers for a guard of honor. Let us hope that there are not more of these in any part of our country than can be profitably used as instructive object-lessons.

The sacred and eternal points of agreement that draw us together are stronger than temporal and transient points that divide us in spirit. Our sympathies should be stronger than our antipathies. We agree wonderfully in our interpretation of the Bible. This fact should have far more significance than the fact that we disagree in our interpretation of some passages in the Constitution of the United States, or of some passages in recent or current history. "Religion is the only remedy for diseased states," says Vinet. Methodists share largely with sister churches the responsibility for the success or failure of Christian civilization in these lands. . . .

It has been said that perhaps there has not been for two centuries in Christendom a public question with so many complications and difficulties as gather around the civil war, its causes, and results. As one of the results, it was inevitable that church lines must largely coincide with geographical and party lines. But, if religion comes in to perpetuate and intensify party spirit, the future of the country is dark indeed. If the light that is in us becomes darkness, how great will be that darkness! This is too great and goodly a land to be given up to the genius of discord and hate. You will let a layman declare, with all possible emphasis, that one of the greatest difficulties in the way of the common man is

13. *Addresses of J. H. Carlisle,* ed. by his son, 126-136.

the fierce temper so often carried into religious quarrels, and into public quarrels by religious men. If the Christians of this land could meet all the great questions now confronting us, not as angels may be supposed to meet them, but as brave, tolerant, large-hearted, Christian and Christlike men, this would do more for the spread of Christianity than all the volumes of evidence that this generation of scholars can write.

In our immediate church relations there are seen strong reasons why we should meet this crisis like Christian men. Two great bodies, with all great points in common, each pledged to spread holiness through these lands, ought to have a clear and full understanding. If such grave interests were not involved it would be amusing to watch the position and attitudes of our churches. Here are two stout, comely Methodist lads, not quite a century old. They have all the sanguine, complacent feelings which are natural to that early stage of historic growth. They are not afflicted with that excessive diffidence which is so painful in some young people. They are not afraid of that which is high or of large designs. A few years ago they had a most unbrotherly struggle. Since that time each has considered it a religious duty to consecrate in prose and poetry, not only the heroic incidents, but the spirit and sentiment, even the moods and tempers, of his story of the fight, while he often suggests to his brother that he ought to let the past go, and never allude to this matter before company.

Each one, with the charming simplicity of youth, says openly to the whole world, "I see the way very clear for me to achieve the great mission to which I am certainly called; but, alas for me! I have a twin brother, and is he not rightly named Jacob? For he supplants me on all occasions in birthright and in blessings." Each one of these Wesley boys is in a great chronic distress about the other's eyesight. Each one is forward on all occasions, in season and out of season, to offer his whole stock of oil of vitriol, his lancet, and his tomahawk, to take the mote out of his dear brother's eye. Surely it is time to put away these childish things. . . .

Our last Sabbath-school lesson carried us to the mount of transfiguration. The astonished disciples came down from that sacred mountain, with its celestial visitors, to find poor human nature torn by a demon at its base. You are here to overlook many and far-reaching interests of your vast organization. If our wishes and prayers can avail, you will find every day in the social and religious intercourse of this place an ever-fresh, enriching influence. In all the prosaic drudgery and claims of a laborious session you will find it good to be here. You will go down to common life when all these claims have been met, perhaps to find a great nation torn by the spirit of discord and strife. If we ask—and what thoughtful patriot has not asked again and again, in sorrow and surprise—"Why cannot we cast out this evil spirit?" the sad answer is at hand, "Because of our unbelief," our want of faith in God and man. We suppose our common Father to be like one of ourselves. We cannot rise to the high conception that North and South, as we often use them, are words which he does not recognize. We unconsciously suppose that he regards, just as we do, state lines and party lines. These are very important and necessary for many purposes. But they do not, they cannot, restrain or bound his all-embracing love, blessed be his name! And we unfortunately lack faith in our fellowman. We too often judge him by the

146

badge or regalia he wears. We do not rightly prize the immortal jewel within. With our backs to the irrevocable past, and our faces turned toward the available future, can we not gather from all the associations and inspirations of this hour some lasting impulse which will connect them with the suffering nation below?

The North and the South! These short words have gathered strange power to move the swiftest instincts of our nature. They have "turned the coward's heart to steel, the sluggard's blood to flame." Must they forever be the watchwords of an undying strife? Must they still represent the gulf across which no love or sympathy can reach? Is there no one high relation which can adjust and subordinate them—no one overpowering sentiment which can unite them? Will not all Christians, of all names, in all parts of this vast nation, surprised and saddened, but made humble and wise by their painful failure, carry this distracted land, the mother of us all, to Him who can give peace and quiet? Brethren, we solemnly pledge you the sympathy and prayers of many thousands of earnest men and faithful women, who will join you and your people in urging to heaven an appeal which may satisfy all the purest longings of patriotism and piety: "The North and the South, thou hast created them";

> "Possess them, thou who hast the right,
> As Lord and Master of the whole."

At both South Carolina Conferences of 1939, with the desire of Dr. Carlisle's heart for reunion of the churches about to be fulfilled, Bishop Clare Purcell read to the Conference as appropriate to the occasion a portion of the above address.[14]

Dr. Carlisle was elected to the first General Conference of his church to which laymen were eligible in 1870, and to each one afterwards through 1898, except that of 1874. He was elected a delegate to the Ecumenical Conference in London in 1881, but did not attend, fearing that the sickness which afflicted him so severely on a train trip would be unendurable on a sea voyage; and to the second one in Washington and did attend.

On a visit to Nashville, Dr. Carlisle met Bishop McTyeire, whose will was law in the affairs of Vanderbilt University. As the Bishop grasped the hand of his fellow-native of South Carolina, he said significantly, "I wish I had known you earlier." [15] It would have made no difference; the Doctor would not have left Wofford.

Dr. Carlisle took seriously his duties as a citizen, but he took little part in political life. In 1860 he was drafted as a member of the Secession Convention by his fellow-citizens, who, whatever may be thought of their determination to secede, certainly, conscious of the mighty issues involved, chose as their spokesmen the best men from all over the State. It is some-

14. *S. C. Conf. Mins.* 1939, 34; *Upper S. C. Conf. Mins.* 1939, 29.
15. J. H. Carlisle, Jr., *op. cit.*

times erroneously said that he alone voted against secession. Not only common knowledge of his contemporaries, but the record of the Convention, where he is recorded by name as answering Yes to the roll call on the question, shows how groundless is that idea. Like many another man of conservative character, in the emotional storm that raged over the State he was swept along with what he later called "the wild passions of that mad hour." [16] His profession exempted him from the draft, and he did not volunteer, although his younger brother, John W. Carlisle, went out as First Lieutenant and became Captain of the company from Spartanburg. Though he admired greatly both Washington and Lee for their characters, he was utterly disinclined to military life and probably could not have endured its strain; for, although he was with slight exceptions always in good health, he was not muscularly strong. Though swept into the tide of secession sentiment, his later view was expressed to me, when, in the 1890's I enquired of him about material for the history of the Secession Convention, he gave me what information he could, and concluded with the remark, "I hope your generation will make better history than that." He rarely talked of the Secession Convention and never wrote of it, though offered an attractive financial inducement to do so.[17] The fact is that the Doctor, though never yielding anything in his respect for the Confederate soldier and the motives of Confederate leaders, came much sooner than most men of his generation to understand the mistakes of Southern policies.

In 1864 Profesor Carlisle was solicited to run for the legislature. He consented on condition that he make no campaign. He remained at home more than usually, to avoid the appearance of electioneering. The grievously wounded Confederate soldier, Major J. L. Coker, elected to the legislature the same year, was the author, tradition says, of the bill introduced in December, 1864, in the House of Representatives greatly to broaden and enlarge the free school system. Instead of the annual appropriation of $74,400 ($37,200 before 1852) for the education of the poor, the amount was to be annually $300,000, and a General Superintendent of the Free School System was to be provided, with a salary of $5,000 a year. Special effort was to be made for the benefit of the children of soldiers. The amount to be spent on each child was to be $5 a month, with a maximum of $50 for the year, and children even above 16 years of age were to be eligible for the benefits if in need. Said the Columbia *South Carolinian:* [18]

16. He used the expression to Dr. H. N. Snyder, who repeated it to me.
17. J. H. Carlisle, Jr., *op. cit.*, 131.
18. Quoted in the *Charleston Daily Courier* of December 20, 1864. Also *ib.* Dec. 24, 1864. *Chastn. Mercury,* Dec. 19, 1864. Carlisle's speech was December 15.

The opening speech was made by Professor Carlisle of Spartanburg, and it is no flattery to that gentleman, or injustice to his eloquent collaborators in the Legislature, to say that it was by long odds the ablest, most impressive and eloquent speech that has been made during the present session. For a wonder, silence reigned in the galleries, while the members, one and all, acknowledged by their attention, the spell by which they were bound.

Leroy F. Youmans, a thirty-year-old army officer in Columbia on leave to sit during the session, said forty-two years afterwards that he had never heard such a speech on education, either before or since. Some members were moved to tears (as South Carolina's rulers before 1860 deserved to be moved for their shameful neglect of popular education).

It is astonishing to read the arguments by which men of some eminence opposed the bill. Said Edward McCready, the father of the historian, "I am opposed to the whole measure. To force people into school [the bill had no compulsory attendance feature] is tyranny. Man fell on account of knowledge. It was education that caused the New England mind to oppress us." He feared " 'the refinement of this people, if the youthful intellect was to be educated in a common mould like that of the North. . . . No one could say that with knowledge came virtue.' Genius will press to success irrespective of difficulties."

Mr. William Whaley effectively demolished the arguments of his fellow-Charlestonian, and the House sent the bill to the Senate with its endorsement.

"What is going on?" asked a Senator as the news of the eloquence of Professor Carlisle spread into the lobbies. "A young teacher from the up country is making a powerful speech in favor of establishing a State Superintendent of Education," was the reply. "Then we must go in and prevent the extravagance of the House, swept away by such eloquence," said the Senator; and kill it the Senate did.[19]

Professor Carlisle's life during the War of Secession has been largely related in a former chapter. During Reconstruction his reverence for law (and, someone has put it, his reverence for even the office itself) governed his conduct. I remember the horror with which he recalled the hanging of John C. Calhoun in effigy by the anti-nullifiers in Spartanburg. His conduct under defeat—submission with self-respect, but without plotting or violence—may be described in his own words long afterwards as recorded by his son: "In the spring of 1865 darkness had settled over the land

---

19. J. H. Carlisle, Jr., Memories of Wofford, MS., 128, 129; L. F. Youmans to H. B. Carlisle. The incident had been related to me before, with less detail. Prof. R. Means Davis of the University of South Carolina said that he remembered as a boy what an impression the speech made.

One by one, group by group, the war-worn Confederates were returning to their desolate homes. A company of Federal soldiers had taken charge of Spartanburg and opened a sort of office where men might take the oath of allegiance. I was standing on the street talking with Capt. John H. Evins, who had his arm in a sling, and the great gravity of the occasion was overwhelming. The courthouse had been long unused except by spiders. The semblance of authority and majesty of the law appeared nowhere. I said, 'Well, Captain, I can stand tyranny and even despotism, but I cannot stand anarchy. I propose to step across the street and take the oath of allegiance. If you have no objection, I would like for you to walk across with me.' Then we took that oath. How well he kept it to the end of his life his noble work in Washington as our chosen representative will attest. I propose to keep it while life lasts." [20]

To the same effect was his statement in declining in April, 1871, nomination as a delegate to the first Taxpayers Convention, a perfectly peaceful means of seeking relief from the abuses of corrupt government: "There are difficulties in any path which promise to lead us from our present position to stability and confidence. The only path before us, in which there are no formidable difficulties, is the one which leads from the point where we now stand, directly, rapidly, easily, to anarchy or despotism"; and from anarchy "any despotism will be welcome as a relief." We must not lose hope, he continued. "A people who in '65 met a shock in all their social and industrial framework, which in suddenness and universality is without a parallel in history, and in 1870 made one of the largest crops ever gathered—this people surely will not rush into *frenzy* or sink into the *apathy* of *despair*. The same patience, firmness and practical wisdom which has done so much in improving the affairs of their everyday life will bring benefit when applied to our political problem."

The words are excellent; but it is hard to excuse a man of Dr. Carlisle's declared principles for declining to serve his people in this peaceful co-operative effort for betterment. He constantly insisted during the Reconstruction period that relief could come only through lawful means, urging that the short cut of lawlessness or violence could lead only to evil, and that relief must be sought by peaceful means. In a long and earnest article in the *Southern Christian Advocate* of January 17, 1872, he urged charity toward the North and restraint of our passions in politics. He sought to show how unchristian and unwise were those who, like at least one South-

---

20. J. H. Carlisle, Jr.'s, Memories of Wofford College, MS., 132-3. John H. Evins was Congressman from the Fourth S. C. District from 1877 to 1884. Dr. Carlisle once remarked with dry humor in a Sunday School convention of the pious Presbyterian, who could not then answer the roll, "Captain Evins was once a Sunday School teacher, but now he is only a Congressman."

ern Governor, refused to celebrate Thanksgiving Day because proclaimed by a Yankee President, and enumerated the blessings for which the South should be thankful despite the possession of the State government by bad men. Let us be Christian, he urged, in our policies, and in public act and private speech.

In June, 1877, the Legislature elected Dr. Carlisle a member of the Commission on School Text Books. The same year Superintendent of Education Hugh S. Thompson wrote, December 1, in his annual report: "I determined, if possible, to call to my assistance in revising the school law the experience, learning and ability of men who were peculiarly fitted to perform the work. Accordingly Prof. J. H. Carlisle, LL.D., Prof. Charles Petty, R. W. Boyd, Esq., R. Means Davis, Esq., Prof. William Hood and Henry P. Archer, Esq., were invited to meet in this city on the 21st of August, for the purpose of considering the free school system of the State and suggesting such changes as would promote its efficiency." The lengthy statute proposed by the Superintendent as the result of this consultation, with a few minor omissions, was adopted practically verbatim by the Legislature in 1878.[21]

In times of moral let-down or disorders the Doctor's sensitive soul was saddened, but his faith in an overruling Providence saved him from pessimism. At the first Faculty meeting of a year near the end of his administration, I recall how gloomily he referred to certain evil aspects of contemporary life; "but," he concluded, "our Lord knew all things, and he was no pessimist." Nor did the Doctor live in the past, deeply as he revered its great men. His face was so definitely turned to the future that he could quote with approval before his class in the early '90's the editor of a Virginia newspaper who congratulated the public that not once in the recent school closings had Lee and Jackson been dragged from their graves to stalk across school or college platforms.

Dr. Carlisle was largely responsible for securing for Spartanburg the Kennedy Free Library. Mrs. Kennedy, the widow of Dr. Lionel Chalmers Kennedy, wished the site of her husband's office, where so many had re-

---

21. S. C. *Senate Jour.* extra session 1877, 416; Supt. of Ed. report in *S. C. Reports and Resolutions 1877-78,* 384, 395-408; *S. C. Stats. at Large,* XVI, 571. It is interesting to note that three of the six men invited by Superintendent of Education Thompson to help in revising the school law were connected with Wofford College: Dr. Carlisle, the President, Charles Petty, an alumnus, and R. W. Boyd, an early Principal of the preparatory department. Some have said, confusing the above facts, that Dr. Carlisle was appointed by Gov. Hampton a member of the State Board of Education. Under the Constitution of 1868 the State Board of Education consisted of the County Superintendents of Education (elected popularly), an unfit and cumbersome body. A section of the law of 1878 enacted there should be four gubernatorial appointees, under the name of the State Board of Examiners, to whom the functions of a State Board were assigned. Dr. Carlisle does not appear as a member. The State Board of Education consisting of the Superintendent of Education, the Governor, and a gubernatorial appointee from each Congressional district was established by the Constitution of 1895.

ceived free service to their bodies, to be the place where they could go for strength freely given for their minds. The time limit for the acceptance of her offer had almost expired, after which the lot would have gone to the Episcopal church. Dr. Carlisle headed the subscription list with one hundred dollars to raise the funds necessary for erecting a building.[22]

This suggests an incident which should commemorate, but no longer does, the name of the great teacher. When the large brick school building which formerly stood on Magnolia Street, incidentally almost on the site of the present Kennedy Library Building,[23] was erected in 1889, it was named the Carlisle School. Dr. Carlisle prepared a rather elaborate address for the cornerstone laying, August 2, 1889.[24] The name was soon forgotten, as with just one white school for many years a specific name was not necessary. When the construction of a little school in the Flatwoods section of Spartanburg County stalled for lack of funds, it was Dr. Carlisle's subscription of ten dollars among the town people, the largest on the list, that helped complete the school and gave it his name.[25]

The Doctor took a much more active part in educational and religious activities requiring travel up to middle age than he did later, and would have done so to a greater extent but for the train sickness which made a journey persecution. Humorous incidents sometimes resulted. Once, as he sat in misery with his head on the seat in front of him, he overheard a lady remark, "How sad to see an old man in that condition." On another occasion, sitting in the baggage car (for looking out through the large open door seemed to relieve the sickness) two young men were passing the bottle. One, thinking from the Doctor's appearance that he had already had some and would like more, offered him the bottle. "Did you reprove him?" someone later asked him. "No," said the Doctor; "he meant it for a kindness." There spoke, not the moralist who abhorred liquor, but the gentleman who would not wound the feelings of another.[26]

The first organization of teachers in South Carolina resulted from a call from Gov. Whitemarsh B. Seabrook for the teachers to meet in Columbia, July 12, 1850. Forty-one men from sixteen districts (as the counties were then called) met. Dr. A. W. Leland was elected President and James H. Carlisle, then a young teacher in Columbia, Secretary. Interest could not be sustained, and the organization called the Teachers' Convention, or

---

22. J. H. Carlisle, Jr., *op. cit.,* 70-71.
23. The first Library stood on the northern side of Kennedy Place, now sometimes called Dunbar Street, just east of the Andrews Building.
24. J. H. Carlisle, Jr., *op. cit.,* 169.
25. Spartanburg correspondence in *Greenville News* for school in town data; J. H. Carlisle, Jr., for Flatwoods incident.
26. The incidents were related to me by Prof. D. A. DuPre.

Teachers' Association, died after a second feeble meeting. The next attempt was in 1870, when "The Educational Institute of South Carolina" was organized. James H. Carlisle was one of the nineteen signing the constitution, and he delivered the "Annual Address," as it was hopefully called, on the subject "Some Mistakes Which a Young Teacher May Make." A very fruitful address, the reporter for the *Charleston Daily News* called it: "For an hour and a half the accomplished speaker held his audience in the closest attention. Rarely have the claims, duties, and responsibilities and character of the teacher been portrayed in a more forcible and striking manner. Learning, wit, quotation, and authority filled the hour as usefully and ably as a Columbia audience has listened to in many a day." We have already in the foregoing chapter given extracts from this address to illustrate Dr. Carlisle's ideals as a teacher. At the 1871 meeting of the Educational Association Professor Carlisle was elected President. Apparently there was no third meeting; but at the time at which it was to have been held there convened in Charleston the State Sunday School Convention, in which Professor Carlisle was very prominent and by which he was elected President. In 1875 we find him addressing the convention of Spartanburg county teachers, and in 1877 informally the Georgia State Teachers' Association. The lapsed Educational Institute of the early 1870's was revived in the form which it has since unbrokenly continued, as the State Teachers' Association in Greenville in 1881. Dr. Carlisle was elected its first President and gave "a wonderful and impressive address" on "The Regrets of the Teacher." It was sought to have him at the 1882 meeting in Columbia "to repeat his address on 'Prizes in Colleges' which he had recently delivered with so much effect before the National Teachers' Association in Saratoga," but it proved impossible. He was surprised on arriving at home to find the unanimous invitation of the Board of Trustees of the South Carolina University to become its President, as he had previously positively refused to allow his name to be presented—the second occasion, I have understood, on which he had been offered the position. Dr. Carlisle's presidency of the State Teachers' Association continued through its meeting in 1884, which was held at Wofford College. In those days Dr. Carlisle of Wofford and Dr. William Moffatt Grier of Erskine were the outstanding figures in the Association. "Their views had more weight than those of any other men, and the last word had not been said on any subject until one or both had spoken." [27]

---

27. Dr. J. L. McCain to D. D. Wallace, Dec. 15, 1923. The account of the teachers' organizations is from D. D. Wallace's *History of the South Carolina Teachers' Association*, 5, 6, 12, 16, 20, 26.

The address at Saratoga in 1882 referred to above exhibited strongly two of Dr. Carlisle's outstanding characteristics: first, his abhorrence of selfishness as a motive of human conduct; and second, his stimulating and liberalizing influence on those with whom he came into personal touch. Mrs. Kellogg wrote the *Boston Herald* of this address on the prize system as an incentive to college students, "every word of which," she said, "should be written in fire to arrest the attention of the country to the evils of over-stimulation." As one gem glows brighter than another, she continued, so this address stands out from the many shining essays at the convention. It was cheered continually from end to end. He said, "You cannot offer a prize for the most generous, the most truthful, the most unselfish or the most humble. You offer them only for accomplishments and achievements which sink to a subordinate rank when we take a wide and generous view of life, in all its manifold relations. He who begins life with the selfish maxim, 'I will not be second,' prepares the way for chronic restlessness and final defeat. It cannot be the will of our Creator that each one of us should try to be first. Our country does not need a generation of men set on fire by their energy."

Mrs. Kellogg, who lost her husband in the war, says that she went to this meeting scarcely feeling it possible to associate with Southerners, but that she was completely won to fraternal feeling by the words and bearing of the Southern gentlemen at the convention. "Old bitternesses have fallen away like worn-out garments, and our hearts could not tell which of our new-made friends of this week received the warmest good-bye, whether Northern, or Southern or Western." [28]

Interesting are the five lectures which he delivered before the State Teachers' Summer School held at Converse College, June 29 to July 13, 1901, on The South Carolina Judge, William C. Preston, John Belton O'Neall, George McDuffie, and Regrets of an Old Teacher.[29] But taken all in all the Doctor's written output was small and by no means worthy of his powers. A little book, "The Young Astronomer, or Helps to a Knowledge of the Leading Constellations," 144 pages, published in 1891 by the Southern Methodist Publishing House, confines itself to locating the leading stars and constellations in the heavens every ten days from January 1 through December, in clear, simple language, and, according to his custom, is interspersed with poems or prose quotations expressive of the moral glory of the universe. His frequent articles in the *Southern Christian*

---

28. J. H. Carlisle, Jr., *op. cit.*, 145-6.
29. Addresses of James H. Carlisle, 164-238. State Supt. of Ed. Report 1901, pp. 15-18; 615-18 in Reports and Resolutions, 1901.

Walter Kirkland Greene Hall

Advocate sometimes contained valuable historical information, but were often so overloaded with quotations that his readers sighed for more of the great teacher himself. In 1886 he edited for the Chautauqua Press a little volume of 252 pages, consisting in its first part of Dr. Samuel Johnson's sketch of the great sixteenth-century school teacher, Roger Ascham, so wise of mind and so beautiful of character, and selections from his small but important work, *The Schoolmaster;* and in its second part portions of Arthur Penrhyn Stanley's *Life and Correspondence of Thomas Arnold,* the great Headmaster of Rugby. Dr. Carlisle's ten-page introduction on Ascham and his fourteen pages on Arnold are so excellently written and show such knowledge and sympathy with these beloved teachers that we are obliged to believe that he must, from a young man, have held them consciously before him as models. In regard to Arnold we know this is true; for among his books we find an exceedingly well worn volume of Stanley's *Arnold,* bearing on the flyleaf the words, "James H. Carlisle Feb. 1852 Copy No. 2 (No. 1 having been lent and *never returned!*)" He was a great lender, but a rather negligent reclaimer, of his books. Perhaps his lost copy No. 1 was bought when issued in 1845, or at all events when he was little over 20. But for that lending or some other slip of time, I am inclined to believe that an old volume of Ascham would tell the same story. How long after the young Carlisle at 27 obtained Copy No. 2 of the life and letters of Arnold he had those striking passages from Arnold printed in large letters and framed for his classroom we do not know; but I know that when I first saw them in 1891 they were very old. Perhaps they were among the *lares* and *penates* which the young teacher brought with him to Wofford. We may as justly apply to James H. Carlisle the words of Gladstone on Arnold which Carlisle in his volume quotes to describe the great teacher: "One of the noblest minds and highest characters of these days. . . . A career of usefulness which we believe we are guilty of no extravagance in terming unparalleled in the life which Dr. Arnold adopted"; or the words about Arnold which Dr. Carlisle uses from a writer in the *Edinburgh Review,* "We never recollect a religious life which so much affected us; which, while reading, we wished so much to make our own; revolving which, we can so little justify ourselves that it shall not be so."

We are impressed even in reading his excellent treatment of Ascham and Arnold, as well as in considering the small extent of his written output, that Dr. Carlisle's mind was receptive rather than creative. He praised intellectual labors in others and valued, as a mind like his did by the necessity of its nature, intellectual greatness; but he would not submit himself to the sustained exertion which great intellectual achievement requires. He was so absorbed in the religious and the moral and was so conservative and intellectually timid as to be incapable of the progressive educational leadership of a Kirkland or an Eliot; but neither of them could have concluded with his impressiveness an informal lecture on the stars under the night skies with the words, "And yet they are not all worth a single human soul." What would have been a vapid commonplace in another's mouth was from him an unforgettable flash of the greatest truth of human existence. The flash was characteristic; for under the stress of thought illuminated with strong feeling his thoughts were a series of emotional explosions, or, better perhaps, of brilliant lightning flashes.

As is sometimes the case with genius, Dr. Carlisle came to maturity early. Dr. Douglas Southall Freeman says that this was the case with Robert E. Lee, in character at least, in contrast with the less brilliant Washington, who continued to grow in every fine quality to the last.[30] There is little in Dr. Carlisle's utterances of later years superior to the keenness of thought and the moral grandeur of the young Professor Carlisle's inaugural address at thirty as Professor of Mathematics in 1855, except the powerful and broad-visioned address before the Methodist General Conference in 1880. His classes from the first had almost the full benefit of his powers. The Doctor's ideas were profound and brilliant, broad in view and sympathetic in understanding, but confined to a comparatively small range of intellectual interests, always dominated by the moral and religious. From the first there are the same elements: moral and religious convictions; a profound sense of the mystery of existence and the sacredness of human relationships; the conviction that only the Christian way of life by men and nations can solve the world's troubles; the keen, swiftly working intelligence; the electric flash of eloquence. He almost seems to have been born full grown.

Though the Doctor was of profoundly religious character there was in him nothing of the fanatic. He said, for instance, there is no fear that any fact discovered by science can contradict divine truth—a noble statement, but one which might have embarrassed an orthodox churchman on cross examination. He regretted, he said to me, the invidious remarks of President Wightman about the State College in his inaugural address and explained them as natural for a clergyman. Though a profound believer in the benefits of church colleges, he took no part in the fight on the State

---

30. Dr. Freeman writes D. D. Wallace, Sept. 7, 1949, referring to Lee's character, not his mental powers, "I believe Robert E. Lee at twenty-five was in character and all other essential qualities much the same man he was in 1861, but George Washington grew immensely in every fine quality between the time he was twenty-five and the time he assumed command of the Continental Army at forty-two years of age."

institutions. He expressed to me his strong disapproval of the clergy's taking the bread and wine of the communion before the laity as a survival of Romanism; but for the ministry he had the highest respect. Take it as narrow Methodism preference or as the fruit of sage observation as you will, he said to me with earnestness that taking them all in all the Methodist ministers outpreached any others in the world. He was uneasy at seeing Wofford graduates go to Harvard for graduate study for fear of Unitarian influence; but he welcomed to Wofford Harvard's great Unitarian President Emeritus Charles W. Eliot. Dr. Eliot, full of vigor, on his seventy-fifth birthday, March 20, 1909, on a Southern tour, delivered to the Wofford student body and a throng of visitors filling the chapel to overflowing a thrilling address on colleges' endowments and mission. The applause at the close of the address had not ceased when Dr. Carlisle, eighty-four years of age, straight and tall, obviously happy in the presence of intellectual greatness, rose and approached Dr. Eliot, who rose to receive the congratulation. In his splendid organ-like voice, Dr. Carlisle said to Dr. Eliot, who stood facing him, "If figures do not lie, I must have been a sturdy lad who had made his way through the labyrinth of the alphabet and was in the dismal swamp of the multiplication table when you were a babe in your mother's arms. Rejoice, O young man, in thy youth, and let thy heart cheer thee, and may you still bring forth fruit in old age, and at eveningtime may there be light!" As they clasped hands the enthusiasm of the audience went even beyond what it had been a moment before.[31]

Dr. Carlisle, though rejoicing, as by his nature he must, in the presence of intellectual greatness, was too humble in the presence of great men. Speaking of Phillips Brooks, whom he greatly admired, he said, "As I walked beside him, I felt myself a pygmy, mentally as well as physically." That was unjust to himself; for, although Brooks had some things Carlisle did not have, in what they both had he was in no respect Brooks's inferior.[32]

---

31. Dr. Snyder in his *Educational Odyssey* (following the *Spartanburg Herald* of March 21, 1909) and Mr. J. H. Carlisle, Jr., in his manuscript Memories of Wofford College each omit a different clause which the principles of textual criticism lead me to include. The words beginning, "Rejoice, O young man," are a very apt weaving of passages from Ecclesiastes 11: 9; Psalm 92: 14; and Zechariah 14: 7, in which the Carlisle MS. has the advantage of putting "eveningtime," as the Scripture does, instead of "eventide" as the others do. There is strong reason for thinking that Dr. Carlisle's unscheduled speech was put together as he sat during the last part of Dr. Eliot's address. His daughter noticed his ceasing to pay attention toward the last; hence the inference. Dr. Snyder errs in making the date March 21, and the *Wofford College Journal* errs in making the day Friday instead of Saturday.

32. Dr. Carlisle and Dr. (later Bishop) Brooks, both six feet four inches tall, the one slender, the other quite robust, were conversing at Chautauqua, when a lady approached and said, "Oh! Dr. Brooks, will you come over to the chapel this afternoon, where there will be members of our own church, just a little family gathering?" Dr. Brooks replied, "If you mean, madam, that only Episcopalians will be there, I do not care to come, for one of the things that I like about Chautauqua is that all denominations are represented." J. H. Carlisle, Jr.'s, Memories of Wofford College, MS., 165-66.

His excessive modesty shrank from compliments. He got a good reply from Dr. Herman Baer when he asked that very direct gentleman, "What do you do when people say things like that to you?" "Do as you did: say nothing and look foolish," replied Dr. Baer. Dr. Carlisle's modesty and delicate sense of propriety went so far as sometimes to be a hindrance. When he was offered the chairmanship of the Board of Education of the South Carolina Conference he declined; and when protested with that he was making a mistake replied, "I could never consent to be a member of the committee that nominates my own Board of Trustees." Dr. Snyder when later offered the same position did not hesitate to accept it as being a means of serving the college; and, he remarked to me, if Dr. Carlisle had accepted it he would have saved himself some future vexations (alluding doubtless to his seeing the Board of Trustees radically revised under circumstances that deeply pained him).[33]

The Doctor's extreme modesty was evident on the occasion when, in 1895, the alumni, speaking through the first graduate, Samuel Dibble, presented to him a gold watch and chain and a number of books. "Can this be the young student and this the young Professor of forty years ago?" he said with barely restrained emotion in response to the beautiful words of the accomplished Mr. Dibble. He expressed his gratitude for the feelings which prompted the act of his old pupils, and professed his unworthiness of such devotion. He wished, he continued, to ask the pardon of any student to whom he had ever been unjust. But his words were few, in accord with his custom on such occasions. A similar scene with a similar reaction was in 1901 when the students, speaking through one of their number, B. B. Lancaster, presented him with a handsome couch. He was deeply touched, saying that "one who could fittingly respond on such an occasion would be unworthy of the occasion." [34] When on his 79th birthday, a large number of the leading men of the city marched to his house and paid him a beautiful tribute in the words of Stobo J. Simpson, saying that his life had been an inspiration to young and old, he replied that if he had lived here for two hundred years instead of fifty, this experience would have repaid him for it all.[35]

Dr. Carlisle's extreme modesty, so inconvenient to those seeking to write of him today, is illustrated by the sketch, presumably supplied by

33. Dr. Snyder to D. D. Wallace, Sept. 7, 1947. See page 116 above on revision of the Board. Dr. Shipp was a member of his own Board of Trustees from 1859 to 1875.

34. The two incidents are from an article on Dr. Carlisle in the *Wofford College Journal*, Carlisle Memorial Issue of November, 1909. *News and Courier*, June 14, 1895, mentions the books. I witnessed both incidents.

35. J. H. Carlisle, Jr., *op. cit.*, 210-2; *Spartanburg Herald*, May 5, 1904.

himself, in Volume 4, e.g., of *Who's Who in America:* Birth; graduation; marriage; LL.D. degree; dates of Wofford professorship and presidency; editorship of lives of Ascham and Arnold; the Young Astronomer; "only that and nothing more."

Dr. Carlisle was an omniverous reader; but he read for information and serious thought, not primarily for the enjoyment of good literature. His library was notably lacking in "mere literature," if I may use the term. Biography was a favorite, for it depicted character. As his son put it, "Pa was just death on anybody's life." He was an extraordinarily rapid reader, seeming to take in a paragraph at a glance. He loved books, and he loved to lend good books. During a month's stay at Chautauqua he bought a good many volumes. The evening before leaving for home, he met his son on the stairs and complained, "Buddie, I have packed all the books in the trunk, but there is no room for the clothes." [36] Like Erasmus' saying, When I get some money I will buy some books, and then perhaps I will buy some clothes.

Dr. Snyder speaks of Dr. Carlisle's ability to quote exactly conversation between himself and a student in relating to the Faculty circumstances back of cases of discipline. This power of quoting himself was illustrated in connection with an article which he sent the *Southern Christian Advocate* voicing his views, very contrary to those of the editor, on an important matter of church policy. Having neglected to keep a copy of his article, and fearing that the editor might destroy it, he dictated a duplicate to his daughter. When the article was returned unpublished, his son and daughter compared the original with the one he had dictated from memory, and found that they differed in one word. [37]

The matter referred to concerned the conduct of the Book Agents, as they were called, managing the Southern Methodist Publishing House. During the War of Secession Federal forces used and abused the publishing house in Nashville to an extent which the church authority estimated at $495,000. Finally the lower house of Congress passed and sent to the Senate a bill to pay the Book Agents for the church $288,000. Its passage by the Senate was endangered by rumors that E. B. Stahlman, acting as lobbyist, was to receive forty per cent of any sum recovered. The fact was that the Book Agents had signed a contract with Stahlman to pay him thirty-five per cent. Senator Pasco wired to ask if the rumor was true that lobbyist Stahlman was to receive forty per cent of any money that was secured for the church. The Agents wired back, "Story is untrue,

36. J. H. Carlisle, Jr., *op. cit.,* 186.
37. J. H. Carlisle, Jr., to D. D. Wallace.

and you are hereby authorized to deny it." Senator Bate also wired, asking whether Stahlman was to receive "forty per cent or any other fee." The Agents wired Bate, repeating their telegram to Pasco. On this assurance Senator Lodge withdrew his amendment that no one should receive any compensation above $5,000, and, March 8, 1898, the appropriation passed. Stahlman received his $100,800. When the facts became known the church was violently agitated. The Bishops offered, August 26, 1898, to return the money if the Senate considered that they had been deceived into appropriating it. A Senate Committee report of January 9, 1899, unanimously adopted, stated that if the Senate had known of the contract with Stahlman, who, they said, persistently denied that he was to receive anything, the bill would not have passed unless amended so as to prevent such a payment; but that, as the misstatements and concealments of the Book Agents injured the beneficiaries of the fund, and not the United States, no further action should be taken.[38]

To the sensitive soul of Dr. Carlisle, to whom the honor of the church was dearer than life, any dereliction of any clergyman was a sorrow. Even late in life he almost pathetically grasped at any evidence that might show Henry Ward Beecher was innocent in his relations with Mrs. Tilton. The conduct of the Book Agents of his own church was one of the deepest griefs of his life.

Dr. John O. Willson, the editor of the *Southern Christian Advocate,* had refused to allow anything in the organ of the church in South Carolina on the Publishing House matter. Dr. Willson was an able, widely beloved, and devoted believer in his church, but the type that seeks to cure a sore by hiding it with a plaster, a type to which shrewd management appeals more than free thought and free speech. I recall that when I delivered the Founder's Day address at Lander College, of which he was then President, he expressed the fear that my having spoken a paragraph in praise of independent thinking might have a dangerous influence.

Determined to get his views before the South Carolina Conference, and to let the preachers, from whom the facts had been concealed so far as possible by the editor of the *Advocate,* know the true state of the case, Dr. Carlisle, who was a lay delegate to the Conference, went to its meeting at Greenwood, but unfortunately he went too late, entirely without any compelling reason for not being on hand, as anyone with a normal

38. Pamphlet reprinting the committee report, citing *Cong. Record,* Vol. 32, Pt. 1, 493; Alfred M. Pierce, *Giant Against the Sky* (life of Bishop W. A. Candler), 77-79; *Daily Advocate* (of General Conference), May 11, 19, 20, 1902.

amount of political acumen would have been, from the first roll call. It was rumored that he would appear on Thursday to address the Conference; but that day before his arrival Dr. R. A. Child introduced the resolution, which was adopted without debate: Whereas we do not think that Annual Conference resolutions can bring this vexed question to a satisfactory settlement, "Resolved, That we have the utmost confidence in the wisdom and integrity of the constituted authorities of the church and are perfectly willing to leave the whole matter to their godly judgment, feeling that if let alone they will bring the whole matter to an honorable and satisfactory conclusion." The parliamentary clincher was then applied, making it impossible to re-open the question at that Conference.[39]

Dr. Carlisle, having arrived after the resolution had passed, rose on the morning of Saturday, December 10, to speak on a question of personal privilege touching the matter. Bishop Duncan ruled that it would be against all parliamentary law, but that if the Conference insisted, he might state his case. The Conference insisted unanimously, at least without a dissenting vote, though some votes were doubtless given unwillingly under the feeling that refusing the great layman a hearing would not be safe. He proceeded to read the correspondence between himself and Dr. Willson, which led to some sharp exchanges between them on the floor. Dr. Carlisle then read his rejected half column article of about 430 words. It was expressed with great moderation. For the first time in the history of this country, it said, thousands of copies of a public document had been sent out from Washington in which a Senate Committee, after long deliberation, charges high officials of our church with deceiving the Senate in a large, critical financial transaction. Five-sixths of the Tennessee Conference have pronounced the conduct of our Agents "wholly indefensible." Whether from haste, inattention, inexperience, or with purpose, our Agents went dangerously near the line, where intentional concealment becomes intentional deception. It will not be safe for the church to approve that venture actively or passively. "It would have been a lighter calamity to our church if a great flood in the Cumberland River had washed away the foundations of our publishing house and that stately building had fallen into ruins. May the great Head of the Church 'direct, control, suggest.' "

It is known that Dr. Carlisle favored condemning the action of the Agents and returning the money. The reading of his letter was followed

---

39. *Conf. Mins.* 1898, 8, 38, 86. The South Carolina Conference in past years had been quite abundant in offering advice to the church's supreme law making body, the General Conference. It was freely charged (but not by Dr. Carlisle) that the resolution and clincher were rushed through in order to forestall Dr. Carlisle's arrival. This the mover of the resolution denied on the floor.

by such applause as to lead many to think that if it had been heard before the passing of the resolution cited above the vote would have been quite different.[40]

The Doctor was defeated for the time being. The greatest and most devout layman in the whole church had been told what he might say and what he might not say in the official organ of his church; the ministers and laity had been forbidden to know of the facts of a critical problem. But the victory of the suppressers, so adroitly evading the moral issue, was brief. The next Conference, in December, 1899, at last informed of the facts, presuming to assist the "godly judgment" of the "constituted authorities" (constituted by themselves and other Methodists, and not by some external, unquestionable authoritarian absolutism), declared that they deplored the deceptive methods used by the Book Agents, and demanded their resignation.[41] (Rev. Barbee, having been re-elected by the General Conference in the spring of 1898 before the facts were known by the Conference, was refused re-election by the next General Conference in 1902. His character was passed by his own Conference only after he acknowledged that he had done wrong.)

Said the Doctor's brother, Captain John W. Carlisle, "The best proof that the church is a divine institution is that what men have done to it has not been able to kill it." [42]

Doctor Carlisle was cordial in manner, and though many a caller may have bored him, I doubt if he ever froze one out. To him even the humble and ignorant was an object of interest. Though a fluent and gifted talker, he had the knack of drawing out the other person, whether a student returned from the university, a scholar of distinction, a simple craftsman, or a rough mountaineer. For instance, as he waited for the family of his host, he talked with the old Negro coachman, who boasted that he had driven for the family for forty years. Said the Doctor, "Well, Peter, you are getting old now. Are you sure you are driving your horses to the right country?" "That was twenty years ago," said the gentleman relating

---

40. *Spartanburg Herald*, Dec. 10, 1898; *Carolina Spartan*, Dec. 14, 1898.

41. *S. C. Conference Mins. 1899*, 41. Those who are familiar with Dr. Carlisle's abhorrence of profanity (his own strength of language needed no expletives) may imagine his feelings in an interview with Senator B. R. Tillman, who sometimes called on the Doctor. While the Publishing House matter was aflame, the Doctor asked Tillman, "Senator, what do the Senators think about the Book Agents?" Tillman replied, "They think they're a set of damned liars, Doctor." There were two shocks for the Doctor; the opinion of the Senators and the language of the Senator. The Doctor repeated the interview to Dr. Snyder, who repeated it to me.

42. This is remarkably similar to the words of a Roman Catholic man of letters, in reference to the corrupt ages of the church: "I believe that the Catholic Church is divine, and the proof of its divinity I take to be this: that no merely human institution conducted with such knavish imbecility would have lasted a fortnight."—A. J. Toynbee, *Study of History*, Somervel's abridgement, 359, n.

it; "but it put me to thinking, and I am sure that it made of me a better man." The Doctor's innate courtesy was such that never in Faculty meeting or elsewhere would he, as I often heard others do, identify a student whom he was seeking to recall to someone else's recognition by any physical peculiarity, such as "that tall, red headed youth," or "the little fellow who walks with a limp." His aversion to the exposure of the human body was so strong that he disliked even the sleeveless shirt and the pants coming almost to the knees that athletes wore in his later days. "Does calling an indecent suit a gymnasium suit make it decent?" he asked.

Dr. Carlisle was very liberal in his attitude toward Negroes. He said to me one day, "Why can we not meet together in public relations and each go his own way socially?" To his class he expressed disgust at men who prate of the superiority of their race and then place themselves in the most intimate relation on an equality with a Negress. Speaking of the painful contrast between situation and opportunity of the more intelligent Negro, he said, "It would try my Christian character to be an educated colored man."

Dr. Carlisle had his lighter side and told well a humorous story that had a worth while point. One that he enjoyed was concerned with his having been engaged to supply the astronomical data for *The South Carolina Almanac,* long a popular Charleston publication. The first year that he sent in his copy the publisher wrote back reminding him that he had forgotten to predict the weather. He wrote back, of course, that he could not predict the weather; and so the editor supplied the predictions himself, which can right safely be done on the doctrine of averages over a long period of years. The printer, observing that there was no prediction for April 12, sent the office boy to ask what to put. The editor said impatiently, "Oh, put a snow storm." As luck would have it, that year it actually snowed on the 12th of April, and for years, Dr. Carlisle would say with a chuckle, the farmers would insist on having *The South Carolina Almanac* "because," they said, "Professor Carlisle's predictions of the weather are so good."

The Doctor often indulged in his cheerful chuckle; but Dr. A. Mason DuPre told me that he never knew him but once to laugh aloud. DuPre, then a young Fitting School Instructor, had been sitting up for weeks with an ill brother and had neglected to shave. He came up to Spartanburg before the opening of school with a heavy beard. The Doctor himself wore a beard, but not at that age, for he came to Wofford clean shaven as photograph of the old Faculty shows.[43] It was too much; but it must

43. Mr. J. H. Carlisle, Jr., in his MS. of Memories of Wofford College speaks of his father shortly before coming to Wofford as "the clean shaven young teacher."

not be taken for the origin of the future Dean's nickname "Amazing DuPre." The Doctor laughed aloud, and the young instructor took the implied advice and was clean shaven ever afterwards. Dr. Carlisle's son tells us that in reading Mark Twain aloud he laughed until tears ran down his cheeks and had to pass the book to someone else to finish. He read little light literature, however. His son tells us that he never knew his father to read but two novels: Dinah Maria Murlock's (later Mrs. G. L. Craik), *John Halifax, Gentleman,* and George Macdonald's *The Annals of a Quiet Neighborhood,* the latter of which he read aloud to the family.[44]

The Doctor took great satisfaction in possessing what he considered was the only known piece of money that George Washington had ever owned. It was literally a half dollar, i.e., half of a Spanish dollar cut in two with a cold chisel, as was sometimes done to make change before our mint had supplied the public with small coins. Washington paid it for his breakfast as he passed through Chester or Lancaster, S. C., on his trip through the Southern States. It passed through only two hands before it came to James H. Carlisle, who gave it to Wofford College, in whose possession it rests.

Dr. Carlisle has left us an interesting self-criticism. He would sometimes say to his son while they sat on their piazza, "Buddie, if I have made any mistake, it has been that I have stressed character more than scholarship." [45] A few have ventured to say something of the same thing; but it would be more correct if both he and they had said that in stressing character so constantly he had neglected to give enough attention, both for himself and his pupils, to scholarship. I have myself said the same thing, both orally and in the text of this book, long before I saw this statement. The Doctor often emphasized that the two should go together; but certainly in his later years he did not keep them in proper balance.

Nothing is easier than to point out Dr. Carlisle's deficiencies as a college President, or the lack of certain qualities usually possessed by strong men, though men have hesitated to do so because of reverence for his character. The Doctor recognized his limitations and accepted them. They were a part of the man, but they were not the man, and so are a part of the history of Wofford College. But why complain of a diamond because it is not a steel spring?

James H. Carlisle was a genius in righteousness, and in every fiber of his being a gentleman in the highest sense, and even in physical endowment, with his height of six feet four inches, of a majesty of bearing such

44. J. H. Carlisle, Jr., *op. cit.,* 196.
45. J. H. Carlisle, Jr., *op. cit.,* 27.

as one feels a great and good king should have. He was a great spiritual force which stimulated young men to be their best. Inadequately as he used his great powers of intellect, distinguished strangers recognized his greatness when brought into personal contact with him. For instance, President Franklin Carter of Williams College, Mass., said to Miss Virginia Lee McMaster (now Mrs. J. R. Foard) of Columbia, S. C., "The only persons I know in South Carolina are Dr. James Woodrow and Dr. James Carlisle, and both of them are too big for their State." "They are both my cousins," replied Miss McMaster.[46]

Because Dr. Carlisle projected himself into no famous movement or institution and wrote no great book, it was sometimes hard to convince those who had not come into personal contact with him of his greatness. Horace understood the efficacy of the written page: *Exegi monumentum aere perennius.* The injustice to the fame of a great man who erected no such monument is illustrated by Dr. Carlisle's absence from the *Dictionary of American Biography.* At least two persons, one being myself, when requested by the editor to suggest names of South Carolinians, named Dr. James H. Carlisle. By an oversight as the editor wrote me, his name was overlooked, but, he said, it would be included in the supplementary volume to be issued later. When the supplementary volume was being prepared another editor was in charge. I wrote to him of these circumstances, and received in reply the question, What has he done? Not only did I answer to the best of my ability, but so, at my request, did several prominent educators in different States, who urged in the strongest terms the propriety of his being included; but the reply of the editor was that the board had decided that it was not possible to include him as there were so many other names of more importance. This is the only instance I have ever found of anyone's agreeing with Dr. Carlisle that his life ought not to be written, as there was nothing to write, he having been "only a teacher." The opinion of Walter Hines Page was different. When he delivered the commencement address at Wofford in June, 1908, he took occasion to learn all he could, by report and by personal contact, of Dr. Carlisle. In the October, 1908, number of *The World's Work* he wrote:

---

46. Mrs. Foard to D. D. Wallace, Aug. 16, 1949. Rev. James Woodrow (1828-1907), uncle of Woodrow Wilson, was a member of the remarkable group of intellectuals in Columbia closely connected by family ties, the Howes, Wilsons, and Woodrows. He was an outstanding leader in the intellectual history of South Carolina. After earning his Ph.D., at Heidelberg, Germany, he was offered a lectureship there, but preferred to return to his professorship of Natural Science in Oglethorpe University, Georgia. He served the Confederate government in Chemistry, was editor of the *Southern Presbyterian Review* from 1865 to 1885; for many years Professor of Natural Science in Connection with Religion in the Presbyterian Theological Seminary in Columbia, S. C., from which he was forced on account of his teaching of evolution. He was President of the University of South Carolina 1891-7.—*Dictionary of American Biography.*

And who is Dr. Carlyle? A man who went to the college as a teacher of "astronomy and moral science" in 1854, when it was founded, and who has been there ever since, a part of the time as teacher, a part of the time as president, and again as teacher. . . . Doubtless neither philosophers nor astronomers regard him as a great contributor to their departments of learning. Yet it is doubtful whether there be an astronomer or a philosopher at any institution or in any community in our whole land who has exerted so strong an influence upon the young men who have come in contact with him. They do not say that he taught them astronomy or that he taught them philosophy, but they do all bear testimony to his giving them in greater measure than any other man a right adjustment to life and a moral uplift—a kind of influence that the oldest of his pupils, who are now themselves far on in middle life, remember with an affection that has grown since their youth; and throughout the area of the college's influence, men and women say, "We must send our sons to Wofford College because Dr. Carlyle is there. . . ."

Possibly the great business of teaching may get some hint from this simple story.[47]

Though Wofford College was not on the Carnegie Foundation for the Advancement of Teaching, Dr. Snyder secured from the Foundation in 1906 a pension for Dr. Carlisle of $1,050 a year, which, with his small pension from the college (the first it ever granted), made his income slightly larger than it had ever been.[48]

Though Dr. Carlisle's tall figure was of great majesty, particularly when he walked, even in young manhood he possessed little physical strength. Early in his married life his wife asked him to dig some holes for the planting of rose bushes. He came in from the task completely exhausted and never repeated the experiment.[49] Yet his health was practically always good. He was so unwell shortly before and after commencement in 1883 as to need a short rest in the mountains.[50] His only exercise was walking daily, at a slow pace, down street the three-quarters of a mile or more to the book store and back, in whose rear room in those days there took place some informal high discourse among some remarkable men.

At the time of his last illness it happened that the stale old prank had been played, rarely performed at Wofford, of removing the bell clapper. Dr. Snyder told the students in chapel that the old man lying ill missed the accustomed sound, and the clapper was at once replaced. The Doctor remarked, "The old bell is back on the job."

His illness, from his fainting spell on Monday until the end on Thursday,

47. Walter Hines Page in *World's Work*, XVI, 10749-50 (Oct., 1908); reproduced in *Wofford College Journal*, Nov., 1908, 93-94.
48. *Spartanburg Herald*, Oct. 27, 1906.
49. J. H. Carlisle, Jr., *op. cit.*, 197.
50. *Southern Christian Ad.*, June 23, July 7, 1883.

October 21st, 1909, was calm. "What is your profession?" he asked the trained nurse who was brought in. "I am a nurse." "You have a wide field of usefulness before you," he said. On one of the last mornings he asked the time. "Six o'clock," was the reply. Mistaking the gray dawn for the early evening, he said, "The boys will have a long evening to study." Unaware of his surroundings now, he began, in a perfectly natural voice to deliver a lecture to a class, verbatim, says his son, the same as he had made forty or more years before. At times he questioned a student and paused for his answer, and even told a Latin joke on the word nephew. Suddenly the voice ceased, and the teacher, in imagination in his classroom and teaching with his last word, was gone.[51]

Tributes to the great teacher were innumerable. Perhaps none was more understanding than that by Judge Charles A. Woods of the United States Circuit Court of Appeals, his old student of the class of 1872:

What was the source of this power? Dr. Carlisle wrote no great book; he made no great discovery; he took little part in the public councils of the people; he was not foremost in any department of learning; as a college executive he was not without faults. Varying answers to this question will be given. As it seems to me, his power came from three main sources: First, his character, his attaining to a simple, unselfish life without guile, his striving humbly to lead his people to the highest things. This in a strong, aggressive man is the greatest element and source of power. Doubtless there are many other things apparently more useful and powerful; but he made good his belief that it was not the glittering, but the steady and white light that imparts life.

To this character there was added in him the most profound optimism. He had unfailing faith that truth and virtue would in the long run prevail over falsehood and vice. And, what was more important in his influence in inspiring others to strive for righteousness and enlightenment, he was always insistent on the capacity of the average man to take charge of his own heart and mind and elevate himself. More than this, his own convictions were so strong on these subjects and his personal magnetism so great that the least aspiring could hardly come within this sphere of his influence without feeling the chief end of life to be the attainment of the highest will power and its consecration to the acquiring of knowledge and the doing of good.

The third element of his power was eloquence. I do not mean by eloquence merely brilliant expression, polished gesture, rounded periods, or artistic polish. Some of these he had without effort. But his was the eloquence that moved the emotions too deeply to admit of outward demonstration, which carried conviction to the mind and aroused the whole man to the best of aspirations and possibilities. He who could listen and not feel that he had been under the influence of a great human power was indeed poor in spirit." [52]

---

51. J. H. Carlisle, Jr., *op. cit.*, 214-16.
52. C. A. Woods, in Watson's *Carlisle Memorial Volume*, 148-9.

Charles Forster Smith, who had known many great men, said of Dr. Carlisle, "He is the only man I ever knew with whose motives I was always satisfied." Happily we may disagree with that; for there have been men of humbler gifts of equal moral integrity; but the remark is representative of the almost worshipful regard in which he was held. Said others, he was the greatest influence for good in my life. Mr. Ed L. Archer, at the memorial services, Sunday, November 7th, burst out with the words, "Dr. Carlisle showed men what God is like." A bold expression of a rough, strong man, but not words of impiety; for, except as a mighty power, how else can men know God but as righteousness shines through human personality?

CHAPTER XI

PRESIDENT SNYDER'S ADMINISTRATION TO WORLD WAR I, 1902-17

THE SAME day, June 7, 1902, on which the Trustees accepted the resignation of the third President, Dr. James H. Carlisle, they elected by a vote of 11 to 2, immediately made unanimous, as the fourth President of Wofford College, Prof. Henry Nelson Snyder, who since 1890 had been head of the department of English. He was in 1902, 37, having been born in Macon, Ga., January 14, 1865, while his parents were there on account of the duties of his father, Captain Henry Nelson Snyder, in the Quartermaster's Department of the Confederate Army. Thus this scion of distinguished Tennesseean ancestry bore a Georgia label. His mother for two years superintended a Confederate hospital, and was also an historical author. The family saw hard lines back in Nashville after the war; but the perfection of pronunciation and the ease of manners of the Georgia-born Tennesseean were sufficient testimony to his cultural background. At Vanderbilt University he came under the influence of the same men who as very young professors had done so much to open a new era in scholarship at Wofford a few years before, as related in a previous chapter—William M. Baskervill, Charles Forster Smith, and James H. Kirkland. Smith spotted him as good Greek material and turned him into that study. He desired the teaching fellowship in English under Baskervill, which, however, was not available; and so he became teaching fellow assistant in Latin to Dr. James H. Kirkland. In this he lost nothing; for his love for English literature was already established, and he thus secured the exacting and inspiring professional association with another great character and great scholar.

Young Snyder showed his future bent while a university student by winning the oratorical medal and by becoming editor in chief of the Annual. In the latter capacity he had the experience of being hauled up before the Trustees and Faculty on account of an article, the author of which he refused as a matter of honor to reveal, severely criticizing a department of the university. He would have been deprived of his teaching fellowship, to which he had just been appointed, but for the intervention of Chancellor Garland. He for one, he declared, would not be "a party toward

169

having any one of these young gentlemen violate what he might regard as an honorable pledge. There are more important things than printing unfounded attacks on a department of the university, and one of them is to preserve a loyalty to a sense of honor among its students." That settled it.[1]

Professor Snyder's energy and charm as a teacher of English extended into public address, and consequently he soon found himself in such demand as to make him uneasy lest this diversion might impair his further development as a scholar. He found protection against this danger by a year's study in Europe. Leaving the excellent young scholar Olin D. Wannamaker of the class of 1896, who had pursued graduate studies at Vanderbilt University, in charge of his classes, he sailed in September, 1900, and was soon at work at the University of Göttingen. A tour of France, Italy, and England followed a year's intensive study. He almost completed his thesis and intended to return to Germany for his examinations for the Ph.D. degree in the summer of 1903, but this was pushed aside by his election as President of Wofford College.[2]

Simultaneously there came the offer of the presidency of a respectable Middle Western college. This and the possibility of a professorship in Leland Standford were pushed aside, and his long presidency of forty years at Wofford began. Two years later came another invitation to a college presidency. It was then that Dr. Carlisle made to him the notable statement of his own attitude, quoted at page 133 above, i.e., his decision to be a teacher rather than an administrator.

Any man who accepted the presidency of Wofford College in 1902 was obliged to be a different type of President from what Dr. Carlisle had been. To begin with, no man could duplicate Dr. Carlisle, and also the college required more of an administrator than the Doctor was willing, if indeed able, to be. No one ever spoke of "President" Carlisle. The term did not fit him, and would have seemed to diminish his stature. That does not alter the fact that the time had come when there must be a President, at least to a considerable degree, of the modern administrative and business type. Dr. Snyder remarked to me shortly after his election, without the slightest intention of a slur or a boast, that he would be a different kind of President from Dr. Carlisle. Yet he, of course, sought to carry on the Doctor's ideals. Like Dr. Carlisle, he had the gift of public speech, though not the moral fervor overpowering in its intensity; but his facility in meeting varied occasions was even greater. He was, in fact, an almost unrivaled master in the art of speech. There was in his voice a vibrant quality ap-

1. Snyder, *Educational Odyssey,* 43.
2. *Ib.,* 95, 96; Trustee Mins., June 7, 1902.

Henry Nelson Snyder
President, 1902-42
Honorary President
1902-49

Walter Kirkland Greene
President since 1942

Arthur Mason DuPre
First Dean of the College,
1920-40, except 1925-26.
Acting President, 1920-21

pealing to the emotions. His vocabulary at times bordered on the sentimental in the choice of soft, flowing words. I sometimes wondered what he would do if deprived of the use of words such as "sheer"; sheer beauty; sheer greatness; "fruitful" years; "keep faith"; "tossed away in a fever of blinding emotionalism." Not much clanging clash of hammer on anvil. It was a style well suited to its purposes, for it appealed to the emotionalism ready to be stirred in any but the hardened intellectual or the morally indifferent by such a master of the sheer artistry of the spoken word. He understood the moods and capacities of an audience and played upon them as skillfully as a movie producer does through the screen. The presidency of a college like Wofford makes more kinds of demands than does the headship of many colleges or universities; and Dr. Snyder proved that the Trustees were right in guessing that he possessed the needed variety of aptitudes. Taken all in all he proved eminently suited to his task by reason, first, of his well-balanced character, moderation, and tact; second, by his personal influence with the preachers of the Conference; and third, by his skill in keeping the Faculty harmonious.

The new President did not drift. At the first he definitely determined on two rules by which to steer his course, and, if we may anticipate, right well did he follow them. The rules were, he tells us:

"(1) That I would be very economical in applying the privileges of prerogative, and (2) that I would always strive for the golden virtue of patience in my human relations, official and personal."

With the installation of the new President was inaugurated a new relationship between the President and the Trustees. Since the founding of the college it had been the custom for the annual and semi-annual report on the condition of the college to be the report of the Faculty, composed by the President with their criticism and suggestions and rendered by him in their name, though in his later years as the size of the Faculty grew Dr. Carlisle ceased to consult them on the annual report. The old custom was now frankly abandoned for the general modern practice of the report's being the report of the President, without consultation with the Faculty. Also the Trustees required the new President to meet with them, thus making him a member of the Board without vote. (President Shipp had been a regularly elected member of the Board.) Along with this went the devolving of responsibility for the operation of the college upon the President to a degree not existing under Dr. Carlisle. The fact that the system has become virtually universal is sufficient testimony of its inevitability. Dr. Snyder did not, however, entirely give up his teaching, but in order to keep

171

in touch with student life taught one or more classes throughout his administration.[3]

Having sufficiently introduced the new President to those not privileged to know him for themselves, let us glance at the college when he assumed its leadership. Physically much needed to be done. Dr. Carlisle was indifferent to physical conditions. Absorbed in thought, he would eat until satisfied from whatever dish was near him, or even point to what he desired without interrupting his ideas to speak a word. The deterioration of his house was serious—125 broken or cracked window panes out of about 330; sunken floors, so that in the dining room one might in one corner ride up and down like a child upon a joggling board. With perfect content, he would remark, as he looked out over the campus from his front porch, "We should not complain. Only a millionaire could afford to live in a park like this." Bare earth paths led before the residences to the main building. In 1892 or '93 Professor Pritchard, with his class in surveying, marked out the walk from the railroad end of the campus out to Church Street in an accurately surveyed parabola, on which Treasurer and Business Manager J. K. Davis and Applied Mathematics Prof. E. H. Shuler later constructed the present cement paved walks. The campus was so unlighted that even a resident might get lost at night in the heavy darkness of the forest of pines. Prof. D. A. DuPre was planting the beautiful water oaks and elms that have taken the place of many of the pines as they fell before storms or were otherwise removed. Mr. Davis has carried the improvement still farther, including roadway pavement, and, to trespass beyond our chronological limits, President Greene has carried the process notably further.

President Snyder was sparing in his allotment of money for physical improvements, for his principle was to put his limited resources into teachers and teaching instead of parks and parking. It is impossible to doubt that at the time his distribution was wise.

In the summer of 1902 the college chapel was entirely done over and the entire main building was equipped with steam heat and electric lights. The remade chapel added greatly to the comfort of audiences, especially for the Lyceum entertainments during the winter months; for the large stoves that had for some years been used were both unsightly and ineffective. The wonder is that only once, so far as I know, had a classroom caught on fire from that system of heating. In 1903, through the generosity of Rev. S. A. Nettles, the Y.M.C.A. hall was entirely refitted. Bishop W. W. Duncan

---

3. Snyder, *Educational Odyssey,* 198-9.

was thanked in June, 1902, for improvements at his own expense on several of the Faculty houses.[4]

On assuming the Presidency Dr. Snyder found the practice of members of the Board of Trustees borrowing from the college, always, of course, on excellent security. It will be recalled that at the very first the Trustees had made loans to two Professors and at least one Trustee. Apparently this had not again been practiced until about the 1900's. President Snyder was warned that if he criticized it he would "get in bad" with Bishop Duncan, the Chairman, for both he and his son and his brother were borrowers. On the contrary, when he objected to this as bad practice, the Bishop said heartily, "You are right and it must be stopped." The loans were promptly paid and the practice was at an end.[5]

An advance of great importance for the teaching of science was brought about through the action of the head of that department. Prof. D. A. DuPre was of the class of 1869 and an intimate friend of Mr. John B. Cleveland of that class. They often dined together and talked of old times and of the future of the college. Prof. DuPre believed that with the aid of Dr. Carlisle, for whom Mr. Cleveland entertained a deep respect and affection, Mr. Cleveland could be persuaded to give the college a science hall. Said Dr. Carlisle, relating it to his son, "I said to Professor D. A. DuPre, if you will write the reasons why Wofford needs a science hall, I will write Mr. J. B. Cleveland and tell him why he should give it." [6] The joint letter was written. The result is recorded in the following reply:

Spartanburg, S. C., October 31, 1902.

Dr. James H. Carlisle,
Prof. D. A. DuPre,
Wofford College,
Spartanburg, S. C.

My dear Sirs:

It is my intention to build on the Campus, site to be selected by you, a Hall to be devoted to Science, and present same to Wofford College.

I have requested Prof. DuPre to take charge of the matter and get plans and specifications. He told me this morning that plans had been virtually decided upon, and I now authorize you to make necessary contracts in order to have

4. Trustee Mins., June, 1902; *Conf. Mins.*, 1902, 28; Cat., 1901-2, 31.
5. H. N. Snyder to D. D. Wallace, Jan. 30, 1948; *Trustee Minutes.*
6. J. H. Carlisle, Jr., *Memories of Wofford College*, MS., 66.

the work completed as soon as practicable, though I presume nothing much can be done before Spring.

Yours respectfully,

Jno. B. Cleveland.[7]

Mr. Cleveland had been elected a Trustee in 1900, and remained on the Board until his resignation in 1914. He was for many years the outstanding citizen of Spartanburg in his interest and help in civic movements. The value of the Science Hall has been put down in official reports as $25,000; but Mr. Cleveland never allowed the cost to be known nor consented to allow it to bear his name. It was characteristic of his modesty. On one occasion his intimate friend Mr. Alf Moore expressed surprise at his casual allusion to his having been offered an honorary degree by the University of South Carolina, which he had declined on the ground that he was not a scholar and deserved no such distinction. "I never heard of that, Mr. Cleveland. Did you ever tell anybody about it?" said Mr. Moore. "Well," replied Mr. Cleveland, "I *might* have mentioned it to my wife." [8]

Along with this enlargement of the physical facilities for scientific studies there was added to the ever faithful, industrious D. A. DuPre the energetic young Coleman B. Waller, A.B. from Wofford in 1892 and Ph.D. from Vanderbilt in 1902. He was teaching mathematics at Clemson when invited to Wofford in 1903, and before taking up his work here in chemistry and biology prepared himself further by a year's study at Johns Hopkins. Ingenious in the devising of apparatus, clear and attractive as a classroom lecturer, quick in repartee, an active church worker and citizen, a delegate to the General Conference of the Methodist Church in 1914, he was possessed of a natural ability which, with the necessary labor, would have won him distinction; but the lightning that would have made him a very great scientist never seemed to strike.

The next building that rose on the campus, the Whitefoord Smith Library, was made possible by the bequest of $10,000 by Miss Julia Smith, the daughter of our first Professor of English Literature—appropriately named for the cultured scholar and gifted preacher who began to teach at Wofford in the spring of 1856. Here again Prof. D. A. DuPre was responsible for a valuable addition to the college's resources. Miss Smith said to Professor DuPre, the intimate friend of her family, whom

---

7. Letter in possession of Mrs. Helen DuPre Moseley. Dr. Snyder writes in his *Educational Odyssey*, 160: "Then I knew that to do its work effectively Wofford must have two buildings— a library building and a science building. . . . Providence gave the new president a good start. Through the influence of his predecessor and the professor of natural sciences, an alumnus, a classmate of the latter, was easily persuaded to furnish the science building." As we shall later see, Prof. D. A. DuPre was responsible also for the securing of the library building.

8. Mr. Moore related the incident to Mr. J. W. Norwood, who repeated it to me.

174

Whitefoord Smith Library

she made the executor of her will, that she desired to bequeath $10,000 for some memorial to her father. Professor DuPre suggested that the most fitting monument would be a library building for the college, and urged Miss Smith's friend Mrs. W. A. Rogers to re-enforce his arguments. The result was the bequest of $10,000 to Wofford College for the erection of the Whitefoord Smith Library.[9] To this sum President Snyder persuaded the Trustees to add $10,000, which made possible the erection of a library adequate for the next thirty years, and then the finest building on the campus. It has been doubled in size, in still more excellent physical form in 1949, as part of President Greene's plans for Wofford expansion.

Before the construction of the Whitefoord Smith Library the college library was located in the large room immediately to the east of the chapel, and as the number of volumes increased, spread into the recitation room to the east of that. The Whitefoord Smith Library was opened to students January 3, 1910. The formal opening, with suitable exercises in the chapel, occurred February 24, 1910.[10]

We may note here that the house immediately to the west of the DuPre house and now occupied by President Greene was built in 1911 under an arrangement with Dr. C. B. Waller by which he paid part of the cost, on condition that the college might at its option repay him and assume complete control.[11] The large three story President's house of the original plant stood south of Carlisle Hall. It was sold along with a strip of land constituting part of the right of way, to the Carolina, Clinchfield and Ohio Railroad. It had already been seriously damaged by its proximity to the Southern Railway and suffered additionally from the nearer tracks of the Clinchfield and after a few years was condemned and torn down. The infirmary, just west of Carlisle Hall, was the residence of Prof. David Duncan and later successively of Professors Woodward, Gamewell, A. M. DuPre, and Salmon. It was taken for an infirmary when the government took over the college in World War II, the large expense involved being a donation to the college in 1943 by Drs. S. O. and H. S. Black.

In 1933 the children of Rev. James W. Kilgo, D.D., of the class of 1881, as a memorial to him, donated $1,000 for constructing in the library a large fireproof vault for the use of the South Carolina Conference Historical Society and Wofford College for the preservation of the irreplaceable manuscripts of the Conference, etc.[12] Without injury to internal arrange-

9. Mrs. Helen DuPre Moseley to D. D. Wallace, June 27, 1949. Miss Julia Violetta Smith was born in Columbia, S. C., October 3, 1842, and died in Spartanburg, S. C., January 10, 1906.—Gravestone.
10. *Wof. Col. Jour.*, Jan., 1910 (erroneously dated December, 1909), 228; March, 1910, 347.
11. Trustee Mins., June 5, 1911.
12. *Tr. Mins.*, June 1, 1934.

ment or any effect on outward appearance the vault was built under the southwestern end of the main reading room. Using the heavy external walls of the library for three of its sides made possible its construction with the available funds.

The commencement exercises of June, 1904, were unlike any either before or after, for they consisted of the celebration of the first half-century of the life of the college. A personal invitation was sent to every discoverable former student. Incidentally, this afforded me an opportunity to observe Dr. Carlisle's remarkable memory. I was assigned the task of taking the original college register from the beginning and asking the Doctor to locate the residence in 1904 of every man as I called his name. Often of course, he had lost track of places of residence; but so rarely as to be incredible did he fail instantly to remember the man. The joyous occasion brought a flock of alumni, members of the Conference, and other friends. Between seventy-five and a hundred preachers were present, including every Presiding Elder, as we then called District Superintendents, in the Conference. As then usual, the gymnasium exhibition and Junior debate occupied the evening hour at 8:30 P.M. Friday and Saturday. Junior class exercises were held on the campus Saturday afternoon. Sunday morning, June 5, the kingly and eloquent Bishop Charles B. Galloway preached the baccalaureate sermon. Sunday at 8:30 P.M. the beloved President Emeritus James H. Carlisle, as for so many years before, gave his annual address to the Senior class, using as his subject the Sunday school lesson of the day, this time, as he treated it, Pilate's Dilemma— the tragedy of a man's acting on the lower instead of the higher motive. Monday morning President Ira B. Remsen of Johns Hopkins University spoke on the History of Laboratories at the "dedication" of the John B. Cleveland Science Hall. Bishop W. W. Duncan of the class of 1858 was scheduled to speak Monday night on Wofford College, Fifty Years of History, but a torrential rain, accompanied by wind that tore branches from trees, caused his address to be postponed to Tuesday morning, when both he and Dr. Charles Forster Smith of the class of 1872 spoke, the latter on the Making of a Scholar. Tuesday night in the college chapel, as was the custom until 1915, Rev. R. D. Smart of the class of 1868 delivered the alumni oration. The alumni then adjourned to the banquet in the dining room of Converse College, the attendance being too large for any dining room on Wofford Campus, Carlisle Hall of 1912 not then having been built. The speeches, the principal ones having been prepared beforehand, were of such quality as to make it an occasion to remember. Chancellor Kirkland (1877) spoke on The College in Relation to Education;

176

Judge Charles A. Woods, of 1872, on The College in Politics, in which he powerfully denounced lawlessness, particularly lynching, a murderous assault upon the State itself; Bishop Galloway on Wofford and her New Endowment; for the alumni resolved at this commencement to raise an endowment of $100,000 for the college. The incident that stood out above all others to my mind was Bishop Galloway's almost impassioned declaration, "I declare, as prophet, priest, and king in my own household, that I will not send a child of mine to a Methodist institution unless it is equipped to give him the education that he needs." President Snyder closed with a talk well summarizing the significance of the occasion. On Wednesday the 8th eleven of the graduating class of twenty-two delivered their speeches, and Chancellor Kirkland delivered the baccalaureate address on Wofford's progress and her imperative need for enlarged equipment and increased endowment. There were receptions in the literary society halls Friday, Saturday, Monday, and Tuesday nights from ten to twelve.[13]

Turning our attention to the subject of finance, we note at about the turn of the century two movements of the same character and purpose which originated separately, but soon fused into one. The first was more than nationwide in scope; the second, the Wofford College aspect of the larger movement. "The Twentieth Century Movement" began in England in 1898, when Robert W. Perks, a member of Parliament and a leading Wesleyan, proposed at his church's conference that year at Hull that they should seize the psychological moment of the coming of a new century to inspire their members to raise a million guineas for religion and education. It was adopted with enthusiasm. Not only the idea, but the essential methods of organization, quickly spread to Methodists throughout the world and to other denominations as well. The rolls of contributors were to be signed and preserved, under the slogan "A million guineas from a million Methodists." In the Southern Methodist Church the movement took the direction of strengthening the colleges by adding to their resources $1,500,000.[14]

The South Carolina Conference took upon itself in 1898 the responsibility for the share, i.e., $100,000, assigned it to be raised for the Twentieth Century Education Fund. By December, 1899, one-third of the amount had been subscribed.[15] The Trustees of Wofford College, in an article signed by the entire Board, in the *Southern Christian Advocate* of June 21, 1900, appealed to the Methodists of the State to raise the $100,000 assessed

---

13. *Wofford Catalogue,* 1904-5; *Charleston News and Courier* reports of commencement. Dr. Carlisle's printed address is bound in the college's file of catalogues.
14. Stephen J. Herben in *Chautauquan,* XXXI, 16 (April, 1900).
15. *Conf. Mins.,* 1899, 22.

against them by January 1, 1901. The Conference Board of Education recommended in 1904 that in dividing funds not specifically assigned Wofford and Columbia Colleges should share equally. Along with the effort to raise the $100,000 assigned to the South Carolina Conference as its share of the Twentieth Century Education Fund went the effort to add a sum totaling $100,000 to the endowment of Wofford College. The Conference expressed its enthusiastic support of both movements. Wofford did not rely entirely upon the organized plans which the preachers were directed to take in each charge, but put her own representatives into the field. The task was at first laid upon President Snyder, Prof. John G. Clinkscales, and Rev. W. A. Rogers; but September 10, 1904, Rev. R. A. Child, D.D., was employed as Financial Agent for this special purpose. Furman, it was urged, had just raised $125,000. Surely the Methodists, though less numerous, could be relied upon to raise $100,000 to honor the college's semi-centennial.[16]

The plan worked out by Dr. Snyder was as follows: He would deliver an address, often two, on a Sunday in some church or churches on the need of the college for the support of the church, and the church's need for the services of the college. He would then leave Dr. Child to solicit subscriptions in the community during the next week. The next Sunday the same program was initiated in another community, and so on throughout the State. By the end of a year subscriptions totaled $103,000. The General Education Board of New York City offered to give $25,000 if the college raised $100,000. In addition there soon came the legacy of Miss Julia Smith of $10,000 for building a library to the memory of her father, Dr. Whitefoord Smith. Dr. Snyder approached Andrew Carnegie in the hope that his generosity to libraries would prompt him to add an amount sufficient to erect a library building adequate to the needs of the college as $10,000 could not do. Carnegie ignored the reference to the library, but offered to contribute $20,000 when the contributions being raised for the endowment reached $90,000 "in cash or the equivalent."

But the goal was not yet quite in sight, and the President was racking his brain as to where the lacking $10,000 would come from. Without warning he received a telephone call from Mr. Ed Archer to call at the shabby little office that he maintained in town; for Mr. Archer was a farmer living about three miles to the northeast of the city on a place which he had converted from barren red hills to one of the most productive spots in the county. That was his gospel—his faith as shown by his works. He had

16. *S .C. Conf. Mins.,* 1903, 30, 17; *Trustee Mins.: Wof. Col. Journal,* January, 1904, 188-91, reproducing appeals by Chairman W. W. Duncan and Editor W. R. Richardson from *So. Christian Ad.*

been called to preach when a young man, but his voice had failed him, and plunged him into rebellious despair. He talked it over with the Lord, and the Lord told him that he had the gift of making money; that is your field of service. He became an apostle of better farming, education, and a productive, practical Christianity, utterly intolerant of laziness and incompetence.

Would $5,000 help you? he asked Dr. Snyder. Would it! The next morning came another telephone call. Would $5,000 more help? asked Mr. Archer. With his characteristic thrift, Edgar Lycurgus Archer of the class of 1871 stipulated that no Financial Agent should receive any commission of his ten thousand, for no Agent had had anything to do with getting it. Trustees, Nov. 22, 1909, thanked Mr. Archer for his gift of $10,000, and Dr. Child at same time is recorded as waiving his right to any commission on it.[17] And so the campaign wound up with a larger success than had been even planned for.[18]

We must not suppose that the consummation of the semi-centennial drive for adding $100,000 to the endowment came so quickly as the rapid narrative above might be taken to indicate. It is one thing to take subscriptions; it is another to collect the money. June 4, 1910, the endowment stood at $137,494.78, instead of approximately $60,000 when Dr. Snyder became President in 1902.[19] But by December, 1910, only $70,000 had been collected for the movement launched in January, 1904. There remained $24,000 of past due notes and $15,000 of notes not yet due.

A pressing need of the first decade of the twentieth century was for a large dormitory to accommodate the increasing number of students. For awhile the Trustees sought to meet the need by building cheap two story cottages; but the demand outgrew these, though most are still in use for one purpose or another, but not now as student dormitories. Enrollment in the year 1899-1900 was 143. With a few set-backs due to hard times or the elevation of entrance standards, it grew in 1907-8 to 287 and in 1913-14 to 334. The old custom of every member of the graduating class delivering a speech, continued through 1902, became a burden to even a patient commencement audience. In 1903 nine spoke and twenty were excused. In 1905 ten out of twenty-nine spoke, and in 1910 only one. Later two were selected, one by the class and one by the Faculty, until in 1944 only one spoke, and after that the present plan was adopted of having no student to speak.

As the number of students grew the college faced two alternatives: either

17. S. C. Conf. Mins., for 1909, p. 26.
18. Snyder, *Educational Odyssey*, 162-9.
19. *Educational Odyssey*, 162.

it must have increased resources, secure more quarters and a larger teaching force, or it must limit the number of students. In 1908 Financial Agent Child had virtually finished taking pledges for the $100,000 addition to the endowment and was seeking $50,000 for a new dormitory.[20] The need for enlarged eating facilities was almost as pressing. The old Wightman Hall, occupying the large ground floor room entered through the door in the eastern tower, called in later years College Hall, with its kitchen in the yard, ended with June, 1908, and its dining room was fitted up as a classroom for Dr. Carlisle and Dr. Snyder, Dr. Carlisle's recitation room having been at their request given as their hall to the Carlisle Literary Society, organized preliminarily October 26 and formally November 4, 1905.[21]

Carlisle Hall was the answer to both the need for a dormitory and the need for better boarding facilities. Its genesis was an enthusiastic meeting of the alumni at commencement. Considerable subscriptions were offered on the spot. Ed Archer suggested that the dormitory be called Carlisle Hall, and so it was by unanimous consent. Ground was broken for the building November 6, 1911. Toward the estimated cost of $50,000, without furnishings, the Trustees had $15,000 in cash and $10,000 in notes and a loan of $25,000.[22] It was opened for use in September, 1912, especially for Freshmen and Sophomores, fitted up for 160 tenants and for 200 in the dining room.[23] After a few years, the cottages back of the college being no longer used for student dormitories, students of all classes were placed in Carlisle Hall. From the first the Hall was under a system of student government so far as conduct was concerned, but of course without being exempted from the regular authority of the Faculty or Discipline Committee.

1911 was a good year, during which there was added to the resources of the college $48,724.66, a larger amount than in any year since its founding, said the Trustees. This consisted of the payment of $20,000 by Andrew Carnegie, his exacting conditions as to actual collection of $90,000 as a prerequisite having at last been met; $8,125 from the General Education Board, who, less exacting in conditions, had previously contributed a large part of their conditional $25,000 pledge of 1907, $12,500 collected by Financial Agent R. A. Child, and $8,099.66 collected toward the library building.

To conclude this summary, when the First World War broke out in

20. S. C. Conf. Mins., 1908, 29.

21. *Wofford College Jour.*, Oct., 1908; *Carlisle Soc. Mins.*

22. *S. C. Conf. Mins.*, 1911, 31. Mrs. Preston Brooks Allen made a considerable contribution and desired the building to be called by the name of her husband (January 16, 1856-March 8, 1901), whose portrait and a tablet to whom were placed in the large lobby, called the Allen Room.—*Trustee Minutes*, Nov. 22, 1909.

23. *Wof. Cat.*, 1911-12, 36; *Wof. Col. Jour.*, Oct., 1912, 42.

James H. Carlisle Memorial Hall

1914, the endowment had reached $188,154, and the debt of the college, incurred mainly in the erection of Carlisle Hall, stood at $51,846.[24]

Intellectual and moral ideals are the ultimate justification of colleges; but nevertheless the financial foundation for their work is essential. Money is a mighty power in education. Says Dr. Snyder in his *Educational Odyssey:* "It is clear enough that these two boards, the General Education Board and the Carnegie Foundation, together with the initial Duke benefactions to Trinity College at Durham, N. C., and the Candler millions to Emory in Atlanta, started reforms destined to change the whole face of Southern education and to affect permanently the entire structure of Southern life, if education possesses the potent force attributed to it." [25] The church was aware of the need, part of the proof of which is the movement for increased educational resources during the first decade of the twentieth century which we have been tracing.

June 13, 1914 (to look a little forward), Dr. Snyder read to the Board of Trustees the offer, on certain conditions, of the General Education Board of New York to donate $33,000 to the college, an offer which the Trustees accepted with thanks. Dr. Snyder's close touch with the leaders in educational and eleemosynary foundations was a source of very considerable benefits of this kind. We may remark, too, that his constant and harmonious relations with the members of the Conference gave him great influence in shaping the church's educational policy. He was soon a member and for long the chairman of the Board of Education of his Conference, which nominates the members of the Trustees of the various church schools, and was allowed in fact to name his own Trustees. He succeeded, of course being aided by better times, in having the Conference greatly increase the amount of the educational collection.

Restless discontent with the presence of Greek letter fraternities had long smoldered in the college before it became a really troublesome issue. Dr. Carlisle disliked any system which put a formal badge of distinction, other than of a necessary official nature, on certain individuals. There are a certain number of members of the South Carolina Conference, he would say, who by common consent stand out above others; but what would be the feeling of their fellow preachers if these men were to organize themselves into an exclusive secret club, with a badge? With his habitual moderation he never went beyond quiet admonitions calculated to prevent presumptuous conduct.

The democratic swing of the times and some indiscreet conduct on the

24. *S. C. Conf. Mins.,* 1910, 33; 1911, 31; 1914, 38; *Trustee Mins.,* Nov. 22, 1909; *S. C. Conf. Mins.,* 1909, 26.
25. Page 183.

part of fraternity men brought matters to a crisis early in President Snyder's administration. College politics offered a field for organization, trading, and plotting ("cliquing," it was called) by which fraternities sought to get the most honors for their members, or by mutual agreement to obtain at least an equitable share. In this situation there arose several non-fraternity leaders of an aggressive egalitarianism and, doubtless, a certain amount of unsatisfied ambition. Several were of decided ability and determination, and in time organized the non-fraternity students into a group to contend for their rights, and for the abolition of the fraternities.

In June, 1903, the Trustees received petitions both from the anti-fraternity men and from the fraternities, the petitions supported by arguments by Mr. W. C. Owen and Mr. L. Q. Crum, respectively, but on account of the importance of the issues involved, postponed action. The anti-fraternity men were organized as the Philanthropeans. Pending action it was ordered that neither a fraternity nor an anti-fraternity organization should initiate any student until he had been in college for a year; and moreover the Board reserved the right, on the recommendation of the Faculty, to abolish without further notice any organization considered hurtful to the college or its members. Agitation continued, and feeling became so inflamed as to threaten riot, as indeed nearly occurred one night when members of the opposing groups met on the bridge on Church Street over the railroad. The fraternities were finally excluded, not on the merits of the abstract question whether fraternities are good or bad organizations on a college campus (for the members of the Board of Trustees all along preferred fraternities, as men who had themselves attained distinction and remembered the ties of college days and so had no aversion to the system), but because life on the campus was becoming intolerable under the barely suppressed feelings of hostility. The Trustees, June 11, 1906, following the advice of the Faculty, unanimously resolved that no secret organization was to be allowed at the college after the beginning of the next academic year, but that Sophomores might be initiated before that date, as the rule of 1904 had almost guaranteed that right by inference by forbidding the initiation of any student until he had been in college one year. The fraternities then in the college were Kappa Alpha (organized here in 1869), Chi Psi (1869), Chi Phi (1871), Sigma Alpha Epsilon (1885), Pi Kappa Alpha (1891), and Kappa Sigma (1894). In 1904 their active members numbered, 8, 8, 9, 7, 9, and 14 respectively, while the Philanthropeans (the anti-fraternity order organized in 1899) numbered 48.[26] Thus 53% of the student body stood in organized hostile array.

26. *Aurora* (Wofford Annual) of 1904.

Human nature (and no less college boy nature) being what it is, the enforcement of this prohibition was troublesome. Repeatedly announcements of the rule were made from the chapel rostrum. In June, 1911, and 1912, students petitioned the Trustees unsuccessfully for the readmission of fraternities. Rumors of sub-rosa chapters became so rife that a Faculty committee consisting of the President and two Professors were appointed January 27, 1913, to investigate. March 17 they reported that they had made a long and careful investigation of social conditions among the students. Lengthy discussion followed, but no action.[27] As a special admonition there was published in the April, 1913, number of the *Wofford College Journal* Faculty resolutions on the subject to the following effect: Whereas the Trustees have on June 11, 1906, unanimously resolved that there should be no fraternities at Wofford, the Faculty resolve (1) that all such organizations must be disbanded; (2) that any group wishing to form any organization must submit to the Faculty a list of the members, with the object of the organization and the conditions of membership; (3) that no organization shall be permitted which administers a pledge or oath, has formal initiation ceremonies, or has direct or indirect connection with any other college; (4) if after one week any organizations are found not abiding by these rules, they will be treated as violations of college law; and (5) any student initiated into a fraternity during his college course will be treated as a violator of college law.

Soon rumor developed into certainty, which necessitated one of the most painful disciplinary incidents in the history of the college. Nine students, it developed, had gone to Columbia and had been initiated into the Kappa Alpha fraternity by Rho chapter of the order at the University of South Carolina, thus reviving Wofford's Delta chapter. When called one by one before the faculty each acknowledged without equivocation or apparent sense of wrong what they had done. There was no possible course but to require their withdrawal from college, as was done, November, 1913. The incident was the more regrettable as they were all young men of good character and almost all of them of excellent scholastic standing. W. C. Bethea, A. S. Calvert, R. K. Carson, Jr., E. B. Gray, L. A. Grier, and J. P. Wharton were Seniors; C. D. Gray, D. P. Sanders, and J. W. Summers were Juniors. All the nine went to Trinity College, N. C., and in due course all except Sanders took their degrees. Some of the families and friends of the disciplined students bitterly resented the Faculty's taking the action which was thus forced upon them; but in time reason and goodwill asserted

---

27. *Faculty Minutes*. The authority for all statements in this connection is the Faculty Minutes except where otherwise stated.

themselves. A movement for their reinstatement, largely managed by Mr. Luther K. Brice of the class of 1914, was begun. The Faculty concurred, and accordingly the Trustees voted, May 29, 1937:

The Board of Trustees approves the action of the Faculty in re-instating certain students who were suspended from the college in November, 1913, and, on the basis of the work done at Trinity College, confers upon them the degree of A.B. from Wofford College. This action was taken at the request of the Class of 1914, and with the assurance from the Class that such action would be welcomed by each of the former students involved.

From that time the names of the eight who had graduated at Trinity were included in the rolls of their respective classes as published in the list of Wofford alumni.

But to return to the chronological order, which we have violated in order to bring the above case to its ultimate conclusion. October 13, 1915, the Faculty was called upon to consider what, it developed, was a still more serious situation. A Faculty committee reported that a group of students had formed themselves into the Zeta Phi Club. All but one, or possibly two, of the eight acknowledged that they knew that they were violating college law, and they acknowledged, generally, that they had heard the announcements in chapel of the rule against secret fraternities. October 18th Mr. W. G. Ramseur of the Senior class presented before the Faculty a paper from other social clubs on the campus. There were six, with a membership of from five to eleven members, making a total of 49 men who thus openly acknowledged their status as violators of college law, in addition to the eight Zeta Phis. At two that day, said the representative, Mr. Ramseur, they had met and each had appointed two men to represent their cause, with full power to act. Fearing that the Zeta Phis might be severely dealt with, all desired to receive the same treatment as equally guilty as might be meted out to the Zeta Phis. The organizations began some two years ago. They had their badges and did not conceal them, and had constitutions. They had now disbanded, had put aside their badges, and had pledged themselves not to organize again. As acknowledged violators of college law, they only asked for mercy, and for the reinstatement of fraternities.

The Faculty ruled that, whereas the Student Honor System, with the approval of the Faculty, had three years before taken over the enforcement of the law against fraternities, all information in possession of the Faculty should be turned over to them for action. "After long deliberation," the Honor System Council reported, "the Honor System Council has decided to ask the Faculty to deal as leniently as possible under the circumstances with the boys who have been found guilty of violating the college rule concerning fraternities and secret organizations, at the same time, however, to administer justice. The Council believes that a committee consisting of nine men is not competent to render a decision upon such a serious matter in which so many men are involved."

The matter had passed beyond the bounds of an ordinary case of discipline. The Faculty voted that the Trustees be requested to meet with them during the coming session of the Upper South Carolina Conference in Spartanburg in December to go over the entire question of fraternities. Pending that they ruled October 22, 1915, as follows: That in view of (1) the report of the Honor Council, (2) of the voluntary confession of the members of the various organizations, (3) of their pledge as gentlemen that they have disbanded and will remain disbanded, (4) of the whole history of the question of secret organizations, and of the fact that it is now pending before the Trustees and the Faculty and will be finally settled in a few weeks, the matter rests, awaiting such action.

The joint meeting of Trustees and Faculty took place in the Carlisle Society Hall, in which the members of the Faculty were asked severally to express their views. Some emphasized the peace that had prevailed on the campus in contrast with the bitter rivalries that had existed for several years before the exclusion of the fraternities; some favored fraternities on the merits of the question, and others considered that experience had proved the impossibility of combatting the strong tendency of youth in that direction. Better, these held, would be the frank recognition of the organizations, with regulations to guard against abuses, than the undermining of law and good feeling by a succession of secret moves and occasional drastic discipline. The Trustees rescinded their prohibition, and the Faculty, December 17, 1915, after prolonged discussion, adopted the following rules:

There shall be no chapter houses, either owned or rented.

The names of all members must be submitted by each fraternity to the Faculty.

No student shall be initiated until he has been in college for at least five months.

The place of meeting must be approved by the Faculty.

Every fraternity member must sign a pledge that he will abide by the rules of the college on fraternities, and that he will act courteously toward all fellow students.

Several of the old chapters were revived, but two of the oldest and strongest, Chi Psi (1869) and Chi Phi (1871), declined to re-establish their chapters. The latter constituted a loss in traditional and sentimental values; for many alumni were drawn to the college by love for their old fraternities as well as by their distinctly college loyalty.

In October, 1949, there existed at Wofford seven traditional Greek letter college fraternities, the chapters of which are members of the Pan-Hellenic Council, being the following in the order of the dates of the organization of the chapters at Wofford: Kappa Alpha (1869), Sigma Alpha Epsilon (1885), Kappa Sigma (1894), Pi Kappa Phi (1911), Delta Sigma Phi (1916), Lambda Chi Alpha (formerly Theta Kappa Nu of 1926, merged with Alpha Chi Alpha in 1939), Alpha Sigma Phi (1940; Alpha Kappa Pi of 1940 until merged with Alpha Sigma Phi in 1946). Pi Kappa Alpha was re-instituted at Wofford in 1951.

Though they are not Greek letter fraternities in the usually accepted sense, a number of organizations with Greek letter names exist on the campus, most of them intercollegiate, which, in addition to others not announcing themselves in Greek, illustrate how the modern college student is enmeshed with organizations. There may be a few besides the following.

A single date indicates the time of introduction at Wofford; a second date, if any, the time of its disappearance. As a matter of fact, several besides those indicated may be for the time being at least inactive:

Block W., for athletes of distinction.
Senior Order of Gnomes, consisting of twelve outstanding Seniors (1915).
International Relations Club; men of scholarly distinction interested in foreign affairs (1922).
Chi Beta Phi, honorary scientific fraternity (1925). Inactive.
Sigma Upsilon, honorary English literature fraternity (1926). Inactive.
Blue Key, national organization fostering scholarship (1928).
Delta Phi Alpha, German scholarship fraternity (1929).
Scabbard and Blade, fostering distinction in military studies (1928).
Student Christian Association (successor to the Y.M.C.A.) (1938).
Pi Gamma Mu, Social science club (1939).
Ministerial Union (1940).
Phi Beta Kappa, distinguished scholarship fraternity; Beta of South Carolina installed at Wofford 1941.
Pre-medical Society (1946).
Spanish Club (1946).
James F. Byrnes Pre-Legal Society (1947).
Future Teachers of America (1948).
Chemical Society (1949).

Of a somewhat different character are the Student Council, the Baptist Student Union, and the Westminster Fellowship. The Glee Club, the literary societies, and student publications have been treated elsewhere.

The Debating Team, though of transient membership, counts as an organization.

Other fraternities formerly existed at Wofford during the periods indicated as follows. Probably more of them were locals than I have indicated:

Chi Psi (1869-1906, though charter was not surrendered, according to Baird, *Register of American College Fraternities,* until 1909).
Chi Phi (1871-1906).
Delta Tau Delta (1873-75).
Phi Delta Theta (1879-84).
Alpha Tau Omega (1891-96).
Philanthropeans, local, anti-fraternity organization, quite large (1899-1906).
Delta Sigma Phi (1916- ?).
Kappa Sigma Delta, forensic (1921-34).
Pi Kappa Delta (1921-34).
Alpha Pi (1923- ?).
Beta Pi (1924- ?).
Alpha Zeta Phi, local (1924-1934 or later).
Chi Beta Phi, honorary scientific fraternity (1925- ?).
Chi Tau (1925- ?).
Theta Chi Delta (1925- ?).
Sigma Upsilon, honorary English literature fraternity (1926- ?).
Beta Pi Theta, honorary French fraternity (1927- ?).
Alpha Lambda Tau, intercollegiate (1928- ?).
Alpha Chi Delta, Christian leadership fraternity (1923-7).
Phi Alpha Upsilon, founded at Wofford (1933- ?).
Kappa Sigma Kappa (1935-40).
Sigma Tau Alpha, Christian leadership fraternity; succeeded to Alpha Chi Delta (1937- ?).
Gavel, debating club (1937-. Succeeded Pi Kappa Delta, then inactive).

There can be no doubt that the experience of the past, embodying as it does the warning that all organizations must conduct themselves with moderation and fairness or face drastic regulation or even exclusion, has had a salutary effect, and has taught all elements of the college community better how to co-operate as parts of the common college life. Dean A. Mason DuPre stated in his annual report for 1939-40, that during his twenty years as Dean he had kept in touch with the fraternities and had found them co-operative in matters of discipline, even in severe cases. That is encouraging; but to think that conditions are perfect would be to deny human nature. An editorial in the *Old Gold and Black* of November 6, 1937, beginning "Politics at Wofford are *rotten,*" is very bitter against both the fraternity men and the non-frats.

Wofford graduates have always been numerous in the educational field, from the common school to the university. President Snyder in an article in the *Southern Christian Advocate* of January 30, 1908 (reproduced in the *Wofford College Journal* of February, 1908), pointed out that of the seven appointed members of the State Board of Education at that time three were graduates of Wofford. One County Superintendent of Education was a Wofford man, and in his county there were during the past year more school libraries established or improved than in any other county in the State. Of the forty-one County Boards of Education, eleven contained Wofford men, and of the one hundred and twelve town and city Superintendents of Schools listed as many as twenty-four were Wofford men, and this did not include some not mentioned. Dr. Snyder also pointed out the importance of Wofford as a liberal arts institution. The University of South Carolina, he said, with its virtually free tuition, in its college department failed to equal Wofford's enrollment by twenty-one, while Furman University, with a Baptist constituency 20,000 larger than Wofford's Methodists, had on its campus (including in both cases fitting school students) 270 fewer than Wofford.

At about this time, we may note, a majority of all the Supreme Court and Circuit Judges in the State were Wofford graduates—a condition which, of course, was not typical, but which did afford one evidence of the prominence of Wofford men at the bar.

Another student activity concerned college journalism. May 27, 1909, the Faculty declined to grant permission to establish a weekly paper on the campus. Permission was, however, later granted, and the first issue of the *Old Gold and Black* appeared under date of February 10, 1915.[28] A decided change in the character of the *Wofford College Journal,* which had existed since 1889, occurred after the establishment of the weekly. The *Journal* after that neglected local college news, which constituted the peculiar field of the weekly.

Another student activity was the State Oratorical Association, organized in Columbia, November 17-18, 1898, by Furman, Wofford, Clemson, Presbyterian College, and Erskine. The first contest was scheduled for April 28, 1899, at Erskine.[29] Others soon joined, bringing the total to nine. For many years the contests, in April of each year, were held at Lander College in Greenwood or at Winthrop College in Rock Hill, but in later years they rotated among a number of places. In the absence of official records of the winners, I have compiled the following complete list

---

28. A facsimile of the first issue appears in *The Bohemian,* the Wofford annual of 1915, page 157.
29. *Wofford Journal,* May, 1898, p. 29.

from the newspaper files, and for a few of the later years from the records of the colleges. The contests, interrupted by war, have not been resumed since 1943. Intercollegiate debating has meantime been practiced more extensively than ever.

1899 Clemson College won.
1900 Erskine won.[30]
1901 Wofford won. Wofford speaker was Aleri Morrison.
1902 Furman won.
1903 Furman won.[31]
1904 Wofford won, E. K. Hardin being her speaker.
1905 Erskine won.
1906 Furman won.
1907 Wofford won, W. W. Carson being her speaker.
1908 Wofford won, James C. Hardin being her speaker.
1909 Wofford won, Wallace D. DuPre being her speaker.
1910 Wofford won, H. Grady Hardin being her speaker.
1911 Citadel won.
1912 Newberry won.
1913 University of South Carolina won.
1914 Wofford won, R. J. Syfan being her speaker.
1915 University of South Carolina won.
1916 Newberry College won.
1917 Wofford won, T. H. Glenn being her speaker.
1918 Clemson won.
1919 Furman won.
1920 Newberry College won.
1921 University of South Carolina won.
1922 Erskine won.
1923 Presbyterian College won.[32]
1924 Erskine won.
1925 Wofford won, R. A. Dunham being her speaker.
1926 Erskine won.
1927 Erskine won.
1928 Clemson won. C. W. Derrick for Wofford was second.
1929 Erskine won.
1930 Clemson won.
1931 Erskine won.
1932 Clemson won. C. H. Humphries for Wofford won second place.
1933 Erskine won.
1934 College of Charleston won.
1935 Newberry College won.
1936 Erskine won.

---

30. Report in *The State* says that Koger of Wofford was the best speaker, but that his oration did not grade up high enough in composition.
31. Walter K. Greene of Wofford was second. The year before that, illness prevented his speaking. His oration in 1902 was rated three points higher than any other.
32. Paul Hardin of Wofford won second place.

1937 Citadel won.
1938 Clemson won.
1939 Presbyterian College won.
1940 Charleston College won.
1941 Furman won.
1942 Wofford won, her speaker being H. Fletcher Padgett.[33]
1943 Furman won.

Thus, in the forty-five contests, Wofford and Erskine each won ten times; Clemson and Furman each six times; Newberry College four times; the University of South Carolina three times; the Citadel, the College of Charleston, and Presbyterian College each twice.

A further instance of Wofford student distinctions is their record as winners of Rhodes scholarships:

John Lee Hydrick, of the class of 1908, awarded scholarship in 1908;
J. Lyles Glenn, Jr., of the class of 1912, awarded in 1914;
Edwin F. Moseley of the class of 1916, awarded in 1920;
John Q. Hill, of the class of 1947, awarded in 1948.[34]

An activity concerning Wofford graduates is the reorganization of the Alumni Association in 1915. A new Constitution was adopted, making all former students at Wofford members of the Association. The fine old motto of 1859, Τρόφιμοι τόν τροφὸν τιμῶμεν—We the adopted honor [the mother] who nourished us—was retained. Local Associations were to be formed in each county and leading town, in addition to those already existing. The Alumni oration, as that year, was in future to be delivered at the annual banquet instead of in the chapel, unless for special reasons some other plan should be adopted. Classes were to hold reunions one, three, and five years after graduation, and every five years thereafter. The rule of secrecy was omitted.[35]

---

33. H. Fletcher Padgett as a high school student won the National Legion High School Oratorical contest, carrying an educational scholarship of $4,000.—Columbia *State,* Apr. 15, 1939.
34. Rhodes Scholarship Trust files.
35. D. D. Wallace in *So. Christian Ad.,* July 22, 1915.

CHAPTER XII

INTELLECTUAL AND ADMINISTRATIVE
PROBLEMS, 1902-1929

HAVING carried some topics forward to their completion for purposes of clearness, we must now turn back for others that have been allowed to drop out of their chronological order. The first concerns the advancement of academic standards. This was accomplished, first, by raising the standard for admission to the Freshman class; and, second, by a progressive elevation of the standard of instruction through the use of more advanced textbooks, and in some departments certainly, and in all let us hope, by more modern and exacting standards of teaching. Dr. Snyder in his *Educational Odyssey* speaks affectionately of the days before the breaking out of "the Ph.D. rash." It is an expression of impatience at those who possess little besides the degree, and it is a fact that many of the greatest teachers in the history of the college have not had the degree; but I dare say no one would be quicker than they to acknowledge that they would have been still better teachers if they had had the benefit of the wider knowledge of their subjects and the keen discipline of the graduate school. Dr. Snyder himself would have been a German university Ph.D., but for the fact that his election to the presidency of Wofford College made it impossible for him to complete the small amount of further work required. It is also true that President Snyder came more and more to emphasize that new instructors should possess this testimonial of at least their technical preparation; and it is also true that those possessing the degree generally exhibit through the thoroughness of their work and their requirements of their students the benefit which they had derived from their training in advanced university studies. Moreover the continuance of research after taking the degree, unless carried to such excess as to prevent proper preparation for classroom work, vitalizes teaching as nothing else can do. It will hardly be contended that Wofford Professors who have been most active in research and publication, as Dr. James A. Chiles for instance, have been backward in either the preparation or the presentation of their classroom work.[1] Dr. Chiles's alma mater, Central College, Missouri, in 1948 presented him with an engraved plaque for distinguished scholarship.

---

1. Dr. Chiles has issued the following works, all from the press of Messrs. Ginn and Company: *German Prose Composition*, 1914; *German Composition and Conversation*, 1931 and 1946;

The Ph.D. rash has come to be, for the college full Professor almost as much a requirement as A.B. for a teacher in a first class public school or an M.A. as a condition for advancement in the better kind of high school. With all the shortcomings of Ph.D.dom, of which I myself have sometimes been quite impatient, the Ph.D. rash is indicative of a distinct advance in the standards of American education. Character and personality are the fundamentals of good teaching; but let us not forget that a great personality has more to give in proportion to what he himself has received and achieved.

Not only has there been advancement in the general level of academic standards, but there has been change in the content of those standards. This has involved both gain and loss. The gain has been scientific and technical; the loss cultural and moral. With the multiplication of new sciences and the vast increase in the demands made upon the preparation of the specialist, there has grown up a great body of "educated" men who have no common ground of culture, no common basis of intellectual life, no common background for their thinking. Even conversation among members of a modern faculty has become difficulty unless one or the other of the persons has a curiosity to induce his differently educated colleague to enlighten him on the content of the other's intellectual world; and sometimes the inclination, or even the capacity, to do so is found wanting.

As modern civilization developed in such abundance, majesty, and power Americans lost interest in the wonders of Greece and Rome and were satisfied to contemplate greatness nearer home. I once heard a high school teacher of Latin and Greek say that the man who invented the electric light did more for the world than Plato. What a valuation of the relative importance of physical and intellectual light! Needless to say, the offender soon shifted to an occupation better suited to his tastes and talents.

Of necessity the demands of modern branches of learning forced the neglect of the ancient cultures; but the really scholarly mind accepts the fact with regret and not with a sneer. Whether he would or not, modern man must strive to master the forces of nature and control the deafening whirl of modern machinery and the powers of atomic energy, with its possibilities of annihilating or of energizing modern civilization. In other

---

Intermediate German Readings, 1940; Chiles and Wiehr, *First Book in German,* 1935; Chiles and Wiehr, revised edition of the same, 1948. The *German Composition and Conversation* was used by the Federal government in London and perhaps elsewhere during the Second World War for soldiers who would need to know German. Dr. Chiles founded here in 1929 the honorary German scholarship fraternity Delta Phi Alpha, of which there are now sixty-five chapters.

words, modern education perforce has become more and more scientific and less and less cultural and moral.

Wofford has not escaped this world-wide movement; for, as Dr. Carlisle once put it when speaking of some of the excesses of modern democracy which had invaded South Carolina, when the tide rises along the shore of the Atlantic Ocean it enters not only every great harbor, but pushes into every creek and rivulet. The building of the John B. Cleveland Science Hall was thus one of the most significant moves in the history of the college. It was followed by the immediate doubling of the scientific teaching force, a movement which has continued to this day. Some of the brightest minds of the modern Faculty have come here to teach the sciences, and it has been found harder to keep these departments well manned, for the reason that one great corporation after another tempts away our brilliant young chemists. In this way Wofford lost Victor C. Edwards, here from 1909 to '17, to the DuPont Company, and Herbert E. Vermillion, here from 1939 to '41, to the Texas Company. So serious has this practice become as a national phenomenon that university Presidents have warned great corporation executives that if they want good chemists for their service in the next generation they had better leave the best ones in the universities to prepare young men to take their places.

The Wofford College catalogue of 1907-8 for the first time set up definite "units" as necessary for admission. But let us remember that there were definite requirements laid down in the early catalogues of extensive preparation in Latin and Greek, etc., though they were not called units. This new system was in response to the movement by the Association of Southern Colleges and Secondary Schools for the purpose of elevating educational standards. President Snyder and Dr. A. G. Rembert represented Wofford as one of the nine institutions at the organization of the Association in Atlanta, November 6, 1895. Chancellor Kirkland of Vanderbilt, himself a Wofford man, taken all in all our most distinguished graduate, was the moving spirit and continued until his death, August 5, 1939, to be its dominant member. Of the ten institutions which soon signed the constitution and by-laws, only six were then able to meet the requirements for the proposed uniform standards of entrance to college: Vanderbilt University, the University of North Carolina, the University of the South, the University of Mississippi, Washington and Lee University, and Trinity College (now Duke University).[2] Vanderbilt University at that time required fourteen

2. Higher Education in the South, in *Southern Association Quarterly*, August, 1947, 478 *passim*. Both Mims, *Life of Chancellor Kirkland*, 130-1, and Snyder, *Educational Odyssey*, 123-4, err in confusing the number of institutions represented with the number of persons present.

units for entrance, but the Association was able to set the standard only at ten. A unit was defined as a course of five hours a week in some subject through a high school year.

Wofford had been requiring, in a not very effective way, about eight and a half units. She began her effort for classification with the best by publishing in her catalogue of 1907-8 that, beginning with the following September, Freshmen must present eight and a half units. The next catalogue, that of 1908-9, announced that they must present fourteen units, on not more than four of which conditions might be allowed, and that these conditions must be worked off by the end of the second year. It was an act of some boldness. President Snyder was the moving spirit. He warned that it might so reduce patronage as to necessitate cutting salaries; but every member of the Faculty voted for it. I well remember the sense of moral elevation in the determination for better standards, and the purifying willingness to suffer the consequences, which seemed to move every member. And cut enrollment it did; but there was no cut in salaries. The considerable drop in the autumn of 1908 was attributed to a combination of causes; raising the standard of entrance, destructive floods, the low price of cotton, and the money panic.[3] From 287 in 1907-9 enrollment sank to 216 in 1909-10, after which it began again to rise. The cut in the Freshman class was more decided, the figures for successive years being as follows: 1907-8, 95; 1908-9, 82; 1909-10, 54; 1910-11, 92. The catalogue of 1914-15 announced, in support of schools that were striving to do their part in elevating standards, that the college would next fall admit no student on certificate from any high school which maintained a four year course unless he had completed the four years of his school; for one of the greatest difficulties that the high schools had had in seeking to raise their standards was that colleges had been admitting high school students who had completed only three years of high school work. For admission to the Freshman class in 1920 fifteen units were required, on not more than two of which the student could be conditioned. The catalogue for 1921-22 announced that Wofford was a member of the Southern Association of Colleges and Secondary Schools, and that the requirement was therefore that no student would be admitted to the Freshman class without fifteen units, either on the certificate of an accredited school or on examination. She was fully qualified by standards of entrance and quality of work years earlier, but could not be fully accredited until her Professor of Greek ceased to teach also in her Fitting School.

The system of admission on certificate continues; but, sad to say, the actual preparation furnished by different schools differs widely. It has

---

3. Report of Com. on Education, *S. C. Conf. Minutes*, 1908, 28.

proved much easier to erect a series of magnificent school houses than to fill them with teachers of as high grade as the architecture of the buildings in which they teach.

The passing grade was 60 before 1906. In June, 1906, it was made 70 for all classes except Freshman, and for Freshmen was made 70 on a second examination. In June, 1916, the passing grade of 70 was enacted for all classes. From at least that early a passing grade of 80 was required in all M.A. courses.[4]

The growing number of students and the increasing complexity of college affairs called for certain administrative changes. The strength of the industrious, energetic D. A. DuPre, who in addition to his teaching duties had discharged also those of Treasurer since 1890, was no longer equal to the heavier tasks which the college's development imposed upon his aging shoulders. In June, 1920, he resigned the treasurership, along with which had gone also the duty of general supervision of buildings and grounds. Joseph K. Davis, a Wofford graduate of the class of 1910, was given these duties as a full time position, and has discharged them with satisfaction to his employers ever since. Davis has never forgotten the business methods that he learned in the office of the Southern Railway in Washington.

The growth of the institution, the extensive extra-collegiate demands upon the time of the President, and finally his absence for more than a year in the church-wide educational drive made a necessity what had already been needed—the creation of the office of Dean.[5] Fortunately the man was ready in the person of Prof. A. Mason DuPre, who on June 4, 1920, was elected by the Trustees the first Dean of Wofford College. Dr. DuPre, as we may call him, for he was given the degree of LL.D. by Furman University in 1933, had long been and was to continue for many years Professor of Latin and Mathematics—a rather poor way, in my opinion, to use a man of first rate ability, though ranking as a full professor, as a kind of assistant to those departments in charge of older men called respectively Professor of Latin and Professor of Mathematics, instead of giving him his own department to build up in a way commensurate with its needs and his own capacity. Such are the sacrifices sometimes demanded in a small institution.

As a young man in Abbeville, where he was born November 22, 1869, Mason DuPre was clerking in a store when he heard a sermon by that missionary of light and learning Dr. A. Coke Smith. So stirred was he

4. Fac. Mins., June 1, 1916; catalogues.
5. Snyder, Educational Odyssey, 203; Tr. Mins., June 4 and 5, 1920.

that he formed the resolution on the spot, "I'm going to college." He was thinking of Clemson, just about to open, when Rev. Marion Dargan said to him, "You are going to Wofford;" and to Wofford he came.[6] He was about five years older by the calendar and many years older in maturity than the average student. An incident before his coming to college, while he was acting as deputy for his father, then Sheriff of Abbeville County, illustrates several aspects of his character. Hearing a commotion among the prisoners in the cell room, he went up to inspect. Everything became quiet, and the young deputy looked around in a thoroughly nonplussed state of mind, a state of mind, however, which he did not reveal. Covering his frustration with the stern remark, "I've seen all I need to," he withdrew. Later one of the prisoners, or rather then ex-prisoner, told him that they had been sawing through the bars, and were raising the general racket so as to prevent the sawing from being heard. When they heard the deputy coming they put a blanket over the place, and when he said, "I've seen all I need to," they supposed that he had detected their work, and so that was the last of the attempt to escape. Many a time this same august, know-it-already manner brought from a less serious culprit a full statement to the Dean of what the student had been up to.

Dr. Mason DuPre was one of the most striking characters in the history of the college. He was possessed of a mind of very considerable ability, marked by great clearness and analytical powers. Accuracy was to his mathematical instincts a religion, and rarely was he convicted of error of either fact or judgment. He was so conservative that he was led to assert on a few occasions that it was not correct to say that he never changed his mind.

An activity that we should not overlook is Dr. DuPre's teaching for many years the men's Bible class at Central Methodist Church Sunday School, which gave him an outlet for his views on practically anything having a moral or religious aspect. He was a strong believer in prohibition, and was for awhile Chairman of the State Committee of the Anti-Saloon League for South Carolina. He was for some years a member of the Board of Stewards of the church; but his positive and aggressive nature did not fit him well into deliberative bodies. Another extracurricular activity was a year's service as President of the State Teachers' Association.

The Dean was thought to like to be considered like Dr. Carlisle, for whom he entertained great veneration. He was indeed like Dr. Carlisle in his tall, imposing figure, and, more important, in his devotion to the

6. A. M. DuPre to D. D. Wallace.

highest moral standards and his conservatism; but in other respects he was very unlike. To begin with, Dr. DuPre's character was essentially that of the soldier, as Dr. Carlisle was not—the soldier of stern discipline and rugged conduct, much more like Stonewall Jackson than the gentler and better balanced Lee. Another difference was that Dr. Carlisle shrank, perhaps too much, from action that would wound feelings. The Dean sometimes inflicted deep wounds in his quick anger, using occasionally a violence of language which his best friends could not approve. In short, he was intensely masculine, with the faults and virtues of a positive, high-strung nature. It is well that he was a good man, for he would have been a terror as a bad one.

As remarked above, the Dean's character was essentially that of the upright, Christian military officer. I never knew anyone who was more positively and consistently convinced that he was right. And he generally was right; for he carefully considered any situation before he took a stand. He was best suited for executive positions in which a large degree of authority was permissible. Even here he would sometimes go to extremes of self-assertion. For instance, while he was sitting in the college Faculty as Headmaster of the Fitting School, the Faculty decided to send back to the school a student unfitted for college. The Headmaster declared with positive deliberation that he refused to accept him back. The President commented upon such a determination in defiance of the decision of the Faculty, with no result except a re-assertion of his position by the Headmaster. That settled it; for it would have been most inconvenient to give up any Headmaster just then, or that particular Headmaster at any time; and no one doubted that he would have resigned rather than submit.

Another occasion of self-assertion occurred while the Dean was acting as President during the absence for a year of President Snyder on the Christian Education campaign of 1920-21. When a certain proposal was made, he said, essentially, "As the officer responsible for the administration of the institution, I will not permit that." There was a dead silence, for never before in the history of the college had the executive head assumed the right of veto over Faculty action, a right which the President was not given by the Trustees until after the accession of President Greene. The relations between President and Faculty had been worked out by custom, with almost a complete absence of friction. Questions of relative authority were unlikely to arise among the small group of teachers during the early years. The respect for Dr. Carlisle had been so great, and his tolerance of Faculty opinion so nearly unlimited, unless strongly moved, that clashes were unlikely.[7] President Snyder was so persuasive and moderate and so skilled in adjusting differences that the issue had not arisen.

In the instance of Dean DuPre's threatened veto, the astonished silence was broken by his distant relative Prof. D. A. DuPre (who had not made the proposal) quietly saying, "You will at least allow us to think." The proposal was dropped; for no one was willing to do anything to precipitate a conflict with an officer whom all respected and whose temorary tenure of the executive headship made it the more needful that he should be supported by a united Faculty.

As Dean Dr. DuPre was eminently successful, and for nineteen years enabled the Faculty to rest in the serene confidence that his fair and firm administration of discipline would keep the ship on an even keel. President Snyder testified to the fact that he carried a very large part of the executive and administrative labors of the college. Also, said Dr. Snyder, Dr. DuPre did not like very much going around to places; [8] but there was one assembly in which he took pleasure; that was the annual meeting of the Southern Association of Colleges and Secondary Schools, for there he could exercise his talent for the framing and enforcement of regulations and standards.

I have spoken as though the responsibility for discipline rested entirely with the Dean after the creation of his office; but such an idea would not be exact. June 4, 1921, a year after creating the office of Dean, the Trustees added the Discipline Committee, in whose hands all matters of discipline should rest, without reference to the Faculty. The Committee was to consist of the Dean, the President of the College, and an elected Faculty member without any specified term. I was the elected member, and so remained for years until leave of absence for writing my *History of South Carolina,* taking me away from Spartanburg for a great part of four years, caused me to resign. The harmony of the Committee was exemplary, though never by mere acquiescence in the Dean's proposals. He was more open to argument by his colleagues on that small committee than in the meetings of the whole Faculty. June 2, 1923, the Trustees voted that the Dean, with the approval of the President, should be allowed to dismiss a student; but that was in fact already the case, for they constituted a majority of the Committee. This was merely a little more expeditious.

Dean DuPre was rigorous, but scrupulously fair. It did not save a student, for instance, who left town for the week end without permission that in Greenville he attended Sunday School; for when he walked into the Men's Bible Class he found Dean DuPre the visiting teacher of the day. His piety

---

7. But see page 96 above.
8. Dr. Snyder to D. D. Wallace, August 9, 1949.

FACULTY 1924-25

Left to right: A. M. DuPre, Dean and Prof. Latin and Mathematics; J. G. Clinkscales, Prof. Mathematics; D. A. DuPre, Prof. Geology; D. D. Wallace, Prof. History
and Political Science; J. A. Gamewell, Prof. Latin; J. A. Chiles, Prof. Modern Languages; A. G. Rembert, Prof. Bible, Greek, and Psychology; C. B. Waller, Prof.
Chemistry and Biology.

FACULTY 1924-25

Left to right: W. L. Pugh, Prof. English; J. L. Salmon, Asst. Prof. Modern Languages; A. M. Trawick, Prof. Religious Education; W. C. Herbert, Prof. Bible, Greek, and Mathematics; E. H. Shuler, Asst. Prof. Applied Mathematics; J. M. Rast, Asst. Prof. Economics and Sociology; J. W. Harris, Jr., Asst. Prof. English; C. S. Pettis, Asst. Prof. Physics and Chemistry.

availed him nothing; and let us hope that the suffering of his penalty was assuaged by a sense of humor which could enjoy the irony of his situation. A more extreme case was that of a student who left town without permission and had the misfortune of a severe automobile accident, which automatically revealed his transgression. The Dean quietly waited until the miscreant's term in the hospital was over and then imposed the usual penalty of so many days suspension from college for having left town without permission.

Nothing could have preserved the popularity of so rigorous an officer except the sense among the students of his absolute fairness. As a matter of fact Dean DuPre was not only thoroughly respected, but was one of the most beloved teachers in the history of the college. But despite his strictness as a disciplinarian, he was not severe as a teacher, but was kind, sympathetic, and helpful toward his pupils. He was clear, thorough, and effective. The pressure of administrative duties prevented his ever showing what he might have done with full opportunity in either of those two splendid mental disciples, Latin or Mathematics. He might have built one of them into a strong department, as Snyder did English or Rembert Greek, and have saved them from their sadly declined state.

I sometimes differed with Dean DuPre in Faculty meetings, and still believe that in some instances I was right, as, for instance, when I urged adopting the plans of the Carnegie Foundation for the Advancement of Teaching for Faculty insurance, and he urged instead the makeshift group insurance, which broke down in a few years because of its impracticability for a small group constantly growing in average age. But then, as generally, it was useless to oppose him, even in a matter having no connection with his own particular duties. After he spoke the Faculty ceased to think, but docilely agreed, so much easier is it to follow a clear mind and strong will that has thoroughly gained public confidence than to think for one's self. They would rather risk being wrong with the Dean than risk not being right with somebody else.

A. Mason DuPre (or, as the boys called him "the old Dean," or "old Mas," or sometimes "Amazing DuPre") was indeed an unusual person. With all his strength he was sensitive to irritation and took his duties a little super-seriously. I sometimes thought that he lived in unnecessary apprehension of student disorders; for the herd instinct of human beings holds them generally to normal lines of action; but he was constantly alert to that other possibility of the herd instinct which can turn them toward mass disorder.

Dr. DuPre resigned the Deanship May 30, 1925, and was succeeded for a year by Prof. W. C. Herbert, who had had successful experience as Headmaster of the Wofford Fitting School and for years, in addition to his teaching duties, acted as Registrar of Wofford College. Dr. DuPre consented to resume his duties as Dean after a year. He sought again to resign in 1937, but consented to serve to September 1, 1940. On his retirement his colleagues at a dinner in his honor presented him with a gold watch, and in 1945 at a dinner given by the college in honor of his fifty years of service they presented him with a gold ring. The Trustees named him Dean Emeritus; but he disliked the idea of decrepitude associated with Emeritus. He preferred and was given the title of Honorary Dean. He died in Spartanburg, S. C., October 29, 1949. (Not October 28, as sometimes stated.) On his retirement the Alumni Secretary, LeRoy H. Cox, was made Dean and served until he entered the military service during the Second World War. He was followed in 1942 by the present Dean, Dr. C. C. Norton, Professor of Sociology and Political Science. Dr. Norton spent the summer of 1939 in South Africa studying a problem that vexes that region even more than it does ours, the relations of the Negro and the white men.

The earliest summer schools at Wofford have been noted above.[9] The Wofford Summer School of 1909, with a term of four weeks, was designed especially for teachers, particularly those of high schools, and looked forward to developing to such an extent as to grant the degree of Licentiate of Instruction, L.I. The Faculty was learned and able: Dr. Snyder, President and instructor in Literature; W. G. Blake, Principal of the Spartanburg High School, Geometry and Arithmetic; Mrs. H. S. Browne, of Spartanburg City Schools, Primary Methods; W. A. Colwell of Wofford, Modern Languages; D. Wistar Daniel of Clemson, English Literature; A. Mason DuPre of Wofford Fitting School, Algebra; S. H. Edmunds, Superintendent of Sumter City Schools, Grammar and Rhetoric; Frank Evans, Superintendent of Spartanburg City Schools, Geography and Physiography; Miss Caroline McMakin, of the Spartanburg City Schools, Music; W. H. Morton of Converse College, Physics and Physiology; A. G. Rembert, of Wofford, Latin; J. A. Tillinghast, of Converse College, History and Civics; Patterson Wardlaw of the University of South Carolina and the veritable dean of education in the State, Pedagogy. The same Faculty served in the summer of 1910, with the addition of an instructor in Agriculture.

Not only did Wofford fear the competition of Winthrop, with her prestige as a college for teachers and the resources of the State when she inaugurated her summer school; but a number of the strongest members of the Wofford Summer School Faculty took work at Winthrop, and our promising two

9. Page 95.

year beginning of a high grade summer school of college grade went by the board. However, Headmaster A. M. DuPre instituted summer sessions of the Wofford Fitting School, in 1910, designed to enable students to make up deficiencies. This was continued by his successors until it was superseded by the summer school conducted on a college level by members of the college Faculty. In 1926 the scope was enlarged to include courses for teachers who were ambitious to improve their professional preparation or to gain academic credits. With 1927 the college catalogue for the first time recognized the existence of the Summer School, although it had previously been noted in the Fitting School catalogue and had for some years issued its own bulletins. The bulletin in the spring of 1927 was more pretentious and announced an enlarged program. H. N. Snyder appeared as President of the Summer School instead of W. C. Herbert as Director. This circular and the college catalogue announced considerable variety of regular college credit courses, both for enabling ambitious students or teachers to advance themselves, and for affording opportunity for students needing to make up failures or back work. Both curriculum and enrollment expanded, until the summer came to rival the winter session and to be counted as a regular part of the college year, with diplomas awarded during the summer session just as in June.

All this time, however, the college assumed no financial responsibility and received none of the fees, the entire plan being managed independently by such Professors as participated. The college merely set standards and credited in its records the results reported. The situation was regarded with dissatisfaction by the Trustees, but continued until after the installation of President Greene, when the summer session was assimilated in all respects to the authority and management of the college. We thus have the gradual development of a thoroughly collegiate summer term as a regular part of the college year from 1909; but, as indicated above, it was not except for the first two years and again from 1927 of collegiate grade.[10] The Fitting School catalogue in 1914 begins to state the enrollment in the Fitting School summer session—28 in 1913; but the college catalogue, though describing

---

10. *Catalogue Wofford College and Wofford College Fitting School,* at end of Fitting School part, 1910-11, 1917-18, and so on; *So. Christian Ad.,* June 6, August 22, 1912; Aug. 21, 1913; Aug. 6, 1914, etc.; Bulletins Summer School. The Bulletin of 1923, the earliest to which I have access, speaks of the session of that summer as the fifteenth. That treats the succession as unbroken beginning with the session of 1909. The 1927 bulletin of the enlarged school says that "The Wofford College Summer School" has for the past fifteen years been devoted mainly to the needs of college and high school students needing to make up conditions or back work, basing this apparently upon the fact that in 1913 the old summer session of the Fitting School included making up college back work in its announcement of services; but it was still the summer session of the Fitting School. Copying the statement without change for several years, and finally for the next year changing fifteen to sixteen caused confusion. Again in later catalogues repeating carelessly the number of years stated in the previous year's catalogue made the confusion still worse, until finally all reference to the length of time the summer school had operated was dropped.

the college Summer School from 1927-1928 did not even mention its student enrollment until 1929-30, when the 217 of the previous summer (1929) are added to the regular 1929-30 session's 463, though not dignified by being listed in the roll of students. From its small beginnings the Summer School has grown until in 1948 it enrolled 722 persons in comparison with 720 for the winter session. The total number of persons enrolled during the college year September, 1947-August, 1948, including the afternoon classes for advanced students mentioned in the next paragraph, eliminating all duplicating of names, was 1205, the largest in the history of the college.[11]

An attempt by Professors Trawick and Wallace, with the approval of President Snyder, to enlist the interest of young business men and women or teachers in night classes met so little response as barely to require mention. Later there developed, however, an important addition to the services rendered by the college, namely, afternoon classes running through the regular fall, winter, and spring terms, primarily for ambitious teachers wishing to improve their professional training, to gain credits, or to obtain a Master's degree. These were organized to satisfy requests, which in 1927 were becoming urgent. After the report of a Faculty committee on M.A. courses, the Faculty authorized, September 19, 1927, a few courses especially suited to meet the needs of teachers, to meet on Tuesday and Friday afternoons. The popularity of the move proved its need, and soon a considerable number of high grade young men and women were in attendance, constituting a kind of graduate school of the college. In 1929-30 the enrollment was 63, all but 18 holding A.B. or B.S. degrees. The courses offered were increased as demand justified, though the work was mostly confined to languages, education, history, and sociology. Standards, of course, were those of the college, and results were entered in the college records, and in due time degrees, if won, were awarded by the College.

Though the Faculty endorsed and fully credited the work of the afternoon classes, the college assumed no financial responsibility. Fees were collected and paid out to the Professors concerned by a selected member of the Professors participating. It was creditable to the Professors concerned. both in the summer session and in the afternoon classes for advanced work, that their initiative created two highly serviceable and creditable advances in the intellectual life of the institution, as well as being interesting to observe as a sociological process in institutional development. The slower moving body of the college corporation finally and very properly taking over the developed additional organs of institutional life is similar

---

11. For enrollment annually since the founding of the college, see Appendix I. The college Catalogue has not always eliminated duplicate names.

to the process in a larger field to the State's having taken over education after the church's initiative had shown both the necessity and the method. Regularly private initiative leads in a new idea, and the cumbersome, slower moving corporate body later takes over, develops, and supports what it did not have the initiative to invent.

The Faculty in 1949 discontinued giving the degree of Master of Arts, although allowing those who had already entered upon such courses to pursue them to the attainment of the degree.

During the summer of 1909 a summer school for preachers and religious workers was conducted by the college. Among the lecturers were Bishop James Atkins, Dr. Gross Alexander of Vanderbilt University, and Dr. J. M. Buckley, the editor of the *New York Christian Advocate,* the latter of whom wrote for his paper a notable appreciation of Wofford College and of its President Emeritus Dr. Carlisle, the reverence and affection for whom, he said, he had never found equaled.[12] Dr. Coleman B. Waller of the Wofford Faculty lectured in untechnical terms on some practical aspects of Biology. The continuance of the institute in 1910 without expense to those in attendance, except the cost of their food, was made possible by contributions by laymen in the State. The 1910 session was from August 31st through September 6th. The courses offered were as follows:

Eight lectures on the educational side of the preacher's work, by Dr. Henry F. Cope, of Chicago, General Secretary of the Religious Education Association, and a member of the staff of the *Sunday School Times:*

1. What is religious education?
2. Laws of the spiritual life.
3. Practical aspects of psychology for the preacher.
4. Practical aspects of pedagogy for the preacher.
5. The Church as an educator.
6. The Sunday school as an educator.
7. Social forces and aims.
8. Training efficient workers for the kingdom.

Six lectures by Dr. Charles L. Goodell, of the Calvary Methodist Church of New York, on the evangelistic side of the preacher's work:

1. The mystery of Godliness. (Sermon Sunday morning.)
2. The men for the new age. (Sermon Sunday night.)
3. The minister and his own soul.
4. The minister and his own soul (concluded).

---

12. Reprint in *So. Christian Ad.,* Sept. 9, 1909.

5. The minister and his work.
6. The minister and his work (concluded).

Six lectures by Dr. John A. Rice, formerly President of the Columbia College and then pastor of a leading Methodist church in New Orleans, on Biblical Studies:

1. The makers of Israel.
2. Proverbs: the wisdom of a people.
3. Job: the tragic ideal.
4. Ruth: the world and the saint.
5. Jonah: the saint and the world.
6. The modern man's Bible.

President Henry N. Snyder lectured on The English Bible as Literature; The Moral Aspects of Shapespeare's Art; and Robert Browning, a Poet of Faith in an Age of Doubt. Dr. Coleman B. Waller of the Wofford Faculty lectured on some practical aspects of Biology, to the instruction and pleasure not only of the attending ministers, but of the other instructors as well. Dr. A. G. Rembert of the Wofford Faculty gave a course intended to make easier the mastery of the Greek Testament for preachers who had not had the advantage of thorough collegiate instruction in the language. Attendance was fifty-four as against thirty-nine the year before.[13]

The Institute was allowed to lapse, but the South Carolina Conference took up the idea and gave it a somewhat different development. At their 1919 session they instituted a Board of Managers to organize the South Carolina Methodist Training Conference, and invited the Upper South Carolina Conference to participate, which they did. The first session of the Training Conference was held at Wofford College June 15-25, 1920, with an enrollment of 199 preachers and religious workers. Dr. John A. Rice was Chairman of the Commission and Dean of the Training Conference, Rev. Leo D. Gillespie, Secretary, and Rev. J. Emerson Ford, Bursar. Among the lecturers the first year was Bishop E. D. Mouzon. Professor A. M. Trawick's first connection with Wofford College was as a lecturer at several sessions of this Conference. With the summer of 1924 the Training Conference, under the changed name, but with the same officers, was transferred, as the South Carolina Methodist Pastors' School, to Columbia College, where it has continued to meet ever since. The central location of Columbia

---

13. The lectures were reported by Rev. A. D. Betts in *Southern Christian Advocate* of Sept. 8 and 15, 1910. Extensive circular by D. D. Wallace, Secretary of the Committee, in *ib.*, May 26. Unfortunately we lack similar full data about the Institute of 1909.

and, doubtless, a feeling that the sister institution should share in Conference interests, accounted for the change.[14] Without envying her sister institution, Wofford is conscious of a distinct loss in the absence of the stimulating influence of the great thinkers, teachers, and preachers who have made the Institute and the Pastors' School a valuable addition to the life of the church.

14. *S. C. Conf. Mins.*, 1920, 56; 1924, 76, etc., for various years, under Reports.

Chapter XIII

FINANCES AND MISCELLANEOUS INCIDENTS
1920-29

IT IS necessary to interrupt the flow of our narrative to notice several disconnected incidents. During the year 1901-2 the widow of Rev. J. Thomas Pate gave the college one thousand volumes of her husband's excellently balanced library.[1]

A troublesome question which arose incidentally from the growth in numbers of the Faculty concerned the fact that the older full Professors were given large brick residences in addition to their money salaries, whereas their confreres of equal rank were without this additional compensation. When the college was founded it was taken for granted that the Professors would be furnished with houses, and a sufficient number were built to take care of all contingencies for many years. After several years of agitation by the unpossessed the Trustees, June 13, 1908, voted that a full Professor, after ten years' service in any and all ranks, should either be supplied with a house or should be given $250 a year in lieu of a house, but was not to have this compensation if a faculty house was vacant and he refused to occupy it. It may be mentioned also that, as the Trustees were able, they gradually increased salaries in order to meet rising cost of living which has so cruelly affected persons living on fixed incomes; and although they have acted as liberally as possible, they have by no means been able to keep their Faculty from declining to a relatively lower economic (and consequently social) level. Occupations whose pay formerly ranked along with the Professors' now draw double the salary of the learned. The condition is nationwide, and threatens distinctly to lower the quality of college teaching, especially in personality, breadth of mind, and force of character.

Another provision for the welfare of the Faculty concerned life insurance or annuities. Prof. Wallace urged that the college and the Faculty members co-operatively take advantage of the terms offered by the Carnegie Foundation for the Advancement of Teaching. Prof. A. M. DuPre urged instead a plan of group insurance, under which the college would pay for a $5,000 policy on the life of each Professor. The Faculty preferred the latter, and accordingly in October, 1921, there was given each Professor, with the

---

1. *Tr. Mins.*, June, 1902.

exception of two whose age was too advanced, by an old line life insurance company a certificate contracting to pay to his beneficiary $5,000 upon his death while employed by the college. In the case of the two older men the college promised to pay for life $300 a year to the widow, if the wife survived the husband.

The defect in the plan was that the group insured was too small. Fifty is generally considered a minimum, and even that number in such a group as a college Faculty would have proved insufficient to assure a fairly level cost to the employer, year after year, as the number of old men who continue in employment is likely to be much greater than the number of young men who are taken on. After several years of uneasiness at the mounting cost, the Trustees, October 25, 1930, adopted the following in place of the group insurance: Each of the fourteen Professors covered should have the choice of receiving annually in cash the amount that his insurance was then costing the college, or could elect instead to have his then wife, if she became a widow, receive annually for life $300, with the same privilege to his minor children if only they remained beneficiaries for not more than ten years. About half chose the one alternative and about half the other. The plan operated on this basis until modified by mutual agreement under the retirement and annuity plan inaugurated under President Greene.[2]

Several moves to improve thinking and living in the college may be briefly noted. February 5, 1912, the Faculty adopted President Snyder's suggestion for a course in The Making of Modern Civilization, intended, as was being attempted at various institutions, to give students an appreciation of the unity and significance of the world's civilization. Each Professor was to give a lecture explaining the bearing of his own field of thought. The work was not integrated into regular courses as academic requirements and credits and so did not last long.

The size of the student body at Wofford, particularly until recent years, has been so moderate as to make for intimate contact between professors and students. Some time before 1912 The College Council was organized with the definite purpose of bringing students and Faculty into closer touch. President Snyder and Dr. C. B. Waller represented the Faculty, and officers of various student organizations represented the students.[3] In 1913 the Faculty approved the plan of President Snyder's dividing the classes into groups and appointing a Faculty adviser for each group. Students were urged to consult their Faculty Adviser on anything, personal or academic,

---

2. *Trustee Mins.,* June 4, 1921; June, 1927; June, 1928; October 25, 1930.
3. *Wofford Col. Jour.,* Nov., 1912, 44.

as they desired. Little seemed to come of the plan, as questions of curriculum, etc., had to be carried to the proper authority for official action, and the purely personal consultations between students and teachers continued to follow the natural lines determined by the personality of teachers and pupils. Probably Prof. A. G. Rembert was more frequently consulted by troubled boys than was any other, simply because he was what he was—sympathetic, patient, brotherly. Professors Salmon and Bourne have more recently grown into a similar position.

Another idea of President Snyder's was to have the Faculty members from time to time give simple parties in their homes for the students of their group. The occasions were agreeable and had considerable possibilities; but I do not remember its having been practiced but once by each Professor, though, aside from this, some few Professors gave student parties. The college, like the church, has been troubled with the problem of dancing. The Trustees in 1916 forbade the formation of dancing clubs or the giving of dances by any organization of students. The result has not been satisfactory. Students request friends in town to get up dances and invite the students to them, and so it has gone until the rule has tended to become a dead letter, if not actually a promoter of hypocrisy.

A trivial incident in this connection may relieve the weight of serious history, and also shed some light on why the authorities objected to dancing. It came to the ears of the Discipline Committee that there had been a college dance at the country club. Students understood to have been present were summoned. One was a large, powerful young man of serious and studious habits, earning his college expenses at least in part. Dr. Snyder asked, "Mr. Pressley, were you at the dance at the country club?" With the solemnity of a judge, Pressley answered, "Yes, Sir." "Did you dance, Mr. Pressley?" "No, Sir." Dr. Snyder then asked with some puzzlement, "If you did not dance, Mr. Pressley, why were you there?" "I was bouncer, Sir," answered the serious Mr. Pressley. "Bouncer? What do you mean, Mr. Pressley?" asked the still more puzzled Dr. Snyder. "Bounce them off the floor if they get disorderly," explained Mr. Pressley. Having learned the nature and the necessity of a "bouncer," President Snyder probably looked upon student dances no more favorably than he had done before. All of which has a bearing on the question, Was the turning down of the petition of the students to be allowed to have dances on the beautiful, smooth floor of the Andrews Field House the wisest way to meet what Dr. Carlisle, with an inclusive wave of his hand, would have called "this whole question of dancing"? [4]

4. *Trustee Mins.*, Jan. 22, 1912.

In November or December, 1909, was formed the Student Body Organization, with its constitution and officers.[5] Later followed the Student Honor Council, which undertook at first the trial and disciplining of students found guilty of cheating on examination, and finally extended its functions to noticing any student conduct of dishonorable character. The Faculty considered it a good way of stimulating a sense of student honor and responsibility, and even went so far as to turn over to the students the whole conduct of the examinations after the Professor had delivered the questions and left the room. Until the middle '90's cheating on examinations was rare at Wofford. It was an old Southern tradition that gentlemen would not associate with a cheater. In the spring of 1894 my own class expelled a fellow member, in effect because of being convinced of his having cheated on examination, though technically he was convicted (evidence in the other case not being sufficiently conclusive to satisfy some) of having cheated an ignorant Freshman by misrepresenting the facts in the sale of a textbook. As the spirit of commercialism spread from the North, where college cheating was understood to be common, it produced the same results here. Dishonesty extended to the copying of essays for prizes. For instance, I had two of the finest examples of historical writing in the past quarter century handed to me by students who evidently had a poor opinion of the extent of my reading. It was harder, though, to catch the man who bought his material from one of the firms that circularizes students with offers of such service.

A large part of the explanation rests with the popularizing of college education. Great numbers of students from families having little touch with standards of honor among gentlemen poured into the colleges, bringing with them their lower standards of personal honor. As in the State at large, so in the colleges, in shoving aside the dominance of the old aristocracy modern democracy has lost also some of the virtues of the old regime. Will the modern college, with its heterogeneous student body and its multiplied utilitarian courses, many of which have little or no bearing on morals or gentlemanliness, be able to leaven the whole lump?

For a while the Student Honor System worked well, but it was gradually undermined by a decline in the sense of honor. May 31, 1916, a committee of the Faculty met with a committee of students to consider means of diminishing the evil. The students testified that students who sought to enforce the system incurred ill will (which, I may add, went so far at times as to threaten physical violence against informers), and that in their

---

5. *Wof. Jour.*, Dec., 1909, 160.

opinion two-thirds to three-fourths of the students cheated at some time during their college course. Most thought that there was some improvement. The Student Body sought to improve the system in 1926 and adopted a form of examination book which remained in use as long as the system lasted, and may, for that matter, be used indefinitely. December 13, 1940, a proposal to abolish the honor system and leave the matter of honesty in examinations to the Faculty was voted down in Student Body meeting and an effort was promised to attempt to vitalize the system. The mention of the system in Student Body meeting about October 1, 1942, brought hoots and derisive laughter. Finally, in January or February, 1948, the students voted to abolish the system and rely wholly on the Faculty for regulating conduct in examinations.[6]

In 1908, for $18,200 the college sold to the South & Western Railroad Company (the Clinchfield) five and eight-tenths acres along the southeastern border of the campus. About half of the money was applied to the endowment and the rest to the expenses of the Financial Agent of the college in his endowment and buildings campaign. The railroad was being built around the campus in March, 1909.[7]

This leads naturally to a statement of the general financial condition of the college at this period. Figures for the year 1914-15, for instance, are as follows:

	1914-15	%
Tuition and matriculation	$12,311.60	42
Laboratory and other fees	547.50	2
From endowment investments	11,114.51	38
From gifts	259.50	1
From annual church assessment	5,325.92	17
Total income	$29,559.03	100
Salaries for instruction	$20,700.00	66
Supplies and expenses	286.38	1
Books and equipment	635.26	2
Administration and general	3,300.00	10
Business administration and expense	1,513.11	5
Operation and maintenance of physical plant	4,950.87	16
Total expense	$31,385.62	100

6. *Old Gold and Black*, Dec. 14, 1940; Feb. 21, 1941; Oct. 3, 1942; Feb., 1948. The editor expressed regret that no one who had known the deceased was present at his death.

7. *Tr. Mins.*, Nov. 27, 1908; December 10, 1909; *Wof. Col. Jour.*

Endowment Investments:	1914	1919
Stocks and bonds	$ 24,668.00	$ 22,618.00
Notes and mortgages	147,837.50	151,385.30
Rental property	13,185.30	15,185.30
Cash uninvested	1,571.33	685.45
Buildings and furniture	225,400.00	225,400.00
Grounds	150,000.00	150,000.00
Equipment and books	20,350.00	25,000.00
Sinking funds for payment of debt on student dormitory		14,200.00
Total Endowment and Plant	$583,012.13	$604,474.05

Endowment was growing. In 1916 it was $204,988; the debt was $53,403, but was being steadily reduced, as, e.g., in the next year by $10,220. Total income that year was $38,628.[8]

Practical interest in the college by the church was on the increase, as manifested not only by the much larger contributions through the Conference assessment for education, but through energetic moves to increase both equipment and endowment of all the schools belonging to the church. In 1912 the Conference created the Educational Commission for the purpose of raising funds for all their schools. In 1913 Rev. W. I. Herbert was appointed as Commissioner of Education to travel throughout the State in pursuance of these plans. Depression and alarm, particularly disturbing in a State whose chief product, cotton, sank to ruinously low price levels on the outbreak of war in Europe, necessitated some delay. The Commission, meeting in the office of President Snyder June 2, 1916, determined that the time to act had come. They therefore determined (1) that active measures be taken for accomplishing the object of their creation, namely, the raising of $400,000 for paying off the debts and bettering the equipment and endowment of our colleges; (2) that one Commissioner be elected to carry out the work throughout the State for the two Conferences; and (3) that the $300,000, or such sum as should be raised, should be apportioned as follows: to Wofford College and Carlisle Fitting School $140,000; to Lander College $65,000; to Columbia College $95,000. To this all three Presidents heartily agreed.

Rev. F. H. Shuler was elected Commissioner of Education, to give his whole time to canvassing. Results were disappointing, but were better in the cities in which the institutions were located. Spartanburg, which did much the best, for instance, subscribed in the spring of 1917 $40,000 to the

---

8. The statement of endowment in 1916 as larger than the stated figure in 1920, several pages below, may be due to loan funds being included in one figure and not in the other, etc.

endowment of Wofford, of which $16,000 was promptly paid. Bamberg in proportion to size and means did about as well. But during 1918 the campaign lagged, partly on account of the large demands being made upon the people for war purposes, and partly on account of the lethargy of the laity and even of some of the ministers. Commissioner Shuler resigned and each institution was advised to seek to obtain the balance of its apportionment.[9]

Wofford's resources were still small, the productive endowment in 1919 being only $189,189, and loan funds $14,158. Yet debt was being steadily reduced, leaving in that year a debt of only $29,829. Gifts and legacies during the year amounted to $11,119. The tuition fee was timidly raised in 1918 to $45 instead of $40 a year, and by a bolder move in 1919 to $60—very modest indeed compared with the tuition fee today of $250 a year, matriculation $70, medical and other fees (not including room and board) bringing the total fees to $390 a year. Matriculation had already been raised to $20. Among accessions of this period were the gift from Mrs. E. L. Archer of $5,000 in 1919 [10] and the bequest by Mrs. Ann Jeter of Columbia of $5,000.

College life during the period was violently changed by the plans of the government to secure the services of young men for the armed forces and yet disrupt the life of the colleges to the least degree possible. The government to a large extent took over the management of the colleges and turned them into a mild form of military camps. The students were organized into military units under the title of Reserve Officers Training Corps. The courses of study were reshaped to serve military needs. The war ended so soon that the students were not sent as a body to the front, and hence the disruption of college life was much less than in World War II, as will be narrated in due course. In the First World War, however, numbers of students went directly into the armed forces instead of remaining in college as members of the R.O.T.C. The college made liberal allowances in granting their degrees to men who were near graduation.

The college commencement of 1919 was largely devoted to honoring the six hundred and thirty-seven known Wofford men who had served in World War I, beginning with the class of 1882 and extending through those of latest enrollment in the college or Fitting School, and especially honoring the seventeen who gave their lives for their country. The Alumni Banquet was presided over by Lieutenant James C. Dozier, who had been a Freshman at Wofford in 1915-16, and had been awarded the Congressional Medal of

---

9. *Min. S. C. Conf.*, 1914, 40; 1916, 30-31; *Upper S. C. Conf. Mins.*, 1918, 48; *Trustee Min.*, June 2, 1917.

10. *Wof. Bulletin*, July, 1919, 12. Not to be confused with the $4,956.61 later received as a request.

Honor for "intrepidity and gallantry beyond the call of duty." The Alumni speaker was Capt. J. Lyles Glenn, Jr., of the class of 1912 who had distinguished himself in the Hoover relief commission's work in Belgium before the entrance of the United States into the war, and who won the *croix de guerre* as an American soldier. Both men bore wounds received in the war.

Sunday night, June 1, was a memorial service in honor of Wofford's war dead. President Snyder delivered a moving address narrating the service of each of the seventeen Wofford men who lost their lives.

Lieutenant William Augustus Hudgens of the class of 1897
Lieutenant Ernest Fripp McWhirter, of the class of 1904
William Montague Nicholls, a Freshman at Wofford during 1907-8. Lieutenant of artillery in the British army
John Theodore Monroe, of the class of 1913
Lieutenant Frank Gibbes Montgomery, a student at Wofford from 1910 to '13
Earl A. Davidson, a Freshman at Wofford during 1910-11
Lieutenant Thomas D. Lake, of the class of 1914
Lieutenant Thomas Carlisle Herbert, of the class of 1914
Lieutenant Hubert McCree Smith, a Freshman and Sophomore, at Wofford 1911-13
Clarence A. Lewis, of the class of 1916
Robert Thomas Fletcher, of the class of 1916
Thomas Raysor Summers, a Freshman at Wofford 1913-14
John M. Thomas, a Freshman at Wofford 1916-17 [11]
Frank L. Chennault, student at Wofford 1913-17
Arthur Welling, student in Wofford Fitting School 1907-8
Charles Dewey Graham, student at Wofford Fitting School 1916-17
Melvin Claude Rogers, student in Wofford Fitting School 1910-11 [12]

The South Carolina Methodist Conference having been divided, to begin with the 1915 session, a slight amendment to the charter of Wofford College became necessary. It was enacted in 1916 that in future the South Carolina Conference, consisting of the southeastern part of the State, should elect six members of the Board of Trustees, and the more populous Upper South Carolina Conference, consisting of the northwestern part of the State, seven members.[13] The Conference having been reunited, meeting as one in 1948, the amendment of 1916 fell into abeyance.

The endowment was reported to the Conference in November, 1920, as $193,091; loan funds an additional amount of $16,786; income for the academic year 1919-20 $50,694; debt $27,829. There were some features

---

11. Catalogue and the student's signature in college register show that his middle initial was M and not H, as in the *Wofford Bulletin* of July, 1914.
12. Memorial issue of *Wofford College Bulletin,* July, 1919.
13. Acts of S. C. Legis. for 1914-16, 1203.

of college finance that needed to be tightened up. For instance, the Trustees noted in June, 1921, that interest on the "loan" to the Fitting School at 4% had not been paid since 1916. The minutes of May 30, 1925, speak of "the $10,000 endowment loan to the Fitting School." The cottages built to accommodate the growing number of students were being carried at $20,000 as part of the endowment, out of which they had been built. The year before this brought in nearly 7% gross, which was better than formerly, but, considering insurance and repairs, represented a rather poor showing. The college had also borrowed from student loan funds to the extent of more than $3,000. All these, it was emphasized, would be replaced out of the first proceeds of the Christian Education Movement (to be presently noticed), as the use of endowment funds for such purposes was, to say the least, of doubtful wisdom. The policy was later declared to be to lend no money to church institutions or to any individual to sue whom would involve peculiarly disagreeable circumstances.

Another reform, made at the instance of Treasurer Davis and with the approval of President Snyder, was converting the part of the endowment invested in bank stocks into securities on which there could be no double liability, as there was then on the owners of stocks in banks in case of failure. Textile stocks were also being converted into other securities. Insurance on buildings was increased and put in better shape. In the academic year 1920-21 the college income of $55,710.10 was derived from the following sources: tuition and matriculation fees, $23,462.49; Conference assessment $15,984.78; endowment income $12,752.83; General Education Board $2,500; miscellaneous $1,010. The small proportion of total income derived from endowment was disturbing.

An important addition to the college, from both a scholarly and a personal standpoint, was the creation of the new chair of Religious Education, which was filled by Rev. Arcadius McSwain Trawick, who, after a wide experience in religious and sociological work, came to Wofford in 1921 from Scarritt Bible and Training School then situated in Kansas City, Mo. Fully justified was the judgment of President Snyder, who said in connection with the new chair that it must be filled by a man who would hold it up to a par with the other departments of the college. A very strong preacher, though not popular in style, a profound thinker on religious and philosophical questions, gifted with a rich sense of humor and an engaging personality, Professor Trawick has had few equals in broad and accurate scholarship in the history of the college. Though in the strange vagaries with which the lighting of honorary degrees strikes, he was never "Doctored," the college community instinctively and habitually called him Doctor, for they could not imagine that one so well deserving the title could be without it. Unaggressive almost to the point of passivity, he quietly awaited whatever Providence had in store for him. He took little part in Faculty discussions, and none in wrangles, as he was philosopher enough to realize that most questions that agitate Faculties could be settled either way without serious influence on human destiny.

The crying need for educational and moral forward moves emphasized by the World War, and the tempting prospect offered by the flush times that continued for some time after it, prompted the churches to movements to increase their educational and religious endowments. The movement in the Southern Methodist Church took the form of the Christian Education Movement, which proposed to raise $33,000,000, to be apportioned among the different Conferences, and by them on down to the charges and individual members. The quota expected to be raised in the South Carolina Methodist Conference was $1,202,000;[14] for the Upper South Carolina Conference doubtless a little more. The South Carolina movement for raising $300,000 for the church's institutions in this State and the wider Christian Educational movement for the whole Southern Methodist Church thus somewhat overlapped. President Snyder was made Associate Director of the latter. Entering upon this duty October 1, 1920, he had to be away in Nashville or speaking and conferring over the whole South for more than a year. Dean A. M. DuPre became Acting President during that time.[15]

The Christian Education Movement was to mean much to Wofford College. A welcome assistance was the pledge of the General Education Board of New York to give the college two dollars for every three raised by the movement, a strong reason for spurring collections.[16] As with the Twentieth Century Movement twenty years before, so now we seem to have jumped into the tide of business prosperity too late to be fully borne on to fortune. The depression of 1921 interfered with the collection of pledges. Yet the college went steadily forward during the '20's. President Snyder's report to the Trustees on the year 1923-24 may be summarized as a good picture of the college's condition at this period. Enrollment, he said, had increased during the last four years and is now 467. We need another dormitory, to cost about $100,000, and perhaps even more a community house to cost about the same, as suggested by the ladies of the campus a year ago. Two of our new young professors lack personality,

14. *S. C. Conf. Mins.*, 1922. I have not been able to find figure for Upper Conf.; but it would be a little larger, probably.
15. *Fac. Mins.*, Oct. 4, 1920; Snyder, *Educational Odyssey*, 203.
16. *S. C. Conf. Mins.*, 1923, 65.

but we will allow them further trial (which, we may remark, proved fruitless, as personality is not something easily augmented). A Professor of Economics should be employed, as the burden on one man to teach History and Economics is too much. Scholarship among the students is far from satisfactory, and we are seeking means of eliminating the unprepared from the lower classes.

Expenses at various colleges in the State were stated as follows:

	Tuition		Fees	Total	Board		Room	Total	Total
Charleston	$40.00	plus	$11.00	$ 51.00	$252.00	plus	$45.00	$297.00	$348.00
Erskine	60.00	plus	40.00	100.00	175.57	plus	48.80	224.37	324.37
Furman	60.00	plus	55.00	115.00	174.00	plus	60.00	234.00	349.00
Newberry	50.00	plus	27.50	77.50	162.00	plus	18-45	180-207	294.50-357.50
Presbyterian	50.00	plus	48.00	98.00	172.00	plus	50-75	222.-247	345.00
Univ. of S. C.	40.00	plus	38.00	78.00	162.00	plus	10-40	172-202	250-280
Wofford	60.00	plus	25.00	85.00	144.00	plus	32.00	176.00	261.00
Clemson	40.00	plus	35.00	75.00	144.00	plus	31.00	175.00	250.00
Citadel	....		....	....	....		....	....	250.00

In the death of Mr. James F. Hammett of Anderson, the college has lost a valuable friend. For the past four years he has on January 1 sent a check for $1,200 to be used as a loan fund, in blocks of $200. His will contained a bequest of $20,000 to Wofford College.

Additional statistics were given as follows:

Campus		68 acres valued at	$200,000
Main Building	cost $30,000	present value[17]	$100,000
Gymnasium	cost 5,000	present value	8,000
Science Hall	cost 25,000	present value	50,000
Library	cost 23,000	present value	40,000
Dormitory	cost 55,000	present value	100,000
Professors' residences	cost 25,500	present value	60,000
	$163,500	present value	$558,000

Library, 22,642 volumes; value $25,000
Annual appropriation for new books.............................. $1,000
Total value of scientific apparatus................................ $8,900
Museum, value $1,500
Furniture and fixtures, value $11,000

Grand Total for campus, buildings and equipment $605,400.00
(Including Fitting School) $683,691.78

Endowment for general maintenance, $281,996.77; other purposes, $15,507.50; total endowment, $297,504.27.

Amount of endowment invested in dormitories or other college buildings, $10,-554.50.

Unsecured notes and subscriptions receivable by college, $500,000.

17. More correctly, cost of replacement.

Additions to endowment during past year, $39,124.92.
Indebtedness, none.
Financial Campaign now in progress:
Christian Education movement $500,000.
Retirement funds none.

Income		*Expenditures*	
Tuition and fees	$31,960.25	Administration	$ 6,389.38
Endowment	17,017.52	Instruction	45,628.37
Conference collections	13,943.00	Operation and Maintenance	7,724.39
Other income	742.08	Books for Library	1,024.78
	$63,662.85		$60,766.92
Surplus			2,895.93

The college proper, the report continues, has no debt; but the Fitting School, now being discontinued, is indebted to the college to the extent of $9,500, being $6,000 balance on cost of constructing the recitation hall, and $3,500 deficit from operations. We are charging this to the Christian Education Fund, and are expecting to pay it out of collections from that. We have endowed loan funds of $15,507.50. As the Board knows, we receive $2 from the General Education Board for every $3 we collect. In South Carolina during the last two years our collections have been so small that we are humiliated when we hand in our pro rata. Of $100,000 due from South Carolina Methodists, we report only $20,000 collected, and half of that from residents of the city of Spartanburg.

Number in Faculty, 20;
Number of Methodists, 15; other churches, 5;
Ph.D.'s, 5;
M.A.'s, 9;
Bachelor of Arts or Science, 6;
How many carry over 16 hours a week? 3; 41 classes have over 30 men;
Number of students, 467;
Ministerial students, 26;[18]
Members Methodist church, 350; other churches, 104; of no church, 13;
Units for Freshman admission, 15;
Alumni, 1563.

1925-26 was a banner year. The enrollment reached a higher figure than ever before, namely 498. The increase of $280,345 in the endowment was the greatest that had ever occurred in any one year.[19] This was due to two

---

18. Dr. Snyder says elsewhere in report, 41.

19. The statement of a committee of the Trustees May 29, 1937, that the year 1936-37 saw larger additions to the endowment than any former year is incorrect. Detailed statement of the sources of the $280,345 increase are found in the *Upper S. C. Conf. Mins. for 1926*, page 50.

large donations: $100,000 from Mr. Benjamin N. Duke of New York; $75,000 from the General Education Board of New York, and $50,000 from the citizens of Spartanburg.[20] Mr. Duke's gift was made contingent upon the college's raising $50,000 in addition by June 1, 1926. The Spartanburg Chamber of Commerce promptly undertook meeting the condition, and as promptly did so.[21] The Benjamin N. Duke donation was peculiarly gratifying, for the reason that the college was feeling severe disappointment at Wofford's having been entirely left out of the benefits of the Duke Foundation, established in 1924, conferring such large benefits on Duke University, Davidson College, and Furman University.[22]

Mr. Benjamin Duke's donation in effect went much further than indicated by its nominal amount of $100,000. Mr. Duke asked Dr. Snyder whether he should make the donation without conditions, or on condition that some amount be contributed by others. Dr. Snyder chose the latter, and placed the amount to be raised from other sources at $50,000. This the Spartanburg Chamber of Commerce asked the privilege of raising, and did so promptly. The General Board of Education had also pledged to give the college two dollars for every three that the college raised. The Duke donation was in securities of a par value of $100,000, but of a market value of $120,000. Add to this the $50,000 given by Spartanburg businessmen, and the amount given by the General Education Board, and the real addition to resources due to the Duke donation sums up a value of about a quarter of a million.

Other noteworthy donations of this period were the gift of Mr. and Mrs. T. P. Sims in 1912 of $1,000 for establishing a scholarship for some orphan boy from Spartanburg, Union, or Fairfield County;[23] the bequest in 1925 by Mr. L. E. Caston of the 1878 class of $5,000; the gift of

---

20. President Snyder's report to American Council on Education, Washington, D. C.

21. *Trustee Mins.*, March 22, 1926.

22. Dr. Snyder told me today, January 28, 1949, my note states, sitting in the parlor of the St. John Hotel, in Charleston, that he was confident, on the basis of statements to him by persons intimate with Mr. James Buchanan Duke, the founder of the Duke Endowment, that if Mr. Duke had lived he intended to do something for Wofford College. He also told me (which I already knew) of statements from persons intimate with Mr. Duke of his deep resentment of what he considered Spartanburg's unfair treatment of him when he was building the Piedmont & Northern Railroad—electric interurban. Mr. Boyce Lee, Mayor of Spartanburg, was a strong friend of Mr. Knox, manager of the "local company," owned in Pittsburg, Pa., and was instrumental in thwarting Mr. Duke's plans for developments in Spartanburg. All the above, of course, except what relates to Mr. Duke's possible intentions toward Wofford College, is common knowledge. But it must be remembered that Mr. Duke desired such concessions as to the use of streets, etc., that many persons on the merits of the matter considered them excessive. Mr. Warren DuPre, for instance, said to me at the time, that he would rather see grass growing in our streets than agree to such demands. The idea, which I have sometimes met, that Dr. Snyder turned down an offer of a donation from Mr. James B. Duke is so absurd as hardly to merit denial. In securing the gift of $100,000 from Mr. Benjamin N. Duke Dr. Snyder had the co-operation of President William P. Few of Duke University, a Wofford alumnus of 1889, as Dr. Snyder told me, and as an entry in the *Wofford Trustee Minutes* indicates.

23. At another time Mrs. Sims gave another $1,000.—Conversation with President Snyder.

$1,500 by Mrs. B. Hart Moss as a book purchasing fund in honor of her father, Mr. Samuel Dibble, the first graduate of the college; the gift in 1928 by Dr. and Mrs. W. C. Kirkland of $1,000; the bequest in 1929 by Mr. John B. Cleveland of $1,000; and in 1928 the pledge by Mr. Isaac Andrews of $20,000 towards a field house, the total cost of which, $41,650, was met by the college's borrowing the necessary funds pending the payment several years later by Mr. Andrews, the building being named in his honor the Andrews Field House.[24]

Such was the condition of the college just before the great depression, with large enrollment, full treasury, growing endowment; the loyal support of the church; a Board of Trustees of able and devoted leaders in their professions or businesses; a rapidly growing body of alumni occupying their full share of positions of responsibility in this and other States; a President in the full maturity of his intellectual powers and still of remarkable physical vigor; an enlarged Faculty with only three diminished in energy by years, when it received its full share of the impact of the economic cyclone which burst upon the country in October, 1929.

24. Trustee report to Upper S. C. Conference, *Conf. Mins.*, 1930, 58.

CHAPTER XIV

DEPRESSION AND RECOVERY, 1929-37

NOT ONLY is the story of depression disagreeable, but the necessary array of figures is wearisome. Yet behind those figures is a moving story of patience and heroic determination not to succumb. Attendance was off sharply in 1928-29, but this cannot be attributed to the depression, whose advent was announced dramatically by the stock market crash of October, 1929. The steady decline for the next three years, however, needs no other explanation. The tide turned for the better with 1932-33, beginning a healthy growth in number for six years and from then until the devastating effects of World War II at a fairly steady level. Income suffered a corresponding decline, which by the year 1932-33 had become alarming. Debt had risen from $67,617 in 1925 (or $88,967 in 1928, to use a later date) and to $187,300 in 1933. Though endowment was still stated at over $700,000, $250,000 of it was reported as unproductive. Steadily increasing failure of borrowers to pay interest or principal threw quantities of real estate on the hands of the college, which required years to liquidate, which was ultimately done without net loss.[1]

Like many others, the authorities of the college did not realize how profound and prolonged was to be the deflation of the inflated prosperity of the middle '20's. President Snyder's report to the Trustees on the year 1930-31 was on the whole rather cheerful. Dr. Rembert's health forced him late in the year, bitterly to the disappointment of that inveterate worker, to allow others to take over his work. Prof. D. A. DuPre's death September 6, 1930, had left Geology uncared for; but the highly competent Prof. W. H. Morton of Converse College took it over for two years. Dr. Pugh was collaborating in preparing a dictionary of the English language before 1600; Dr. Chiles was about to issue another textbook in German, and Dr. Wallace was on his four years' leave of absence begun in June, 1929, for writing the *History of South Carolina*. President Snyder's activities had been incessant: the General Board of Christian Education in Nashville; the Hymnal Commission in Cincinnati; The Association of American Colleges in Indianapolis; visits to New York, the University of North Carolina, Duke University, in the interest of the college; meeting eight out of twelve

---

1. Treasurer J. K. Davis to D. D. Wallace, May 7, 1948.

220

of the District Conferences in South Carolina; addressing graduating classes in thirty-three high schools.

The steadily mounting deficit presented disagreeable alternatives. To drop some professors and put heavier loads on those remaining would involve losing our rating with standardizing agencies and would be a high price to pay for balancing our budget. Far better to bring back income to what it was. This involved several things dim with doubt as to their possibility. Suggested President Snyder: 1. We should as quickly as possible add one hundred to the number of our students. 2. We should seek to increase the income from Conference assessments, which I believe the preachers and people will do. 3. We should canvass alumni and friends for annual donations for a number of years (what, we may remark, came to be called the living endowment). The work of Mr. Henry W. Fair, of the class of 1892, as President of the Alumni Association, in aiding Dr. Snyder in organizing the alumni all over the State was so highly appreciated as to receive the special acknowledgment of the Board of Trustees, as recorded in their Minutes of June 4, 1938. 4. We should approach men of wealth in Spartanburg for contributions to the college.

To much the same effect as President Snyder's statement to the Trustees was the report of the Board of Christian Education of the Upper South Carolina Conference in the fall of 1931. Our colleges, says the report, have reached a crisis. We recommend that each of the two Conferences in the State appoint three ministers and three laymen from each Conference to constitute a commission to study the situation and recommend what ought to be the educational service which Methodism should offer its constituency and the State.

The commission was appointed, and made its report to each of the Conferences in 1932. Opinion within the commission differed considerably, but by mutual adjustment the following was agreed upon (we condense):

The commission has sought to conserve each institution and its contribution. *First,* as to the kind of education which we should provide: Institutions conferring academic degrees must be maintained at Grade A standing. Education should be provided for as large as possible a part of our constituency, and costs should be kept low enough for parents to meet them. There should be something more distinctive in the church college than is often implied merely in the name. "Without apology, the church college must teach religion" and should relate itself to the organized religious life of the community. This should extend beyond the distinctly religious courses such as Bible study and should extend into the courses in philosophy, theology, and psychology.

Second, as to our educational situation and emergency problems: examination shows that for the most part our faculties are well trained and devoted to their tasks. We are sure that conditions, though not ideal, compare favorably with those of former generations. The two women's colleges, with their small endowments and enormous debts, are in worse condition than is Wofford, whose general endowment is $700,199, and which has in addition endowed loan funds of $39,798, and a debt of $135,394. Wofford is a member of the Southern Association of Colleges and Secondary Schools and is fully approved by the Association of American Universities; but her endowment does not admit of much expansion of buildings, equipment, or faculty. Increased endowment is the imperative need of all three colleges. The church should increase its subventions. Only about one-fourth of the 2,300 Methodist students in colleges in South Carolina are in our Methodist colleges. Unpaid student accounts are a considerable cause of the college deficits.

One of our most serious problems is that of competition. We are competing with ourselves, a ruinous plan, wasteful and suicidal policy. We recommend that the Carlisle Fitting School be discontinued as a church school and sold or leased.[2] We also recommend that certain changes should be made by the Trustees of each institution, after consultation with this commission or its successor, but that changes should not be made except by the votes of both the commission and the Trustees voting separately.[3]

It is obvious from this report, and from the one of a similar commission in 1937 reviewed a few pages below, that the movement for the consolidation of institutions which was voted by the Conferences in 1947 was already strongly under way.

In 1933, salaries and other expenses at Wofford were cut to an extent, it was calculated, to save something over $20,000. President Snyder told the Trustees in June, 1933, that the students had done well during the depression. The Faculty, too, had large opportunity for the moral heroism for which they had been accustomed to hear their predecessors of the Civil War and the Reconstruction period praised. There was some grouching (and there was some in those earlier days too), but not much; a few harsh words, but not many. The Trustees paid the Faculty in full for several years, partly on borrowed money, but with the year 1932-33 they began to suffer. The Trustees guaranteed, February 15, 1933, that salaries for that scholastic year would ultimately be paid in full; and that from September 1, 1933, all officers and teachers should receive pro rata only what the income of the college warranted. That did not help to pay the grocer's bill; for, since September 25, 1932, the Professors said in an address to the Trustees June 2, 1933, they had received only the October salary and a small part on November. I do not see, said President Snyder, how they have lived with seven months' salaries unpaid. He was forced into a sort of inconsistency; for, whereas a few years before, irked by the

---

2. It was leased in 1932 to Prof. James F. Risher, the Headmaster, and sold to him in 1938.
3. *Mins. Upper S. C. Conference,* 1932, 46.

surplus of playboys in American colleges, he had openly said there were too many students in colleges, he was now seen working the flesh off his bones trying to keep the flesh on the bones of his Faculty by bringing in more students.

The Trustees ordered that $23,000 worth of securities be sold and back salaries paid, or that the Professor might take his pro rata share of these securities, or take real estate which the college had had to take in on delinquent endowment loans. Otherwise he would receive three notes bearing 5% and payable September 1, 1934, 1935, and 1936. After paying what the college income justified, gradually increasing from year to year, the Trustees, June 3, 1939, restored salaries to the pre-depression level.

The Faculty suggested to the Trustees that, without discounting the value of athletics, the appropriation for that purpose might be reduced. The Athletic Director in 1932 was receiving $5,000 (about half paid by the college and half by the alumni or other subscribers), when the highest salary paid a Professor was $3,250. This was reduced to $4,000, and on the expiration of his contract to a still lower figure. May 27, 1931, the President reported to the Trustees that the college had lost on athletics $40,145.82. Almost $10,000 of this was written off as a permanent loss in 1926, and in 1933 the balance, then amounting to $32,375.71. However in 1933-34 athletics for the first time in years ended the year with a profit. For the year 1939-40 the deficit was only $1,778.[4]

The President's report to the Trustees in 1931 refers to one of the largest gifts to the college, namely the expenditure ultimately of about $30,000 by Mr. William A. Law, with the co-operation of his brother, Mr. John A. Law, for steel and concrete grandstands, etc., for the Athletic Field, which Dr. Snyder very properly thought ought to be named Law Field; but Mr. Law insisted that it be called Snyder Field. William A. Law, of the class of 1883, was one of the most distinguished graduates of the college. He was one of five brothers who graduated at Wofford, the others being John A. Law of 1887, Thomas A. Law, of 1892, Andrew M. Law of 1896, and Robert A. Law of 1898. Robert is one of the leading Shakespeare scholars of the world; the others attained eminence in finance, except Thomas, who died young. Their father, Rev. Thomas H. Law, D.D., for more than forty years missed only one commencement. Called to Philadelphia to handle the Southern business of the Merchants National Bank, William A. Law became in time its President, and of the First National with which it merged, from which position he passed to the Presidency of the Penn Mutual Life

---

4. Trustee Mins. June 5, 1926; May 27, 1931; June 4, 1932; June 3, 1933; June 2, 1934; May 31, 1940.

Insurance Company. He was killed by an accidental shot while hunting in North Carolina. His friend Mr. H. Clay Williams, of the Reynolds Tobacco Company, gave the college in 1937 in memory of him $50,000 as an endowment of the William Adger Law scholarships.[5] That same year Mr. T. B. Stackhouse, of the class of 1880, then living in Columbia, gave the college $50,000, and Bishop E. D. Mouzon bequeathed it his splendid library.[6] Other donations during the period were $1,000 from Mr. Hough Milton Stackhouse, a Freshman in 1859; a bequest of $30,000 from the estate of Mrs. Annie Naomi McCartha Shirley of Columbia, as a loan fund for ministerial education; a bequest of approximately $23,000 from Mr. W. Frank Walker; $833 from the estate of Mr. Joseph A. McCullough; and $3,000 from the estate of Mr. F. A. Sondley of the class of 1876.[7] Thomas W. Smith of the class of 1871, April 10, 1930, sent in a letter with trembling hand $500 as an expression of what the college had done for him.[8] Bernard Baruch early in 1939 gave Wofford (as he did about the same time to a number of South Carolina colleges) $10,000.[9] The bequest to the college by Mrs. E. L. Archer, who died November 30, 1941, amounted to $4,956.61 [10]

Beginning in 1934 the $187,300 debt was steadily paid off, until in 1942 the college was entirely free of debt. Though we may say the college was out of the depression by 1937, with salaries being paid at 90 per cent, thoughtful men realized that much remained to be done for strengthening its position.[11] A committee of the Trustees had this to say in reviewing the President's and Dean's reports for the year 1936-37:

We are still facing the future with increasing anxiety and concern as this great institution is compelled to carry on with such limited funds in a field of ever enlarging demands with the keenest sort of competition from heavily endowed church institutions and also from large tax-supported state colleges and universities. We also face a future of changing standards and ideals of education. Along what lines in the future this college must chart her course must be considered. We are unable at this time to make any definite recommendations, but this much we are clear in our thinking, that we shall forever hold to the ideals of Christian character and unselfish service for which the institution has stood through all the years. As to the future of Wofford and its general policy in the coming years

5. *Trustee Mins.*, May 29, 1937.
6. *Ib.*
7. *Ib.*, June 2, 1934; May 30, 1936; President to T. B. Stackhouse, June 22, 1937.
8. Letter in Dr. Snyder's files.
9. *Old Gold and Black*, Apr. 1, 1939.
10. Papers of the estate, Spartanburg Probate Office. Mrs. Archer bequeathed the residue of her estate (after a few small personal bequests) in equal parts to the Epworth Orphanage, The Georgia Cleveland Home for aged ladies, and Wofford College.
11. Treas. books on salaries.

another committee will make a fuller report. This is worthy of the careful consideration of every member of this Board, for in the near future a change of leadership is imperative because of the growing age of those who now lead us.[12]

Admirable is the wisdom, excellent the foresight, of the committee who prepared this report—Reverends Peter Stokes, George C. Leonard, and R. F. Morris—conscious of difficulties; confident of the future, and thoughtfully preparing to meet it. Next those problems must engage our attention.

---

12. *Tr. Mins.*, May 29, 1937.

225

CHAPTER XV

PRESIDENT SNYDER CLOSES HIS LONG ADMINISTRATION, 1937-42

THOUGH Wofford College strives to stimulate the religious life of its students, it makes no attempt to draw them from the church to which they or their families belong. It is interesting to note the distribution of students by denominations. The enrollment on October 1, 1940, is doubtless typical for recent years. Of the 480 undergraduates then in college 260 were Methodists; 144 Baptists; 23 Presbyterians; 17 Episcopalians; 9 Lutherans; 2 each Roman Catholics and Quakers; and 1 each Jew, Associate Reformed Presbyterian, Pentecostal Holiness, Seventh Day Adventist, and Greek Orthodox; while 18 were of no church connection.[1]

A sort of outline picture of the college in 1937 as it was emerging from the Great Depression may be sketched from the report of the President to the General Board of Education, November 30, 1937, a somewhat scrappy sketch, however, as it consists of answers to a questionnaire:

Yes, the growth of Junior colleges has affected our enrollment; but what we have lost in the two lower classes is partly made up by the students that we received from them for our upper classes. Probably this condition will continue, with our Freshman class remaining relatively stable and our upper classes growing.

In the past our students have been drawn very largely from Methodist families, but of recent years the number from other denominations has grown. Recognition of the good work we do will probably result in our holding our Methodist constituency and drawing still more largely from other denominations.

Yes, I think that an increase of at least 30% in student fees is advisable, and in fact do not see how else we can remedy our shrinking income. Some advance is being contemplated. I cannot approve of charging, as you suggest as a possibility, more to students able to pay, as it would result in unhappy divisions among students, and invite insincerities and concealments. I would, however, advise the increase in scholarships and funds for student loans. Funds for these purposes are easy to raise, but we shall not proceed to that until we have met more pressing needs.

We are contemplating special efforts for the increase of endowment and plant and equipment. The diminution of upkeep during the depression calls for increased expenditures for that purpose, and certain buildings need to be enlarged, the library, for instance. The alumni do not raise a regular annual fund for the college, but we contemplate appealing both to them and to the general public for

---

1. President's report to Board of Ed., Methodist Church, Nashville, Tenn., Dec. 18, 1940.

meeting the above needs. During the depression a group of alumni contributed a small amount toward current expenses.

It is hard to say whether the present tax laws encourage or discourage gifts. Under normal conditions the high income tax laws, with exemptions for gifts, would tend to increase giving; but when men of wealth feel that they are being treated as public enemies they fall into a somewhat hysterical state of fear and uncertainty, sit tight and do nothing. "The 'atmosphere' must clear up."

Research is not carried on except as the individual professor does it on his own initiative. The college makes no provision for it. Salaries were cut during the depression, but have now been restored to within 8% of the pre-depression level. Current income for the year 1936-37 was sufficient to meet current operating expenses.

I think that the colleges in this section, especially those of our class, need to make a thorough study of themselves, their potentially continuing constituencies, the special values which they must strive to preserve, the necessary adjustment which they must make to meet new needs, how each differs from others of its class, whether this difference is worth carrying on, and finally of just how much money is required for buildings, equipment, and endowment to fit a college to render its particular kind of service in its own field. There must follow from such a study a long range program to secure the funds needed to enable the institution to do its work without too much pinching.

We are unavoidably struck by the similarity between this statement by the old President so soon to retire of the needs of the college and the program for realizing these aims so vigorously undertaken by the new President on his installation five years later. This continuity of aims is a feature of the development of the life of the institution which can be observed at several stages and constitutes strong evidence of the soundness of these proposals and advances.

President Snyder's report outlined above chimes perfectly with the contemporary thought of the South Carolina and the Upper South Carolina Methodist Conferences. The two Conferences in 1939 and again in 1940 designated the five-year period from 1940 through 1944 for special effort for Wofford, known as the Promotion Program. The General Committee on Promotion in February, 1941, adopted a comprehensive plan for the physical and financial improvement of the college and the organization of the alumni as a permanently assisting body. Dr. Snyder was named as Director-in-Chief of the movement—a high compliment, but rather a cruel burden to lay upon a man of his age and strength.[2]

We must remember, however, that the two Methodist Conferences of the State had in mind an even broader movement comprehending the systematization and improvement of the entire educational equipment and

2. A detailed account of the Wofford Promotion Movement is given in the *So. Christian Ad.,* of Feb. 20, 1941, by Dr. J. Emerson Ford, one of the chief leaders of the movement.

program of the church. In 1937 the two Conferences asked the Bishop to appoint a joint commission on their colleges. This was clearly a continuation of the method of procedure of 1931 in the appointment of a joint commission for the same purpose, and carried farther, as will be seen, the policy of that commission as announced in its report of 1932 outlined in the last chapter. In both Rev. J. Emerson Ford (who was elected a member of the Wofford College Board of Trustees in 1938) was a leading member and very influential in their findings. The report of the Commission of 1937, presented in 1938, deals with difficulties which had vexed the Conference for years, arising largely out of the fact that they were seeking to support three colleges—one for men and two for women. We consider, said the Commission, that the appointment of one Board of Trustees for the three institutions would not meet the needs, as each institution would still have its own problems. There are other alternatives:

1. Shall we leave the colleges as they are to succeed or fail academically and financially?
2. Shall we seek to obtain endowments sufficient to maintain all three as accredited senior colleges?
3. Shall we merge all three into one institution?
4. Shall we merge the two colleges for women?
5. Shall we choose the one that shall survive and close the others?

The Commission returned to these questions the following answers:

1. Wofford College should be maintained as a four year grade A college, with co-education in the Junior and Senior classes, and with dormitory facilities for women.
2. Columbia College should be maintained as a four year grade A college for women.
3. Lander should be made a Junior college for girls, with co-education for local patrons.[3]

The movement was never allowed to cease, as attested by the activities of Trustees and Conference up to the very end of President Snyder's administration, and much was done for laying the foundations in thought and sentiment for the bold structure which President Greene proposed on assuming office. A serious heart attack at Junaluska, N. C., in the summer of 1940 kept Dr. Snyder from his office until January 1, and from full time duties until February 1, 1941;[4] but the "Five Year Plan," or "Promotion Program," as it was called, was being systematically pushed to the very day

---

3. *Upper S. C. Conf. Mins.*, 1938, 69-71.
4. President Snyder's report for 1940-41.

of his retirement. Continuity of thought and purpose was maintained in the story of institutional development by the new President.

Another item illustrating the continuity of development, and the recognition by various thinkers that adjustments were required as the institution grew in size and the Faculty in numbers was the order of the Trustees, June 1, 1935, that a committee be appointed to report a set of by-laws for governing the relations of Trustees, President and Faculty. Such a set of rules was reported to the Trustees May 29, 1937, and was referred back to the committee for further consideration. This, like the expansion program, passed over for completion into the new administration.

A striking similarity will be observed, indicating the continuity of development, between the recommendations of the Conference committee of 1938, detailed above, and the plan finally adopted in November, 1947, at the joint session of the South Carolina and the Upper South Carolina Conferences:

Wofford College shall be maintained as a standard grade A college primarily for men, but may become co-educational if the Trustees considered that the demand warrants.

Columbia College shall be maintained as a standard grade A college for women.

Lander College shall be offered to the city or county of Greenwood or some responsible body representative of the community, to be used exclusively for educational purposes, and not to be disposed of without the consent of the two Conferences. The name Lander must be surrendered if the college comes to be operated on any lower standard, e.g. as a junior college. In case of refusal of Greenwood to accept the institution, it shall be sold and the proceeds divided between the other two Methodist colleges in the State. [An eleemosynary corporation of Greenwood citizens accepted the college on these terms.]

Wofford and Columbia Colleges shall remain in their present locations, and be placed under the control of one Board of thirteen Trustees, and administered by a single Chancellor or President [the term President was adopted when the plan went into effect, with President Walter K. Greene of Wofford College as President]. South Carolina Methodism shall at once enter upon a campaign to raise $600,000 for Wofford and $400,000 for Columbia.

The plan promptly went into effect, with Dean C. C. Norton, Dean at Wofford since 1942, being made Dean of Administration at Wofford and Dr. Oscar W. Lever, up to that time Professor of Philosophy at Wofford, Dean of Administration at Columbia. The burdensomeness of the double presidency and other disadvantages led the Conference in November, 1950, to abandon the plan and to return each institution, as of February 1, 1951, to its own separate board of Trustees and President. Dr. Greene, who in October, 1950, had given notice of his resignation as of August 1, 1951, was made President of Wofford under its restored independence.

Having carried the movement for the consolidation of the colleges to its conclusion, let us turn back to take up matters which have been passed over chronologically. On Sunday, November 5, 1939, at 1:50 in the afternoon, the campus community was shocked to witness a spectacular fire bursting through the roof of Carlisle Hall.[5] The fire swept through the attic, but was effectively checked by the city fire department. We might mention also the burning of Bobo Cottage one spring day in the early 1900's as the result of students' somewhat carelessly carrying out the President's suggestion to burn up all old papers and trash; and the quite damaging, but not completely destructive, fire the afternoon of January 29, 1917, that burned off the roof and other parts of the Wilbur E. Burnett Gymnasium—incidentally much to the joy of certain students who abhorred the compulsory exercises.[6] "Several days ago," says the *Wofford College Journal* of January, 1912, "a fire in the old Kappa Alpha house (the cottage in the southwestern corner of Calhoun Street and the circular driveway, last occupied before being torn down on account of the building of the Spartanburg County Auditorium by Prof. Bourne) was extinguished by a student 'bucket Brigade' before the city fire department arrived."

A gratifying evidence of religious activity was the request of various student organizations in September, 1941, that in order to stimulate religious interest on the campus, the students be allowed to designate one of their number for each Thursday to conduct chapel exercises that day. The Faculty gave its unanimous approval.[7]

An incident occurred in the spring of 1937 which showed, without intention or anticipation, how the feelings of class prejudice may be suddenly and dangerously roused. Peter R. Moody, of Cooleemee, N. C., a village almost fifteen miles north of Salisbury, N. C., a member of the class of 1937, was a frequent contributor to the *Wofford College Journal*. A class exercise in modernistic poetry, entitled "To a Cotton Mill Worker," was so good that it was desired for publication, and appeared in the April, 1937, issue of the *Journal*. It addressed the lower type of mill worker in language describing both his own degraded character ("Your shoulders are humped and your head is bent") and the degrading conditions under which he lived so as to be offensive both to the average cotton mill worker, whom it did not intend to satirize as a class, and to the cotton mill owner or executive. Moody concluded (employing a term particularly offensive to cotton mill operatives):

---

5. City Fire Department Records.
6. City Fire Dept. Records.
7. Faculty Minutes, Sept. 29, 1941; *Old Gold and Black,* October 3, 1941.

Listen, lint-head, you are just another poor, illiterate cotton mill worker. You stand with a thousand others just like you . . . tending a power loom, all for forty cents an hour. . . . You are dead! You died on your sixteenth birthday when you went to work in the cotton mill.

It would have passed as merely a particularly good piece of college student writing but for the fact that two newspapers in the community pounced upon it. One, regarded as representing the mill owner interests, was perhaps offended by the implication of guilt on the part of the mill owners as contributors through bad conditions to such a product, and, seeing an opportunity to ingratiate itself with the workers, denounced young Moody in terms of extreme violence. The other paper, the real labor journal, joined in the chorus of condemnation, but not in such mob-rousing vehemence as the supposed mill owners' organ. Such anger flamed among the thousands of mill operatives in and around the city as to threaten, on the part of a few hotheads, physical violence. A group actually came on the campus one night and called for Moody; but no students responded. The men went away, threatening to "get him" on the street. Dr. Snyder telephoned to the labor leader in that village and called his attention to the lawless trespass already committed, and invited him to conference. He consented to come, but late at night telephoned that an interview was useless and that there would be no more trouble. The danger of mob violence was for several days thought very real. Dr. Snyder wrote a conciliatory letter to the Secretary of the Central Labor Union regretting the publication of the poem and assuring the Secretary that Moody held no such opinions of the mill workers as a class, and Moody himself wrote the Secretary a similar letter.

A member of the legislature from Spartanburg County interrupted the processes of legislation to introduce a resolution, buttressed by lengthy whereases, declaring that Moody was proved by what he had said about this large class of our citizens, praised affectionately in the whereases, to be either insane or a criminal and dangerous to the public if allowed at large; and therefore resolved that the Superintendent of the State Hospital be requested to send a psychiatrist to examine him. The legislature, with the primary election four months off, actually passed this resolution. "Just think what he said about us," said a preacher-operative legislator from another county with tears in his eyes to Dr. Snyder. Dr. E. L. Hoerger was sent to Spartanburg, and after an hour's interview with Moody reported to Dr. Snyder (but not in the same words as he used to the alarmed law makers) that Moody had more sense than the members of the legislature.

Moody's father was an employee of a cotton mill company, who, it is said, manifested their indignation or their desire to please their operatives (it is not clear which) by proposing to discharge the elder Moody; but other mill executives, it is understood, shamed them out of that.[8]

The whole affair was deeply significant of class prejudices and explains many things in South Carolina politics and social life. Within the past fifty years the cotton mill operatives have advanced mightily in worldly welfare and education and normal recognition as a valuable class of society; but their reaction in the Moody affair revealed like a lightning flash how deep is still the chasm between them and other elements of our society. And I am free to say that the so-called upper class of our society has much to answer for on account of the mingled aloofness and disdain with which it too long treated the textile workers as they gradually rose in the social and economic scale.[9]

Neither the Moody incident nor any other embarrassment which has occasionally arisen from student publications has ever caused the Faculty to institute a censorship. *The Wofford College Journal* has several times editorially criticized college policies, and the weekly newspaper, *The Old Gold and Black,* has a few times rather roughly ridiculed a Professor for riding his hobby in class instead of devoting his time more exclusively to rendering instruction in the subject for which he was employed.

A talkative teacher is always in danger of drifting into becoming what Dr. Snyder once called "Professor of Allerlei Gewissenschaft"—i.e. to say, things in general, but what the boys less elegantly call "running rabbits." It is strange that a teacher deeply interested in his subject should be willing to use on anything else part of the insufficient time allowed him to give the men all he wants to of what he is trying to teach. In such matters, in which a friend hesitates to speak to a colleague for fear of offending, the less considerate college journalist may render a needed service, and, it is to be hoped, accomplish some good. It is a hard disease to cure. But the courtesy and consideration of students toward Professors at Wofford has been excellent. Occasionally student criticism, and, in one case that I recall, radicalism, have been angrily condemned by some members of the Faculty. There is no pre-publication censorship; but college publications are forbidden to publish anything profane or obscene or reflecting upon a Professor. As a matter of fact such offenses have been extremely rare.

We may note here an instance of student action for solving some of the problems that arise in college journalism. In December, 1935, The Student

---

8. That was Dr. Snyder's information, communicated by him to me.

9. My account of the Moody affair is from my own observation of the events, conversations with Dr. H. N. Snyder, Dr. Snyder's and Moody's letters in *The State* of April 24, 1936, and *House of Representatives Journal* for April 22, 1936 (II, 1445-6.) See also *"Letters,"* May 25, 1936; published quarterly by Time, Inc., pp. 1-2.

Publications Union drew up a constitution for the three student publications (*The Wofford College Journal, the Old Gold and Black,* and the annual, *The Bohemian*), which was overwhelmingly adopted by the Student Body in January, 1936. It was for financial supervision and the election of staffs, and not for censorship. The Publications Board, it was enacted, should consist of eight members—four representing the Faculty and four the students, the latter being two Seniors and two Juniors elected by their respective classes by ballot. Staff members may not be members of the Board. Funds for college publications shall be allocated to the respective publications according to their needs, but existing allocations are to continue unless some special need dictates a change. Compensation of staff members shall be fixed by the Board. The staffs shall be elected by the Board; but retiring staffs shall have the right to nominate two men for editor and two for business manager, and others may be nominated by student petition signed by forty students; but the Board is not confined to these nominations in choosing staffs. Funds shall be under the control of the Board, and strict accounts and reports be required of the Business Manager.[10]

As noted above, a group of good singers in the late '60's were accustomed to sing together as serenaders for the delight of the maidens of that day; but apparently what would be called a modern Glee Club did not exist until about 1902. It was a sufficiently established college institution to have its officers listed in the October, 1904, *Journal* along with those of the literary societies, etc. In the early days in its home concerts or on its short trips it was accompanied by athletes, who added to the entertainment with their gymnastic stunts. Under Prof. Wilson B. Price, a high class musician, talented as a chorus trainer, who began his work with the Club in the year 1922-23 and served almost continuously for twenty-five years, i.e., through 1946-47, both the character of programs and the excellence of performance rose to a high level, which has been sustained since his retirement by Prof. Samuel R. Moyer of the regular college staff.[11] The Glee Club, on its tours through the State, has been an agency for presenting the college before the public in an extremely favorable light.

We have noticed the history of the Literary Societies from their origin through 1872, when the Trustees for the first time made membership compulsory for all students. So long as the societies remained almost the sole organized extracurricular activity, they absorbed a large part of the stu-

---

10. *Old Gold and Black,* Jan. 18, 1936. Originally the editors and business manager of the *Journal* were chosen by the two literary societies in joint session.

11. *Old Gold and Black,* Feb. 10, 1940; Price to Wallace. I thank Mr. S. R. Moyer for information on the Glee Club from his master's thesis on the history of music in Spartanburg County.

dents' energies. Debates sometimes lasted until midnight, and habitually the debates and other literary exercises consumed the entire night session, so that for many years it was the custom to have an additional session Saturday morning for miscellaneous business. But as other interests developed, either diversions in town, other student social or intellectual organizations, or athletics, interest was dissipated over so many fields as to leave the societies more neglected. The tendency began earlier in the Calhoun than in the Preston Society and went further there. During this indifference and absolute flippancy on the part of some which began to undermine the Calhoun Society in the early 1890's, turning debates into a farce or ending the session by a motion to adjourn almost immediately after the first roll call on account of the flimsiest reason, or no reason at all except indifference to the exercises, the Preston Society continued for a good many years the serious performance of its duties. It happened that the Calhouns had a number of bright men more or less flippantly inclined, while the Prestons enjoyed the leadership of an able and seriously minded group, led by D. Wistar Daniel and W. E. Willis of the class of 1892, for instance, to whom the society offered a really desired forum in which to display or develop their talents.

The Calhouns, it should be said, at the same time enjoyed the leadership of some men of the same character and aims, such as Thomas ("Tony") G. McLeod and William J. Cocke of the class of 1892; but one is struck in looking over the rolls fifty-seven years later by the enormous preponderance of able and serious-minded upper classmen who in 1892 belonged to the Prestons. That is natural; for, when a certain kind of student becomes conspicuous in any organization, students of that kind naturally flock into it, and students of the opposite kind avoid it. That was the misfortune that overtook the Calhouns to such a degree that the elements seriously desiring to use the society for its legitimate purposes were unable to stem the tide under the purely democratic rules that governed the societies. I was then a Sophomore member of the Calhouns, from the mere influence of tradition, my father having been a Calhoun, and saw with pain the development of these tendencies.

As the size of the student body increased, the membership of the societies, on account of the Trustees' rule of compulsory membership, swelled to unwieldy proportions and increased the evil of flippant and indifferent members, or students who, though falling into neither of these classes, simply did not care for that sort of thing. For several years in the 1920's the Preston Society was so large as to divide itself into two sections to meet on separate nights.[12] The Carlisle Society was organized preliminarily October 26, and permanently November 4, 1905. In answer to their request they were given in 1908 Dr. Carlisle's recitation room to the west of the chapel as their hall.[13] What they lacked in the handsome paintings and comfortable furniture of the older societies, they made up in the earnestness of the men conducting the new undertaking.

Increased college enrollment led in the college year 1920-21 to the organization of the Snyder Literary Society.[14] Gradually the hostile influences referred to above, particularly the increasingly intense absorption in intercollegiate athletics, restricting the outside reading of many students to the sports page in the newspaper, continued to sap the literary societies. After years of discussion in Faculty meetings and futile attempts to devise means of improvement, the rule was modified so as to require compulsory membership only during the student's first year in college, in the hope that the required tasting of the refreshing waters would cause those appreciating the benefit to continue membership. The results were disappointing, as the causes producing disintegration were constantly increasing, particularly the intense student interest in intercollegiate athletics, and the multiplication of the varieties of athletic contests, and the enlarging of the number of events. Intercollegiate debates, which had at one time stirred great interest, came to be attended at times by hardly a person except the contestants and the judges; for even a good debate is a rather tame affair to the average student compared with a snappy football or baseball or basketball contest between rival colleges, with college patriotism stirred to its height and with brass bands and organized cheering increasing an excitement already running high.

About 1937 the Calhoun and Snyder Societies united as the Calhoun-Snyder.[15] Finally, January 22, 1943, this society and the Carlisle Society met together to form plans for combining into one as the Carlisle-Snyder. Despite Faculty urging not to drop the historic name Calhoun, they continue to call themselves Carlisle-Snyder, as any addition would make the name too long.[16]

June 1, 1935, membership was made entirely voluntary, with the proviso

12. C. R. Spell in *Journal,* December, 1936, 11.
13. Carlisle Society Mins.; *Wof. College Jour.,* Oct., 1908.
14. College catalogue and *The Bohemian* for the college year closing in June, 1920, make no mention of the Snyder Society; both, for the year ending June, 1921, give the Snyder along with the other societies.
15. The college catalogue for 1937-8 contains the first reference to the Calhoun-Snyder Society.
16. Faculty Mins., Feb. 2, 1943.

that none but society members could participate in the public literary or oratorical exhibitions.[17]

Both the Calhoun and the Preston Societies accumulated libraries which were considerably used. They grew by donations as well as by purchases. Dr. Carlisle, Dr. Whitefoord Smith, and Dr. A. Coke Smith were givers of books, we know, to the Preston Society's library, and doubtless to that of the Calhoun Society also. In 1870 the Preston Library contained about 1,000 volumes; in 1885, 1,334; in 1894, 1,642.[18] It was estimated when the Society libraries were united with that of the college in October or November, 1894, that the Calhoun library contained about 3,000 volumes; the Preston about 2,500 volumes (probably considerable overestimates, judging from the more careful Preston figure just above), and the college library immediately before the union about 4,000 volumes.

A Preston treasure is the gavel made from wood from the old Hanover, Va., courthouse in which Patrick Henry delivered his famous speech in the "Parson's cause" in 1763. It was presented to the Society in 1895 by the Treasurer of Randolph-Macon College.[19] The plaster bust of William C. Preston was presented to the Society bearing his name by Dr. James H. Carlisle, who found it in possession of I. B. Glass, the postmaster of Columbia, who gladly gave it to Prof. Carlisle when he explained the purpose for which he desired it. The crack, not affecting the face, occurred from a jolt while Prof. Carlisle was bringing it to Spartanburg. Preston himself gave the plaster bust of his great uncle Patrick Henry, but was unable to present it in person as he desired, on account of ill health.

The most valuable painting on the campus is the life-size portrait of Calhoun, owned by the Calhoun Society, a replica by Albert Guerry of his portrait of Calhoun in the South Carolina Senate chamber, a portrait of which there are apparently several replicas. One of Guerry's last works is the fine portrait of Dr. James H. Carlisle in the college chapel. The portrait of Bishop Wightman, by his brother Thomas, long in the Calhoun hall, now in the Faculty Room, is a fine piece of work.

A late comer in college journalism is *The Bohemian*. It had a predecessor as an annual called *The Aurora,* a very creditable book issued in 1904. That was entirely too sissy a name for red-blooded college youth, and so when the annual was revived in 1908 it was called *The Bohemian*. Since then it has continued as a creditable student publication.

Dr. Snyder was fortunate in his secretaries; for, I suppose, next to having

17. *Tr. Mins.,* June 1, 1935; Faculty Mins.
18. C. R. Spell as above.
19. C. R. Spell as above.

a good wife, as he certainly did in the lady who so charmingly presided over his hospitable table, it is important for a college President to have a good secretary. Early in his administration was Daniel L. Betts of the class of 1910, who served as Secretary and managed Carlisle Hall. Small in stature but tall in efficiency, Betts, who was once humorously introduced as "the young man who writes Dr. Snyder's speeches," was in fact a large cog in the college machinery. Capable, active, conscientious, he created a vacancy not easily filled when he left the college and later went as a missionary to Brazil. President Snyder was served from 1925 to '29 and again from 1933 to 1942 by a young woman from New Hampshire, Miss Dorothy Woodward, possessed of all the qualities of an ideal secretary; high intelligence, industry, good cheer, fidelity, and above all loyalty to duty and employer. She helped other officials with their correspondence, and, after Dr. Snyder's retirement, served as Registrar from 1943 or '44 until 1947. These faithful, efficient handlers of innumerable details did their part in making President Snyder's administration a success.

Old students remember with a sort of tenderness the nicknames by which they called their teachers. After Prof. Henry N. Snyder spent a year in Germany he was Heiney. Rembert, as he sat screwed up with legs tightly crossed and shooting caustic remarks at lazy pretenders (if any such dared long to remain in his classes) was Knotty; Trawick, with his kindly round face and thick-set body was Pug; D. Duncan Wallace was inevitably Dunk; A. Mason DuPre was Amazing DuPre, or more often Old Mase; another was Skinny; Salmon was of course Fish; Waller was Frog, perhaps because he dissected so many of them; the venerable head of the scientific department was Uncle Dan; Clink was sufficient without the scales; Herbert, Headmaster of the fitting school while it had military drill, as he strode around in uniform and puttees earned the title of "Colonel" for life; Chiles was "Graveyard," whether from his solemn manner or from the large number of men he "flunked" has not been determined; Norton was Cutie, a tribute perhaps to his Hitleresque mustache; the Professor of Latin who loved to expound the beauties of the *ut* clause was Ut (and his young son Little Ut), until time and affection substituted Uncle Gus; one with a birthmark was Blaze Face; another who had lost a foot was Peg; Shuler was also Peg, doubtless because of his surveying stakes; Nesbitt was Chuck; and, as said Paul, to enumerate all those, of whom the world was not worthy, time would fail.

President Snyder in his later years saw four of his older colleagues pass into the Great Beyond. With his kindly disposition and the lack of adequate resources, President Snyder never worked out any systematic plan for retiring men as their efficiency declined, or they reached an arbitrary age limit. He kept them on part work and salary, and moreover he determined to make them an asset so far as possible to cancel their burden as a liability. "What to do with your old men?" a college President once asked him.[20] "Why, capitalize them among the real assets of the institution. They represent in a living way its past; they are its traditions at their best; and it is they the alumni enquire about and visit when they come to the campus. So I paid special and sincere attention to these older men; told about them in public addresses; and took them with me to alumni gatherings. And as time went on and their infirmities increased, as tactfully as I could, I would ease them into teaching one course. . . . Capitalize their service, their character, their personality; hold to them as long as life lasts; and memorialize them as among the enduring records of the institution. The dividends will be richly humane and satisfying. Daniel DuPre, James [21] Augustus Gamewell, Arthur Gaillard Rembert, John G. Clinkscales—I saw them walking into the sunset, showing what kind of persons men become who through a long life have loved truth, and freedom, and honor, and courtesy, qualities still as valid as they were when Chaucer more than five hundred years ago ascribed them to his 'verray parfit gentil knight.' Their homes were meccas for visiting alumni, paying grateful tributes of affection and reverence to men who taught them science, Latin, Greek, mathematics, but also something that went deeper; something that called to an urge toward upright and serviceable living. Isn't this, I ask it again, one of the elements in what we are trying to say when we talk so much about a 'liberal education'? If it isn't, it ought to be, and if a college President is not dumb and blind to what really counts, he will be greatly pleased to have such 'old men' around, and will know what to do with them."

This is such a fine expression of the "old men" problem that we are tempted to forget the difficulties it overlooks. It worked fairly well when Wofford was a small institution; but even President Snyder had more troubles under it than in his kindly spirit he cared to speak of. Just when the student should be protected from the old man who has outlived his efficiency, and just when he should be deprived of the services of a mind rich with accumulated knowledge and experience, still vigorous and progressive though past a certain arbitrary age limit, I shall not attempt to say. Dr. Snyder's treatment of the "old men" problem is suffused with kindly sentiment; but the passage that immediately follows on the younger man who at, say fifty, has become negligent and unprogressive is unsparing of that academic un-

20. Snyder, *Educational Odyssey*, 248-49.
21. Should be Joseph.

worthy. All this does not tell us how to mingle justly the kindly sentiment of his first paragraph and the rigorous academic integrity of his second; but it at least helps us to realize how hard it is to be a good college President.

The first of the old men to go was Prof. Daniel Allston DuPre, who died after a brief illness, September 6, 1930. He was born at Eagle Point Plantation, his maternal grandmother's home, near Boydton, Va., May 15, 1848. He was largely of Huguenot ancestry. His was the good fortune of a gentle decline in physical strength without impairment of mental faculties and the happiness of being able to continue to do good by the imparting of knowledge to the last. Industrious to a degree, ever faithful to every duty, par excellence a gentleman by nature and of a distinction of manner which few possess, he taught unconsciously more than his subject. Yet, with all his polish, and a temperament, it was often said, as sensitive as a woman's, he was decided in his views and did not hesitate to express them positively. His sensitive nature sometimes caused him to speak impatiently, especially at shilly-shally proposals regarding discipline, a subject on which his ideas were strict. For instance, on one occasion when the Faculty was puzzling over a vexing problem, a certain bright young Professor from a distant part of the country, not well versed in Wofford circumstances and traditions, kept again and again urging his views while the rest of the Faculty tended rather to silent thought. At last, as he started up again, Prof. DuPre burst out, "Let somebody talk who has some common sense." The remark was not inconsistent with his habit of thought, but was the widest departure from his manner of expression that I ever witnessed. Never, however, was he impatient with a student. Indeed, he sometimes seemed too much to suffer fools gladly. He was one of those who deserve to be honored because they put the best that they had into their tasks.

The next of the old men to go was Dr. Rembert. Their temperaments, their tastes and competence as scholars, interested in the same fields of language and literature, made Rembert and Snyder friends from their first meeting. The reference in the President's report to the Board of Christian Education of the South Carolina Conference October 17, 1933, was singularly discriminating:

On the 18th of July, 1933, Wofford College, Methodism, and the cause of education suffered a great loss in the passing of Dr. Arthur Gaillard Rembert. For more than forty years as Head Master of the Fitting School and as Professor of Greek, Psychology, and Bible at Wofford, he exercised an extraordinary influence. He was a great teacher, a man of the highest spiritual qualities, and a sympathetic and understanding friend. Many generations of Wofford students owe to him some of the best inspiration of their lives as well as counsel and guidance in critical moments of experience. Few men exercised a better influence than did Dr. Rembert.

Dr. Rembert was born in Charleston, May 30, 1860. In his intellectual qualities, and even in his physical appearance, he illustrated the qualities of the Huguenot, which was prominent in his ancestry. He was both a lover of books and a lover of men. Probably no other member of the Faculty ever came into intimate, friendly personal relations with more students than did he. In the face of the dying interest in the classics, his keeping Greek alive at Wofford was the achievement of a great teacher and superb schoolmaster. He said to me once, "I suppose it is all right for a man to feel at one period of his life that Greek is the most important thing in the world." No number of extra classes in order to help men to keep up was too much for him. As he grew older and his Greek classes perforce grew smaller, his broad scholarship enabled him to take over completely satisfactorily the teaching of Greek, Psychology and Bible. He was a member of the State Board of Education from 1904 to 1916. The University of South Carolina conferred upon him in 1915 the degree of LL.D.[22]

The next of the old guard to go was Dr. Joseph Augustus Gamewell, who died July 7, 1940. Born in Rutherfordton, N. C., January 3, 1850, and graduating at Wofford in 1871, young Gamewell, after teaching a few years in Kentucky, happened along in Spartanburg in 1875 just at a time when his services were needed in the preparatory department. After a few years he was given college work in English and Latin, and soon in Latin alone. His father, Rev. W. A. Gamewell, was one of the original Board of Trustees and at his death in 1869 was its Chairman. When Professor Gamewell died at ninety years of age he had been connected with the college (including his years in the preparatory department) for sixty-five years, a longer time than any one else in its history.

Professor Gamewell was gentle in disposition, but ready to stand for the right. Many years ago, when the minister nominated for steward a member who, without the minister's knowing it, had the bad habit of profanity, Steward Gamewell openly objected to a profane swearer's being on the board. The man thanked the Professor for the reproof, stopped his bad habit, and was for many years a useful member.

Professor Gamewell was a man of excellent ability; but, to put it mildly, he did not use his talents to the extent of their capacity. In the summers of 1902 and 1906 he studied at Cornell University. His classes were pleasant, for he was of most amiable manner, and in fact possessed to unusual de-

---

22. State Supt. of Education *Reports;* Green's *Hist. of Univ. of S. C.,* 470.

gree the faculty of making men feel at once his good will. Friendliness seemed to radiate from him, as with his slow drawl he would call students by their names without any handle or chatted with them on the campus. With his ability and charm he could have made his Latin, that queen of cultural and disciplinary studies, one of the most effective departments in college; but he was so slack that students of scholarly inclinations were tempted to turn to other work. Even the lenient Dr. Carlisle was worried about his middle aged colleague's easy-going ways. Trustees sometimes growled dangerously, but neglected to do anything very decisive until he acquired a veritable vested right to his own easy-going ways, all the while gathering more and more kindly affection, until he was for the last years of his life a veritable institution. What more striking evidence of the affection of his colleagues than that they should have in 1937 taken the unusual step of voting their own fellow member the degree of LL.D.? When in the fall of 1939 not enough students elected Latin to form a class, the *New York Times* editorially congratulated the aged scholar who could now enjoy the fruits of culture undisturbed by young ignoramuses.[23] *Life* pictured him walking across the campus as probably the oldest college Professor in the country, and a radio station in Newark, N. J., of the Mutual Broadcasting Company put his life in its Collegiate Review of February 11, 1939.[24] About the same time he was given a banquet by a large number of alumni, when he had been teaching Latin sixty-two years and conducting the Lyceum for thirty-nine years.

The only thing about which I ever knew him to show enthusiasm was the Lyceum, which was his darling for the last decades of his life. It was his best contribution to the intellectual life of the college, for it was the one thing that he did with his whole heart, and therefore did well.

The last of the old guard to depart was Dr. John G. Clinkscales, who died January 1, 1942. He was born May 28, 1855, in Abbeville County, S. C. His geniality and his gift for popular speaking had made him widely popular before he came to Wofford from a professorship in Clemson College in 1899, bringing with him a huge mustache which he could tie behind his neck—something of a distinction in an age when the idea still lingered that there was some connection between hair on the face and scholarly wisdom. Even Dr. Snyder wore a Van Dyke beard for several years (if I may be pardoned for reviving the memory). It was a joke when I was a graduate student at the university that no man could take his Ph.D. degree without a beard; but scholarship has now passed from the Van Dyke into the Gil-

---

23. In full in Wof. Bulletin, December, 1939.
24. *Old Gold and Black*, Feb. 11, 1939.

lette era. Even physicians often carried around huge germ traps on their faces (Mormon elder face mats, they were sometimes called).

Dr. Clinkscales' popularity and his interest in church affairs caused his election as a delegate to the General Conference of the Methodist Church in 1902. He was brought to Wofford primarily as a field agent to bring the college before the public and induce boys to come to Wofford; and right well did he perform those functions. He was not a deeply learned mathematician. He studied at Johns Hopkins in the summer of 1902 and at Cornell in the summer of 1906; but ordinarily his summers were given to representing the college in the field. In 1904 he published a charming little volume, *How Zach Came to College,* describing in story form how that North Carolina mountain boy and his brother who heard the college bell one evening as they were camping with their "truck" to be sold the next day, went to the speaking, and determined themselves to stand one day on that rostrum. They both became graduates, Zach Whiteside a Baptist preacher in his mountain valleys, and his brother a useful farmer citizen. In 1916 he put out a little volume, *On the Old Plantation,* an idyllic story of an old time Negro. Ill health forced his becoming Professor Emeritus in June, 1938.

Dr. Clinkscales manifested moral courage by running for Governor in 1914 on the platform of State-wide compulsory education, something no candidate in South Carolina had ever had both the intelligence and the courage to do. In or about 1912 Governor Cole L. Blease was uttering his denunciations against compulsory education, medical inspection of school children, and other humane progressive measures for the benefit of the masses (saying he would telegraph a pardon to any father for killing a doctor who said his daughter was impure, as an appeal to the ignorant who had no idea of what medical inspection of school children was like). Dr. Clinkscales said, in his indignation at such demagogy and the ignorance that made it profitable, that unless some man ran next time on the platform of compulsory education, he would.[25] He kept his promise, and though falling into third place among the anti-Blease candidates in the first race, did a noble work in stirring interest in his ideas. Various forces defeated him. First, his platform was too advanced. Second, both Manning and Cooper were able and experienced politicians, with much superior organizations. Third, Dr. Clinkscales, though handsome and erect, manifestly had not the physical stamina demanded by such an ordeal. His having to withdraw for some days from the campaign created an unfavorable impression from this standpoint. And fourth, the outbreak of World War I shortly before the election impressed

---

25. I thank Mr. Chas. O. Hearon for calling my attention to this.

the voters with the necessity for a Governor of the wide and successful experience of Manning in the management of large private business and public affairs.[26]

In his long administration of forty years—one of the longest in the history of American education—Dr. Snyder won an extraordinary degree of affection from students and alumni. He had the satisfaction of seeing the resources of the college increased during his administration by a million and a half dollars, much of it due to his influence in that direction.[27] It was a satisfaction for him to be able to close his letter of resignation to the Trustees in June, 1942, with these words:

As I look back over fifty-one years, I am not aware that I have had any ambition other than the welfare of Wofford College, have ever let any personal interests come before the interests of the College, have allowed any sort of prejudice or dislike prevent my trying to advance what is best for everyone with whom I have had official relationship, have ever at any time failed to give myself without counting the costs to the effort to make Wofford a really great small college.

Such things I am saying at this time as a sort of apology for the many mistakes I have made—mistakes, as the old saying goes, of the head, not of the heart.

These more than fifty years have been happy years. The Board of Trustees has been co-operative to the highest degree and has given me great freedom to do what I wanted to do,—perhaps more freedom than I ought to have had. At times I may have misused it, I do not know. But I do know that this is the main reason why I have remained here when, up to fifteen years ago, there was never a year in which I could not have left Wofford College, and possibly to my advantage. But here I took my stand because, unhampered, I was permitted to express what ability and purpose I had in trying to unite religion and learning in the training of men at Wofford College.[28]

Partly from affection, and partly from the modern dislike of the fine old word Emeritus, strongly suggestive of old age, in this era which eschews anything over forty, he was given the title of Honorary President; but I insist that he was President Emeritus just the same; for Emeritus means "on account of merit."

---

26. There were ten candidates, under our stupid primary rules that allowed any crank who chose to pay the entrance fee to run, even though he could expect only a few hundred votes, serving merely to reduce to a worse absurdity that other abomination, the county to county speaking tour with all candidates speaking from the same platform on the same day at each county seat in succession. In the first primary, John G. Richards, the leading Blease candidate, received 26,081 votes; Richard I. Manning 25,397; Robert A. Cooper 25,053; John G. Clinksclaes 17,126. (Official count in *Spartanburg Herald*, Sept. 2, 1914.) In the second primary Manning defeated Richards by 73,969 to 45,099.—*News & Courier*, Sept. 15, 1914.

27. *Old Gold and Black*, Oct. 18, 1940; Snyder, *Educational Odyssey*, 199, etc.

28. From Dr. Snyder's MS. Part of the quotation is in Dr. Snyder's *Educational Odyssey*, 270.

Chapter XVI

DR. SNYDER AS MAN AND TEACHER

EACH of the Presidents of Wofford College has had his own elements of strength and usefulness. Dr. Wightman was the great preacher, the bold leader for Christian ideals of education, and also a man of executive gifts; but his tenure from 1853 to 1859 was too brief for him to carry his policies to completion. Dr. Shipp was primarily the scholar, though he was not lacking in energy in practical affairs. His demeanor and personality were not suited to the almost insuperable difficulties that weighed upon him during almost the whole of his administration from 1859 to 1875. Dr. James H. Carlisle's administration from 1875 to 1902 has been sufficiently described in former chapters to make it plain why he has been called "Wofford's spiritual endowment"; but vigorous, executive leadership he deliberately refused to assume, and, as a matter of fact, he appears to have been little suited to it. Dr. Henry Nelson Snyder proved himself versatile, widely accomplished, and active as a college executive. Dr. William P. Few summarized it well: Dr. Carlisle gave Wofford character; Dr. Snyder preserved that and gave Wofford academic excellence; the next President must be a builder.

Dr. Snyder has entered so largely into the history of the college as narrated above that some repetition may be unavoidable in speaking of him here as a man and teacher. So superb was he as a teacher of English that I have never been able to get over a sense of disappointment at his having sacrificed that for executive duties. Though he wrote excellently, his best work was in the classroom. He contributed many articles of value to the *Southern Christian Advocate,* usually on topics connected with the history and ideals of Wofford College. In 1906 he published *Sidney Lanier—a Study in Interpretation;* in 1927 *The Persistence of Spiritual Ideals in English Literature;* in 1928 a compilation, *Old Testament Narratives,* and in 1947 the valuable and charming autobiography, *An Educational Odyssey.* In the earlier years of his professorship and presidency he contributed a number of articles to the *Sewanee Review,* the *South Atlantic Quarterly,* and the (Southern) Methodist *Quarterly Review.*

As a teacher Dr. Snyder so effectively held his students that questions of conduct virtually never arose. He was rarely harsh, and even then gently

244

harsh. For instance, on one occasion a student persisted in asking what appeared to everybody else rather foolish questions, until both Professor and class were wearied. The teacher finally closed the quizzing by saying, "Well, Mr. Blank, we live to learn, and I hope you'll live a long time."

Dr. Snyder's gift as a lecturer on literature brought invitations from great summer schools ranging from Chicago and Chautauqua to Alabama and Texas, in which his sympathetic penetrating interpretation of great authors stirred deeply the love of good literature. Engagements of that sort had often to be declined after he became President; but other demands became so numerous as to be a burden even to a man who naturally enjoyed an exercise in which he was so apt. He not often told anecdotes, but was abundant in a subtle humor and in amiable chaffing when anyone invited it; but he never "shot fish in a barrel." Dr. Buckley of the *New York Christian Advocate* called it "dignified colloquialism." I never saw him at anything less than perfect ease before an audience but twice. Once was when we put him up in a turbulent political convention to conclude the debate for the prohibition forces. The liquor opposition objected, interrupted, and heckled, and his talk was quite ineffective. He was not suited to that sphere and moreover it was an occasion in which persuasion was impossible. His forte was rather in persuasion and reasonableness, not in the clashing clang of hammer on anvil. The other occasion was when, at a banquet, the presiding officer by a strange slip announced him just as the plates were placed before the guests. He was too kindly to embarrass the rex, and so, in evident embarrassment on his own part he proceeded to speak. Soon he was handed a note from mine host saying that his waiters must be released by a certain hour. The speech ceased for the time being, and when the meal was disposed of the speaker took up his theme exactly where he had dropped it and carried it effectively to the end.

Perhaps the most important speech that Dr. Snyder ever made was at the Southern Educational Conference (the "Ogden Movement") in the spring of 1902, where he had gone at Dr. Carlisle's request to substitute for him in speaking on the influence of the denominational college. After the speech a tall, imposing gentleman approached him and said, "You ought not to be allowed to speak in public." "Why not?" "Because I disagree with everything you said, and now I want to do everything you advocated. You are a dangerous man." That was George Foster Peabody, ardent believer in education by the State and not by the church. Dr. Snyder was later told that that speech and a letter which he wrote decided the General Education

Board to take up the small church college instead of devoting itself only to non-denominational institutions.[1]

Dr. Snyder was an extraordinary artist of the spoken word, and therefore very skilled in presenting a subject. If I may be allowed the left-handed compliment, he could make a given amount of thought go wonderfully far. It was a useful gift; for a different method would have been ineffective with many of his audiences when, as President of a small college, he labored incessantly, as he himself put it, to carry education to the plain people. He was capable of charming audiences in the universities, and, had he chosen to turn in that direction, would have been known as one of the country's leading lecturers on literature; but he chose the other route and stuck to it. Repeatedly offers came from other colleges. In 1908 the Trustees of the University of South Carolina made a tremendous effort to persuade him to come there as President. The students at Wofford assembled before his house, and through an address by E. R. Mason, now a leading member of the Conference, begged him to stay here.

When Dr. Snyder was about fifty years old Senator Tillman of the Clemson College Trustees sent one of the outstanding members of the Board to seek him as President of that institution. He declined to consider the offer for two reasons: first, although he approved of the work of Clemson, he felt himself unsuited to that sort of education, all of his preparation and preferences being for the liberal arts college. In the second place, if he should accept he would insist on an elevation of academic standards which would largely empty their dormitories and raise such protest over the State as to necessitate campaigning for his ideas, with unpleasant consequences. About ten years later "a diamond studded trustee" of a Western State University sat in on his lectures at Junaluska and afterwards made him a most tempting offer. No, said Dr. Snyder; too old for such a change. The disappointed trustee replied that they had tried a technical man as President, then a politician, and so on, and that now they wanted to get a man of intelligence and character.

So highly was Dr. Snyder's success as a college President esteemed that the President of a prominent college in the South, who had made a notable success as a financial manager (having been taken from the ranks of business), offered Dr. Snyder, some years after his retirement, twenty-five dollars a day to visit him in his home for two weeks and just talk with him and members of his Faculty; for, he said, I'm a business man, but I want to learn how to be a college President.[2]

1. Dr. Snyder to D. D. Wallace, August 9, 1949.
2. The incidents of the above two paragraphs are from conversations with Dr. Snyder.

So incessant were the compliments showered upon him, both in this way and by word of mouth to his face, that one wonders that it neither made him arrogant nor warped his judgment. Praise did not embarrass him as it did Dr. Carlisle, but it did not turn his head. His humorous self-esteem was harmless. Both by nature and in answer to his constant prayer after he became President his character was well balanced: "Lord, help me not to let my feelings interfere with my thinking!"[3] Emphatically, Dr. Snyder lived intelligently.

Dr. Snyder saw little advantage in the maulings of angry combat. His preference was for reasonableness, adjustment of differences; and in this he was unusually successful. Hard would it be to find a Faculty through so many years kept in harmony with each other. Outstanding occasions when he stood boldly as a combatant were in the dispute over the relations of Vanderbilt University to the Methodist Church, in which he opposed the church's abandoning all connection because it could not control; and in the movement for the reunion of the Northern and Southern branches of Methodism, in which he stood strongly for reunion. His co-operation with the South Carolina Methodist Conference, to whom the college belongs, was constant and effective. He was a member of the Board of Education of the Upper Conference from 1930, and from 1931 through 1943 was President of the Board,[4] and so virtually had the power of nominating the Trustees of all the educational institutions from that Conference, and at the same time maintained the most cordial relations with the South Carolina Conference, though not eligible by residence to a membership on its Board of Education.

The church quite naturally drafts its college Presidents into numerous activities. Dr. Snyder was a member of every General Conference of his church, except that of 1926, beginning with 1906 and ending with 1940, and of the Uniting Conference at Kansas City in 1939 and the Southeastern Jurisdictional Conference at Asheville in 1940.[5] He was a member of the commission for Methodist unification from its origin in 1914 to the completion of its task in 1939. He was a member of the General Board of Education of the Southern Methodist Church from the Board's origin to 1942, and represented that church as a member of both the Joint Hymnal Commissions of the Northern and Southern Methodist Churches. He was also a member of the ritual commission of the Southern church. He served as Associate Director of the Christian Education Movement of his denomination in 1920-21. Not to attempt an absolutely complete catalogue, we may say

---

3. Snyder to D. D. Wallace.
4. *Upper S. C. Conf. Mins.*, 1930-43.
5. *Conf. Mins.*

that few if any other laymen in the history of the church ever held more church positions or for a greater total number of years of service. In 1916 he became a member of the South Carolina State Board of Education and served for twenty-two years, and was President of the South Carolina Association of Colleges from the second year after its organization continuously until 1942.[6]

President Snyder never made a mistake in selecting a full Professor; though he did sometimes, when trusting to testimonials instead of personal inspection, bring in young men for subordinate positions whose disappointing personalities necessitated their being dropped.

Dr. Snyder was prevented, by being elected President of Wofford, from completing his work for the degree of Doctor of Philosophy at Goettingen; but he was awarded the honorary degrees of Litt.D. and LL.D. by the University of South Carolina and LL.D., by Furman and Duke Universities. Though Dr. Snyder was primarily the scholar, he was possessed of excellent business judgment and was behind several of the improved methods of investment adopted by the Board of Trustees. It would be hard to defeat the proposition that he turned the income at the disposal of the college to the directions calculated to produce the greatest possible educational results.

Dr. Snyder was in fact a well balanced President. Though possessed of considerable emotional power, he was governed almost entirely by his intelligence. On the side of his own scholarship and of his sympathy with scholarly work by his Faculty he left nothing to be desired. Particularly after his serious heart attack in the summer of 1940, the clearness of his planning for future developments exceeded his energy for execution; so that excellent ideas for forward movements remained for his successor to take over—another illustration of the continuity of the institution's life. It was through his agency that the Board secured the services of his active and able successor. It was characteristic of the scholar that President Snyder took such deep satisfaction in the awarding to Wofford College in August, 1940, by the unanimous action of the Senate of the Phi Beta Kappa Society, which enters only institutions of high order of scholarship, a charter for Beta chapter of South Carolina, the only other chapter in the state being Alpha of South Carolina at the University. Beta chapter was installed January 14, 1941, by the President of the order, Dean Marjorie Hope Nicholson, of Columbia University. In effectively presenting the claims of the college for that distinction Dr. Snyder shares the honor with Dr. John W. Harris, then a member of the Wofford Faculty.

---

6. These data are mainly from Dr. Snyder's *Educational Odyssey*. Dr. Snyder became a member of the State Board of Education in 1916, not 1914, as he says. He succeeded **Dr. A. G.** Rembert, who served 1904-16.—*Supt. of Ed. Reports*.

Of the gifts to Dr. Snyder expressive of the affection and esteem felt for him was a surprise in the form of twelve or fourteen hundred dollars handed him on his 1935 birthday by a committee representing the alumni with the suggestion that he use it toward buying a new automobile. President W. P. Few of Duke University presided, and Presidents W. L. Baker of the University of South Carolina and S. J. Derrick of Newberry College and young ladies representing Converse and Columbia Colleges participated.[7] On the annual Home Coming Day (October 12 that year) in 1940, and called Snyder Day, the alumni again expressed the same feelings in presenting him with a very handsome silver service on the completion of his fifty years of service at Wofford College as Professor and President. At a meeting of the alumni on the campus September 11, 1942, to welcome the new President, an unscheduled feature was the presentation by the Faculty to the Honorary President, as Dr. Snyder had recently become, of a gold watch as an expression of their appreciation of him as friend and leader.[8] The third of their awards of a plaque to men of distinguished public service by the South Carolina American Legion (the first two having been to President David B. Johnson of Winthrop College and David L. Coker), given at no stated periods, was to Dr. Snyder in 1929. The years since retirement were not idle. For many months his weekly talks over the radio were a widely enjoyed feature. Often he was the speaker to interpret the significance of an important occasion. He served continuously since its organization as President of the Spartanburg Foundation, a non-profit organization of business men transacting large financial operations for the benefit of the community. Thus, though freed from official duties, he continued to serve the college, the community, and the church through his touch with their intellectual and spiritual life, virtually to the day of his death, September 18, 1949. Long will he be remembered as one of the chief builders of Wofford College.

---

7. *Wof. College Jour.*, Jan. 19, 1935.
8. *So. Christian Ad.*, Sept. 24, 1942.

Chapter XVII

PRESIDENT GREENE'S PROGRESSIVE PROGRAM

ON RETIRING from the presidency of the college in June, 1942, after having been at its head for forty years, Dr. Snyder gave the Trustees his help in the delicate and important task of finding a successor. Largely through his influence his old pupil Walter K. Greene of the Wofford class of 1903 accepted the presidency of his alma mater in August, 1942. Walter Kirkland Greene was born in Greenwood, S. C., February 22, 1884. He was not only a high grade student in college, but was the crack second baseman on the famous baseball team of that day, which lost only two games in the last three years of his college course. Since assuming the presidency he has had the satisfaction of witnessing a similar record of remarkable success in the series of twenty-four football games in 1948 and 1949, without a defeat under the efficient coaching of Phil (W. P.) Dickens,* and a very fine record in basketball also, following the fine coaching of Joel Robertson. Dr. Greene received the degree of Master of Arts from Vanderbilt University in 1905, and the degrees of Master of Arts and Doctor of Philosophy, respectively, in 1921 and 1923 from Harvard, and the degree of LL.D., from Mount Union College, Ohio, in 1943 and the degree of Litt.D. from Furman University, South Carolina, in 1951. After teaching at several places, he served as Dean at Wesleyan College, Macon, Ga., from 1921 to 1928, and as Professor of English at Duke University from 1928 to 1942, from 1930 to 1942 being also Dean of Undergraduate Instruction there.

This history is written so soon after the beginning of the administration of President Greene that to extend it into his term would be merely fragmentary. We shall therefore confine ourselves to a statement of his announced program of promotion and rehabilitation, which, even this early we may note has already achieved notable success. Dr. Greene has brought to the task which he took up in the summer of 1942 great energy and ability, and the outlook of an educator accustomed to the ways and viewpoint of a large, up-to-date university. He is a strong believer in the value of the Christian ideal in education, and, like his predecessors, he emphasizes the achievement of this ideal as the dominant purpose of his administration.

---

* Five of the twenty-four games were ties.

Apparently a distinctive contribution will be the upbuilding and expansion of the physical plant, systematic business administration, and vigorous executive leadership. Again, therefore, we note with a change of President a change in personality and method. It will be well with the old college if he successfully blends these forward-looking qualities with the heritage of the past.

As we look back across the first century of the life of Wofford College we observe a steady development, except when interrupted by the disturbances of war. There are seven distinguishable eras: First, the years of early promise; second, the trials of Civil War and Reconstruction, when it seemed that the very life of the college might go out with the Confederacy through which it lived; third, the Carlisle era, divided into the struggle for recovery and the establishment of security; fourth, the era of development under President Snyder until checked by the shock of the Great Depression of 1929; fifth, the Great Depression, which again brought the college into difficulties and dangers; sixth, recovery and development; and seventh, the era just beginning with a new President and new methods, which is still on the lap of the gods. Through it all there has existed a continuous co-operation and a deep loyalty to her institution on the part of the church, without which what has been achieved would have been impossible.[1]

As to what this seventh era may become, President Greene writes in the *Wofford College Bulletin* of March, 1944, on The Program of Promotion and Rehabilitation:

By the action of the two Conferences of South Carolina Methodism, Wofford College was granted a period of five years—1940-1945—to inaugurate and complete its program of promotion and rehabilitation.

In 1940-41 President H. N. Snyder organized twelve District Alumni Associations in the State, and initiated, as the first phase of the program, the Reimbursement Roll Call of alumni in South Carolina outside of Spartanburg County. The Reimbursement Roll Call was rudely interrupted in December, 1941, by the outbreak of war with Japan.

I accepted the presidency of Wofford College in August, 1942, and worked out a program of promotion and rehabilitation for the College.

A complete statement of these plans was made in a handsomely illustrated issue of the *Wofford College Bulletin* of September, 1945, entitled "The Wofford of Tomorrow." It contains a map of the campus with the location of buildings, existing and contemplated, and drawings of the

---

1. Rev. M. L. Banks, of the class of 1894, in his address before the South Carolina Conference Historical Society, clearly presents the history of this co-operation.

proposed new structures. There follows a history of the original endowment and its loss through the War of Secession the account of which has already been outlined in this volume. The *Bulletin* concluded as follows:

Within the foregoing pages is set forth a clearly-defined picture of what is planned for THE WOFFORD OF TOMORROW.

The body is the temple of the spirit. This is as true of a college as it is of an individual. Wofford must have a body commensurate with its soul if it is to be the effective Christian college of liberal arts *that it ought to be* and that its friends and alumni *should want it to be.*

It must be remembered that Wofford College is *an immortal thing* with changeless values in a changing world. Whoever plans for its service in the closing decade of its first hundred years must also plan for its service when the dawn of a second hundred years breaks over its majestic towers. Great men and good men, nourished within its halls, have their entrances and exits; but *Wofford still remains*—the immortal symbol of invisible realities.

President Greene adopted the plan of stating specific objectives and inviting friends of the college to direct their gifts, if they preferred, to one or another of these aims. Twenty-seven objectives were specified, as follows. It is interesting to note that items 2, 3, and 4 have a strong sentimental appeal, as designed to replace the endowment lost by the War of Secession:

Objectives	*Goal*
1. General Endowment	$300,000
2. Benjamin Wofford Endowment	50,000
3. South Carolina Conference Endowment	11,000
4. The 1855-1864 Memorial Endowment	25,000
5. The Living Endowment (Annual Gift)	30,000
6. Endowed Scholarships	50,000
7. Student Loan Funds	(no amount stated)
8. James H. Carlisle Chair of Religion and Philosophy	50,000
9. Henry N. Snyder Chair of English Language and Literature	50,000
10. Unrestricted Funds	(no amount stated)
11. Endowed Library Funds	(no amount stated)
12. Athletic Fund	(no amount stated)
13. Mrs. E. L. Archer Estate	4,956.61 received
14. Wofford Day Fund	11,648.31 received
15. Main Building (Remodeled)	100,000
16. Carlisle Hall (Remodeled)	30,000
17. Wilbur E. Burnett Hall (Remodeled)	12,000
18. Snyder Hall (New Dormitory)	200,000
19. New Dormitory	150,000
20. The Enlarged Library	30,000

252

21. New Science Hall 27,000
22. Swimming Pool 80,000
(Mr. Isaac Andrews in 1949 pledged $80,000 to enlarge the
Andrews Field House, towards building which he had given
$20,000.)
23. Honorary Society and Fraternity House 30,000
24. War Memorial Chapel 50,000
25. Student Activities Building 100,000
26. Central Heating Plant 75,000
27. Campus Improvement 50,000

TOTAL $1,500,000

At this writing, several of these plans have been carried to completion and some with much greater expenditure than was proposed. Others await favorable conditions. Abnormally high building costs would cut in two the results attained if more were done immediately than is pressingly necessary. As of July 11, 1949, the endowment stood at $876,731.41, and the grounds, buildings, and equipment (the "plant fund") at $1,060,979.84. The current $1,000,000 movement for Wofford and Columbia Colleges, on which approximately $800,000 has been pledged, is the largest in the history of the institutions.[2]

Treasurer's books do not contain the record of Wofford's best endowment, the devotion of her 9,117 former students, of whom 6,535 are living as of October 1, 1950. Through 1949 the college has awarded 3,268 A.B.'s, 461 B.S.'s, 253 A.M.'s and 1 M.S. Eliminating repetition of names, these degrees have been awarded to 3,773 persons, of whom 11 Bachelors and 26 Masters are women.[3] The college has always conferred the A.B. degree, the ancient mark of liberal culture. From 1870 through 1884, and again from 1931 to the present she offered the Bachelor of Science degree. There have been four periods in the history of the Master's degree at Wofford. Before 1878 any graduate of three years standing received the Master of Arts degree merely by applying. By the rule adopted in 1877 by the Trustees on the recommendation of the Faculty, the degree was conferred on Wofford graduates who completed with distinction a prescribed course of postgraduate study, without any requirement of class attendance.[4] The third period begins with the afternoon and summer school classes, for study in which A.M. was granted to any Bachelor degree holder, man or woman, from a recognized college, the first degree under this plan being awarded

---

2. Treasury books.
3. I thank Registrar S. F. Logan and Director of Public Relations and Alumni Affairs L. H. Cox for assistance in compiling these figures. For detailed figures, see Appendix I. Two Wofford women A.B.'s hold also Wofford A.M.'s.
4. *Tr. Mins.*, June 25, 1877, Cat. 1876-7, page 21.

in 1909. The fourth period begins with 1949, when the giving of the Master's degree was discontinued, except as to persons already having completed part of their work.

Early in President Greene's administration the government's military necessities seriously disarranged the normal life of the college. The government took over the entire plant as a school for soldiers preparing for the air service. Men from all over the eastern half of the United States were sent in for successive training periods of six weeks. Our own students of military age were drafted into the army and were sent wherever military policy dictated, instead of being left in the college for training. The Faculty conducted classes in subjects prescribed by the military as suited to their training needs. The 570 soldiers (the level at which the corps was sought to be kept) so fully taxed the available space that the students undrafted, on account of youth or other reasons, were housed in town and, with great generosity on the part of those institutions, were taught at Converse College or at the Spartanburg Junior College, Seniors and Juniors going to the former, Freshmen and Sophomores to the latter. This arrangement began with February 22, 1943. Some of the girls called it "the Wolf-ord invasion," and called the boys "wolfesses." One girl declared that "It's a good thing in that it stimulates class work, but that ain't all." Another testified that "it definitely makes us more conscious of our appearance"; and a third could only exclaim, "Oh, my dear, I think it's wonderful." [5]

The policy of the government was that the college should not make anything out of the arrangement, nor should it lose anything. All expenses, salaries included, were paid by the government. Physical improvements were installed, particularly in the culinary department, and the Professor's house nearest to Carlisle Hall was equipped as an up-to-date infirmary. The cost of the latter, approximately $5,000, was met by a gift from the brothers Dr. Samuel Orr Black and Hugh S. Black, being part of the various contributions of these alumni to the college totaling about $50,000.[6] Of this approximately $39,700 will go for a new science hall. The following from the *Southern Christian Advocate* of January 10, 1946, gives the account of the contribution of the Black brothers towards another college purpose:

A gift of $30,000 to Wofford College by Drs. Sam O. Black and Hugh S. Black of Spartanburg for the construction of an honorary society and fraternity house on the campus has been announced by Dr. Walter K. Greene, president. The building will be a part of the expansion and improvement program in the

---

5. *Old Gold and Black*, Feb. 13, 20, March 20, 1943.
6. President Walker K. Greene to D. D. Wallace, August 4, 1949.

Wofford of Tomorrow, a plan outlined last September for the raising of $1,500,-
000 for postwar construction and endowments. The proposed building will be
headquarters for literary societies, honorary organizations and the eight Greek-
letter fraternities at Wofford.

The doctors making the contribution to Wofford's expansion are alumni of
the college and natives of Spartanburg County. Both have been engaged in medical and surgical practice in the city for many years. They, in association with
their father, the late Dr. Hugh Ratchford Black, founded the Mary Black Clinic in
1924, and have operated it since that time.

In announcing the gift, Dr. Greene said: "This is the second important gift
that these two outstanding citizens of our state have made to Wofford, their
alma mater. In 1943, through their generous gift, one of the residences on the
campus was converted into an infirmary in honor of their distinguished father,
Dr. Hugh Ratchford Black, who, among his manifold responsibilities, was also
Director of Student Health at Wofford College. This building will provide the
much needed space for the meeting of the literary society, and of the many
honorary societies of the college such as the International Relations Club, Pi
Gamma Mu, Sigma Upsilon."

When the government suddenly terminated its contract and turned the
plant back to the college authorities, June 30, 1945, the institution was
left in difficult circumstances. The bulk of the older material from whom
students are drawn was still in the service. Salaries were cut for a year or
more, but, with the flood of students whom the disbandment of the armed
forces sent into the colleges, the back amounts were soon paid in full. There
followed, under the government's liberal educational policy for ex-soldiers,
an enormous expansion of student bodies here as all over the country.

On Sunday, February 17, 1946, at 3 p.m., there was held in the college
chapel a memorial service in honor of the Wofford men who had died in the
Second World War. President Greene presided, and Honorary President
Snyder delivered the address. The roll of the dead was read by Dean C. C.
Norton, as follows:

ROLL OF HONOR[7]

Lafayette Bagnal Adams, '37
  Sumter, S. C.
William Heyward Alexander, '45
  Woodruff, S. C.
David Buist Anderson, Jr., '37g†
  Moore, S. C.

Everett Lee Bass, '41g
  Concord, N. C.
Roy Volney Bishop, '40
  Inman, S. C.
Evander Cullen Bryant, '37g
  Marion, S. C.

---

7. This list includes all Wofford men known by the College to have given their lives or to be
missing in action.
† "g"—graduated.

Ralph Sherwood Bryant, '37g
Marion, S. C.
William Price Buhrman, Jr., '40
Sanford, Fla.
Volney Lee Byars, '41g
Drayton, S. C.
Charles Benedict Church, '32g
Henderson, N. C.
Wendell Eugene Cole, '46
Spartanburg, S. C.
Joe Foch Compton, '42
Cliffside, N. C.
Sheldon Marchus Dannelly, '39g
Ehrhardt, S. C.
William Thomas Dixon, '46
Gaffney, S. C.
Ben Rogers Easterling, '39
Florence, S. C.
Henry Paul Elias, '41
Spartanburg, S. C.
James Aubrey Faust, '43g
Spartanburg, S. C.
John Dixon Ferguson, '45
Great Falls, S. C.
Thomas O'Connor Fowler, '42g
Switzer, S. C.
John Hobson Franks, '44
Spartanburg, S. C.
Earl Pinckney Furman, Jr., '44
Allendale, S. C.
Claude Edgar Gatlin, Jr., '45
Great Falls, S. C.
Irwin Philip Gibbons, '41
Turbeville, S. C.
Fred Edward Gillespie, '42g
Walhalla, S. C.
William Henry Gladden, Jr., '39g
Rock Hill, S. C.
Homer Lee Glenn, '40
Starr, S. C.
Horace Edward Graveley, '27g
Belton, S. C.
Walter Keith Hale, Jr., '43g
Spartanburg, S. C.
Lyles Glenn Hardin, '35g
Rock Hill, S. C.
Walter B. Haynes, '38
Pacolet, S. C.

James Belle Heins, Jr., '38g
Blythewood, S. C.
George Albert Hendley, '45
Spartanburg, S. C.
Ernest Geter Hewitt, Jr., '46
Laurens, S. C.
Carley McLeod Hinson, '33
Mullins, S. C.
Brian Floyd Hodges, '38g
Spartanburg, S. C.
Frank Connor Hodges, '29g
Hodges, S. C.
William Eric Johnson, Jr., '39g
Spartanburg, S. C.
Julian Kilgo Joliff, '43
Gatesville, N. C.
Drew L. King, '26g
Poplar Creek, Miss.
Warden Henry King, Jr., '43
Hartsville, S. C.
James Madison Lee, '38
Pacolet, S. C.
Eugene Evans Little, '40
Jonesville, S. C.
John Jacob Little, '35g
Pageland, S. C.
William M. McLeod, '21g
Columbia, S. C.
Joe Huntley Marlowe, '45
Conway, S. C.
Theodore Palmer Mason, '36g
Woodruff, S. C.
James Howard Morris, '47
Spartanburg, S. C.
James Oren Moseley, '45
Spartanburg, S. C.
Fred Moran Nanney, '42
Wellford, S. C.
Francis DeLorme Newman, '38g
Oswego, S. C.
Michael Clarence Oakman, '46
Spartanburg, S. C.
Edward William Owens, '42g
Sumter, S. C.
Maxwell Farmer Parrott, '38g
Arcadia, S. C.
Norman Eugene Priester, Jr., '41
Allendale, S. C.

256

John Edward Raftery, Jr., '45
 Upper Darby, Pa.
Thomas Center Reed, Jr., '36
 Sumter, S. C.
William Walter Ritter, '37g
 Newberry, S. C.
Roy Robertson, '35g
 Caroleen, N. C.
Eddie Monte Robinson, '43g
 Union, S. C.
Simon Kittrell Rowland, Jr., '41g
 Sumter, S. C.
James Shands, '40g
 Spartanburg, S. C.
James Otto Smith, '44
 Wellford, S. C.
John Wesley Speake, '31g
 Spartanburg, S. C.

Gordon Sefton Stevens, '39
 Smithfield, N. C.
Roach Sidney Stewart, Jr., '41g
 Lancaster, S. C.
Leonard TaVelle Thompson, '36g
 Spartanburg, S. C.
William Forney Thompson, '46
 Spartanburg, S. C.
David A. Wallace, '25g
 Spartanburg, S. C.
Lawrence Frederick Watson, '45
 Spartanburg, S. C.
Richard Roger Watts, '40g
 Union, S. C.
Guy Wilson Wilkes, Jr., '42g
 Chester, S. C.
Allen Owens Wood, '40g
 Spartanburg, S. C.

REPORTED MISSING IN ACTION

Wilson Kirby King, '42

Bennettsville, S. C.

I have of necessity mentioned many distinguished Wofford graduates as their lifework touched in some distinct way the life of the college. Some may ask, Why no extended list of distinguished Wofford alumni, for certainly there is no lack? Any such list would be invidious, unless it was confined to men holding some official position, and even that would be unsatisfactory; for such a list would include some men far less worthy than others who were omitted because of not coming within the arbitrary restricted lines. Again, Why so little mention of active members of the Faculty at the present time? There are today men of ability on the Wofford Faculty whom a future historian can single out with more propriety and justice than can now be done. I do wish, however, to say a word for the teacher who is just a good teacher—the man who does not occupy any administrative post that constantly gets him into the limelight; who does not write books or articles; who has not the talent that causes him to be publicized in the papers as delivering commencement addresses at this, that, or the other high school; nor possesses the camaraderie that makes him "popular," but who year after year just keeps on faithfully teaching men what they profess to have come to college to learn, and which he has been engaged to teach. Without him the college would not be worth the efforts of its friends to sustain it. There is no yardstick whereby one can measure the service of the teacher who does faithfully the work of passing on to the next generation the knowledge and culture of the past and the implements for the intellectual life of the future. In this work the small Christian college has an important place. In the fiftieth anniversary edition of *Who's Who in America* the editor says, "That institutions of 300 students or less . . . can report almost four times as many Who's Who biographies per current student as the largest and richest institutions of the country should be significant news to all interested in our smaller colleges and universities and what they stand for in the American educational scene." [8] As doubtless the large majority of those small colleges are under the control of churches, we must consider the religious atmosphere as a large influence in the shaping of the character of students for successful lives—values which we must never surrender or compromise.

The church, the community, the alumni, and the friends of the college are responding generously to the move of President Greene, forward-looking and energetic, and his vigorous young Faculty for making Wofford a better and stronger institution than it has ever been. Proud of our past, but never willing merely to rest upon it, we trust that those yet to come may derive satisfaction from what we do in our generation, as we take pride in what those did who went before us.

---

8. *Who's Who in America*, 1948-49, 14.

APPENDICES

APPENDICES

ENROLLMENT, GRADUATES, AND DEGREES 1854-1950
NO PREPARATORY STUDENTS INCLUDED

Year	Regular fall & winter terms	Afternoon classes	Summer school	Total enrollment, duplicate names eliminated	A.B.	B.S.	A.M. (1 M.S. among 7 Masters 1934-5)	D.D.	LL.D.	Litt.D.
1854-5	24	...	...	24	...	...	...	...	...	...
1855-6	35	...	...	35	1	...	...	...	...	...
1856-7	60	...	...	60	6	...	...	...	...	...
1857-8	61	...	...	61	12	...	...	...	...	...
1858-9	70	...	...	70	14	...	...	...	...	...
1859-60	76	...	...	76	16	...	...	...	...	...
1860-1	79	...	...	79	15	...	1	...	...	...
1861-2	33	...	...	33	0	...	...	...	...	...
1862-3	27	...	...	27	0[1]	...	3	...	...	...
1863-4	18	,,,	...	18	2	...	3	...	...	...
1864-5	00	...	...	00	0	...	...	...	...	...
1865-6	18	...	...	18	0	...	...	2	...	...
1866-7	46	...	...	46	2	...	4	2	...	...
1867-8	56	...	...	56	4	...	3	...	...	...
1868-9	90	...	...	90	14	...	...	1	...	...
1869-70	100	...	...	100	4	2	4	...	...	...
1870-1	94	...	...	94	15	...	2	1	...	...
1871-2	104[2]	...	...	104	17	...	10	...	...	...
1872-3	96[3]	...	...	96	14	1	5	...	...	...
1873-4	103[4]	...	...	103	13[4]	..	9	3	...	...
1874-5	About 92		About	92	16	2	5	...	...	...
1875-6	86[5]	...	...	86	18	3	4	...	1	...
1876-7	70	...	...	70	11	1	5	...	...	...
1877-8	76	...	...	76	12	2	2	...	...	...
1878-9	66	...	...	66	9	3	4	...	...	...
1879-80	83	...	...	83	7	3	2	1	...	...
1880-1	About 78[6]		About	78	2	..	1	...	...	...
1881-2	About 85[6]		About	85	11	...	2	...	...	...
1882-3	About 65[6]		About	65	7	...	...	...	...	...

1. There was no graduate in 1862-3, and the catalogue so stated for over seventy years. In 1933 the college conferred "honorary Bachelor of Arts" on H. M. Stackhouse, who might have graduated in 1863 but for war. Since 1935 the list of graduates in the catalogue has incorrectly put him down as graduating in 1863.

2. Catalogue list of 1873-4 seems wrong in saying 105 for 1871-2.

3. Catalogue of 1873-4 cannot be correct in giving 112 as number of college students. Catalogue of 1876-7 states 96, which is 3 more than the Treasurer's books show paid college dues.

4. 103 by count of names. Catalogue errs badly in saying 93. Also, Trustee Minutes name a thirteenth graduate, John Theodore Perkins, whose name has always been omitted from the catalogue.

5. Catalogue of 1876-7 says 76. Report of Faculty to Trustees says 86.

ENROLLMENT, GRADUATES, AND DEGREES 1854-1950
NO PREPARATORY STUDENTS INCLUDED

Year	Regular fall & winter terms	Afternoon classes	Summer school	Total enrollment, duplicate names eliminated	A.B.	B.S.	A.M. (1 M.S. among 7 Masters 1934-5)	D.D.	LL.D.	Litt.D.
1883-4	About 75[6]			About 75	10	1[7]	1	...	...	...
1884-5	72	...	...	72	5	...	2	...	...	...
1885-6	72	...	...	72	5	...	2	...	...	...
1886-7	64	...	...	64	7	...	...	...	...	...
1887-8	72	...	...	72	6	...	2	...	...	...
1888-9	89	...	...	89	16	...	...	...	...	...
1889-90	112	...	...	112	11	...	1	2	...	...
1890-1	138	...	...	138	19	...	3	...	...	...
1891-2	158	...	...	158	29	...	1	...	...	...
1892-3	139	...	...	139	11	...	5	...	...	...
1893-4	156	...	...	156	19	...	6	3	1	...
1894-5	144	...	...	144	34	...	5	2	...	...
1895-6	153	...	...	153	25	...	5	1	1	...
1896-7	155	...	...	155	18	...	2	...	1	...
1897-8	161	...	...	161	21	...	3	...	...	...
1898-9	131	...	...	131	9	...	2	...	...	...
1899-1900	143	...	...	143	17	...	1	...	...	...
1900-1	188	...	...	188	27	...	5[8]	...	...	...
1901-2	182	...	...	182	25	...	5[9]	1	...	...
1902-3	196	...	...	196	27	...	1	1	2	...
1903-4	196	...	...	196	21	...	3	1	1	...
1904-5	220	...	...	220	29	...	2	2	1	...
1905-6	248	...	...	248	22	...	4	...	...	...
1906-7	286	...	...	286	29	...	2	...	...	...
1907-8	287	...	...	287	37	...	3	...	...	...
1908-9	268	...	...	268	56	...	2[10]	...	1	...
1909-10	216	...	...	216	38	...	4	...	1	...
1910-1	239	...	...	239	42	...	1	1	1	1
1911-2	266	...	...	266	47	...	2	...	...	...
1912-3	308	...	...	308	38	...	...	...	...	...
1913-4	334	...	...	334	61	...	1	...	...	...
1914-5	289	...	...	289	49	...	3	3	1	2
1915-6	328	...	...	328	61	...	8	...	1	1
1916-7	289	...	...	289	62	...	3	1	1	...
1917-8	274	...	...	274	54	...	10	...	...	...
1918-9	294	...	...	294	31	...	6	...	...	...
1919-20	283	...	...	283	41	...	...	...	...	...

6. Catalogue and Faculty report lump college and preparatory students these years. I arrive at my figures from Treasurer's books.

7. After 1884 the college did not offer B.S. until 1931.

8. *Southern Christian Ad.* report of commencement gives 5 by name in 1901 and 5 by name in 1902. Omitted from catalogue list.

9. Marvin V. Bennett, omitted from catalogue list.

10. Grange S. Coffin omitted from catalogue list. See Faculty Mins., June 4, 1909.

ENROLLMENT, GRADUATES, AND DEGREES 1854-1950
NO PREPARATORY STUDENTS INCLUDED

Year	Regular fall & winter terms	After-noon classes	school Summer	Total enroll-ment, du-plicate names elimi-nated	A.B.	B.S.	A.M. (1 M.S. among 7 Masters 1934-5)	D.D.	LL.D.	Litt.D.
1920-1	343	...	...	343	60	...	...	3	...	...
1921-2	345	...	...	345	42	...	1	...	...	...
1922-3	440	...	...	440	61	...	...	...	...	...
1923-4	446	...	...	446	76	...	...	1	...	...
1924-5	474	...	...	474	86	...	...	...	...	...
1925-6	498	...	...	498	96	...	...	...	3	...
1926-7	413	...	...	413	67	...	...	1	...	...
1927-8	479	25	...	504	68	...	2	...	...	...
1928-9	425	29	217[11]	671	86	...	3	...	...	...
1929-30	400	63	230	693	63	...	8	...	...	...
1930-1	350	47	256	653	84	...	6	2	...	1
1931-2	400	46	161	547	68	...	2	...	...	...
1932-3	385	21	75	481	58	6	4	...	2	1
1933-4	412	12	109	533	58	8	2	1	3	1
1934-5	435	32	121	564	56	15	6[12]	...	...	...
1935-6	476	23	117	594	61	36	1	1	1	1
1936-7	482	28	137	624	68	30	3	2	2	...
1937-8	493	22	124	621	49	47	2	...	1	1
1938-9	486	38	139	635	70	38	1	...	...	...
1939-40	461	30	170	625	59	31	1	1	...	...
1940-1	483	29	165	628	56	25	4	...	...	2
1941-2	476	81	186	681	52	34[13]	3	...	...	...
1942-3	404	26	168[14]	564	42	32	1	...	...	...
1943-4	96	56	87	230	13	9	1	2	...	1
1944-5	110	53	237	371	5	5	1	2	1	...
1945-6	279	49	540[15]	719	8	11	2	3	...	1
1946-7	664	20	712	1108	58	30	3	1	1	...
1947-8	720	42	722	1205	62	40	5	2	...	...
1948-9	690	33	633	1104[16]	174	34	6	2	2	1
1949-50	624	...	493	921	160	12	8	1	2	1

11. Number in summer school not given before 1928-9. Names of summer school students not given before 1934-5; therefore impossible before 1934-5 to eliminate duplicate names; but the number of duplicates, I know from having taught during these years, was small.

12. In addition to the six A.M.'s, one M.S. degree was granted this year, the only one so far in the history of the college.

13. Geddes Marion Cox, wrongly entered in 1943-4 catalogue p. 71, note, as Marion C. Geddes, received B.S. in December, 1942, but did not appear in list of 1942 graduates until the wrong entry here noted.

14. First two terms, ten weeks, summer school.

15. Catalogue for 1946-7 in reporting summer school attendance for summer of 1946 merely adds together the attendance for each of the two terms, thus counting 258 names twice. My count of duplicates to be eliminated for the 1947 and 1948 summer schools differs slightly from the figures of the catalogue. It is extremely difficult to eliminate duplicates with absolute accuracy.

16. I thank Registrar S. F. Logan for compiling this figure and other help.

ENROLLMENT, GRADUATES, AND DEGREES 1854-1950
NO PREPARATORY STUDENTS INCLUDED

Year	Regular fall & winter terms	After-noon classes	Summer school	Total enroll-ment, du-plicate names elimi-nated	A.B.	B.S.	A.M. (1 M.S. among 7 Masters 1934-5)	D.D.	LL.D.	Litt.D.
Honorary A.B. & A.M. degrees										
1878	...	...	...	...	...	...	1[17]	...	...	...
1892	...	..	...	...	...	..	1[17]	...	...	...
1933	...	...	...	...	1[17]	...	...	...	...	...
TOTALS					3,268	461	253 and 1 M.S.	53	32	15

The total of Bachelor's and Master's degrees which the College has awarded is thus 3,983. Master's degrees earned by advanced work in summer school or afternoon classes by persons not holding Wofford Bachelor's degree, 43, to whom are to be added the two Professors in the College noted above who were awarded the Master's degree merely as a recognition of their scholarship and ability.

---

17. Honorary A.M. to Prof. W. M. Baskervill in 1878, and to Prof. John C. Kilgo in 1892, both at the time members of the Wofford College Faculty; honorary A.B. to H. M. Stackhouse in 1933, who might have graduated in 1863 but for the war. See text for details. Of the 253 A.M. degrees, 58 were awarded before 1878 merely on application of graduates of at least two years' standing.

APPENDIX II

HONORARY DEGREES AWARDED BY WOFFORD COLLEGE, WITH DATES AND PERSONS

Compiled by S. Frank Logan and D. D. Wallace

1866	Rev. W. H. Anderson	Kentucky Conference	D.D.
1866	Rev. James A. Duncan	Virginia Conference	D.D.
1867	Rev. S. S. Roszell	Baltimore Conference	D.D.
1867	Rev. A. A. Porter	Presbyterian Church	D.D.
1869	Rev. A. A. Morrison	Louisville Conference	D.D.
1871	Rev. W. A. Finley	Corvallis College, Oregon	D.D.
1874	Rev. W. H. Potter	North Carolina Conference	D.D.
1874	Rev. S. B. Jones	South Carolina Conference	D.D.
1874	Rev. J. S. Kennedy	Holston Conference	D.D.
1876	Warren DuPre	President of Martha Washington College, Abingdon, Virginia	LL.D.
1878	Prof. W. M. Baskervill	Professor in Wofford	M.A.
1880	Rev. F. X. Forster	Central College, Missouri	D.D.
1890	Rev. A. M. Chreitzberg	South Carolina Conference	D.D.
1890	Rev. R. D. Smart	South Carolina Conference	D.D.
1892	Rev. John C. Kilgo	Professor in Wofford College	M.A.
1894	Rev. George W. Yarborough	North Georgia Conference	D.D.
1894	Hon. Samuel Dibble	Orangeburg, S. C.	LL.D.
1894	Rev. J. C. C. Newton	China	D.D.
1894	Rev. G. W. Walker	President of Paine Institute, Augusta, Georgia	D.D.
1895	Rev. John C. Kilgo	President of Trinity College, North Carolina	D.D.
1895	Rev. R. J. Bigham	North Georgia Conference	D.D.
1896	Hon. G. D. Shands	University of Mississippi	LL.D.
1896	Rev. J. O. Willson	South Carolina Conference	D.D.
1897	Rev. W. B Murrah	President of Millsaps College, Mississippi	LL.D.
1902	Rev. B. F. Wilson	President of Converse College, South Carolina	D.D.
1903	President R. E. Blackwell	Randolph Macon College	LL.D.
1903	Associate Justice Charles A. Woods	South Carolina Supreme Court	LL.D.
1903	Rev. J. M. Lander	President of Granbery College, Brazil	D.D.
1904	Benjamin J. Sloan	President of University of South Carolina	LL.D.
1904	Rev. J. W. Wolling	Missionary to Brazil	D.D.
1905	P. A. Sondley	Asheville bar	LL.D.
1905	Rev. F. L. Beaty	South Carolina Conference	D.D.
1905	Rev. W. C. Power	South Carolina Conference	D.D.
1909	Prof. Andrew C. Moore	Acting President Univ. of S. C.	LL.D.
1910	Prof. Charles Forster Smith	University of Wisconsin	LL.D.
1911	Prof. William P. Few	President of Trinity College, Durham, North Carolina	LL.D.

1911 William A. Webb.............President of Central College, Missouri..Litt.D.
1911 Rev. R. E. Stackhouse........South Carolina Conference...............D.D.
1915 Prof. Albert Shipp Pegues.....Southwestern University...............Litt.D.
1915 D. Wistar Daniel............Clemson College.......................Litt.D.
1915 Rev. W. C. Kirkland........South Carolina Conference...............D.D.
1915 Rev. R. S. Truesdale........South Carolina Conference...............D.D.
1915 Rev. Edward K. Hardin......Baltimore Conference...................D.D.
1915 Thomas M. Raysor...........Orangeburg, S. C......................LL.D.
1916 James Perrin Smith..........Leland Stanford University, California...LL.D.
1916 Prof. S. H. Edmunds.........Sumter City Schools, South Carolina...Litt.D.
1917 Prof. W. W. Wannamaker.....Duke University, North Carolina.......Litt.D.
1917 Rev. Charles C. Jarrell.......Emory University, Georgia..............D.D.
1921 Rev. D. E. Camak...........Upper South Carolina Conference.......D.D.
1921 Rev. A. N. Brunson..........Upper South Carolina Conference.......D.D.
1921 Rev. W. B. Campbell........President Kentucky Wesleyan College....D.D.
1924 Rev. B. Rhett Turnipseed.....Upper South Carolina Conference.........D.D.
1926 Gov. Thomas Gordon McLeod..Governor of South Carolina...........LL.D.
1926 Prof. W. Laurens Walker.....Superintendent State School for
                                 Deaf and Blind, South Carolina.........LL.D.
1926 Prof. N. Gist Gee...........Lander College, South Carolina........LL.D.
1927 Rev. Claude L. Smith........Brazil Conference......................D.D.
1931 Rev. R. O. Lawton..........Lander College and Upper South
                                 Carolina Conference..................Litt.D.
1931 Rev. Peter Stokes............South Carolina Conference..............D.D.
1931 Rev. C. C. Herbert..........South Carolina Conference..............D.D.
1933 Julius A. Mood.............Sumter, S. C........................LL.D.
1933 United States Senator
     Ellison Durant Smith........Florence County, South Carolina.........LL.D.
1933 Nathan M. Salley..Litt.D
1933 H. M. Stackhouse...........Who might have graduated in 1863
                                 but for war...........................A.B.
1934 L. L. Dantzler..............University of Kentucky ....Litt.D
1934 Judge J. G. Stabler..........South Carolina Supreme Court........LL.D.
1934 Prof. T. C. Easterling........Superintendent Marion City School, S. C. LL.D.
1934 President B. E. Geer.........Furman University....................LL.D.
1934 Rev. T. Grigsby Herbert......South Carolina Conference...............D.D.
1936 Bishop Paul B. Kern.........Methodist Episcopal Church South......LL.D.
1936 Pres. John W. Speake........President of Lander College,
                                 South Carolina.........................D.D.
1936 Dr. P. M. Hamer.............University of Tennessee...............Litt.D.
1937 Prof. Joseph Augustus
     Gamewell ....Wofford College......................LL.D.
1937 Dean D. D. Peele ....Columbia College, South Carolina.......LL.D.
1937 Rev. J. Emerson Ford.......South Carolina Conference..............D.D.
1937 Rev. W. L. Mullikin..........Upper South Carolina Conference.........D.D.
1938 Prof. W. D. Roberts.........Superintendent, Epworth Orphanage.....LL.D.
1938 Prof. R. L. Meriwether.......University of South Carolina..........Litt.D.
1940 Rev. J. Marvin Rast.........President Lander College, S. C..........D.D.
1941 Prof. Louis B. Wright........Huntington Library, California.........Litt.D.
1941 Prof. J. M. Steadman.........Emory University, Ga................Litt.D.
1944 Francis Marion Kinard.......Dean of Department of Arts and Sciences
                                 Clemson College, S. C................Litt.D.
1944 Leo Darby Gillespie..........Upper South Carolina Conference........D.D.

1944 Rev. Francis Eldon Dibble....South Carolina Conference..............D.D.
1945 Henry R. Sims...............President Winthrop College, S. C.......LL.D.
1945 Rev. James E. Ellis...........Secretary General Board of Education,
                                  Brazil Conference......................D.D.
1945 Rev. Francis A. Buddin.......North Texas Conference................D.D.
1946 Prof. James Milton Ariail.....Columbia College, South Carolina.....Litt.D.
1946 Rev. Homer L. F. Shuler.....South Carolina Conference..............D.D.
1946 Rev. William B. Garrett.......Upper South Carolina Conference.......D.D.
1946 Bishop Cyrus Bassett Dawsey..Brazil Conference......................D.D.
1947 Rev. John Owen Smith.......Upper South Carolina Conference.......D.D.
1947 Miss Wil Lou Gray.........South Carolina Department of Education LL.D.
1948 Rev. Rembert Bryce Herbert..South Carolina Conference...............D.D.
1948 Rev. Fritz Chester Beach.....Upper South Carolina Conference........D.D.
1949 Howard Bobo Carlisle........Attorney at Law,
                                  Spartanburg, South Carolina............LL.D.
1949 Rev. Wallace Duncan Gleaton..South Carolina Conference..............D.D.
1949 Rev. J. R. T. Major.........South Carolina Conference..............D.D.
1949 Prof. Robert Adger Law......University of Texas...................Litt.D.
1949 Samuel Lander Prince........Dean of Law School, University of
                                  South Carolina......................LL.D.
1950 James Francis Byrnes........Attorney at Law; Statesman...........LL.D.
1950 Rev. Paul Hardin, Jr.........North Alabama Conference..............D.D.
1950 Edward Watson Rushton......Superintendent Orangeburg City Schools Litt.D.
1950 William Laurens Walker......President South Carolina School for
                                  Deaf and Blind .....................LL.D.

267

APPENDIX III

TRUSTEES OF WOFFORD COLLEGE 1851-1951

I ask lenient judgment of errors (extremely easy to creep into a list of this kind) either of names or dates in connection with Trustees, or in the list in Appendix IV of Professors.

Dates of service by a Trustee are to be interpreted as follows: 1851-58, e.g., means that the Trustee was elected at the end of the Conference Year 1851 (usually November or December) and served until the end of the Conference Year 1858. To find who were the thirteen members of the Board at any particular June other than the years for which complete lists are given (e.g., 1907) drop from the last complete list (i.e., 1891) any who have ceased to be members at the desired date (June, 1907). Add to those remaining the names of any added since the last complete list and still serving, not neglecting to examine the next complete list (1911). No difficulty will arise unless a Trustee has died or resigned between the close of the last Conference Year and the following College Commencement. If his place has been meantime filled by the Board pending action by the next Conference, it would make it appear from this list that there was one too many Trustees. Our list, giving only terms by whole years, has no way of indicating such a temporary vacancy.

The original Board of 1851:

Rev. W. M. Wightman, D.D., 1851-53; 1857-59; 1870-82
    President of the Board, 1851-53; 1874-82. (Sometimes called Chairman)
Clough Beard, 1851-53
Rev. Charles Betts, 1851-72
Simpson Bobo, 1851-61; 1863-85
    President of the Board, 1869-74; 1882-85
Rev. H. H. Durant, 1851-53; 1857-61

Rev. W. A. Gamewell, 1851-69
    President of the Board, 1867-69
R. C. Leitner, 1851-53
Rev. A. M. Shipp, D.D., 1851-53; 1859-75
Rev. James Stacy, 1851-53
J. Wofford Tucker, 1851-57
Rev. H. A. C. Walker, 1851-66; 1869-83
    President of the Board, 1853-66
Rev. T. R. Walsh, 1851-57
Harvey Wofford, 1851-77

Trustees elected after 1851 and before 1870, but not holding after 1870:

G. Cannon, 1861-63
Rev. W. G. Connor, 1866-67
J. H. Dogan, 1856-70
Rev. J. W. Kelley, 1867-68
Rev. W. A. McSwain, 1853-61

Rev. H. H. Durant, 1851-53; 1857-61
W. J. T. Miller, 1857-70
Rev. J. R. Pickett, 1853-70
Rev. C. S. Walker, 1853-57
R. J. Boyd, 1868-70

Members of the Board at Commencement, July, 1871:

Dr. W. M. Wightman, 1851-53; 1857-59; 1870-82
    President of the Board, 1851-53; 1874-82

Simpson Bobo, 1851-61; 1863-85
    President of Board, 1869-74; 1882-85
Rev. A. M. Shipp, D.D., 1859-75

---

[1] Trustee Minutes, July 13, 1858, quoting Conference Journal of December, 1857, show President W. M. Wightman was in December, 1857, elected Trustee in place of Rev. T. R. Walsh. College catalogue 1858 and 1861 (we have none between those years) seems to err in naming Walsh as Trustee and omitting Wightman, and Wightman's successor Trustee Shipp elected in 1859.

268

Rev. W. C. Kirkland, 1912-38
A. M. Chreitzberg, 1914-48
John A. Law, 1914-46
Rev. Geo. C. Leonard, 1914-45

J. B. Humbert, 1914-48
Rev. J. R. T. Major, 1927-48
Rev. Wm. V. Dibble, 1930-35

Elected to the Board of Trustees after 1930, but not serving to 1948:

Rev. R. F. Morris, 1933-43
Marvin W. Adams, 1934-44

Rev. Peter Stokes, 1927-30; 1935-39
J. R. Conner, 1944-45

The Board of Trustees at Commencement, June, 1948, and until November 1, 1948, when the union of Wofford and Columbia Colleges went into effect:

H. B. Carlisle, 1907-48
    President of the Board, 1939-48
A. M. Chreitzberg, 1914-48
J. B. Humbert, 1918-48
Rev. J. R. T. Major, 1927-48
Rev. E. K. Garrison, 1932-48
Rev. J. E. Ford, 1938-48

Rev. W. D. Gleaton 1939-48
H. S. Sims, 1939-48
Rev. R. L. Holroyd, 1943-48
J. R. Williams, 1944-48
Rev. C. E. Peele, 1945-48
A. B. Boyle, 1946-48
J. A. Chapman, 1946-48

The Board of Trustees of Wofford and Columbia Colleges, elected October and taking office November 1, 1948, and serving, with one brief exception, until the Board for Wofford College alone took office February 1, 1951.

Hugo S. Sims, Chairman
    Orangeburg, S. C.
J. Emerson Ford, Vice-Chairman
    Nashville, Tenn.
Dwight F. Patterson, Secretary
    Laurens, S. C.
Edwin B. Doyle
    Sumter, S. C.
Robert M. Carlisle
    Spartanburg, S. C.
James A. Chapman
    Spartanburg, S. C.
Pierce E. Cook
    Charleston, S. C.

Joe Edens
    Columbia, S. C.
Leo D. Gillespie
    Batesburg, S. C.
R. Bryce Herbert
    Sumter, S. C.
J. Carlisle Holler
    Hartsville, S. C.
Raymond L. Holroyd
    Greenville, S. C.
H. Lester Kingman
    Lancaster, S. C.

Board of Trustees elected 1950 to take office February 1, 1951, on the dissolution of the union between Wofford and Columbia Colleges:

Hugo S. Sims, Sr., Chairman
    Orangeburg, S. C.
Rev. J. O. Smith, Vice-Chairman
    Spartanburg, S. C.
Dwight F. Patterson, Secretary
    Laurens, S. C.
Sam Orr Black, Sr.
    Spartanburg, S. C.
Robert M. Carlisle
    Spartanburg, S. C.
James A. Chapman
    Spartanburg, S. C.

Rev. Wallace D. Gleaton
    Columbia, S. C.
Rev. H. Lester Kingman
    Columbia, S. C.
Hugh W. Perrow
    Cameron, S. C.
Rev. R. Wright Spears
    Florence, S. C.
Rev. C. L. Woodard
    Charleston, S. C.
Rev. John M. Younginer
    Walterboro, S. C.

(Frank W. Raysor resigned without serving.)

APPENDIX IV

FACULTY MEMBERS AND TERMS OF SERVICE IN
WOFFORD COLLEGE 1853-1951

Errors of a year as to time of service may creep in, especially as long ago the catalogue was frequently issued after commencement, and occasionally even after the opening of the fall term, thus making it difficult at times to tell to which year some names refer. Trustee Minutes do not always solve the doubt, especially as to men in lower positions.

The first time a man's name appears I give his full record of service; later if his name occurs again I give only his standing at that time and refer if necessary in a note to his former entry. In order to make up the complete list of the Faculty for any year for which a complete list is not given (e.g., 1907), take all the men in the last complete list (i.e., 1891), who were still serving at the desired date (i.e., 1907), not neglecting to look ahead to the next complete list (i.e., 1911) for men who were serving at the date in question (e.g., 1907). Drop all names from the last complete list whose dates show that they did not serve to the date in question.

Faculty members elected in 1853, preparatory to the opening of the College in 1854:

William M. Wightman, D.D., 1853-59. President and Professor of Mental and Moral Science, 1853-59

David Duncan, A.M., 1853-81. Professor of Ancient Languages, 1853-81; Emeritus, 1877-81. Treasurer for many years

James H. Carlisle, A.M., LL.D., 1870. Professor of Mathematics (or Mathematics and Astronomy), 1853-89. Professor of Moral Science and Mathematics (or Astronomy), 1889-1902. President Emeritus and Professor of Astronomy and Ethics, 1902-09. In early years Secretary of the Faculty

Warren DuPre, A.M. (LL.D. after leaving Wofford). Professor of Natural Science, 1853-75

Herman Baer, 1853-55, Tutor in Modern Languages and Hebrew and Assistant in Preparatory Department. Though elected in 1853, from the Treasurer's books his actual service apparently began with the organization of the Preparatory Department in January, 1855, and lasted only through December, 1855; the very able Mr. Baer, a converted German Jew, taught elsewhere after his services were dispensed with at Wofford (the nature of his subjects sufficiently indicates the small demand for his services), and, at his request, was in 1858 granted the degree of A.B. in recognition of his having privately studied the entire college curriculum—the only instance of the kind in the history of the college.—*Trustee Mins.*

Faculty members elected after 1853, but not serving into year 1870-71:

R. W. Boyd, A.B., January, 1855-59

Richard King, A.B., 1859-?[1] Principal of Preparatory Department

George Cofield, January-July, 1860. Teacher in Preparatory Department. During 1859

---

1. *Trustee Mins.*, Nov. 1859.

and 1860 the Preparatory Department was moved down town, perhaps with the idea of separating it entirely from the college.—*Trustee Mins.*

Faculty in year 1870-71:

A. M. Shipp, D.D., 1859-75. President and Professor of Mental and Moral Philosophy

David Duncan, A.M., 1853-81. Professor of Ancient Languages

Warren DuPre, A.M., 1853-75. Professor of Natural Sciences

James H. Carlisle, A.M., LL.D., 1853-1909. Professor of Mathematics. See 1853 list for successive departments

Whitefoord Smith, D.D., 1855-59; 1860-93 (re-elected April, 1860, after a brief presidency of the Columbia Female College). Elected December, 1855; began service in spring of 1856. Professor of English; Emeritus, 1885

Rev. A. H. Lester, A.M., 1866-73. Professor of History and Biblical Literature

John W. Shipp, A.M., 1868-75. Principal of Preparatory Department

Faculty members added after 1870-71, but not continuing through years 1890-91:

W. W. Duncan, D.D., January, 1876-86. Professor of Mental and Moral Philosophy. Financial Agent

Charles Forster Smith, A.M., 1875-79.[2] Junior Professor of Greek and German, 1875-76. Professor of Ancient Languages and German, 1876-79

W. M. Baskervill, A.M., Ph.D., 1876-78, 1879-81. Principal work was English, but taught also at times Latin, Greek, and German

J. H. Kirkland, A.M., 1878-83. Tutor in Languages, 1878-80. Assistant Professor of Greek and German, 1880-81. Professor of Greek and German, 1881-83

Frank C. Woodward, A.M., 1881-88. Professor of English and French

J. T. Littleton, A.M., 1883-86. Professor of Greek and German

John B. Henneman, 1884-85. Instructor in Subcollegiate Department

A. Coke Smith, A.M., D.D., 1885-89. Professor of Metaphysics and Political Science. Financial Agent

Granville Goodloe, M.A., 1886-90. Professor of Greek

J. H. Marshall, 1886-90. Instructor in French and German

A. W. Long, B.A., 1888-90. Professor of English

Faculty in 1890-91:

J. H. Carlisle, A.M., LL.D., 1853-1900. President, 1875-1902; Emeritus, 1902-09. For department by classes, see 1853 list

Whitefoord Smith, D.D., 1855-59; 1860-93; Emeritus, 1885. Professor of English

D. A. DuPre, A.M., 1872-1930.[3] Co-Principal of Preparatory Department, 1872-75. Junior Professor on leave in Europe, 1875-77. (Elected full Professor, 1876.) Professor of Natural Sciences, 1877-78. Professor of Chemistry, Physics and Geology, 1878-1902. Professor of Physics and Geology, 1902-23. Professor of Geology, 1923-30. Treasurer, 1890-1920

J. A. Gamewell, A.M., LL.D., 1875-1940. Assistant Professor, 1876-78, in Preparatory Department. Assistant Professor of English, 1878-81. Professor in Charge of Introductory Classes, 1881-85. Professor of Latin, 1885-1940. For many years Secretary of the Faculty

E. B. Craighead, A.B., 1890-93. Professor of Greek and French

H. N. Snyder, A.M., LL.D., Litt.D., 1890-1949. Professor of English and German,

2. On leave for two years after this, but never taught here after 1879.
3. The date 1872 is fixed by Prof. DuPre's M.S., autobiographical notes, for which I thank Mrs. Helen DuPre Moseley.

1890-93. Professor of English, 1893-1942. President, 1902-42. Honorary President (i.e., Emeritus), 1942-49

Rev. John C. Kilgo, A.M., 1888-94. Financial Agent, 1888-94. Acting Professor of Metaphysics and Political Science, 1891-94

S. R. Pritchard, A.M., 1890-93. Professor of Mathematics

Additions to Faculty after 1890-91, but not serving into 1910-11:

J. B. Thomas, A.M., 1893-95. Assistant Professor of Mathematics

D. B. Easter, A.M., 1893-95. Assistant Professor of German and French

C. C. Herbert, A.B., 1892-93. Assistant in English and German

Hugo G. Sheridan, Sr., 1892-96. Headmaster, Carlisle Fitting School

Rev. C. B. Smith, 1894-99. Professor of Metaphysics and Political Science. Financial Agent

W. G. Blake, A.M., 1895-99. Assistant Professor of Mathematics

A. B. Cooke, B.A., Ph.D., 1895-1909. Assistant Professor of German and French, 1895-1901. Professor of German and French, 1901-09. On leave in Germany and France, 1899-1900

S. M. Tucker, 1895-96. Librarian

J. Easterling Walker, 1896-1899. Librarian

William Wertenbaker, 1896-97. Instructor in Gymnasium

A. M. Chreitzberg, A.B., 1897-99

C. H. Leitner, A.B., 1898-1900. Instructor in Gymnasium

R. A. Stewart, A.B., 1899-1900. In charge of German and French

Miss Lily McMakin, 1899-1901. Librarian

Mrs. David Johnson, 1901-04. Librarian

O. D. Wannamaker, 1900-01. Acting Professor of English

E. S. Williamson, 1903-04. Acting Professor of Chemistry and Biology

R. O. Lawton, 1904-05. Assistant in English

A. C. Daniel, Jr., B.A., 1904-07. Instructor in Gymnasium

J. W. Boyd, A.B., 1905-06. Assistant in Mathematics

Mrs. J. D. Holler, 1904-05. Librarian

W. E. Willis, 1896-1901. Headmaster, Carlisle Fitting School

H. G. Sheridan, Jr., 1901-06. Headmaster, Carlisle Fitting School

C. C. Alexander, A.B., 1905-06. Assistant in English

J. B. Guess, A.B., 1905-06. Assistant in Biology

P. K. Switzer, 1905-06. Assistant in Chemistry

M. L. Spencer, M.A., 1906-10. Assistant Professor of English

D. C. Corbin, B.A., 1906-07. Instructor in Physics and Mathematics

T. H. Brewer, M.A., 1906-07. Supply Professor of Psychology and Philosophy

J. L. Hines, Jr., B.S., 1907-09. Instructor in Physics and Mathematics

C. W. Watson, A.B., 1907-08. Instructor in Gymnasium

W. S. Hogan, Jr., 1906-09. Headmaster, Carlisle Fitting School

G. S. Coffin, 1908-09. Assistant in Latin

A. R. Bressler, A.B., 1908-10. Instructor in Gymnasium

Faculty for the year 1910-11:

H. N. Snyder, 1890-1949. President 1902-42. For complete data see under 1890-91

D. A. DuPre, 1872-1930. Professor of Physics and Geology. For complete data see under 1890-91

J. A. Gamewell, 1875-1940. Professor of Latin. For complete data see under 1890-91

A. G. Rembert, A.B., A.M., LL.D., 1887-1933. Headmaster Wofford Fitting School, 1887-97. Professor of Greek, 1893-1911. Professor of Greek, Psychology and Bible, 1911-33

J. G. Clinkscales, A.B., A.M., LL.D. Professor of Mathematics, 1899-1915. Professor of Mathematics and Astronomy, 1915-40. Emeritus, 1938-42

D. D. Wallace, A.M., Ph.D., Litt.D., LL.D., 1899- Adjunct Professor of History and Economics, 1899-1901. Professor of History and Economics, 1901-47. Absent teaching in University of Michigan part of 1917-18. On leave (except for one hour a week) 1929-33 writing History of South Carolina. Retired 1947 under age limit rule

C. B. Waller, A.M., Ph.D., 1904- (Elected 1903; on leave for study 1903-4.) Professor of Chemistry and Biology. Retired 1947 under age limit rule

W. A. Colwell, M.A., Ph.D., 1909-14. Professor of French and German

J. B. Peebles, B.A., 1908-12. Assistant Professor of Applied Mathematics

R. L. Wiggins, Jr., A.M., 1909-12. Acting Assistant Professor of English. Absent on leave 1911-12 and did not return

Rev. E. K. Hardin, M.A., 1909-10. Assistant Professor of Psychology, Philosophy, and English Bible. Absent on leave, 1909-10. Appointed to St. John's, Rock Hill, Dec. 1910

V. C. Edwards, A.B., 1909-17. Instructor in Chemistry and Physics

A. Mason DuPre, A.B., A.M., LL.D., 1895-1949. Assistant Headmaster Wofford Fitting School 1895-7. Headmaster Wofford Fitting School, 1897-1912. Professor of Mathematics and Latin, 1912-42. Professor of Mathematics, 1942-47. Dean, 1920-40, except 1925-26. Registrar, 1925-26. Dean and Registrar, 1933-37. Honorary Dean (i.e., ex-Dean), 1940-49. Acting President, 1920-21. Retired Professor under age limit rule 1947-9

R. L. Keaton, 1910-14. Instructor in Gymnasium

Miss Mary Sydnor DuPre, 1905- Librarian

W. W. Mooney, M.A., 1909-12. Assistant Professor of Latin

J. D. Guilds, 1909-20. Headmaster Carlisle Fitting School

Additions to Faculty after 1910-11 but not serving into 1930-31:

J. Lyles Glenn, A.B., 1912-14. Instructor in Greek

J. M. Steadman, Jr., A.B., A.M., 1912-14. Headmaster (jointly with A. W. Horton) Wofford Fitting School

A. W. Horton, A.B., 1912-16. Headmaster Wofford Fitting School (Jointly with A. M. Steadman, Jr.) 1912-14

J. W. Scott, M.A., 1913-15. Assistant Professor of Chemistry and Biology

E. T. Spigner, A.B., 1914-17. Instructor in Greek

C. L. McCoy, 1915-6. Instructor in Gymnasium

H. A. Bedient, A.B., 1917-8. Acting Assistant Professor of Chemistry and Physics

Leslie Moser, A.B., 1916-18. Instructor in Gymnasium

F. P. Wyche, 1916-18. Headmaster Wofford Fitting School

A. S. Libby, M.A., 1917-18. Acting Professor of History and Economics

Capt. J. L. Erler, 1919-20. Professor of Tactics and Military Science

J. P. Major, 1919-20. Director of Athletics

Capt. G. R. F. Cornish, 1920-24. Professor of Military Science and Tactics

S. G. Hammond, A.B., 1920-21. Instructor in Mathematics

J. F. Gorsuch, 1920-21. Director of Athletics

J. P. Major, 1921-6. Director of Athletics

Capt. F. W. Hardee, 1921-25. Assistant Professor of Military Science and Tactics

D. F. Pasmore, Ph.D., 1922-24. Assistant Professor of Modern Languages

J. F. Maxwell, A.B., 1922-23. Instructor in Mathematics

F. N. Egerton, Jr., M.A., E.E., 1923-24. Assistant Professor of Physics

W. C. Duncan, A.B., 1920-3. Headmaster Carlisle Fitting School

J. E. Powell, A.M., 1924-25. Assistant Professor of Modern Languages

J. M. Rast, A.M., 1925-27. Assistant Professor of Sociology and Economics, 1924-25. Not here 1925-26. Assistant Professor of English, 1926-28
Capt. J. R. Boatwright, 1925-27. Professor of Military Science and Tactics
Capt. J. W. Starkey, 1925-27. Assistant Professor of Military Science and Tactics
E. C. Kirkland, M.A., 1925-26. Acting Assistant Professor of English
A. E. Terry, B.Ph., 1925-29. Assistant Professor of Modern Languages
M. J. Chaudon, L. es C., E.E., 1925-28. Assistant Professor of French
Capt. H. L. Hagan, 1925-30. Assistant Professor of Military Science and Tactics
E. H. Gregg, 1925-26. Assistant in English
L. K. Hagood, A.B., 1923-25. Headmaster Carlisle Fitting School
M. G. Gault, A.B., 1925-28. Headmaster Carlisle Fitting School
J. O. Bailey, M.A., 1926-27. Assistant Professor of English
Lieutenant T. C. Scaffe, 1926-34. Director of Athletics
D. W. Carpenter, A.M., 1928-29. Acting Assistant Professor of Physics
T. B. Stroup, A.M., 1928-29. Assistant Professor of English
J. F. Risher, A.B., 1928-32. Headmaster Carlisle Fitting School. (Continues in control, having leased the school in 1932 and bought it in 1938)
E. C. Morgan, A.B., 1929-30. Instructor in English
T. H. Daniel, A.B., 1929-32. Lecturer on Law
Capt. D. C. Smith, 1929-34. Assistant Professor of Military Science and Tactics

Faculty in 1930-31:

H. N. Snyder, M.A., Litt.D., LL.D., 1890-1949. President and Professor of English. For full data see under 1890-91
A. M. DuPre, A.M., LL.D., 1895-1949. Dean, and Professor of Mathematics and Latin. For full data see under 1910-11
W. C. Herbert, A.M., 1918- Headmaster Wofford Fitting School 1918-24. Professor of Mathematics and Greek, 1924-25; Professor of Greek and Education, 1925-47. Professor of Education, 1947-; Dean, 1925-26; Registrar, 1926-33; 1937-43
D. A. DuPre, A.M., 1872-1930. Professor of Geology. Died Sept. 6, 1930. For full data see 1890-91
J. A. Gamewell, A.M., 1875-1940. Professor of Latin. For full data see 1890-91
A. G. Rembert, A.M., Litt.D., LL.D., 1887-1933. Professor of Greek, Psychology, and Bible. For full data see 1890-91
J. G. Clinkscales, A.M., LL.D., 1899-1942. Professor of Mathematics and Astronomy. For full data see 1910-11
D. D. Wallace, A.M., Ph.D., Litt.D., LL.D., 1899-. Professor of History and Economics. For full data see 1910-11
C. B. Waller, A.M., Ph.D., 1904-. Professor of Chemistry and Biology. For full data see 1910-11
W. L. Pugh, A.M., Ph.D., Litt.D., 1911-. Professor of English Language and Literature, 1911-47. Retired on age limit plan 1947
J. A. Chiles, A.M., Ph.D., 1914-. Professor of Modern Languages. Retired 1947 under age limit rule
A. M. Trawick, A.B., B.D., 1921-. Professor of Religious Education. Retired in 1947 under age limit rule
C. C. Norton, A.M., Ph.D., 1925-. Professor of Political Science and Sociology. Dean, 1942-49; Dean of Administration, 1949-
E. H. Shuler, B.S., 1912-. Professor of Applied Mathematics
J. W. Harris, A.M., Ph.D., 1920-35. Instructor in English and French 1920-21. Assistant Professor of English 1921-28. Professor of English 1928-35
J. L. Salmon, A.M., 1921-. Assistant Professor of Modern Languages, 1921-28. Professor of Modern Languages, 1928-

C. S. Pettis, B.S., M.S., 1924-. Assistant Professor of Physics 1924-28. Professor of Physics 1928-

W. H. Morton, B.S., Sc.D., 1930-2. Acting Professor of Geology

W. R. Bourne, M.A., 1922-. Student Assistant in Modern Languages, 1922-23. Not here 1923-25. Assistant Professor of English and German 1925-26. Assistant Professor of German 1927-33. Assistant Professor of French 1933- Dean of Students 1946-48.

R. A. Patterson, A.M., 1916-. Assistant in Chemical Laboratory 1916-23. Instructor or Assistant in Chemistry, Biology, and Physics 1923-31. Assistant Professor of French 1930-31; Assistant Professor of Chemistry and Biology 1931-45; Associate Professor of Chemistry and Biology 1945-

C. L. Epting, Jr., M.A., 1929-32. Acting Assistant Professor of History and Economics

J. M. Rast, A.M., 1926-28. Assistant Professor of English

K. D. Coates, A.B., 1928-. Instructor in English 1928-32. Assistant Professor of English 1932-45. Associate Professor of English 1945-

T. H. Daniel, A.B., LL.B., 1929-32. Lecturer on Law

Capt. H. F. Teate, 1930-7. Professor of Military Science and Tactics

Capt. D. C. Smith, Jr., 1928-34. Assistant Professor of Military Science and Tactics

Lieutenant T. C. Scaffe, 1926-34. Director of Athletics

Miss Mary S. DuPre, 1905-. Librarian

H. R. Black, M.D., 1919-33. Consulting Surgeon

J. L. Jeffries, M.D., 1919-24. Attending Physician 1919-24. Consulting Physician 1924-42

S. O. Black, M.D., 1919-. Attending Surgeon 1919-42. Director of Student Health 1942-

H. S. Black, M.D., 1924-50. Attending Surgeon 1924-42. Director of Student Health 1942-50

Added to Faculty after 1930-31, but not holding into 1950-51:

R. G. Stone, Ph.D., 1932-33. Acting Assistant Professor of History and Economics

J. N. Holcombe, A.B., LL.B., 1932-36. Lecturer on Law

L. S. Winton, A.M., 1934-35. Instructor in Mathematics

F. E. Lowance, Ph.D., 1935-39. Assistant Professor of Mathematics

Albert Stanbury, A.M., Ph.D., 1935-46. Assistant Professor of English

Capt. Bob Childs, 1935-38. Assistant Professor of Military Science and Tactics

J. L. Carson, B.S., 1934-42. Director of Athletics

D. H. Montgomery, A.B., B.D., 1936-39. Director of Activities and Associate in Religious Education

F. J. Bostick, A.B., LL.B., 1937-41. Lecturer on Law

Major C. C. Loughlin, LL.B., 1937-42. Professor of Military Science and Tactics

O. B. Ader, Ph.D., 1938-42. (On leave 1942-43, but did not return.) Assistant Professor of Mathematics

J. F. Risher, A.B., 1928-. Headmaster Carlisle School

LeRoy H. Cox, A.B., 1939-49. Director of Alumni Affairs and Public Relations; Acting Dean 1940-42. Absent on military and other government service during several years

H. E. Vermillion, Ph.D., 1939-41. Instructor in Chemistry

LeGrand Tennis, Ph.D., 1939-47. Instructor in Modern Languages, 1939-43; Assistant Professor of Modern Languages, 1943-46; Associate Professor of Modern Languages, 1946-47

Major Harry Henry, 1939-40. Assistant Professor of Military Science and Tactics

Capt. W. C. Guy, A.B., 1940-41. Assistant Professor of Military Science and Tactics

H. L. Bomar, A.B., LL.B., 1941-42. Lecturer on Law

Capt. B. W. Rushton, A.B., 1941-42. Assistant Professor of Military Science and Tactics

O. W. Lever, A.M., Ph.D., 1943-48. Professor of Philosophy and Assistant to the President until made Dean of Administration of Columbia College in 1948
J. S. Rowland, A.M., 1947-50. Instructor in Sociology
W. P. Cavin, A.M., 1946-50. Assistant Professor of Chemistry
Lieutenant Colonel E. W. Grimmer, 1942-43. Professor of Military Science and Tactics
Lieutenant E. L. Culler, 1942-45. Assistant Professor of Military Science and Tactics
F. L. Petoskey, 1942-47. Director of Physical Education
Miss Dorothy E. Woodward, 1943-47. Registrar
M. L. Infinger, M.A., B.D., fall term 1946. Assistant Professor of Economics and Business Administration
D. L. Linn, A.B., 1947-49. Instructor in Physical Education
L. L. Dunlap, A.B., 1947-49. Instructor in Biology
Capt. J. E. Lance, Jr., 1947-50. Assistant Professor of Military Science and Tactics
S. R. Graves, A.M., 1947-50. Assistant Professor of Modern Languages
R. E. Watkins, A.M., Ph.D., 1947-50. Professor of Ancient Languages
Colonel G. M. Nelson, B.A., fall term 1947. Professor of Military Science and Tactics
Wm. H. Ford, A.M., 1947-50. Professor of Economics and Business Administration
Major A. L. Woods, 1946-48. Acting Professor of Military Science and Tactics
Bernard M. Cannon, A.M., 1948-50. Associate Professor of Sociology; Dean of Students
Wm. B. Owsley, A.M., Ph.D., 1948-50. Professor of Biology

Faculty in 1950-51:

Walter K. Greene, A.B., A.M., M.A., Ph.D., LL.D., Litt.D., 1942. President
Lt. Col. Howard D. Balliett, A.B., 1948-51. Professor of Military Science and Tactics
William R. Bourne, A.B., A.M. (1922), 1925. Professor of Modern Languages
Charles E. Cauthen, A.B., A.M., Ph.D., 1943. Professor of History and Political Science
James A. Chiles, A.B., A.M., Ph.D., 1914. Emeritus Professor of Modern Languages
Kenneth D. Coates, A.B., A.M., 1928. Professor of English
Lester H. Colloms, A.B., B.D., Ph.D., 1949. Professor of Philosophy
William C. Herbert, A.B., A.M., 1918. Professor of Education
Harold E. Hunter, B.S., M.S., 1947-Feb. 1, 1951. (Resigned February 1, 1951.) Professor of Mathematics
William B. Hunter, Jr., A.B., A.M., Ph.D., 1946. Professor of English
James C. Loftin, B.S., M.S., Ph.D., 1941. Professor of Chemistry
Charles F. Nesbitt, A.B., B.D., A.M., Ph.D., 1939. Professor of Religion
Clarence C. Norton, B.S., A.M., Ph.D., 1925. Professor of Sociology
Raymond A. Patterson, A.B., A.M., 1916. Professor of Chemistry and Biology
Charles S. Pettis, B.S., M.S., 1924. Professor of Physics
William Leonard Pugh, A.B., A.M., Ph.D., Litt.D., 1911. Emeritus Professor of English
John L. Salmon, A.B., A.M., 1921. Professor of Modern Languages
William W. Scheerer, A.B., A.M., 1947. Professor of Physical Education
Hugh T. Shockley, A.B., A.M., 1947. (Deceased May 23, 1950.) Acting Professor of Economics and Business Administration
Edward Hampton Shuler, B.S., 1912. Professor of Applied Mathematics.
Arcadius McS. Trawick, A.B., B.D., 1921. Emeritus Professor of Religion
David D. Wallace, A.B., A.M., Ph.D., Litt.D., LL.D., 1899. Emeritus Professor of History
Coleman B. Waller, A.B., A.M., Ph.D., 1904. Emeritus Professor of Chemistry
John T. Doby, A.B., M.S., 1950. Associate Professor of Sociology
Philip Stanhope Covington, A.B., A.M., 1947. Associate Professor of English
Robert D. Fridley, A.B., B.D., 1947-51. Associate Professor of Religion.
Walter R. Leonard, A.B., A.M., Ph.D., 1949. Associate Professor of Biology

Virgil S. Ward, A.B., A.M., 1947. (On leave of absence.) Associate Professor of
Education and Psychology
William P. Cavin, A.B., A.M., 1946. (On leave of absence.) Assistant Professor of
Chemistry
William R. Burnie, A.B., A.M., 1950. Assistant Professor of Modern Languages
Lewis P. Jones, A.B., A.M., 1946. (On leave of absence.) Assistant Professor of History
Capt. John E. Lance, Jr., 1947. (Resigned June 5, 1950.) Assistant Professor of
Military Science and Tactics
Gordon H. May, A.B., A.M., 1946. Assistant Professor of Mathematics
Lawrence O. Vickers, A.B., A.M., 1950-51. Acting Assistant Professor of Psychology
Major Samuel S. Wood, A.B., 1950. Assistant Professor of Military Science and Tactics
Deck W. Andrews, A.B., 1948. Instructor in Economics and Business Administration
John W. Boozer, B.S., M.S., 1945-51. Instructor in Chemistry
Robert M. Davis, B.S., M.A., 1950-51. Instructor in Biology
Harry L. Harvin, Jr., A.B., A.M., 1949-51. Instructor in History
Louis G. McCullough, Jr., A.B., 1949. Instructor in Physical Education
Augustus McK. Chreitzberg, Jr., A.B., A.M., 1949. Instructor of Chemistry
Alfred L. V. Ingram, A.B., 1949-51. Instructor of Economics
Samuel R. Moyer, A.B., 1948. Instructor of Art and Music Appreciation
Joseph S. Rowland, Jr., A.B., A.M., 1947-Jan. 1, 1951. (Resigned Jan. 1, 1951.)
Instructor of Sociology
George W. Whitaker, Jr., A.B., A.M., 1947-51. Instructor of English
James S. Worley, A.B., A.M., 1950. Instructor in Economics
Master Sgt. George R. Leitner, 1950. Instructor of Military Science
Master Sgt. James A. Poindexter, U. S. Army, 1950-51. Instructor of Military Science
Master Sgt. Charles W. Wroten, 1950. Assistant in Military Science
William P. Dickens, B.S., 1947. Director of Intercollegiate Athletics
George C. Stapleton, B.S., 1948. Assistant in Physical Education
Joel E. Robertson, A.B., 1947. Assistant in Physical Education
Wilbur O. Stevens, B.S., 1947. Assistant in Physical Education

OFFICERS OF ADMINISTRATION

Walter K. Greene, A.B., A.M., M.A., Ph.D., LL.D., Litt.D. President
Clarence C. Norton, B.S., A.M., Ph.D. Dean 1942-49; Dean of Administration since
1949
Joseph K. Davis, A.B., 1920. Treasurer
Samuel F. Logan, A.B., A.M., 1947. Registrar
Philip S. Covington, A.B., A.M. Dean of Students since 1950
Mary S. DuPre, 1905. Librarian
Herbert Hucks, Jr., A.B., A.M., B.A. in L.S., 1947. Associate Librarian
Robert D. Fridley, A.B., B.D., 1947-51. Director of Religious Activities
William P. Dickens, B.S., 1947. Director of Intercollegiate Athletics
Samuel R. Moyer, A.B., 1948. Director of Music
William W. Scheerer, A.B., A.M., 1947. Director of Intra-Mural Sports
Sam O. Black, M.D., 1919. Director of Student Health
Hugh S. Black, M.D., 1924-50. (Deceased May 22, 1950.) Director of Student Health
Sam O. Black, Jr., M.D., 1925. College Physician
Larry A. Jackson, A.B., 1949-51. Alumni Secretary
William C. Morris, A.B., 1949-51. Director of Publicity
Harold S. Smithyman, 1946. Accountant
Mrs. Sumter S. Wingfield, A.B., 1941. Assistant Librarian
John R. Curry, 1947. Superintendent of Grounds and Buildings

FACULTY MEMBERS, 1853-1951, WITH TERMS OF SERVICE

Warren G. Ariail, Jr., A.B., 1949. Athletic Trainer
Mrs. Elizabeth R. Brockman, R.N., 1947. Nurse
Mrs. Inez B. Helms, 1933. Hostess at Snyder Hall
Mrs. Irene C. Sullivan, 1950. Hostess at Greene Hall
Mrs. Annie Daniel, 1950. Hostess at Carlisle Hall.

APPENDIX V

ALMA MATER

On the city's northern border,
  Reared against the sky,
Proudly stands our Alma Mater
  As the years go by.

Chorus

May it ever be our watchword,
  "Conquer and prevail."
Hail to thee, our Alma Mater,
  Dear old Wofford, hail!

Cherished by thy sons forever
  Memories sweet will throng
'Round our hearts, dear Alma Mater,
  As we sing thy song.

When we from thy halls are parted,
  And life's battle's on,
Thy great spirit shall inspire us
  Till eternal dawn.

The motto on the Wofford College seal, Intaminatis fulget honoribus (She shines with undimmed honors) is from Horace's Odes and Epodes, Carminum, Liber III, Ode II. I thank Prof. Herbert Hucks, Jr., for locating the passage.

INDEX

281

Index

Moss, Mrs. B. H., 219.
Mount Union College, 250.
Mount Ariel Academy, 40.
Mount Bethel Academy, 40.
Mouzon, E. D., 107, 120, 204, 224.
Moyer, Samuel R., 233.
Murray, A. B., 33.

Nabers, Z. L., 73, 117.
Nash, J. W., 111.
Nesbitt, Charles F., nickname, 237.
Nettles, S. A., 172.
Newberry College, 189, 190.
New York Christian Advocate, 245.
New York *Times,* 241.
Nicholls, W. M., 213.
Nicholson, Dean Marjorie Hope, installs Phi
  Beta Kappa, 248.
Nicknames, faculty, 237.
Norton, C. C., dean, 106, 200, 255; visits
  Africa, 200; dean of administration, 229;
  nickname, 237.

Ogden Movement, 245.
Oglesby, N. D., 73.
Old Gold and Black, 233; not censored, 232.
Olin, Stephen, 27, 42, 53.
Oliver, R. C., 105.
Oratorical Association, 188-190; winners in,
  189-190.
Organizations, student, 186-187.
Orr, Maud S. (Mrs. D. D. Wallace), 9, 14.
Owen, W. C., 182.

Padgett, A. L., 73.
Padgett, H. F., 190 and n.
Page, W. H., 166.
Palmer, General W. J., 70.
Palmer, J. J., 73.
Pasco, Senator, 159-160.
Passing grade, 195.
Pastors' School, Methodist, 204.
Pate, J. T., 119.
Patterson, W. S., 74.
Peabody, George Foster, 245.
Pearson, R. L., 74.
Pegues, W. L., 68.
Perks, R. W., 177.
Petigru, J. L., 142.
Petty, Charles, 63, 151 and n.
Phi Beta Kappa Society, installation of
  Wofford chapter, 248.
Pickens, Gov. F. W., 66-67, 73.
Pickett, J. R., 68, 80.
Pitts, W. A., 117.
Plant Fund in 1949, 253.
Political Economy, (and History), chair
  established, 124.
Preparatory Department, 76.
Presbyterian College of S. C., 9, 188, 189,
  190.
Presbyterian Church, student members, 226.
President's house, 175.
Preston Society, 64, 79, 234; library, 236.
Preston, William C., 236.
Pressley, T. I., 208.
Price, T. R., 88.
Price, Wilson B., 233.
Prince, G. E., 125.
Prince, N. L., 125.
Pritchard, S. R., 112, 172.
Professors, term, 42.
Promotion program, 227 *et seq.*
Pugh, W. L., 220.
Purcell, C., 147.

Quakers, students, 226.

Railroad, to Columbia, 65.
Ramseur, W. G., 184.
Randolph-Macon College, 27, 40, 42, 50, 52,
  53, 87, 88, 94, 126, 236.
Religion, revivals, 62.
Religious Education, chair established, 214.
Rembert, A. G., mock duel, 91; and Dr.
  Carlisle, 91; headmaster, 105; on athletics,
  107-108; library, 120; represents college,
  193; and summer school, 200; and Pastors'
  School, 204; and students, 208; illness,
  220; nickname, 237; mentioned, 238;
  sketch, 239-240.
Remsen, I. B., 176.
Reserve Officers Training Corps, 212.
Residences, for faculty, 206.
Retirement plan, 207, 237-239.
Revivals, 62, 77.
Reynolds, J. S., 114.
Rhodes scholars, 190.
Rice, Dr. John A., 204.
Richardson, W. R., 123.
Risher, J. F., 107.
Robertson, Joel, 250.
Rogers, M. C., 213.
Rogers, W. A., 79, 178.
Rogers, Mrs. W. A., 175.
Roll of Honor, World War II casualties,
  255-257.
Roper, D. C., 137.
Rules, for students (1858), 60; on relation of
  faculty, trustees, etc., 229.

Salaries, original, 63; in 1860's, 68-69, 75;
  (1854-1900), 69-70; (1870), 80; (1890),
  114; cut and restored, 222-223; cut after
  World War II, 255.
Salmon, J. L., house, 175; and students,
  208; nickname, 237.
Sanders, D. P., 183.
Scarritt Bible and Training School, 214.
Science Hall, 173, 176.
Scholarships, endowed, 252.
Seabrook, W. B., 152.
Seay, W. B., 43.
Secretaries to Dr. Snyder, 236-237.
Seventh Day Adventists, students, 226.
Scarborough, W. H., 34.
"School System," 93-95.
Sheridan, H. G., Sr., 106.
Shipp, A. M., trustee, 42, 170; professor,
  51; president, 65, 66, 68, 70, 76, 78,
  244; resigns at Vanderbilt, 80-81; rela-
  tions with J. H. Carlisle, 80; writings,
  81; death, 81; residence, 103.
Shipp, J. W., 76, 80.
Shirley, Mrs. A. N. M., 224.
Shockley, H. T., 121 n.
Shuler, E. H., 172, 237.
Shuler, F. H., 211-212.
Simons, Albert, 49 n.
Simpson, S. J., 158.
Simpson, T., 74.
Sims, Mr. & Mrs. T. P., 218 and n.
Slavery, and early Methodists, 22.
Sloan, Benjamin, 56.
Smart, R. D., 79, 176.
Smith, A. C., 77.
Smith, A. Coke, birth and death, 98; finan-
  cial agent, 80, 98, 102, 104; professor,
  98, 103, 104; urges Fitting School, 104;
  suggests *Journal,* 107; resigns, 112; made
  bishop, 98; gifts, 103; anecdotes, 114;
  inspires A. M. DuPre, 195; contributes to
  Preston Society Library, 236.
Smith, C. F., professor, 84, 86, 93, 112,
  114; on Carlisle, 168; addresses, 176.
Smith, E. D., 107.

285